Oliver Bell Bunce

The Romance of the Revolution

True Stories of the Adventures, Romantic Incidents, Hairbreath Escapes, And Heroic Exploits

Oliver Bell Bunce

The Romance of the Revolution
True Stories of the Adventures, Romantic Incidents, Hairbreath Escapes, And Heroic Exploits

ISBN/EAN: 9783744673310

Printed in Europe, USA, Canada, Australia, Japan

Cover: Foto ©ninafisch / pixelio.de

More available books at **www.hansebooks.com**

THE ROMANCE

OF

THE REVOLUTION:

BEING

TRUE STORIES OF THE ADVENTURES, ROMANTIC
INCIDENTS, HAIRBREADTH ESCAPES,
AND HEROIC EXPLOITS

DAYS OF '76.

ILLUSTRATED.

PHILADELPHIA:
PORTER & COATES,

CONTENTS.

	Page
Introduction,	11
Stories and Anecdotes of Washington,	31
Adventures of Marion,	46
A Romantic Story,	58
Capture, Imprisonment and Escape of Gen. Wadsworth,	62
Gallant Enterprise of Major Barton,	69
An Interesting Story,	75
A Thrilling Narrative,	82
The Story of an Old Soldier,	86
Adventures of the Brothers Sammons,	92
Narrative of Frederick Sammons,	102
Deborah Sampson,	110
Joseph Bettys,	117
Mr. and Mrs. Fisher,	122
Thrilling Adventure of Lieut. Slocumb,	131
Execution of Col. Isaac Hayne,	139
Adventures of Major General Clinton,	142
Adventures of Lieut. Richard Dale,	144
Miss Moncrieffe,	147

CONTENTS.

	Page.
An Extraordinary Adventure,	150
Miss Moore,	162
Adventures of Mr. Ferris,	165
Exploits of Sergeant Jasper,	172
An Act of Mercy Rewarded,	176
Captain Nathan Hale,	179
Capture of Captain Harper,	184
A Desperate Encounter,	190
Anecdotes of Col. Horry,	193
A High Spirited Family,	197
Escape of Captain Plunkett,	201
Attempted Abduction of Gen. Schuyler,	203
Adventures of Dr. Caldwell,	206
Colonel Willett,	209
Intrepid Conduct of Major James,	212
A Novel Situation,	214
The Death of Major Henley,	218
Adventures of Col. Harper,	221
Narrow Escape of Col. Snipes,	225
A Scene in the Forest,	228
A Gallant Combat,	231
A Gallant Enterprise,	233
Narrative of Baroness Reidesel,	236
Lydia Darrah,	249
Capture of President Daggett,	252
Murder of Mr. and Mrs. Caldwell,	255
Captain Cunningham,	259
Adventure of a Soldier,	261
Adventures of Gen. Putnam,	263

CONTENTS.

	Page
Incidents at the Battle of Oriskany,	265
Adventure of Col. Cochran,	268
Anecdotes of Sergeant McDonald,	270
A Romantic Incident,	272
Heroism of a Young Girl,	273
A Spy in Burgoyne's Camp,	275
Capture of a Tory,	277
Captain Huddy,	279
Colonel Fisher,	281
An Escape from the Prison Ship,	284
A Daring Youth,	286
Cruelty of the Tories,	288
Affecting Scenes,	290
A Story of a Dog,	292
Dicey Langston,	294
Wonderful Escape from Indians,	296
A Patriotic Girl,	302
Trials of a Patriot,	304
Mrs. Shubrick,	318
The Privateer,	321
The Maiden Warrior,	323
Major Israel Fearing,	326
Captivity of Ethan Allen,	328
A Fair Exchange,	334
A Patriot's Sufferings,	335
Col. John Small,	336
Adventure by two Ladies,	338
Capture of Gen. Woodhull,	339
British Barbarity,	340
Adventure of Charles Morgan,	341

	Page
EXPLOITS ON THE FRONTIERS,	344
DAVID ELERSON,	344
ATTACK ON MR. SHANKLAND'S HOUSE,	346
DARING ADVENTURE OF A CAPTIVE,	348
A GALLANT DEFENCE,	349
HEROISM OF A WOMAN,	350
A STIRRING INCIDENT,	351
A DARING FELLOW,	352
A FEARFUL ENCOUNTER,	355
MISCELLANEOUS ANECDOTES,	359
INCIDENTS ON THE BORDER,	414
STORY OF NANCY HART,	423
APPENDIX,	433
HISTORY OF THE SONS OF LIBERTY,	433
A REVOLUTIONARY RELIC,	438
APPOINTMENT OF GEORGE WASHINGTON,	440

INTRODUCTION.

The leading events of the War of Independence, are familiar to every American; but there has been much recorded of stirring incident which is not familiar to the American people, and much remains yet to be disclosed, connected with even the prominent actors in the drama. From time to time, during the last fifty years, various sketches have appeared, recounting strange passages in the war; and these sketches have been sometimes replete with extraordinary adventure and romantic situation of the most novel and thrilling kind; but they have never, till now, been collected in any permanent form, and have been in danger, from merely appearing in the transitory periodicals of the day, of passing into utter oblivion. And, to preserve these legendary pictures from such oblivion, and to perpetuate them in the affections of the American people, was the object of this work; to collect these, and other fragments of history, as combined, would present a history of the romance of the Revolution, and a chronicle of the individual heroism, exploits, and adventures of those engaged in that struggle.

And it is only by such a history, that we can have a forcible illustration of the age, and be enabled to understand and appreciate all that our forefathers did and suffered for the cause they espoused. Ponderous histories, that merely chronicle the movements of armies, or the actions of governments, give but an inadequate conception of an era. We must look into the hearts of the people, see their motives and passions, if we would understand the merits of a contest. If we would understand how England, with all her wealth and greatness, could not conquer her wretched starving colonies, we must go to the firesides of her opponents and see in the virtues there nourished, and the love of freedom there fostered, a solution to the mystery. And to see and feel this legend were a thousand-fold more potent than cold and dignified history. By it, the living and breathing age is portrayed and brought home to our sympathies, in all its vivid reality. The fireside reminiscence, treasured with sacred reverence, that gives a fearful page of suffering, and cruelty and blood, wreaked on those our memory recalls in life, will sooner than the most studied eloquence of the historian, send us to our pillow with tearful sympathy, and thrilling gratitude for dangers past. Such fragments of history, although they are often excluded as unsuited to the dignity of history, are the surest preservers of a people's patriotism, and the most certain link between the present and former ages.

This volume, therefore, in being the legendary part of the history, will promote a better knowledge of the spirit of the time, than can be derived from most any other source. Not that it is claimed to possess anything new, but the minute details of individual suffering and bravery, have been gathered together; the broken and diffuse rays have been centered into one focus, and the result is a romantic history, scarcely to be equalled. By this the reader sees, not the action of armies, but of the people. He enters directly into their spirit. He suffers, dares, and forbears with them. He feels all their manifold grievances, and bears with them the burthen laid upon their shoulders. All the minute springs of the contest are developed, and in the battle we see the impulse of each heart, and the despair or joy of the individual combatant; rejoice with him in the accomplishment of his cherished revenge, or weep over his untimely fate. In short, we are transported to the scenes, and become actors in the drama, whereas, in the loftier air of history, we are only spectators.

It is undoubtedly a truth, that injustice promotes injustice; a wrong begun is only maintained by wrong continued. The first contest of England with America, sprang from tyranny; she was the aggressor, the offending party; and it seems to have been a moral consequence, that a war, thus unrighteous, should have been characterised by an entire violation of every humane and honorable purpose. The chivalry of the British soldier was compromised by an invasion so monstrous, and this principle once banished, there was nothing to restrain the sway of brutal passion, and cruelty and blood-thirstiness, were suffered to grow and foster in every breast. Never has England been engaged in a contest which has left so uneffaceable a stain as the struggle with America. The long established reputation of her army for courage and humanity, was sacrificed for the stigma of cruelty and ferocity; and this stigma became affixed upon all concerned in the war. What say the present English historians, of Rawdon, Tarleton and Cunningham? What can future ages say of those arch-instruments of wrong and oppression? Their history remains a monument of England's wrong; and by their deeds alone could future ages determine the merits of the contest. Those who are impelled to a course by a sense of right, those who are engaged in the defence of a principle, never are guilty of cruelty and oppression; the sacredness of their cause, preserve their names unstained, and their souls unblemished.

But perhaps the fact that we were rebels, aside from the injustice of their invasion, may have goaded them on to ferocity. English history shows that that's a name on which the English bestow no sympathy, and for those thus ranked they allow no mercy. Such beings are without the pale of humanity, and are not to be treated with any faith, with whom no obligations are binding, and to whom no pity is due. With such severity, at least, were the rebel Scots treated on the sanguinary field of Culloden. We are all familiar with the atrocities committed on that day; how, by the commands of the inhuman butcher, the Duke of Cumberland, the hapless Scots were shot down, bayoneted, and murdered, long after they had surrendered, and even while they were begging for quarter.

But, indeed, the extent which British cruelty was inflicted upon us in the memorable contest of the Revolution, is scarcely appreciated by our countrymen. Nothing equals the determined, blood-thirsty fury which characterised it in some quarters of the union. It was almost a war of extermination in the South. There young lads were often shot down, that they might not live to be full-grown rebels, and mothers brutally murdered, that they might bring forth no more enemies to the king. Among the people in villages, and in the open country, existed the greatest suffering, and often were manifested the noblest heroism, the loftiest patriotism, and the grandest fortitude. With such ferocity were they pursued by the British soldiery, that their only retreat became the army. At no moment were they safe. Neither in their beds, by their firesides, nor on the high ways. Daily and nightly murder frightened the time with their trocities. Reckless marauders traversed the country in all directions; sparing neither age, sex, nor infancy. Nightly, the red flame glared upon the horizon, and houseless children hung over the desecrated and butchered forms of their parents. Bitter the hatred, malignant the revenge, that, on such occasions, would spring into existence, destined to find retribution in torrents of blood.

It is claimed, that these atrocities were mostly chargeable upon the tories. This is partly true; but it would have been impossible for any class of beings to have exceeded the ferocity of the Hessian hirelings. And the fiercest renegade in the whole South, could not have equalled the dark deeds of Tarleton. And as an evidence that not the tories, nor the marauders alone, but the British army, and not the mere ignorant and brutalized privates, but many of the officers, the high-minded, honorable and chivalric officers, were cognizant of the cruelties and atrocities practised, we subjoin an extract from a letter, written by an officer in General Fraser's battalion, engaged in the unfortunate Battle of Long Island, which shows the spirit that actuated our enemies in that oppressive war. This is the extract: "The Hessians and our brave Highlanders gave no quarters; and it was a fine sight to see with what alacrity they despatched the rebels with their bayonets, after we had surrounded them so they could not resist! We took care to tell the Hessians that the rebels had resolved to give no quarter—to them in particular—which made them fight desperately, and put to death all that came in their hands." What are we to think of such savage and diabolic conduct?

But of all atrocities, those committed in the prisons and prison-ships of New York, are the most execrable; and, indeed, there is nothing in history to excel the barbarities there inflicted. It is damned as this? Within these ships were crowded all classes and all ages, from infancy to decrepid age, and here they lived in darkness, with scarcely sufficient air to breathe, and that so foul a light could not burn in it; some dead, dying, or delirious with fever; prayers and blasphemies filling the air; their bodies over run with vermin; crowded up to dead and corrupted bodies; no food but what was polluted and repugnant to the stomach, often crazed with thirst; no relief, no pity, no hope; nothing but death —death in its most horrible forms—suffering and anguish! The imagination cannot picture the scene in all its horrors. Sometimes a dying wretch would creep to the guard and beg a drop of water to quench his raging thirst; his answer would be a curse, a kick, or perhaps the thrust of a bayonet, which would end his agony at once.* On one occasion, while quite a large body of prisoners were gathered at the grate at the hatchway to obtain fresh air, a sentinel for mere pastime thrust his bayonet down among them, and twenty-five next morning were found to be dead. And this demoniac spirit was practised more than once.† We turn from the contemplation of this picture with sickening horror. Great God! can it be possible, that deeds like these could have been enacted by thy creatures?

---

* At one time two young brothers were sent on board the Jersey. The elder took the fever and in a few days become delirious. One night, as he was dying, he became calm and sensible, and begged for a little water. His brother with tears entreated the guard to give him some, but in vain. The sick youth was soon in his last struggles, when his brother offered the guard a guinea for an inch of candle only, that he might see his brother die. Even this was refused. "Now," said he, drying up his tears, "if it please God that I ever regain my liberty, I'll be a most bitter enemy." He regained his liberty, re-joined the army, and when the war ended, he had eight long and one hundred and twenty-seven small notches on his riff ock!—*Life of Silas Talbot.*

† History of Martyrs.

In examining the history of the revolution, we are struck by the vast difference in the physical condition of the two armies. On one side was luxury and ease, on the other every kind of privation. Our invaders had gold to command every want, while our own soldiers had only principle by which to fight and starve When the British soldier went into the field he had comfortable clothing on his back and plenty of food in his stomach; he was animated by martial array, and inspirited by the confidence of victory. He had also his comfortable quarters, and he was rarely oppressed by onerous duties. But the American fought naked and starving. Death was only a relief from misery, his prospects were dark, and when in the battle, he had nothing but his consciousness of right to animate him. It is wonderful to think how the army was kept together. It is difficult to realize how even the loftiest patriotism could keep men in the field, where the chances of success were so small, and their suffering so great. Nothing but their noble self-devotion, unparalelled in the world, kept them together. How can posterity believe that in the battle of Eutaw Springs, as stated by Greene himself, that hundreds of his men were as naked as they were born! Their loins were galled by the cartouch-boxes, and a folded rag, or tuft of grass, saved their shoulders from the same injury by the musket.* What magic was it that held men together in such a guise! What was it, but a principle of right, that mighty lever which no power can restrain, and which will eventually accomplish its triumphs!

Not only the men, but officers and all suffered alike. Major

---

* Johnson's Life of General Greene.

Garden* states that often there was but one uniform among a dozen officers, and that these took turn in wearing it when invited to head-quarters. Garden gives another anecdote to show the privations of the officers. Dr. Fayssoux called at the hut of General Ruger, of the southern army, but was refused admission by the sentinel. The Doctor insisted upon his right to enter, which the sentinel denied, when the General hearing the altercation, desired the sentinel to let his friend pass. "Pardon me, Doctor," said the General, who lay upon the ground wrapped up in his military cloak, "for giving you so ungracious a reception; but the fact is, the chances of war have robbed me of every comfort, and I confine myself to solitude, and an old cloak, while my washerwoman prepares for a future occasion, the only shirt I own."

The many acts of chivalrous heroism which were performed by those who thus suffered and forebore in our revolutionary contest, if the truth could be told, and they possessed that distance which lends enchantment to view, would be found to possess more real chivalry, than the chronicles of that age affords in which our fondness for the dim, uncertain events that are traced upon the horizon of the past, has made us stamp as peculiarly the age of romantic bravery. If motive constitutes an evidence whereby the actions of men should be judged, then assuredly the deeds of our forefathers, must in the impartial judgment of every age, and in the verdict of the future, which shall from a higher point of view look and pronounce judgment on the actions of all the past that shall be spread out before it, and all alike be surrounded by the softening and harmonious lines of distance, be admitted to as

---

* Garden's Anecdotes of the Revolution.

lofty eminence, as all the half-fabulous wonders performed by the poet-sung heroes of the olden time. If by motive, our heroes should be judged, they would rank above many of those it is the pride of the world to honor. In old Greece and Rome two passions combined to urge men on to heroism—a love of glory and love of country In the middle ages it was purely a passion for glory, a thirst for renown in prowess, that actuated and controlled those mailed warriors. But with the hero of the Revolution, an unmixed and pure patriotism; a true, undivided, and earnest devotion to his country, for which he would often sacrifice glory itself, for which he would be content to bear the "scorns and whips of time," was the sole passion of his breast. Those who figured in the chivalrous ages, possessed more of the "pride, pomp and circumstance of glorious war," than did our plain, simple, uncouth, and "unnamed demi-gods." They were surrounded by a glorious halo, through which men look entranced. A barbaric splendor accompanied all their movements, and the soft touches of love, and the gilded decoration of art, invest them with a softened and marvellous coloring. With flaunting banners, caparisoned steeds, silken canopies, brilliant costumes, jeweled weapons, and nodding plumes; with attending pages, glittering retinues, and imposing pomp; with a dramatic show and glitter of war that fired and delighted the imagination, and steeped men's senses in bewildering wonder,—by all such means they presented a gorgeous spectacle. And then again in their huge castles, with battlements and towers, and ramparts, with tapestried halls, and brilliant feasts, where beauty and song swayed, and controlled their impulses; in this and these, and in their reverence for beauty, to which alone they bent a knee or yielded service, do we find the romance that surrounds them.

and our proneness to deify them. Wrest them, however, of all this glitter and show, and come close where all the ruggedness of their characters may be examined, and we find that their chivalry often was degraded into brutality, and their heroism no more than modern annals attribute to the meanest of those who took up arms, not for their own selfish advancement, but for the glory of their country. The reader will find in the following pages, deeds of greater prowess, incidents of an equal romantic chivalry, and instances of as pure, unselfish devotion, as can be afforded by any history whatsoever. The deeds stand out in their naked simplicity, "a plain, unvarnished tale," unexaggerated by poet or romancer.

Perhaps for marvellous adventure, cunning address, great fortitude, and cool daring, no history is so fruitful as that of our border warfare. The imagination of the romancer is dull, and his invention weak, if in such scenes he endeavor to substitute fiction for truth. With these frontier warriors there was no ease, their energies were never allowed to repose, and their watchfulness never at rest. At no hour, on no occasions, could they indulge in a feeling of safety. Their nerves were always strung to the farthest tension, their invention ever alive to avert danger, or to secure a victory. Coolness and courage must ever be at hand, a moment's weakness would often prove fatal. Every man was the cunning general, the wily tactician, the undaunted hero! Stratagems over which we hang in delight, and reckless daring that make us pause in breathless admiration, were daily enacted. Acts of heroism were so common, and heroes so many, that they ceased to create surprise. Not only were the men thus heroic, but women were inspired with a spirit equal to that which has immortalized the Spartan mothers, and children often manifested a fortitude in suffering, and courage in danger, superior to anything in history. The peculiar warfare of the frontier was of kind to nurse such spirits. It developed certain faculties to a marvellous degree. Men were continually indebted, and often dependant for their lives upon their acuteness of hearing and keenness of sight. They were also taught to be close and narrow observers, and to detect the presence of an enemy by signs that would have escaped those less skilled and practiced. Wonderful personal prowess, a capacity for the endurance of fatigue, an insensibility to climate, and an indifference to hunger or exertion, were required and manifested by them. Their warfare required tactics of its own, that were to be acquired in no school but that of bitter experience. Every man was as necessarily compelled to learn the art of war, and to obtain an initiation in all the mysteries of forest warfare, by stern practice, as ever the ancient knight warriors were forced to be instructed in all the arts of the tournament, or the "tented field." They were as much accomplished warriors as Surry or Sidney. They did not possess the graces and the elegancies of war as did those soldiers of song and legend, but they were as thoroughly accomplished in the art itself. In the handling of the spear and sabre, in the mastery of the rifle, they acquired a skill equal to that displayed of old with the battle-axe and sword. In feats of "noble horsemanship," those who knew the art at all, were unexcelled. Putnam, who was frontier bred, and inured in all the mysteries of forest life, when he rode down the precipice at Horse-Neck, performed a feat, that had it been enacted by Surry, the favorite of romance, song and ballad would have made the world ring with it.

But, perhaps, for romance, no part of the Revolution equals the partizan warfare of the South. Its history is invested with a delightful and charming air. The many details of the contest possess nearly every requisite to arrest and gratify the imagination. It only lacked the glitter and pomp of a pageant to fascinate th world. The deeds performed were unfortunately enacted in homespun, rather than in steel, and therefore lose some of their charm They were without martial parade, but the mode of warfare, th strange characters gathered in the bands, the wild forest retreats all combine to give them a romance of their own. It is with peculiar delight that the imagination follows Marion and his followers into their fastnesses. Their retreats were better strongholds than was ever the castle of a Norman knight. They defied the ingenuity and the power of their enemies to expel them. To follow them was to plunge into a region beset with unknown dangers, and once involved into its secret depths, the key of Ariadne was needed to trace the puzzling labyrinth. The herald, or messenger from the enemy, was blindfolded, and led by intricate courses, through vast morasses, and by paths bowered by masses of foliage the sun never penetrated, until at last he would be admitted into the sequestered area where the chief and his men would receive him. And this area, this camping ground, where was organized the daring expedition, the sudden attack, and the cunning stratagem, from which emanated all the schemes that held at bay, and in terror the English leaders; whence sprang the undying patriotism and the undaunted heroism; where Liberty's altar was erected, and where her fires ever burned with a hopeful flame, and never sank nor died, when all around, gloom and horror and wretchedness had wept and extinguished her flame; this noble, imposing area of freedom, what a grand piece of nature's handiwork it was! It was a fit asylum for those true to nature's behests. It was her grandest cathedral, where trees, aged, and with the grey moss streaming in hoary locks from their venerable trunks, loomed up in their mighty strength, and locked their giant limbs in a huge dome, through which the stars gleamed, and the sun shone in a gentle light that fell like the rays through the stained glass of the cathedral, softly upon the virgin moss of the far extending, and lofty aisles. And here, in the midst of these scenes, guarded from access by impenetrable thickets, dangerous marshes, and rugged defiles, where no enemy could penetrate, and which no force, however great, could destroy—here was the home of patriotism in the South—here, in the free air of heaven, sojourned the partizan, Marion. The soft bank of moss was his couch, and truly, the couch of Mars, and nothing but the domed oaks and sycamores canopied his head. No luxurious ease intruded in to the sacred precinct—sacred to the cause of liberty and humanity—for with a Spartan hardihood, those warriors, in fair or foul, amid the severities of summer or of winter, clung to their forest home, and nightly embraced the hardened couch, save when hurling themselves upon the ranks of the enemy, or rushing forth upon the beck of victory.

And glorious indeed were the victories achieved by that noble band. If the accomplishment of great ends by little means be a stamp of greatness, we cannot withhold from Marion the highest rank. It is true that he performed no single great victory, and his army, if it could be called an army, was but a band of a few hundred patriots. But with these few hundred, he kept in check the whole British army. He was the Nemesis of the South; the sure and terrible avenger of wrong. The iniquities of the English leaders, and Tory marauders, were visited with a sudden, rapid and fearful punishment. Their career of bloodshed was known to him; and their midnight expeditions, marked by burning dwellings, reckless murders, with flying families before them, and desolate hearths behind—these were treasured up, and shortly found a retribution. His scouts traversed every section, in many disguises, often assuming as many shapes as Proteus, and hung upon the routes of armies, and watched the actions of men. So keen was their cunning, so exhaustless their resources, that they would visit the same encampment many times, each in a different form; creep into the councils of the enemy; sometimes adroitly capture and carry off persons from the very midst of their armies. By these, Marion was always kept informed of the movements of his enemy, while his own were so rapid and so sudden that his own men were often puzzled to trace and find him.

He usually set out upon his expeditions at about sundown. He would then ride rapidly thirty or forty miles, fall suddenly upon some division of the enemy, who were reposing in false security; scatter them before they could form for defence; continue his journey, attack and defeat another detachment twenty miles farther, and ere the news could spread, he would have disappeared into his fastnesses, where no step could follow, and his enemies without, would gaze in wonder about, as if a meteor had shot down destruction upon them, and suddenly vanished into air

Their expeditions were beset with great difficulties, that only patience and hardihood could overcome. They had to swim rivers, penetrate tangled thickets, cross dangerous morasses, and undergo severe fatigues of all kinds, such as prolonged hunger, exhaustion from want of sleep, and often suffering from want of clothing sufficient to protect them from the weather. When pursued, and many a huge army was sent to destroy him, he was more cunning than the fox, and still dangerous as the lion. He would as certainly lure his enemy into his toils, as they would attempt to follow him. He would fall upon their camps, cut off their provision, dash upon them like a thunderbolt, in advantageous places, and suddenly disappear, lead them into ambuscades from which they would only be extricated by fearful loss, puzzle bewilder and send them back defeated, disgraced and utterly confounded.

His brigade formed a picturesque and motely group.—Their costumes were formed of every imaginable kind and color, such as their own resources could provide, or their swords capture from their enemies. Sometimes the contrast presented by them, would be highly amusing. There would be the huge backwoodsman, with his rough boots and flannel shirt, mounting some silken or golden remnant of an English officer's regimentals, often times ridiculously in keeping with his own habiliments; here would be seen a fortunate adventurer bedecked with conquered plumes and scarfs, glittering by the side of ragged, threadbare fustian, there a swarthy negro, with naked feet and a gold embroidered coat, or perhaps with lace and ruffles, and gilded ornaments, but hiding himself in shame for his nakedness. Not only the men themselves, but many of the partisan officers, were suffering from want of clothing, and compelled to adapt such articles as chance threw in their way. But sometimes they were bedecked in vesture, furnished by the hands of fair ladies, and pledged to defend and protect them to the last. The whig ladies of South Carolina, were as high-souled and chivalrous a body of the sex as ever knight broke lance for. During the whole war, they exerted themselves for the welfare of their defenders, and often by their sacrifices, or their cunning, or their patriotism, was some signal service done to the state. They particularly exerted themselves to the procuring of necessaries for the partizan warriors.

Many of those who resided in Charleston, by their ingenuity supplied their friends from the abundance of the British garrison. Notwithstanding all those who passed out into the country, were examined, to prevent smuggling, their resources provided ways to elude the vigilance of the guards, and to carry off articles with impunity. Says Garden,* who served in the South, "The cloth of many a military coat, concealed with art, and not unfrequently made an appendage to female attire, has escaped the vigilance of the guards, expressly stationed to prevent smuggling, and speedily converted into regimental shape, worn triumphantly in battle. Boots have, in many instances, been relinquished by the delicate wearer to the active partisan. I have seen a horseman's helmet concealed by a well arranged head-dress, and epaulettes delivered from the folds of the simple cap of a matron. Feathers and cockades were much in demand, and so cunningly hid, and handsomely presented, that he could have been no true knight, who did not feel the obligation, to defend them to the last extremity."

The privations of these devoted bands were manifold. They were often dependant for food entirely upon the uncertain resources of the forest. They were always without salt, except when captured from the enemy, and even then this necessary condiment was distributed among destitute whig families, rather than preserved for themselves, although the want of it was a serious grievance, and made their ill-cooked meals, barely palatable. We are all familiar with the anecdote of the British officer, who upon visiting Marion's encampment, was invited to dine, and who, after a surprised survey of the forest for any signs of dinner, was shown a few roasted potatoes, on a shingle, which had just been

---

* Major Garden's Revolutionary Anecdotes.

drawn hot from the ashes, and were to be eaten without salt, or any accompaniment. But, even on this occasion, they were uncommonly fortunate; they were often without any food whatever. But with men resolved in their course, confident in the ustice of their cause, and united by the holy instincts of patriot ism, no physical suffering could divert them from their purposes or dampen their spirit.

In these various phases of our great National contest exist the romance which the editor of this volume has endeavored to glean and present to the American public. There can scarcely be found a period in any history, so replete with variety of interest as is presented by this era. In the border struggles on the frontier, and the wild partisan warfare of the south, in the regular army, in the prisons, wherever the contest was an active one, we find romance on every page of its history, romance that's wild and entrancing. It is strange that this fact is so rarely accredited, and that our history is accounted dull and prosy, with all the rich materials which it affords for exciting and gratifying the imagination. But our poets have passed over it, with the dogged belief that romance only existed in armor and a breast-plate. Not so thought the English poet Campbell, who gathered golden fruit where our native romancer would not deign to stoop. Assuredly there are other passages in our history as capable of being immortalized in song as the touching story of Wyoming. Let the pages of this volume bear witness of it. There are many incidents here related, that should go down to fame on the buoyant tide of poetry, but which in prose can scarcely be preserved. It is the minstrel and the poet, more than the historian, who have immortalized the heroes of the past. Achilles and Hector became immortal, only through the pen of Homer. The poet then owes this much to his country, that he should seek to embalm the fame of her heroes for posterity to admire and emulate. Brave and heroic deeds have thrice their force as examples, more readily fire the heart with generous and noble emulation, when written in the glowing imagery of the poet, than when simply coming to us in the cold chronicles of the historian. Let our poets, wh would be great, remember this, and say not, when that which follows in this volume is before them, that there is no material or incident wherewithal to write.

The editor believes that he has gathered a collection of sketches which will be acceptable to the American public. Assuredly, a history of the exploits, heroism and suffering of our forefathers can scarcely be aught else but acceptable, to those who are now reaping the golden fruits of their achievements. He believes that none can peruse them without a more vivid conception of the era of which they treat, and a sincere pleasure in the romantic interest, which is proven to have been wove around the deeds and lives of our ancestors.

ROMANCE OF THE REVOLUTION.

STORIES

AND

ANECDOTES OF WASHINGTON.

On a day in the early part of the revolution, just after the sun had passed its meridian, an American officer could have been seen slowly wending his way along one of the unfrequented roads that wound their way up among the mountains, in the vicinity of West Point; where was then stationed the American army. The officer was unaccompanied, and as the horse, with slow and measured tread moved along the road, with the slackened rein hanging loose upon his neck, his rider seemed buried in a deep reverie. The scene around was one of peculiar beauty, the far mountains heaped up, one above another, against the horizon, and at his feet the Hudson sweeping on with a sweet and placid look. But the thoughts of the traveller were turned inward, and his eyes heeded not the pageant before them, but seemed rather to be reading the dark and obscure future, or trying to penetrate into the mysteries which surrounded the present. His thoughts, however, were apparently not disturbed, but only solemn and deep. It would have been impossible for any one to have looked upon his calm, thoughtful brow, the majestic, but benevolent expression of his countenance, the firm contour though sweet expression of his lips, the mild, penetrating glance of his eye, and the noble proportions of his frame, without detecting the presence of the great WASHINGTON. Presently he drew up before a mansion on the road, dismounted, and approached the house. Almost immediately a door was thrown open, and an aged gentleman, in a civilian's dress, rushed forth and greeted the comer with many, seemingly, earnest protestatious of welcome.

The family in which Washington, on this occasion, was received, was one he had frequently been in the habit of visiting. During the stay of the army at West Point, he frequently dined with its members, and with its head he had at first reposed confidence and friendship. But many suspicions of his honesty were whispered about, and in some quarters he was openly accused of treachery to the American cause. To these suspicions Washington would not heed, but having been invited to dine with him on a certain day and at a certain hour, and this invitation being pressed with so much over-earnestness, and accompanied with an insinuation, that his appearance with a guard was an indication of his want of confidence in his friend's fidelity, and urged to give a proof of his unchanged belief in his honesty, by coming unattended to partake with him a private dinner, Washington's suspicions at last became aroused, and he resolved, by accepting the invitation, to prove at once the truth or falsehood of the suspicions entertained against him. It was to fulfil this engagement that Washington, on the occasion we have described, proceeded to the residence of his suspected friend.

The time appointed for the dinner was two o'clock, but it was not later than one when Washington dismounted at the door of his Lost. He had an especial object in this early arrival. The host proposed to occupy the interim before dinner, by a walk on the piazza. Here conversation occupied the time, and it soon became apparent to the chief that his host's manner was exceedingly nervous and excitable. Without revealing this knowledge Washington continued the discourse, and, while he carefully avoided betraying his suspicions, he skillfully led the conversations to such subjects, that would be most likely to cause his companion to betray his agitation. So poor an actor was he, and so often was his conscience probed by the apparently innocent remarks of the commander-in-chief, that his nervousness of manner became so marked as to give the greatest pain to Washington, at this proof of the infidelity of one on whom he had once reposed unlimited confidence. The American commander in commenting upon the different beauties of the landscape that surrounded them, pointed out the spot where lay the encampment of the enemy, at the same time remarking upon the extraordinary lack of principle that could induce men of American birth to forego the interests of their country, and every consideration of holy patriotism, to enrol themselves among their country's invaders for no other temptation than a little glittering gold. Before the penetrating look which Washington fixed upon him while making these remarks, the guilty traitor quailed, but at this juncture, he was relieved by the sound of approaching horses, and as both guest and host turned to the direction whence the sound proceeded, a company of dragoons in British uniforms appeared upon the brow of the hill, and galloping rapidly along the road towards the house.

"Bless me, sir!" exclaimed Washington; "what cavalry are these approaching the house?"

"A party of British light horse," rejoined his trembling host, "who mean no harm, but are merely sent for my protection!"

"British horse sent here while I am your guest!" said Washington with startling sternness, as he turned upon his guest with an air of command that awed, and caused to quail, the little soul of the betrayer before the mighty spirit that he had aroused. "What does this mean, sir?" continued Washington, as a terrible look gathered upon his brow.

By this time the troops had arrived, and they were seen dismounting from their horses. This gave courage to the trembling traitor.

"General," said he approaching his guest, "General, you are my prisoner."

"I believe not," replied Washington, his manner having regained its former calmness, "but, sir, I know that you are *mine!* Officer arrest this traitor!"

In bewildering consternation the treacherous hypocrite looked from Washington to the men; the one an American officer, and the others seemingly British soldiers. But the puzzle was soon solved. Washington had ordered a company of Americans to disguise themselves as British cavalry, and to arrive at the mansion designated, at a *quarter before two*, by which means he would be enabled to discover the innocence or guilt of the suspected person. The issue proved his suspicions were well founded, and the mode he adopted for detecting the plot admirably displayed his great sagacity. The false friend was handed over to the keeping of the soldiers, and conducted to the American camp as a prisoner. He afterwards, confessed. that he had been offered a large sum to betray Washington into the hands of the English, and at the hour of two, a party of British horse would have surrounded the house, and captured the American chief. At first, Washington meditated making a severe example of the man, but he yielded to the earnest solicitations of his family, and pardoned him

The incident which we next give, relative to Washington, was communicated to an old periodical, from which we copy it.

One pleasant evening in the month of June, during the early part of the war, a man was observed entering the borders of a wood, near the Hudson river, his appearance that of a person above the common rank. The inhabitants of a country village would have dignified him with the title of 'squire, and, from his manner, would have pronounced him proud; but those more accustomed to society, would inform you there was something like a military air about him. His horse panted as if it had been hard pushed for some miles, yet from the owners frequent stops to caress the patient animal, he could not be charged with want of humanity; but seemed to be actuated by some urgent necessity. The rider forsaking a good road for a by-path leading through the woods, indicated a desire to avoid the gaze of other travelers. He had not left the house where he enquired the direction of the above mentioned road, more than two hours, before the quietude of the place was broken by the noise of distant thunder. He was soon after obliged to dismount, traveling becoming dangerous, as darkness concealed surrounding objects, except when the lightning's flash afforded him a momentary view of his situation. A peal louder and of longer duration than any of the preceding which now burst over his head, seeming as if it would rend the woods asunder, was quickly followed by a heavy fall of rain, which penetrated the clothing of the stranger ere he could obtain the shelter of a large oak, which stood at a little distance.

Almost exhausted with the labors of the day, he was about making such disposition of the saddle and his over coat, as would enable him to pass the night with what comfort circumstances would admit, when he espied a light glimmering through th trees. Animated with the hope of better lodgings, he determined to proceed. The way, which was sometimes steep, became attended with some obstacles the farther he advanced; the soil being composed of clay, which the rain had rendered so soft that his feet slipped at every step. By the utmost perseverance, this difficulty was finally overcome without any accident, and he had the pleasure of finding himself in front of a decent looking farmhouse. The watch-dog began barking, which brought the owner of the mansion to the door.

"Who is there?" said he.

"A friend who has lost his way, and in search of a place of shelter," was the answer.

"Come in sir," added the speaker, "and whatever my house will afford, you shall have with welcome."

"I must provide for the weary companion of my journey," remarked the other.

But the farmer undertook the task, and after conducting the new-comer into a room where his wife was seated, he led the horse to a well stored barn, and there provided for him most bountifully. On rejoining the traveller, he observed, "That is a noble animal of yours, sir."

"Yes," was the reply, "and I am sorry that I am obliged to misuse him so as to make it necessary to give you so much trouble with the care of him; but I have yet to thank you for your kindness to us both."

"I do no more than my duty, sir," said the entertainer, "and therefore, am entitled to no thanks." "But Susan," added he turning to the hostess with a reproachful look. "why have you not given the gentleman something to eat?"

Fear had prevented the good woman from exercising her well-known benevolence; for a robbery had been committed by a lawless band of depredators recently in that neighborhood, and as report stated that the ruffians were all well dressed, her imagination suggested that this might be one of them.

At her husband's remonstrance, she now readily engaged in repairing her error, by preparing a bountiful repast. During the meal, there was much interesting conversation among the three As soon as the worthy countryman perceived that his guest had satisfied his appetite, he informed him that it was now the hour at which the family usually performed their devotions, inviting him at the same time to be present. The invitation was accepted in these words:—

"It would afford me the greatest pleasure to commune with my heavenly Preserver, after the events of the day; such exercises prepare us for the repose which we seek in sleep."

After the devotions the host lighted a pine-knot and conducted the person he had entertained, to his chamber, wished him a good night, and retired to the adjoining apartment.

"John," whispered the woman, "that is a good gentleman, and not one of the highwaymen as I supposed."

"Yes, Susan," said he, "I like him better for thinking of his God, than all his kind inquiries after our welfare. I wish our Peter had been home from the army, if it was only to hear this good man talk; I am sure Washington himself could not say more for his country, nor give a better history of the hardships endured by our brave soldiers."

"Who knows, now," inquired the wife, "but it may be himself after all, my dear; for they do say he travels just so, all alone, sometimes. Hark! What's that?"

The sound of a voice came from the chamber of their guest, who was now engaged in private religious worship. After thanking the Creator for his many mercies, and asking a blessing on the inhabitants of the house, he continued, "And now, Almighty Father, if it be thy holy will, that we shall attain a name and a place among the nations of the earth, grant that we may be enabled to show our gratitude for thy goodness, by our endeavors to fear and obey thee. Bless us with wisdom in our councils, success in battle, and let our victories be tempered with humanity. Endow, also our enemies with enlightened minds, that they may become sensible of their injustice, and willing to restore liberty and peace. Grant the petition of thy servant, for the sake of him thou hast called thy beloved Son; nevertheless, not my will, but thine be done. Amen."

The next morning the traveler, declining the pressing solicitations to breakfast with his host, declared it was necessary for him to cross the river immediately; at the same time offering part of his purse as a compensation for what he had received, which was refused.

"Well, sir," continued he, "since you will not permit me to recompence you for your trouble, it is but just that I should inform you, on whom you have conferred so many obligations, and also add to them by requesting your assistance to cross the river. I had been out yesterday, endeavoring to obtain some information respecting our enemy, and, being alone, ventured too far from the camp. On my return, I was surprised by a foraging party, and only escaped by my knowledge of the woods, and the fleetness of my horse. My name is George Washington."

Surprise kept the listner silent for a moment; then, after unsuccessfully repeating the invitation to partake of some refreshment, he hastened to call two negroes, with whose assistance he placed the horse on a small raft of timber that was lying on the river, near the door, and soon conveyed the general to the opposite side of the river, where he left him to pursue his way to the camp, wishing him a safe and prosperous journey. On his return to the house, he found that while he was engaged in making preparations for conveying the horse across the river, his illustrious visitor had persuaded his wife to accept a token of remembrance, which the descendants of the worthy couple are proud of exhibiting to this day.

"In the summer of 1776, when the American army was in New York, a young girl of the city went to her lover, one Francis, and communicated to him, as a secret she had overheard, a plan that was in operation among the government men to destroy the American commander-in-chief, by poison, which was to be plentifully mingled with his green-peas, a favorite vegetable of his, on the following day at Richmond Hill head quarters, where he was to dine. Francis, who was a thorough whig, although supposed to be friendly to the royalists, went immediately to Washington and acquainted him with this diabolical plan for his destruction. Washington having listened with attention, said:

"My friend, I thank you; your fidelity has saved my life, to what reserve the Almighty knows! But now for your safety; I charge you to return to your house, and let not a word of what you have related to me pass your lips; it would involve you in certain ruin; and heaven forbid that your life should be forfeited or endangered by your faith to me. I will take the necessary steps to prevent, and, at the same time, discover the instrument of this wicked device."

"The next day, about two hours before dinner, he sent for one of his guard, told him of the plot, and requested that he would disguise himself as a female, and go to the kitchen, there to keep a strict watch upon the peas, until they should be served up for the table. The young man, carefully, observed the directions he had received, and had not been long upon his post of duty, before a young man, another of the guard, came anxiously to the door of the kitchen, looked in, and then passed away. In a few moments after, he returned and approached the hearth where the peas stood, and was about to mingle in the deadly substance, when, suddenly, he shrunk back as though from the sting of the fork-tongued adder, his color changing to the pale hue of death, and his limbs apparently palsied with fear, evidently horror struck with his own purpose—but soon, however, the operation of a more powerful incitement urged forward his reluctant hand that tremblingly strewed the odious bane, and he left the kitchen, overwhelmed with conflicting passions, remorse and confusion.

"'Harold sleeps no more, the cry has reached his heart ere the deed be accomplished,' said the youth on duty, in a voice not devoid of pity, as he looked after the self-condemned wretch.

"'What Harold!" said the commander-in-chief, sorrowfully, upon receiving the information; 'can it be possible—so young, so fair, and gentle! He would have been the last person upon whom a suspicion of that nature could have fallen, by right of countenance. You have done well,' said he to the youth before him. 'Go join your comrades and be secret.'"

"The young man went accordingly, and Washington returned to the piazza, where several officers were assembled, among whom was the hero of Saratoga, who was waiting for further instructions from Congress before he departed for Canada. In a few moments dinner was announced, and the party was ushered into a handsome apartment, where the sumptuous board was spread, covered with all the delicacies of the season.

"The commander-in-chief took his seat, placing General Gates on his right hand, and General Wooster on the left. When the remainder of the officers and company were seated, and eager to commence the duties of the table, the chief said, impressively:

"'Gentlemen, I must request you to suspend your meal for a few moments. Let the guard attend me."

"All was silence and amazement. The guard entered and formed in a line towards the upper end of the apartment.

"Washington, having put upon his plate a spoonful of peas, fixed his eyes sternly upon the guilty man, and said:

"'Shall I eat of this vegetable?'

"The youth turned pale and became dreadfully agitated, while his trembling lips faintly uttered,

"'I don't know.'

"'Shall I eat of these?' again demanded Washington, raising some upon his knife.

"Here Harold elevated his hand, as if by an involuntary impulse, to prevent their being tasted. A chicken was then brought in, that a conclusive experiment might be made in the presence of all those witnesses. The animal ate of the peas and immediately died, and the wretched criminal, overcome with terror and remorse, fell fainting, and was borne from the apartment."

The victories of Trenton and Princeton were the turning point n our revolutionary war. At that time our cause looked dark ndeed, and defeat in those attempts would have utterly annihi ated the last hopes of the Americans. At the battle of Princeton, independent of the enemy's force in front, Cornwallis had eight thousand ready to close on the rear; and in case of defeat, there would have been no barrier to prevent them from spreading over and occupying every inch of the country. Washington felt the importance of the stake at issue, and his heroic devotion on that bloody but glorious field, is well known. The following touching reminiscence of that ever memorable event, is from the late Col. Fitzgerald, who was aid to the chief, and who never related the story of his General's danger, and almost miraculous preservation, without adding to his tale the homage of a tear.

"The aid-de-camp had been ordered to bring up the troops from the rear of the column, when the band, under General Mercer, became engaged. Upon returning to the spot where he had left the Commander-in-chief, he was no longer there, and upon looking around, the aid discovered him endeavoring to rally the line which had been thrown into disorder by a rapid onset of the foe. Washington, after several ineffectual attempts to restore the fortunes of the fight, is seen to rein up his steed, with his head to the enemy, and, in that position, to become immovable. It was a last appeal to his soldiers, and seemed to say, will you give up your General to the foe? Such an appeal was not made in vain. The discomfitted Americans rally on the instant, and form into line; the enemy halt, and dress their line; the American chief is between the adverse parties, as though he had been placed there a target for both. The arms of both lines are leveled. Can escape from death be possible? Fitzgerald, horror-struck at the danger of his beloved commander, dropped the reins upon his horse's neck, and drew his hat over his face, that he might not see him die. A roar of musketry succeeds, and then a shout. It was the shout of victory. The aid-de-camp ventures to raise his eyes, and oh! glorious sight, the enemy are broken and flying, while dimly amid the glimpses of the smoke, is seen the chief, 'alive, unharmed, without a wound,' waving his hat, and cheering his comrades to the pursuit. Col. Fitzgerald now dashed to the side of his chief, exclaiming, 'Thank God! your excellency is safe,' while the favorite aid, a gallant and warm-hearted son of Erin, a man of thews and sinews, and 'albeit unused to the melting mood,' gave loose to his feelings, and wept like a child for joy. Washington, ever calm amid scenes of the greatest excitement, affectionately grasped the hand of his aid and friend, and then ordered, 'Away, my dear colonel, and bring up the troops, the day is our own.'

The aim of the traitor Arnold was not confined to the surrender of West Point alone. He had projected the betrayal, into the hands of Sir Henry Clinton, of Washington himself, Lafayette, and of the principal staff officers. A trifling circumstance caused its failure. Arnold had invited Washington to dine with him, the very morning the plot was discovered, and Washington was only prevented from being present, by the urgent request made to him by an old officer, near to whose station he passed, that he would remain the night with him; and next morning inspect some works in the neighborhood. Washington, accordingly, dispatched an aid from his suite to make his excuses to Arnold. The messenger arrived at West Point the next morning, and breakfasted with Arnold. During the repast a letter was received, the superscription of which no sooner met the eyes of Arnold, than he hurried from the table; and, in a few minutes afterwards, was on his way to New York. This letter contained information of the arrest of Andre. In the meantime, Washington, with his staff, was seated at the table of the officer whose invitation had delayed the visit to West Point, when a despatch was brought to the chief which he opened, read, and laid down without comment. No alteration was visible in his countenance, but he remained perfectly silent. After some minutes, he beckoned to Lafayette, arose from the table, and followed by the young Frenchman, proceeded to an inner apartment, where he placed the fatal despatch, which revealed the perfidy of Arnold in his hands, and, then giving way to an uncontrolable burst of feeling—fell on his friend's neck and wept aloud. "I believe," said Lafayette, "this was the only occasion throughout that long and sometimes hopeless struggle, that Washington ever gave way, even for a moment, under a reverse of fortune; and, perhaps, I was the only human being who ever witnessed in him an exhibition of feeling so foreign to his temperament. As it was, he recovered himself, before I had perused the communication that gave rise to his emotion; and when we returned to his staff, not a trace remained on his countenance either of grief or despondency." So true it is, that of all human reverses, the betrayal of confidence on the part of one who has been implicitly trusted, is, to a generous nature, the hardest and bitterest to bear.*

Of the coolness of Washington numerous instances are given. At one time while standing with his aids in a situation where he was exposed to the musketry and cannons of the whole British line, Col. Cobb said to him, "Sir, you are too much exposed here. Had you not better step a little back?" "Colonel Cobb," replied he, "if you are afraid, you have liberty to move back."

At the battle of Monmouth, while Washington was personally ngaged in forming the line of the main body, a cannon ball

---

* Robert Dale Owen. The above anecdote which does not appear in any history, was related by Lafayette himself to Mr. Owen, while on a visit to Paris, and recounted by him in a speech delivered in Indiana, in 1840

from the enemy struck at his horses feet, throwing the dirt in his face, and over his clothes. The general continued giving his orders, without noticing the derangement of his toilet.

On another occasion, while Mr. Evans, one of the chaplains of the army, was standing near the general, a shot struck the ground so near as to cover his hat with sand. Somewhat agitated, he took off his hat and said, "see here General." "Mr. Evans," rejoined Washington with his usual composure, "you had better carry that home, and show it to your wife and children."

Major Ferguson, who commanded one of the enemy's rifle corps, thus describes an incident, in a letter to a friend, which occurred just previous to the battle of Brandywine. "We had not lain long, when a rebel officer, remarkable by a hussar dress, pressed toward our army, within a hundred yards of my right flank, not perceiving us. He was followed by another, dressed in dark green and blue, mounted on a bay horse, with a remarkable high cocked hat. I ordered three good shots to steal near, and fire at them; but the idea disgusting me, I recalled the order. The hussar, in returning, made a circuit, but he passed within a hundred yards of us; upon which I advanced from the woods towards him. Upon my calling, he stopped; but, after looking at me, proceeded. I again drew his attention, and made signs to him to stop, levelling my piece at him; but he slowly cantered away. By quick firing, I could have lodged half a dozen of balls in or about him, before he was out of my reach. I had only to determine; but it was not pleasant to fire at the back of an unoffending individual, who was very cooly acquitting himself of his duty; so I let it alone.

"The next day, the surgeon told me that the wounded rebel officers informed him that General Washington was all the morning with the light troops, and only attended by a French officer in the hussar dress, he himself dressed and mounted as I have before described. I am not sorry that I did not know who it was at the time."

ADVENTURES OF MARION.

There are but few characters in the history of the war of the revolution, that can be looked upon with more unqualified respect and admiration, than that of Francis Marion. It is impossible to point out a weakness or failing in his public acts; no emergencies were too great for his resources, and no temptations or suffering too much for his integrity. His patriotism never waned low, and his devotion to his country was never crossed by one selfish consideration. His career, however, does not simply appeal to our judgment, nor only enlist our commendation; it is invested with a romance peculiarly delightful to the imagination. We are charmed by the details of his camp, and follow his enterprises with all the entrancing interest we would feel for the exploits of a favorite character in fiction. But unfortunately, sometimes, when our interest is most excited, the details are most meagre; often when we would hang over the glowing page with pleasure, the record fails and our imagination alone can fill up the sketch. It is a source of regret, which time will rather enhance than remove, that history is so dry and unsatisfactory in reference to Marion. Of all the American leaders, the career of Marion would have afforded the most romantic and thrilling interest. Able biographers, however, have, of late years, gathered together all the knowledge of Marion which their industry could effect, which while we regret it is no more than it is, is sufficiently ull to enable us to appreciate his character and services.

In the gallant and heroic defence of Fort Moultrie, he took an honorable part, and the last gun fired on that day, was directed by him. In the surrender of Charleston, he was saved from captivity by an accident which occured to him during the seige. He was dining with some friends, when the host, after the manner of the mistaken hospitality of the time, locked the door upon his guests until they should be gorged with wine. Marion, who was a man of abstemious habits, and not willing to offend his host by raising a disturbance with his half-tipsy companions, cooly threw up the window and flung himself to the street below. The room was on the second story, the height considerable, and the result was a broken ankle. This severe injury totally unfitted him for action, and he was removed from the city in accordance with the orders for the departure of our officers unfit for duty.

After the surrender of Charleston, the county adjoining was overrun by British troops, while there was no one to head a resistance against them. Moultrie and others were prisoners of war, while Sumpter, Gov. Rutledge, and Horry flew to the north in order to stimulate the energies of the people in that quarter, and gain recruits.

"Marion, meanwhile, incapable of present flight, was compelled to take refuge in the swamp and forest. He was too conspicuous a person, had made too great a figure in previous campaigns, and his military talents were too well known and too highly esteemed not to render him an object of some anxiety as well to friends as foes. Still suffering from the hurts received in Charleston, with bloody and malignant enemies all around him, his safety depended on his secrecy and obscurity alone. Fortunately he had "won

golden opinions from all sorts of people." He had friends among
all classes, who did not permit themselves to sleep while he was
in danger. Their activity supplied the loss of his own. They
watched while he slept. They assisted his feebleness. In the
moment of alarm, he was sped from house to house, from tree to
thicket, from the thicket to the swamp. His "hair-breadth
'scapes" under these frequent exigencies, were no doubt among
the most interesting adventures of his life, furnishing rare material, could they be procured, for the poet and romancer. Unhappily, while the chronicles show the frequent emergency which
attended his painful condition, they furnish nothing more. We
are without details. The melancholy baldness and coldness with
which they narrate events upon which one would like to linger, are
absolutely humbling to the imagination; which, kindled by the
simple historical outline, looks in vain for the satisfaction of those
doubts and inquiries, those hopes and fears, which the provoking
narrative inspires only to defraud. How would some old inquisitive Froissart have dragged, by frequent inquiry from contempo-
raneous lips, the particular fact, the whole adventure, step by
step, item by item,—the close pursuit, the narrow escape,—and
all the long train of little, but efficient circumstances, by which
the story would have been made unique, with all its rich and numerous details! These, the reader must supply from his own
resources of imagination. He must conjecture for himself the
casual warning brought to the silent thicket, by the devoted
friend, the constant woman, or the humble slave; the midnight
bay of the watch-dog or the whistle of the scout; or the sudden
shot, from friend or foe, by which the fugitive is counselled to
hurry to his den. A thousand events arise to the imagination as
likely to have occurred to our partisan, in his hour of feebleness

and danger, from the rapid cavalry of Tarleton, or the close and keen pursuit of the revengeful Tories. To what slight circumstances has he been indebted for his frequent escape! What humble agents have been commissioned by Providence to save a life, that was destined to be so precious to his country's liberties!"

After the restoration of his health, Marion formed his celebrated brigade. Then commenced that species of partisan warfare which the English in vain endeavored to crush, and which kept alive the spirit of patriotism in the South. His name became the terror of the British and Tories. His mode of warfare has been described in an earlier part of this work; our present sketch is merely to present some personal anecdote and adventure.

Marion, who was of diminutive stature, and his person uncommonly light, placed little dependence on his personal prowess. It is related of him that, on one occasion, when he went to draw his sword, he could not because of the rust. Certainly a rich incident in the life of one whose career was so active, but it proves to us that his successes were obtained by the strong power of intellect, and that he ruled his rough, undisciplined men, many of whom were giants in strength, and confirmed in obstinacy, by the mere exercise of moral force. He always rode a high-spirited horse, one of the most powerful chargers the south could produce. When pursuing nothing could escape, and when retreating, nothing could overtake him.

"Being once nearly surrounded by a party of British dragoons, he was compelled, for safety, to pass into a corn-field, by leaping the fence. This field, marked with a considerable descent of surface, had been in fact, a marsh. Marion entered it at the upper side. The dragoons in chase leapt the fence also, and were but a short distance behind him. So completely was he now in their power, that his only mode of escape, was to pass over the fence at the lower side. But here lay a difficulty, which, to all but imself, appeared insurmountable. To drain the ground of its uperfluous waters, a trench had been cut around this part of the field, four feet wide, and of the same depth. Of the mud and clay, removed in cutting it, a bank had been formed, on its inner side, and on top of this, was erected a fence. The elevation of the whole amounted to more than seven feet, a ditch four feet in width, running parallel with it, on the outside, and a foot or more of space intervening between the fence and the ditch. The dragoons, acquainted with the nature and extent of this obstacle, and considering it impossible for their enemy to pass it, pressed towards him, with shouts of exultation and insult, and summoned him to surrender, or perish by the sword. Regardless of their clamor, Marion spurred his horse to the charge. The noble animal, as if conscious that his master's life was in danger, and that on his exertion depended its safety, approached the barrier in his finest style, and with a bound that was almost supernatural, completely cleared the fence and ditch, and recovered himself without injury, on the other side. Marion, immediately, faced his pursuers, discharged his pistols at them, but without effect, and then bidding them ' good morning,' he dashed into an adjoining thicket, leaving the dragoons astonished at what they had seen, and almost doubting if their foe was mortal."

The following incident admirably illustrates Marion's great humanity. He was dining at the hospitable table of Mrs. Moultrie, when it was whispered in his ears, that some of Col. Lee's men were engaged in executing certain tory prisoners. Marion hurried from the table, and seizing his sword, rushed with all haste to the gallows, but reached it in time to save only one poor wretch. Two were already dead. With his drawn sword, and his face flushed with indignation, Marion threatened to kill the first man that made any attempt to continue their infamous proceedings. Rebuked by his words, and overawed by his manner, the men desisted and seperated.

We alluded to Marion's exercise of command by moral force. The following incident, admirably illustrates the means by which he enforced discipline and obedience, and also displays his equal powers of firmness and forbearance.

"He had placed one of his detachments at the plantation of a Mr. George Crofts, on Sampit Creek. This person had proved invariably true to the American cause; had supplied the partisans secretly with munitions of war, with cattle and provisions. He was an invalid, however, suffering from a mortal infirmity, which compelled his removal for medical attendance to Georgetown, then in possession of the enemy. During the absence of the family, Marion placed a sergeant in the dwelling-house, for its protection. From this place, the guard was expelled by two officers of the brigade, and the house stripped of its contents. The facts were first disclosed to Marion by Col. P. Horry, who received them from the wife of Crofts. This lady pointed to the sword of her husband actually at the side of the principal offender. The indignation of Marion was not apt to expend itself in words. Redress was promised to the complainant and she was dismissed. Marion, proceeded with all diligence, to the recovery of the property. But his course was governed by prudence as well as decision. The offenders were men of some influence, and had a small faction in the brigade, which had already proved troublesome, and might be dangerous. One of them was a major, the other a captain. Their names are before us in the MS. memoir of Horry, whose copious details on this subject leave nothing to be supplied. We forbear giving them, as their personal publication would answer no good purpose. They were in command of a body of men, about sixty in number, known as the Georgia Refugee. Upon the minds of these men the offenders had already sought to act, in reference to the expected collision with their general Marion made his preparations with his ordinary quietness, and then dispatched Horry to the person who was in possession of the sword of Crofts; for which he made a formal demand. He refused to give it up, alleging that it was his, and taken in war. 'If the general wants it,' he added, 'let him come for it himself.' When this reply was communicated to Marion he instructed Horry to renew the demand. His purpose seems to have been, discovering the temper of the offender, to gain the necessary time. His officers, meanwhile, were gathering around him. He was making his preparations for a struggle, which might be bloody, which might, indeed, involve not only the safety of his brigade, but his own future usefulness. Horry, however, with proper spirit, entreated not to be sent again to the offender, giving as a reason for his reluctance, that, in consequence of the previous rudeness of the other, he was not in the mood to tolerate a repetition of the indignity, and might, if irritated, be provoked to violence. Marion then dispatched his orderly to the guilty major, with a request, civilly worded, that he might see him at headquarters. He appeared accordingly, accompanied by the captain who had joined with him in the outrage, and under whose influence he appeared to act. Marion renewed his demand, in person for the sword of Crofts. The other again refused to deliver it alleging that 'Crofts was a Tory, and even then with the enemy in Georgetown.'

"'Will you deliver me the sword or not, Major―――!' was the answer which Marion made to this suggestion.

"'I will not!' was the reply of the offender. 'At these words, says Horry in the MS. before us, 'I could forbear no longer, and said with great warmth, 'By G―d, sir, did I command this brigade, as you do, I would hang them both up in half an hour! Marion sternly replied,―'This is none of your business, sir: they are both before me!―Sergeant of the guard, bring me a file of men with loaded arms and fixed bayonets!'―'I was silent!' adds Horry: 'all our field officers in camp were present, and when the second refusal of the sword was given, they all put their hands to their swords in readiness to draw. My own sword was already drawn!'

"In the regular service, and with officers accustomed to, and bred up in, the severe and stern sense of authority which is usually thought necessary to a proper discipline, the refractory offender would most probably have been hewn down in the moment of his disobedience. The effect of such a proceeding, in the present instance, might have been of the most fatal character. The *esprit de corps* might have prompted the immediate followers of the offender to have seized upon their weapons, and, though annihilated, as Horry tells us they would have been, yet several valuable lives might have been lost, which the country could ill have spared. The mutiny would have been put down, but at what a price! The patience and prudence of Marion's character taught him forbearance. His mildness, by putting the offender entirely in the wrong, so justified his severity, as to disarm the followers of the criminals. These, as we have already said, were about sixty in number. Horry continues: 'Their intentions were, to call upon these men for support―our officers well knew that they meant, if possible, to intimidate Marion, so as to [make him] come into their measures of plunder and Tory killing.' The affair fortunately terminated without bloodshed. The prudence of the general had its effect. The delay gave time to the offenders for reflection. Perhaps, looking round upon their followers, they saw no consenting spirit of mutiny in their eyes, encouraging their own; for 'though many of these refugees were present, none offered to back or support the mutinous officers;'—and when the guard that was ordered, appeared in sight, the companion of the chief offender was seen to touch the arm of the other, who then proffered the sword to Marion, saying,' General, you need not have sent for the guard.' Marion, refusing to receive it, referred him to the sergeant of the guard, and thus doubly degraded, the dishonored major of Continentals—for he was such—disappeared from sight, followed by his associate."

What adds to our respect for Marion and his followers, was the patient endurance with which they suffered every kind of privation and hardihood. During the whole early part of his career, Marion slept in the open air. When he took command of the "Brigade," he had one blanket, but on one occasion as he was sleeping soundly, after one of his forced marches, upon a bed of pine straw, it took fire, his blanket was destroyed, and he himself very narrowly escaped destruction. The cap that he wore was shrivelled up by the flames. After this event, he was even denied he poor luxury of a blanket, the cause for which his life and time was wholly surrendered, not being able to afford him another one.

In other places the reader will find sketches of the exploits enacted by Horry, Jasper, and Macdonald, all of whom served under Marion. We propose here to subjoin a few of the most striking adventures and exploits of others of his heroic band. The constant employment which he gave his scouts, and in them it was necessary to repose unlimited confidence, as it was by their fidelity and activity that his own movements were controlled, taught them coolness and audacity.

"They were out in all directions and at all hours. They did he double duty of patrol and spies. They hovered about the posts of the enemy, crouching in the thicket, or darting along the plain, picking up prisoners, and information, and spoils together. They cut off stragglers, encountered patrols of the foe, and arrested his supplies on the way to the garrison. Sometimes the single scout, buried in the thick tops of the tree, looked down upon the march of his legions, or hung perched over the hostile encampment till it slept, then slipping down, stole through the silent host, carrying off a drowsy sentinel, or a favorite charger, upon which the daring spy flourished conspicuous among his less fortunate companions. The boldness of these adventurers was, sometimes, wonderful almost beyond belief. It was the strict result of that confidence in their woodman skill, which the practice of their leader, and his invariable success, naturally taught them to entertain."

Gavin Witherspoon, on one occasion, while performing his duty as scout, performed the following exploit. "He had taken refuge in Pedee Swamp from the pursuit of the enemy, and, while hiding, discovered one of the camps of the Tories who had been in pursuit of him. Whitherspoon proposed to his four comrades to watch the enemy's camp, until the Tories were asleep. But his men timidly shrunk from the performance, expressing their dread of superior numbers. Witherspoon undertook the adventure himself. Creeping up to the encampment, he found that they slept at the butt of a pine tree, which had been torn up by the root. Their guns were piled against one of its branches at a little distance from them. These he first determined to secure, and, still creeping, with the skill and caution of an experienced scout, he succeeded in his object. The guns once in his possession, he aroused the Tories by commanding their surrender They were seven in number, unarmed, and knew nothing of the force of the assailant. His own more timid followers drew near in sufficient time to assist in securing the prisoners."

The following instance of daring is related of Major James, of whose courage the reader will find another instance, in another place. In one of Marion's sudden attacks upon the enemy, James distinguished himself, by singling out Major Gainey, the commander of the enemy's troops, for personal combat. "But Gainey shrank from his more powerful assailant, and sought safety in flight. James pursued for a distance of half a mile. In the eagerness of the chase he did not perceive that he was alone and unsupported. It was enough that he was gaining upon his enemy, who was almost within reach of his sword, when the chase brought them suddenly upon a body of Tories who had rallied upon the road. There was not a moment to be lost. Hesitation would have been fatal. But our gallant Major was not to be easily intimidated. With great coolness and presence of mind, waving his sword aloft, he cried out, 'come on, boys! here they are!' and rushed headlong upon the group of enemies, as if perfectly assured of support. The *ruse* was successful. The Tories broke once more, and sought safety from their individual enemy in the recesses of Pedee swamp."

During the attack on Georgetown by Marion and Lee, a party of the English made an attack upon a small party of the Americans who were in possession of an inclosure that surrounded a house, from which they had but a few moments before expelled the enemy. The royalists were most anxious to recover possession of the ground, and their leader urged them to the attack, by exclaiming: "Rush on, my brave fellows, they are only worthless militia, and have no bayonets." Sergeant Ord, a soldier renowned for his heroic valor, immediately hastened to the gate of the inclosure, and placed himself as barrier to their progress And when they rushed up to force their way in, he laid six of his enemies, in succession, dead at his feet, crying out at every thrust. "Any bayonets here—none at all to be sure!" following up his strokes with such rapidity and force, that the British party fell back dismayed before the unwavering front, and Herculaen strength of their single adversary, and were obliged to retire Certainly, this was a performance not excelled, and, scarcely, equaled, by any of the Homeric heroes.

The following exploit as enacted by one of "Marion's men," was worthy to have been performed by Richard of the Lion Heart, and reminds us of the incident when that "Pearl of Crusaders" dashed up singly before the army of Saladin, and by the simple shaking of his spear held in check the Mahommaden hosts. Colonel Watson, when in pursuit of Marion, came up with his guard at Wiboo swamp, and, immediately, commenced the attack. Horry, who commanded the cavalry, was thrown back in disorder, and the enemy's horse were following up the advantage, pressing closely upon the whigs as they were crossing a narrow causeway when Gavin James, a man of gigantic frame, and mounted on a powerful horse, whirled in front of the advancing column, and discharged his musket, shooting the first man dead. In an instant, a volley blazed from the advancing foe, but, wonderful to state, not a shot took effect. A dragoon rushed forward, but he was, instantly transfixed by the bayonet in the hand of James—another shared the same fate, and fell beside his companion. Awed by a single adversary, the whole column halted, when animated and inspired by such signal daring, the cavalry of Marion turned upon their enemy, and charged with such impetuosity as to scatter the royalists before them.

A ROMANTIC STORY.

At the battle of Eutaw Springs, in the midst of the conflict, as the two armies were hurled on each other with a fearful force, two officers of the same rank became engaged in a desperate personal conflict. Their swords flashed with inconceivable rapidity, now one advanced, and now the other, each bending the whole thought of his soul to the single adversary before him, and growing unmindful of the din around him. They heeded not the crash of artillery, the rapid clang of arms, the loud shriek of pain, nor the wild cry of despair. But it soon became manifest that the loyalist officer, though somewhat inferior to the other in weight, was the better swordsman; this the American perceived, and resolving at all hazards to conquer his foe, he beat down his guard, closed in, clasped him in his firm embrace, and made him prisoner

When the captor and his prisoner met after the battle, it was observed that there was a strong personal resemblance between them. They were both youthful, high-minded, and chivalrous gentlemen; and a strong unanimity of feeling existing between them, with a respect already implanted by their respective bearing in the combat, a familiar acquaintance sprang up, which gradu ally grew into friendship, and ended in a sincere, and ardent mutual attachment, as chivalrous in its nature, as it was romantic in its origin. Some little time after the battle, the American officer returning home, on furlough, requested and obtained permission for his captive friend to accompany him.

They traveled like brother knights of old, each pledged to the other's defence, and bound to consider all alike as common friends or common enemies. Their route lay through a district, which was the sanguinary field of many bloody collisions, and cursed by prowling detachments of tories, who exercised a robber's privilege of warring on all whom it pleased their fancy to construe into foes, or who tempted their avarice, or excited their vengeance. One day, the two heroes were suddenly overtaken by a shower, and throwing their cloaks over their shoulders, they retreated under the shelter of a group of trees. Suddenly there appeared on the road, a party of tories, who with drawn swords, and shouting over their anticipated plunder, dashed toward the spot where stood the two friends. The high-souled American resolved not to fall into the hands of those, whom, every instinct of his nature, and every impulse of his virtuous mind, stamped as men to detest and loathe, and as stinging aspens in the bosom of his country; and, the heroic Briton, scorning the motives that actuated them, and although to make himself known, was but to obtain safety and freedom, also resolved to defend himself to the last, and fall or live, the friend of him by whom he had been so generously distinguished. But their cunning and their valor achieved for them a glorious triumph. With waving swords, and with signals to the rear, as if urging companions behind them to follow, they spurred their horses, and both together dashed upon the approaching enemy. The fury of their onset, the determined vigor with which they whirled their weapons above their heads, and their shouts for their supposed companions to follow, alarmed their opponents, who offered but a feeble resistance, and then fled rapidly, leaving the field to their victorious enemy, whom they outnumbered by many fold.

With numerous adventures that more effectually linked their friendship, they arrived safely at the home of the American officer. Here the Englishman was welcomed, and in the home of his friend he found those who generously admitted into their confidence and friendship, one who had become so attached to one of its promising members. In course of his sojourn here, some remarks were dropped which led to inquiries, and the father of the American, to the unmingled joy of all parties, discovered that the two officers were first cousins. Their striking personal resemblance thus became accounted for, and perhaps their involuntary and mental attraction may be attributed to the same cause.

The joy of the American family in discovering a kinsman so lofty in virtue, and possessed of all generous qualities, and one who brought to their circle, high talents and briliant parts, that daily won upon their hearts, was greatly augmented by the appearance of an attachment springing up between the new found cousin, and a sister of the American. This lady was amiable and highly accomplished, and charmed by the bearing of the generous stranger, she soon yielded to him more of affection and admiration, than was due to a cousin. He also was moved by her beauty and her many amiable traits, and thus they became betrothed, to the unbounded satisfaction of the brother. The Englishman had as effectually been conquered by the beauty of the sister, as by the superior strength of the brother. He was a prisoner, soul and body, in the conquerer's family. The reader may be assured that what we write is not fiction, though it sounds marvelously like legends of knightly love and conquest in the olden time. The facts of the story are given by Dr. Caldwell, author of a life of Gen. Greene, who knew the parties when a boy, and saw them often.

But alas! our romance now becomes a tragedy. The stern front of Mars breaks in upon the scene, and Fate, with his iron hand, rends the happy picture. The youthful foreigner, has been exchanged, and a summons comes demanding his presence in his regiment. The duty is a sad one, but his honor compels him to yield, and the lady, worthy of his chivalrous heroism, bids him go, as she would be the last to wither his laurels. Never went forth mailed knight, followed by prayers of greater loveliness, or accompanied by the blessings of superior beauty. Their parting was a scene of woe and tenderness. The future was a blank with no lankmark that might show them where to hope. Danger and death hovered on the horizon, and gloomy uncertainty racked the present. The lover was to bear arms against his betrothed's brother, and the two friends were again to assume to each other the deadly front of war. But they parted, duty pointing to each his course. Ere the lovers seperated, however, they pledged themselves to remain faithful to each other, and, in the event of a happy reunion, to become united in wedlock. With mingled hopes and fears, the Briton hastened to his regiment, leaving a sad vacuum in the circle where he had brought so much joy, and eft so much sorrow. But his noble heart was soon doomed to ink beneath a blow, that, at once, and forever, prostrated his hopes of happiness, and consigned them to the grave where lay buried his love. But a few weeks after the departure of the officer, the young lady was stricken down by an epidemic, which ravaged alike on the young, the hopeful and the beautiful, as it did on the withered, and the defiled, and her hopeful page of life was closed suddenly and forever.

CAPTURE, IMPRISONMENT, AND ESCAPE OF GENERAL WADSWORTH.

"In the spring of 1780, General Peleg Wadsworth was appointed to the command of a party of state troops in Camden, in the district of Maine. At the expiration of the period for which the troops were engaged, in February following, General Wadsworth dismissed his troops, retaining six soldiers only as his guard, as he was making preparations to depart from the place. A neighboring inhabitant communicated his situation to the British commander at Penobscot, and a party of twenty-five soldiers commanded by Lieut. Stockton, was sent to make him a prisoner. They embarked in a small schooner, and landing within four miles of the General's quarters, they were concealed in the house of one Snow, a Methodist preacher, professedly a friend to him, but really a traitor, till eleven o'clock in the evening, when they made their arrangements for the attack on the general's quarters

"The party rushed suddenly on the sentinel, who gave the alarm, and one of his comrades instantly opened the door of the kitchen, and the enemy were so near as to enter with the sentinel. The lady of the general, and her friend, Miss Fenno of Boston, were in the house at the time, and Mrs. Wadsworth escaped from the room of her husband into that of Miss Fenno.

"The assailants soon became masters of the whole house, except the room where the general was, and which was strongly barred, and they kept up a constant firing of musketry into the windows and doors except into those of the ladies' room. General Wadsworth was provided with a pair of pistols, a blunderbuss and a fusee, which he employed with great dexterity, being determined to defend himself to the last moment. With his pistols, which he discharged several times, he defended the rooms of his window and a door which opened into a kitchen. His blunderbuss he snapped several times, but unfortunately it missed fire, he then secured his fusee, which he discharged on some who were breaking through the windows, and obliged them to flee. He next defended himself with his bayonet, till he received a ball through his left arm, when he surrendered, which terminated the contest. The firing, however, did not cease from the kitchen until the general unbarred the door, when the soldiers rushed into the room, and one of them who had been badly wounded, pointing a musket at his breast, exclaimed with an oath, 'you have taken my life and I will take yours.' But Lieutenant Stockton turned the musket aside and saved his life. The commanding officer now applauded the general for his admirable defence, and assisted in putting on his clothes, saying, 'you see we are in a critical situation, and therefore you must excuse haste.' Mrs. Wadsworth threw a blanket over him, and Miss Fenno affixed a handkerchief closely around his wounded arm.

"In this condition, though much exhausted, he, with a wounded American soldier, was directed to march on foot, while the British wounded soldiers were mounted on a horse taken from the general's barn. They departed in great haste. When they proceded about a mile, they met at a small house, a number of people collected, and who inquired if they had taken General Wadsworth. They said no, and added, that they must leave a wounded man in their care, and if they paid proper attention to him, they should be compensated, but if not, they would burn down their house; but the man appeared to be dying. General Wadsworth was mounted on the horse behind the other wounded soldier, and was warned that his safety depended on his silence. Having crossed over a frozen mill-pond about a mile in length, they were met by some of their party who had been left behind. At this place they found a British privateer which brought the party from the fort. The captain on being told that he must return there with the prisoner and the party, and seeing some of his men wounded, became outrageous, and d———d the general for a rebel, demanded how he dared to fire on the king's troops, and ordered him to help launch the boat, or he would put his hanger through his body. The general replied, that he was a prisoner, and badly wounded, and could not assist in launching the boat. Lieutenant Stockton, on hearing of this abusive treatment, in a manner honorable to himself, told the captain that the prisoner was a gentleman, had made a brave defence, and was to be treated accordingly, and added, that his conduct should be represented to General Campbell. After this the captain treated the prisoner with great civility and afforded him every comfort in his power.

"General Wadsworth had left the ladies in the house, not a window of which escaped destruction. The doors were broken down and two of the rooms were on fire, the floors were covered with blood, and on one of them lay a brave old soldier dangerously wounded, begging for death, that he might be released from misery. The anxiety and distress of Mrs. Wadsworth was inexpressible, and that of the general was greatly increased by the uncertainty in his mind respecting the fate of his little son, only tive years old, who had been exposed to every danger by the firing into the house, but he had the happiness afterwards of hearing of his safety.

"Having arrived at the British fort, the capture of General Wadsworth was soon announced, and the shore thronged with spectators, to see the man, who through the preceding year had disappointed all the designs of the British in that quarter; and loud shouts were heard from the rabble that covered the shore; but when he arrived at the fort and was conducted into the officer's guard room, he was treated with politeness. General Campbell, the commandant of the British garrison, sent his compliments to him, and a surgeon to dress his wound, assuring him that his situation should be made comfortable. The next morning, General Campbell invited him to breakfast, and at table paid him many compliments in the defence he had made, observing however, that he had exposed himself in a degree not perfectly justifiable. General Wadsworth replied, that from the manner of the attack, he had no reason to suspect any design of taking him alive, and that he intended therefore to sell his life as dearly as possible. He was then informed, that a room in the officer's barracks within the fort, was prepared for him, and that an orderly sergeant should daily attend him to breakfast and dinner at the commandant's table. Having retired to his solitary apartment, and while his spirits were extremely depressed by a recollection of the past, and by his present situation, he received from General Campbell several books of amusement, and soon after a visit from him, kindly endeavoring to cheer the spirits of his prisoner by conversation. The principal officers of the garrison also called upon him, and from them all, whom he daily met at the commandant's table, he received particular attention and kindness

"He now made application for a flag of truce, by which means he could transmit a letter to the governor of Massachusetts, and another to Mrs. Wadsworth. This was granted, on the condition that the letter to the governor should be inspected. The flag was entrusted to Lieutenant Stockton, and on his return, the general was relieved from all anxiety respecting his wife and family At the end of five weeks, he requested of General Campbell, the customary privilege of parole, and received in reply, that his case had been reported to the commanding officer at New York, and that no alteration could be made, till orders were received from that quarter. In about two months time, Mrs. Wadsworth and Miss Fenno arrived, and the officers of the garrison contributed to render their visit agreeable to all concerned.

"About the same time, orders were received from the commanding general at New York, which were concealed from General Wadsworth, but he finally learnt that he was not to be paroled nor exchanged, but was to be sent to England as a rebel of too much consequence to be at liberty. Not long afterwards, Major Benjamin Benton, a brave and worthy man, who had served under the general the preceding summer, was taken and brought into the fort, and lodged in the same room with him. He had been informed, that both himself and the general, were to be sent immediately after the return of a privateer now on a cruise, either o New York or Halifax, and thence to England. The prisoners mmediately resolved to make a desperate effort to effect their escape. They were confined in a grated room in the officer's barracks within the fort. The walls of this fortress, exclusively of the depth of the ditch surrounding it, were twenty feet high, with fraising on the top, and chevanx de frise at the bottom Two sentinels were always in the entry, and their door—the upper part of which was glass, might be opened by their watchmen whenever they thought proper, and was actually opened at seasons of peculiar darkness and silence. At the exterior doors of the entries, sentinels were also stationed, as were others in the body of the fort, and at the quarters of General Campbell. At the guard house a strong guard was daily mounted. Several sentinels were stationed on the walls of the fort, and a complete line occupied them by night. Without the ditch, glacis and abattis, another complete set of soldiers patroled through the night, and a piquet guard was placed in or near the isthmus leading from the fort to the main land. Notwithstanding all these fearful obstacles to success, they resolved to make the perilous attempt.

"The room in which they were confined, was railed with boards. One of these they determined to cut off so as to make a hole large enough to pass through, and then to creep along till they should come to the next or middle entry; and there lower themselves down into this entry by a blanket. If they should not be discovered, the passage to the walls of the fort was easy In the evening, after the sentinels had seen the prisoners retired to bed, General Wadsworth got up, and standing in a chair attempted to cut with his knife, the intended opening, but soon found it impracticable. The next day, by giving a soldier a dollar they procured a gimblet. With this instrument, they proceeded cautiously and as silently as possible to separate the board, and in order to conceal every appearance from their servants and from the officers, their visitors, they carefully covered the gimblet holes with chewed bread. At the end of three weeks, their labors were so far completed, that it only remained to cut with a knife the part which were left to hold the piece in its place. When their preparations were finished, they learned that the privateer in which they were to embark, was daily expected.

"In the evening of the 18th of June, a very severe storm of rain, with great darkness and almost incessant lightning came on. This the prisoners considered as the propitious moment. Having extinguished their lights, they began to cut the corners of the board, and in less than an hour the intended opening was completed. The noise which the operation occasioned, was drowned by the rain falling on the roof. Major Benton first ascended to the ceiling, and pressed himself through the opening. General Wadsworth next, having put the corner of his blanket through the hole and made it fast by a strong wooden skewer, attempted to make his way through, standing on a chair below, but it was with extreme difficulty that he at length effected it, and reached the middle entry. From this he passed through the door which he found open, and made his way to the wall of the fort, and had to encounter the greatest difficulty before he could ascend to the top. He had now to creep along the top of the fort between the sentry boxes, at the very moment when the relief was shifting sentinels, but the falling of the heavy rain kept the sentinels within their boxes, and favored his escape. Having now fastened his blanket round a picket at the top, he let himself down through the chevaux de frise to the ground, and, in a manner astonishing to himself, made his way into the open field Here he was obliged to grope his way among rocks, stumps and brush in the darkness of night, till he reached the cove. Happily the tide had ebbed, and he was enabled to cross the water, which was about a mile in breadth, and not more than three feet deep.

"About two o'clock in the morning, General Wadsworth found himself a mile and a half from the fort, and he proceeded through a thick wood and brush to the Penobscot river, and, after passing some distance along the shore, being seven miles from the fort, to his unspeakable joy, he saw his friend Benton advancing toward him. Major Benton had been obliged to encounter in his course equal difficulties with his companion, and such were the incredible perils, dangers and obstructions, which they surmounted, that their escape may be considered almost miraculous.

"It was now necessary that they should cross the Penobscot river, and very fortunately they discovered a canoe with oars on the shore suited to their purpose. While on the river, they discovered a barge with a party of the British from the fort, in pursuit of them, but by taking an oblique course, and plying their oars to the utmost, they happily eluded the eyes of their pursuers, and arrived safe on the western shore. After having wandered in the wilderness for several days and nights, exposed to extreme fatigue and cold, and with no other food than a little dry bread and meat, which they brought in their pockets from the fort, they reached the settlements on the river St. George, and no further difficulties attended their return to their respective families."

GALLANT ENTERPRISE OF MAJOR BARTON.

IN the latter part of 1776, Major General Lee, during Washington's retreat through the Jerseys, unfortunately fell into the hands of the enemy, and was conveyed with triumph into New

York. This circumstance, at the darkest era of our revolutionary contest, greatly depressed the spirits of the Americans, particularly as there was no prisoner in their hands for whom he could be exchanged.

Under these circumstances many enterprises were projected to capture some English officer of equal rank, by which means an exchange could be effected, but it was reserved for Major Barton of the Rhode Island line, to successfully plan and accomplish this purpose.

Shortly after the capture of Lee, the British took possession of the islands of Rhode Island, Canonicut and Prudence, in Narragansett Bay. Major Barton was, at this time, attached to a regiment, under command of Colonel Stanton, that was stationed at Tiverton, on the eastern shore of the Bay. From this place, he anxiously watched an opportunity to effect the object he had at heart. In June 1777, he learned from a prisoner, that General Richard Prescott had established his head-quarters on the west side of Rhode Island, and the prisoner gave a minute description of the house. This account was, a few days after, confirmed by a deserter from the British ranks. Conceiving the favorable opportunity now afforded, he began to make preparations for the execution of his design. But there were serious obstacles in the way. The enterprize proposed was hazardous to the extreme, and its failure liable to bring upon it, condemnation as rash and foolhardy; but then again, if successful, an enviable and honorable renown would be the reward of those concerned. He communicated his designs to Col. Stanton, his superior officer, who gave it his commendation, and permitted him to select from his regiment such men and officers as he desired to assist him in the attack. From an apprehension that his design might become known to the enemy, he did not make a selection of the necessary number of men until the last moment, and then with a desire that he might be accompanied only by volunteers, he ordered his whole company upon parade, and in a brief speech stated that he wished to obtain forty volunteers for an expedition of great hazard, and all that wished to accompany him, should signify it by stepping from the ranks. Without one exception, the whole regiment advanced. He now found it necessary to make the selection himself, and he did so, choosing those whose courage and fidelity were tested. Several officers had personaly volunteered, but not one of the party, save Barton himself, knew of the object in view, but all trusted to the honor and courage of their leader

Some delay was experienced in procuring boats, but on the 4th of July 1777, they embarked from Tiverton for Bristol. In crossing Mount Hope Bay, they suffered from a severe storm, but they arrived at Bristol at midnight. On the morning of the 5th, the Major, with his officers, went over to Hog Island for the purpose of reconnoitering the position of the enemy. Here he revealed the object of the expedition, and his plan for its accomplishment.

It was not until the evening of the 5th, that the party again embarked. Crossing Narragansett Bay, they landed on Warwick Neck, but were here detained by a severe storm which retarded their plans considerably. On the 9th, however, it became clear, and they prepared once more to sail, with the intention of proceeding directly to Rhode Island. Some hours after the set of sun, all was still, and the darkness affording them a protection from observation, the little squadron shot out from the land, and proceeded noiselessly and cautiously on its course. This was a very hazardous part of the enterprise, as there was great danger of being discovered by some of the ships of war that lay near the shore. Cautiously gliding along between the islands of Prudence and Patience, by which means they were secured from observation from the enemy's shipping that lay off by Hope Island, they advanced rapidly to their destination. While passing the north end of Prudence Island, they could distinctly hear the sentinels from the ships, cry out, "All's well.' The night was one of excessive darkness, and this fortunate circumstance, no doubt contributed largely to the success of the plan.

The landing was effected without difficulty. In order to secure a rapid retreat, one man was commanded to remain in each boat, and instructed to be ready for departing at a moment?s notice When all were on shore, the requisite instructions were given and the party advanced rapidly in the direction of General Prescott's head-quarters. The difficulties of Major Barton's situation will be, readily appreciated. Even should he surprise General Prescott, a very few moments would suffice for an alarm to be carried to the enemy, and if so, the whole British army would be upon them before they could get to their forts, Or even should they reach their boats, if an alarm were conveyed to the enemy's shipping, their retreat would, with certainty, be cut off. It was, therefore, necessary to proceed with the utmost caution and care; and to act with equal daring, prudence, and celerity.

The distance to the residence of the English general, was about a mile. The party was divided into five divisions; one to approach the door on the south side, another one on the east, and a third on the west side, there being three doors to the house, while the fourth division was to guard the road, and the fifth to be ready to act on emergencies. They were obliged in order to reach the house, to pass the guard house of the enemy, on their left, and on the right a house occupied by a company of cavalry.

On arriving at Prescott's head-quarters, they were challenged by a sentinel who was stationed at the gate of the front yard. The darkness of the night prevented him from determining the nature of the party approaching, but, as they continued to advance in silence, he again challenged them, demanding, "Who goe there?" "Friends" said Barton. "Advance and give the countersign," was the rejoinder. "Pho!" replied Barton, as he continued to advance close to the person of the sentinel, "we have no countersign—have you seen any rascals to night?" Almost simultaneous with this remark, Barton suddenly seized the musket of the sentinel, and charged him to make no noise on the penalty of instant death. So much had been accomplished in perfect silence. The divisions rapidly advanced to their respective positions, while Barton questioned the bewildered and terrified sentinel, as to whether the General was in the house, who replied that he was. The signal was now given, and in an instant the south door was burst open, and the division there stationed, rushed into the building followed by the Major.

The first person Barton met, was Mr. Perwig, who denied that General Prescott was in the house, and his son also obstinately denied the presence of the English officer. Not being able to find him in their rapid search through the apartments, Barton now had result to stratagem. In a loud voice, he declared his intention of capturing the general dead or alive, and ordered his soldiers immediately to set fire to the house. At this juncture, a a voice which Barton suspected to belong to the General, inquired the cause of the disturbance. Barton rushed to the apartments from which came the voice he heard, and finding there an elderly gentleman, just rising from his bed, he accosted him as General Prescott. To this the gentleman assented, and declared he bore the name and title. "Then you are my prisoner," replied Bar-ton. "I acknowledge that I am," was the rejoinder. He was only allowed time to partially dress himself, when he was hurried off by his captors.

Meanwhile a singular circumstance had occurred. At the very moment when Barton first gained admission into the house, one of the British soldiers managed to escape, and flew to the quarters of the main guard to give the alarm. This man, in the alarm of the moment, rushed forth with no other clothing than his shirt; and having hastily explained the matter to the sentinel on duty, he passed on to the quarters of the cavalry, which was much more remote from the head-quarters of the General. But when the sentinel came to explain the matter to the officer of the guard, it seemed so incredible, that he was laughed at, and was told that he had seen a ghost. He admitted that the messenger was clothed in white, and after being heartily laughed at for his credulity, was ordered back to his station, and the guard went back to their quarters. This was a most fortunate circumstance, for had the alarm of the soldier been believed, nothing could have preserved the gallant Major and his band from destruction.

The whole party with the English general in their midst, marched rapidly toward the shore. When they arrived at the boat, their prisoner, who had been hurried away half dressed, was permitted to complete his toilet. They re-embarked with all possible haste, and had not got far from the island, when the discharge of cannon and three sky rockets gave the signal for alarm But, for some cause, the signal was not understood by those on the ships, and, by this fortunate circumstance, the gallant band was preserved, for it would have been easy for their enemy to have cut off their retreat. Although full of anxiety and apprehension, they bent every nerve to reach their port of destination, and happily succeeded without meeting with any obstacle.

When they had landed, General Prescott said to the Major, "Sir, you have made an amazing bold push to night." "We have been fortunate," was the modest reply. The British commander was conveyed as a prisoner to Providence, while this gallant enterprise soon becoming noised abroad, it was received everywhere with unqualified admiration, and the gallant Major and his party, became the heroes of the campaign. It was not long after the performance of this brilliant exploit, that the prisoner was exchanged for General Lee, to the great joy and satisfaction of the American army.

AN INTERESTING STORY.

ISRAEL Israel, a native of Pennsylvania, after having passed ten years in the island of Barbadoes, and amassed a considerable property, returned to his native land to enjoy his wealth, and to be restored to the society of his family. He married and prepared to pass the remainder of his years in quiet and ease, when the war broke out, and his whole fortune became sacrificed. From the commencement of the struggle, he had resolved to take up arms for the cause of freedom, but his unprotected family entreated so urgently not to be left alone, and exposed to a merciless enemy, that he determined to draw lots with his younger brother, Joseph, to decide which should become a soldier. The chance fell upon the younger, and it became Israel's duty to devote himself to the safety and welfare of his family. He took up his residence on a small farm near Wilmington, in Deleware, while his mother and her family resided at Philadelphia. When this city fell into the hands of the British, the privations and hardships endured by the whig families resident in the town, were all that a rapacious soldiery could inflict. Each household had several soldiers quartered upon it, who took delight in terrifying and plundering its helpless inmates. Such was the condition of Mrs Israel, who was deprived of supplies and in want of the actual necessities. Israel, who watched over them with a continued anxiety, learned of this, and this knowledge determined him to undertake a hazardous journey into the town and to smuggle supplies for his suffering family. A tory neighbor, who professed great sympathy for him, gave him the countersign.

It was towards evening, on a day in the latter part of the year 1777—that darkest era of the American cause —that Israel approached the city of Philadelphia, on the road leading from Wilmington. His large and powerful frame was enveloped in a capacious cloak, which not only was a protection against the weather, but which served to conceal sundry parcels of provisions, and a bag of money. It was sometime after dark when he reached the ferry, when he was hailed by the sentinel, with "Who goes there?"

'A friend," was the reply given with an anxious heart.

"The countersign!"

He promptly gave the countersign.

Pass friend!" replied the sentinel; and with a beating heart, the adventurous whig passed quickly on. The main difficulty was now over, and his enterprise promised a successful issue.

A few moments more sufficed to bring him to his mother's residence, which he found in possession of several soldiers, quartered upon the family. Among them was a fierce and ferocious looking Hessian, whose aspect was well calculated to terrify the timid, and produce disgust among the brave. But he was welcomed with open arms by his family, and their happiness was complete from the fact that the younger brother, Joseph, was there on a secret visit also. But their joy was of short duration. At eleven o'clock, while seated at supper, the tramp of horses was heard without; and almost immediately, there was a clamor at the door, and an imperious voice demanded admittance. The scene of peace within, was instantly changed to one of consternation and dismay. The brothers were frantically entreated to fly. The younger sprang up the stairs, threw off his uniform, and escaped upon the roof of the house. The noise below had now become furious, and further delay in admitting them was impossible. Accompanied by the pale and terrified females, Mr. Israel proceeded to unbar the door, when the intruders, headed by the Hessian sergeant, rushed in, and roughly seized Mr. Israel's arm, exclaiming, "We have caught him at last—the rebel rascal."

With an undisturbed mien, a calmness unshaken by the imminence of the danger, and a consciousness that his brother's safety could only be secured by delay, he shook off his assailants, while he quietly demanded what was meant, and who it was that dared to charge him of being a rebel. The Hessian pointed to Cæsar, a slave Mr. Israel had brought from the West Indies.

The young man turned to the negro with a terrible look, and exclaimed, "Dare you, Cæsar, call me a rebel?" The guilty black hung his head and trembled. "Gentlemen," said Mr. Israel, "there is some mistake here. My brother Joseph is the person meant, I presume. Let me fetch the uniform; and then you can judge for yourselves. Cæsar come with me."

Grasping the arm of the black, the young man led him up stairs, exclaiming in his ear, "not one word you rascal, or I'll kill you upon the spot." He procured the uniform and returned to his captors, and when its entire disproportion became apparent, Joseph being light and short of build, while Israel was of a towering and robust frame, the soldiers acknowledged their mistake and the Hessian officer made some rough attempts at apologising. He then impertinently seated himself at the supper table, from which the family had been driven by their terror, and saying, "as your supper is ready, we will sit down." Mr. Israel controlled his resentment, and the family returned to their places at the table, and patiently endeavored to listen to the coarse and brutal remarks of their untimely guest. The young ladies restrained their terror, but still trembling secretly, for fear that the noble indignation of their brother, would lead him to some act of imprudence. And indeed it was only by a powerful exercise of his self-control that he was enabled to submit to his brutal and disgusting conversation. He gave boastful details of his exploits in slaughtering the rebels, so atrocious in their recital, that Mr. Israel several times grasped his knife, with an impulse to strike down the savage, but the entreating looks of his agonized mother and sisters, restrained the blow.

"That Paoli affair," said he continuing his recital, " was capital! I was with General Grey in the attack. It was just after midnight when we forced the outposts, and not a noise was heard so loud as the dropping of a musket. How the fellows turned out of their encampment when they heard us! What a running about—barefoot and half clothed—and in the light of their own fires! These showed us where to chase them, while they could not see us. We killed three hundred of the rebels with the bayonet; I stuck them myself like so many pigs—one after another—till the blood ran out of the touch-hole of my musket."

The horrible story of the bloody-minded Hessian, was interrupted by Mr. Israel, who starting to his feet, with face pale with rage, and his eyes glancing fire, was about to inflict summary vengeance on the wretch, but his sisters sprang forward, and shriek from the younger one, who fell fainting in his arms, prevented the catastrophe that might have ensued. All now thrown into confusion, the Hessian bade them good night, and left the house.

Relieved from the presence so much dreaded, they now prepared for the sad scene of parting. Before departing, Mr. Israel summoned Cæsar before him, and sternly questioned the black who declared that he had been compelled to do what he had done, and now solemnly promised fidelity for the future. He always remained faithful to his promise. The parting was a scene of subdued anguish and pain, for the danger was not over. Tearing himself from their arms, Mr. Israel left the house, and hastened on his journey homeward. But scarcely had he arrived upon his farm at Wilmington, than he with his brother-in-law, were arrested upon the information of the loyalist from whom he had received the countersign, and carried on board a frigate lying in the Delaware, directly opposite to his farm, where they were confined, in order to be tried as *spies*.

He was treated with the utmost severity in his captivity. Several of his tory neighbors came forward to testify against him, and declared that while the tory population had all come forward to furnish their share of provisions for the royal army, he was heard to declare, that he, "*would sooner drive his cattle as a pres* ent to General Washington, than receive thousands of dollars * British gold for them."

When this speech was told the commander, he gave orders for detachment to proceed to the farm, and drive the cattle down to the water's edge, and slay them in the full view of the prisoners. This order gave an opportunity for the display of one of the most intrepid acts of female heroism that occurred during the whole war.

The young wife of Mr. Israel, had been overcome by anguish, at the fearful fate which seemed to await her husband and brother. She was but nineteen, of a slight and symmetrical figure, considerable beauty, and of a modest, retiring deportment, which gave no promise of that heroism, that a trying moment was about to develop.

From the farm she saw the soldiers land from the ships, and march towards the meadow which contained her husband's cattle. She divined their purpose, and instantly resolved, to thwart it. Calling to a little boy, eight years old, to follow her, she started for the field with her utmost speed. In an instant the bars were down, and she was hurrying forward to drive the herd through the opening. The soldiers called out to her to desist, or they would fire.

"Fire away!" exclaimed she, neither fearing nor hesitating. They fired, and the balls flew thick about her, while the frightened cattle began to run in every direction. Heedless of the continued threats of the soldiers, she headed them off, and drove them toward the barn-yard.

"Do not let one escape, Joe!" exclaimed she, while the bullets continued to whistle around her. And not one did escape! The little boy became so paralyzed with terror, that he fell to the ground, but seizing him in her arms, the heroic woman herself drove them into the barn-yard, and put up the bars. The soldiers either baffled by her courage, or out of respect to it, did not pursue their intentions, and returned to their vessel.

This scene had passed in view of the officers of the frigate, and the two prisoners. The fear and agony endured by the husband and brother, while they saw the peril in which the wife was placed, must have been great, while they openly showed their exultation at her triumph.

At last they were brought to trial. Mr. Israel openly confesse his visit to Philadelphia, stating the cause, which was to carry re lief to his suffering parent and family. Matters looked dark for them, but Mr. Israel having learned that the officers of the court belonged to the order of Masons, and being himself a member, at the close of his story, made the secret sign of the brotherhood to the presiding officer. There was an evident change in his favor at once. The officer's stern countenance softened, and the prisoners were eventually acquitted. The court severely rebuked the informers, for preferring charges against an honorable man, engaged on a mission of love and duty. The prisoners were dismissed with honor; but the magnanimity of a verdict, not based upon principles of justice, but upon a connection foreign to the point at issue, may well be questioned.*

---

* Mrs. Ellet's "Women of the Revolution."

A THRILLING NARRATIVE.

The following Revolutionary reminisence we find in an old periodical, where it is given as a well authenticated fact.

In the autumn of 1777, when Lord Howe had possession of Philadelphia, the situation of the Americans who could not follow their beloved commander, was truly distressing, subject to the every day insults of cruel and oppressive foes. Bound to pay obedience to laws predicated, on the momentary power of a proud and vindictive commander, it can be better pictured than described. To obtain the common necessaries of life, particularly flour, they had to go as far as Bristol, a distance of eighteen or twenty miles, and even this indulgence was not granted them, until a pass was procured from Lord Howe, as guards were placed along Vine street, extending from the Delaware to the Schuylkill, forming a complete barrier; beyond these, through the woods extending as far as Frankford, were stationed the piquet guards—thus rendering it in a manner impossible to reach the Bristol mills, unless first obtaining a pass.

The American forces were then encamped at the Valley Forge, suffering from cold, hunger, and the inclemency of the season. The British rolled in plenty, and spent their days in feastings, their nights in balls, riots, and dissipation; thus resting in supposed security, while the American chief was planning a mode for their final extirpation. A poor woman, with six small children, whose husband was at the Valley Forge, had made frequent applications for a pass. Engagements rendered it impossible for her cruel tormenters to give her one. Rendered desperate from disappointment and the cries of her children, she started alone without a pass, and by good luck eluded the guards and reached Bristol.

About this time, there were six brothers of the name of Doale, renowned for many acts of heroic bravery, but which were in the character of marauders rather than soldiers. They were men full six feet high, stout and active, a fearless intrepidity characterizing their deeds, and they always succeeded in making their escape. A marked partiality to the Americans, rendered them obnoxious to the British, and always welcome to the former, to whom they conveyed what information they could glean in their adventures

Our adventurous female, having procured her flour in a pillow-case, holding about twenty pounds, was returning with a light heart to her anxious and lonely babes. She had passed the piquet guards at Frankford, and was just entering the woods a little this side, when a tall, stout man, stepped from behind a tree, and putting a letter in her hand, requested her to read it. She grasped with eager joy, the letter bearing the character of her husband's hand-writing. After a pause, he said, "Your husband is well, madam, and requested me to say, that in a short time he will be with you; money is a scarce article among us—I mean among them; but on account of your husband's partiality to the cause of liberty, I am willing to become his banker." So saying, he handed her a piece of money, "my means, madam, are adequate or I would not be thus lavish," seeing she was about to refuse it.

"You said, sir," my husband would see me shortly; how do you know that which seems so impossible? and how did you know me, who never——"

"Hush, madam, we are now approaching the British guard suffice it to say, the American commander has that in his head which, like an earthquake, will shake the whole American conti nent, and expunge all these miscreants; but, hark! take the road to the left—farewel." So saying, he departed. She gave one look, but vacancy filled the spot where he stood. With slow and cautious steps, she approached Vine street. Already her fire burned beneath her bread, when the awful word "halt!" struck her to the soul. She started, and found herself in the custody of a British sentinel. "Your pass, woman." "I have none, sir; my children are——" "D——n the rebel crew, why do you breed enemies to your king—this flour is mine—off, woman, and die with your babes." A groan was her only answer. The ruffian was about departing, when the former messenger appeared— his whole demeanor was changed; humble simplicity marked his gait—he approached the guard with a seeming fearfulness, and begged him in a suppliant voice, to give the poor woman her flour. "Fool! idiot!" exclaimed the guard, "who are you? see yonder guard house, if you interfere here, that shall be your quarters." "May be so, sir; but wont you give the poor woman the means of supporting her little family one week longer? recollect the distance she has walked, the weight of the bag, and recollect——"

"Hell and fury, sirrah! Why bid me recollect, you plead in vain—begone, or I'll seize you as a spy."

"You won't give the poor woman her flour?"

"No."

"Then by my country's faith, and hopes of freedom, you shall!" and with a powerful arm, he seized the guard by the throat and hurled him to the ground. "Run, madam, run—see the guard house is alive—secure your flour, pass Vine street, and you are safe." 'Twas done. The guard made an attempt to rise, when the stranger drew a pistol, and shot him dead. The unfortunate man gazed around him with fearless intrepidity. There was but one way of escape, and that through the woods. Seizing the dead man's musket, he started like a deer, pursued by the hounds. "Shoot him down! shoot him down!" was echoed from one line to another. The desperado was lost in the woods, and a general search commenced; the object of their pursuit, in the meantime, flew like lightning; the main guard was left behind, but the whole piquet line would soon be alarmed—one course alone presented itself, and that was to mount his horse, which was concealed among the bushes, and gallop down to the Delaware; a boat was already there for him. The thought was no sooner suggested, than it was put into execution. He mounted his horse, and, eluding the alarmed guards, had nearly reached the Delaware.

Here he found himself headed and hemmed in, by at least fifty exasperated soldiers. One sprang from behind a tree, and demanded immediate surrender. "'Tis useless to prevaricate—you are now in our possession." "Son of a slave! slave of a king! how dare you to address a freeman! Surrender yourself—a Doale never surrendered himself to any man, far less to a blinded poltroon—away, or die;" and attempted to pass. The guard levelled his gun; but himself was levelled in the dust; the ball of Doale' pistol, had been swifter than his own. His case was now truly desperate; behind him was the whole line of guards—on the north of him, the Frankford piquets, and on the left of him, the city of Philadelphia, filled with British troops.

One way, and only one presented itself, and that was to cross the river. He knew his horse; he plunged in—a shout succeeded and ere he reached half the distance, twenty armed boats were in swift pursuit. His noble horse dashed through the Delaware, his master spurred him on with double interest, while the balls whistled around him. The tide was running down, and when he reached the Jersey shore, he found himself immediately opposite the old slip, at Market street. On reaching the shore, he turned round, took out a pistol, and, with steady aim, fired at the first boat; a man fell over the side and sank to rise no more. He then disappeared in the wood. The angry, harassed, and disappointed pursuers gave one look, one curse, and returned to the Pennsylvania shore, fully believing, that, if he was not the devil, he was at least one of his principal agents.

THE STORY OF AN OLD SOLDIER.

The following story is as it was related by an old soldier.

It was in the summer of 1780, at the close of a Sabbath day, that the inhabitants of a retired farm house in Georgia assembled at their evening repast. The venerable farmer, the widow of his son, and her only daughter, a blooming girl of sixteen, composed the little circle. "I should like," said the old man, "to know where our young soldier is now." Tears and blushes appeared at once on the countenance of Kate, and when the mother ferently exclaimed "God preserve him," she could not restrain her sobs; for it was of her cousin Leonard, her betrothed husband that they spoke. "Out with your tears, baby face," cried her grandsire, cheerfully; "he will come home to you soon, nothing less than a captain. What! would you have him stay at home at such a time; ah! if I felt not the aches of seventy in my limbs or could I shake from my gray head a score of years, I would not be now sitting in the chimney corner." Kate smiled at her sire's earnestness. She handed him the Bible and his spectacles, and having listened to the evening portion, and joined in the fervent prayer, the peaceful family retired to rest.

    The dwelling of John Cammel was situated on the side of a hill, at the foot of which ran a deep narrow stream that watered the valley. On the bank of this stream terminated the boundary of the farm, and the vale beyond was mostly a thick wood, where some new settlers had begun to clear small portions of the ground. The huts of these people were the only dwellings within some miles of Cammel's house, which was rendered the more retired by the thick shade of the numerous trees which grew around it. It was built in the plain style, most suitable to a farmer; consisting of one story, divided into a parlor and three sleeping apartments, where the inmates lodged. The servants belonging immediately to the house, occupied the loft above; while the negroes who tilled the farm had their own cottages on the other side of the hill, nearly two miles from the dwelling. Kate and her mother slept in the back room, whose windows looked on the path which wound along the brow of the hill, as it led to the house. It was midnight, and Kate had sunk into an uneasy slumber, when she was startled from it by the indistinct sound of smothered voices. Unsuspicious of evil, and unwilling to awake her mother, she arose, and gently opened the window; she leaned out and listened; all was silent, and she saw nothing but the tall trees that stood smiling in the moonlight. She was withdrawing, when she suddenly perceived something gleam among the thick foliage of the old willow, whose branches trailed to the ground. She fixed her eye upon it—the wind gently waved the leaves—

it was a bayonet which glanced in the moonbeam. At the same instant she saw one of the negroes running toward the house.—"Shut the window," he cried, perceiving her: "the British are here." A mortal wound from a musket prevented his concluding. Kate had heard enough; she attempted to bar the shutters, but ere she could effect it, she heard the report of a gun, and felt its burning contents in her bosom. Darkness came over her, and for some moments she lay insensible. The fresh air which blew from the window on her face, revived her; she crept to the bed to speak to her mother, but it was empty; and the sound of men's footsteps, deep execrations, and horrid oaths, struck her with terror. Amidst the noise and tumult, she distinguished the voice of her faithful nurse, calling from the upper window, and entreating her to come to the loft: "Quick, quick," repeated the woman. Kate rose, and with difficulty walked to the door. It was but to cross the hall and she would reach the stairs of the garret. She entered the hall, and was hastening through it, when she saw the inanimate body of a man lying across a chair. Another glance told her that it was her aged parent. She lingered an instant—but that instant decided her fate. The door of the parlor was opened, and an officer, with several soldiers, rushed into the hall. Approaching the affrighted girl, he addressed her in coarse and jeering terms. She sunk on her knees, and attempted to supplicate his mercy; he rudely grasped her arm, when extreme fear, combined with the agonies of her wound, burst the strings of life, and she expired at his touch. The officer threw her stiffening form from him, with an exclamation of horror, and giving some order to his men, they quitted the house. But there was one who had been a trembling witness to his brutality; who had marked his countenance, as for a moment he stood with his head uncovered, and had heard the name by which the soldiers addressed him. The old negro, the husband of Kate's nurse, had ventured to descend the stairs to seek the ill-fated girl, and had partly unclosed the door which shut him from the hall, when he beheld her situation, without the power of affording her assistance. He now hastened to raise her, and observing the blood which flowed from her bosom, he called to his wife to aid him in carrying her to the loft. But the volume of smoke that burst forth from every part of the house, announced that the marauders had finished their dreadful errand. While the nurse supported the cold form of her foster child, the old man stole out to observe the motions of the enemy. They were marching silently up the hill, and the faithful servants, with their lifeless burthen, fearfully descended to the stream, and crossing over a rough bridge, they followed a narrow path, which brought them in safety to the cottage of a young farmer, who readily opened his door to them.

Leonard Cammel had entered the army a private soldier, but his merit soon gained him promotion. He had just received a lieutenant's commission, and was appointed, in conjunction with myself, then of the same rank, to conduct an expedition, the plan of which was unfolded to us by Colonel Clarke, our immediate commander. As a mark of favor, Leonard was permitted to stop at Cammel's farm for two hours, to see and converse with his friends. I could not but envy his feelings, as I looked on his glowing cheek and sparkling eye, and joined in his bright anticipations. At length we arrived at the farm, and entered the road which led to the place of Leonard's nativity. As we ascended a high hill, Leonard looked around, and turning pale, said 'I do not see the house." We put the spur to our horses, and another moment brought us before the black and smothered ruin. The house was burnt to the ground, and some of the finest trees had shared its fate. The garden, which even in its desolation seemed to own a woman's taste, was trampled, and its flowers were crushed. A bower, which had been shaded by the white roses of the luxuriant multiflora, was levelled with the earth; yet the flowers still reared their pale heads, and perfumed the morning air.

"This is not the effect of accident," exclaimed Leonard, leaning against a tree, as if stunned by the shock, while the soldiers vented their anger in oaths and threats of vengeance.

"Where shall we seek your family?" I inquired.

"Not on earth, I fear," answered Leonard; yet the eagerness with which he led the way to the cottage, showed that he still cherished hope. The old nurse was sitting at the entrance of the hut as we approached; at the sight of Leonard, she wrung her hands, and weeping bitterly, cried, "you have come too late."

"Where is Kate and my grandfather?" was Leonard's eager inquiry; and, without waiting her answer, he rushed into the house. I followed him, and beheld stretched on the bed the lifeless form of a young female; her white arms were crossed on her bosom—her beautiful features were not only convulsed by the agony of death, but of mental terror—and her long brown hair, which flowed over her form, was, in some places, clotted with blood. It was only by speaking of revenge, and urging the imperious calls of duty, that I was enabled to tear the wretched youth from the corpse of his murdered love. Before he departed, he ascertained the name of the officer, who had commanded these fiends. I was not surprised, when the negro, after detailing the whole scene, mentioned the name of G——. "You will easily know him," he continued, "by a scar which covers his cheek."

"I shall know him," said Leonard bitterly; and his deportment then changed from deep dejection to a fierce and feverish eagerness of manner. We were successful in our errand, and, after a few days absence, rejoined Colonel Clarke. One morning, as I was sitting alone, Leonard came to my tent, his face lighted up with a joyful, but ferocious expression. Before I could speak, he exclaimed, "Have you heard the order? we are to attack Fort G——."

"Who defends it?" I asked.

"Who? G——." Alarmed at his fierceness, I said, "What do you think of my friend?" Grasping his sword, while his brow crimsoned with rage, he replied, "of the smoking ruin, and stiff corpse I left behind me."

Colonel G—— was obliged to surrender to our superior force. As at the head of his men, he walked from the fort between the ranks of his conqueror, a musket ball whistled through the air; it was aimed by an unerring hand, and G—— fell to the ground, a dead man. Although every exertion was used, it was never discovered who was the murderer. I dared not question Leonard, but the calm sternness of his countenance spoke of satisfied revenge. Once I ventured to deplore the event, as a stain upon our honor. "Would he had died in battle; he had trusted to our faith; he was unarmed; to harm him then, was faithless and unmerciful." "He showed her no mercy," said Leonard, in a voice which made me shudder

ADVENTURES OF THE BROTHERS SAMMONS

Jacob Sammons, and his four sons, were celebrated in the border warfare of the Mohawk Valley, as staunch and intrepid upporters of the American cause. The whole family, with the exception of one son, who was absent from home at the time were taken prisoners by Sir John Johnson, in his night descent on Johnstown, near which town the Sammons family resided. The particulars of the arrest, and of the subsequent marvelous and perilous adventures of Jacob and Frederick Sammons, we draw from Stone's "Life of Joseph Brant." A more deeply absorbing and wonderful history of escapes by flood and field—the history of adventure can scarcely produce.

"On the night of the attack, Thomas, the youngest, had risen at an unwonted hour, in order to feed his horses, and go over to a neighboring farm to work with his brother. On coming down stairs, however, and stepping out of doors half dressed, to take an observation of the weather—it being yet dark, though day was just breaking—the thought occurred to him, that should any straggling Indians be prowling about, he would stand but a poor chance if fallen upon alone. While standing thus in doubt, whether to proceed or to wait for more light, he was startled by a noise of heavy steps behind, and, as he turned, by the glitter of teel passing before his eyes. At the same instant, a hand was aid upon his shoulder, with the words—'you are my prisoner!' In such perfect stillness had the enemy approached, that not the sound of a footstep was heard, until the moment when the younger Sammons was thus arrested, and the house immediately surrounded. One of the officers, with several soldiers, instantly entered the house, and ordered the family to get up, and surrender themselves as prisoners. Jacob and Frederick, who were in bed, in the second story, sprang upon their feet immediately, and seized their arms. The officer called to them and offered quarter if they would surrender. Jacob inquired whether there were Indians with them; adding, that if there were, he and his brother would not be taken alive. On being assured to the contrary, the brothers descended the stairs and surrendered. The old gentleman was also taken. They were directed to make ready to march immediately. Thomas here remarked to the soldier who yet stood sentinel over him, that he could not travel to Canada without his clothes, and especially without his shoes, which he had not yet put on—requesting liberty to return to his chamber for his raiment. The sentinel refused permission; but Thomas persisted that he must obtain his shoes at least, and was stepping toward the door, when the barbarian made a plunge at at his back with his bayonet, which had proved fatal, but for the quick eyes and the heroism of a sister, standing by, who, as she saw the thrust at her brother, sprang forward, and seizing the weapon, threw herself across its barrel, and by falling, brought it to the ground. The soldier struggled to disengage his arms and accomplish his purpose. At the same time, an officer stepped forward, and demanded what was the matter. The girl informed him of the attempt upon her brother, whereupon he rebuked the soldier, by the exclamation—'you d——d rascal, would you murder the boy?' Immediate permission was then given him, to procure whatever articles he wanted."

With their arms pinioned behind them, the prisoners commenced their march. The course of the tories was one uninterrupted outrage. Houses burned, prisoners made, helpless age, and smiling infancy brutally murdered, and property of all kinds recklessly destroyed. They continued along the Mohawk Valley, for several miles, burning and destroying, and then retraced their steps to Johnstown. Here an English lady interested herself successfully for some of the prisoners, with Sir John, and in going, into the field to select them, she managed adroitly to include young Sammons into the group, for whom an interest had been excited in her bosom. The elder Sammons was also released, having privately made an appeal to the Baronet, based upon early associations and services rendered to him, to which Sir John yielded. Jacob and Frederick Sammons, however, were continued in captivity. The march was resumed, and the captives marched to St. John's, and from thence transferred to the fortress of Chamblee.

"The prisoners at this fortress numbered about forty. On the day after their arrival, Jacob Sammons having taken an accurate survey of the garrison, and the facilities of escape, conceived the project of inducing his fellow prisoners to rise upon the guards and obtain their freedom. The garrison was weak in number, and the sentinels less vigilant than is usual among good soldiers. The prison doors were opened once a day, when the prisoners were visited by the proper officer, with four or five soldiers. Sammons had observed, where the arms of the guards were stacked in the yard, and his plan was, that some of the prisoners should arrest and disarm the visiting guard, on the opening of their door, whil the residue were to rush forth, seize the arms, and fight their way out. The proposition was acceeded to by his brother Frederick, and one other man named Van Sluyck, but was considered too daring by the great body of the pisoners to be undertaken. It was therefore abandoned, and the brothers sought afterwards only for a chance for escaping by themselves. Within three days, the desired opportunity occurred, viz, on the 13th of June, 1780. The prisoners were supplied with an allowance of spruce beer, for which two of their number were detached daily, to bring the cask from the beer house, under a guard of five men, with fixed bayonets. Having reason to suppose, that the arms of the guards though charged, were not primed, the brothers so contrived matters, as to be taken together to the brewery on the day mentioned, with an understanding, that, at a given point, they were to dart from the guard, and run for their lives—believing that the confusion of the moment, and the consequent delay of priming their muskets by the guards, would enable them to escape beyond the ordinary range of musket shot. The project was boldly executed. At the concerted moment, the brothers sprang from their conducters, and stretched across the plain with great fleetness. The alarm was given, and the whole garrison was soon after them in hot pursuit. Unfortunately for Jacob, he fell into a ditch, and sprained his ankle. Perceiving the accident, Frederick returned to his assistance; but the other generously admonished him to secure his own flight if possible, and leave him to the chances of war. Recovering from his fall, and regardless of the accident, Jacob sprang forward again, with as much expedition as possible, but finding the lameness impeded his progress, he plunged into a thick clump of shrubs and trees, and was fortunate enough to hide himself between two logs, before the pursuers came up Twenty or thirty shots had previously been fired upon them, but without effect. In consequence of the smoke of their fire, probbly, the guards had not observed Jacob when he threw himself nto the thicket, and supposing that, like his brother, he had passed around it, they followed on, until they were fairly distanced by Frederick, of whom they lost sight and trace. They returned in about half an hour, halting by the bushes, in which the other fugitive was sheltered, and so near, that he could distinctly hear their conversation. The officer in command, was Capt. Steele. On calling his men together, some were swearing and others laughing at the race, and the speed of the 'long legged Dutchmen,' as they called the flying prisoners. The pursuit being abandoned, the guards returned to the fort.

"The brothers had agreed, in case of separation, to meet at a certain spot, at 10 o'clock that night. Of course Jacob lay ensconced in the bushes until night had dropped her sable curtains, and until he supposed the hour had arrived, when he sallied forth, according to the antecedent understanding. But time did not move as rapidly on that evening as he supposed. He waited upon the spot designated, and called aloud for Frederick, until he despaired of meeting him, and prudence forbade him remaining any longer. It subsequently appeared, that he was too early on the ground, and that Frederick made good his appointment.

"Following the bank of the Sorel, Jacob passed Fort St. John's soon after day break, on the morning of the 14th. His purpose was to swim the river at that place, and pursue his course homeward, through the wilderness on the eastern shore of Lake Champlain; but, just as he was perparing to enter the water, he descried a boat approaching from below, filled with officers and soldiers of the enemy. Concealing himself again in the woods, he resumed his journey after their departure, but had not proceeded more than two or three miles, before he came upon a party of several hundred men, engaged in getting out timber for the public works at the fort. To avoid these, he was obliged to describe a wide circuit, in the course of which, at about 12 o'clock, he came to a small clearing. Within the enclosure was a house and in the field were a man and a boy engaged in hoeing potatoes. They were at that moment called to dinner, and supposing them to be French, who, he had heard, were rather friendly to the American cause than otherwise—incited also by hunger and fatigue—he made bold to present himself, trusting that he might be invited to partake of their hospitality. But instead of a friend, he found an enemy. On making known his character, he was roughly received. 'It is by such villians that you are,' replied the forester, 'that I was obliged to fly from Lake Champlain.' 'The rebels,' he added, 'had robbed him of all he possessed, and he would now deliver his self-invited guest to the guard, which, he said, was not more than a quarter of a mile distant.' Sammons promptly answered him that 'that was more than he could do!' The refugee then said 'he would go for the guard himself;' to which Sammons replied, 'that he might act as he pleased, but that all the men in Canada should not make him again a prisoner.'

"The man thereupon returned with his son to the potatoe field, and resumed his work, while his more compassionate wife gave him a bowl of bread and milk, which he ate sitting on the threshhold of the door, to guard against surprise. While in the house, he saw a musket, powder horn, and bullet pouch hanging against the wall, of which he determined, if possible, to possess himself, that he might be able to procure food during the long and solitary march before him. On retiring, therefore, he traveled only far enough into the woods, for concealment—returning to the woodman's house in the evening, for the purpose of obtaining the musket and ammunition. But he was again beset by imminent peril. Very soon after he entered the house, the sound of approaching voices were heard, and he took to the rude chamber for security, where he lay flat upon the irregular floor, and looking through the interstices, saw eleven soldiers enter, who, it soon appeared, came for milk. His situation was now exceedingly critical. The churlish proprietor might inform against him, or a single moment betray him. But neither circumstance occurred. The unwelcome visitors departed in due time, and the family all retired to bed, excepting the wife, who, as Jacob descended from the chamber, refreshed him with another bowl of milk. She endeavored to persuade him, to secrete himself in the woods for two days, when she would be enabled to furnish him with some provisions, for a supply of which her husband was going to the fort the next day, and she would likewise endeavor to provide him with a pair of shoes.

"Disinclined to linger so long in the country of the enemy and in the neighborhood of a British fort, he took his departure forthwith. But such had been the kindness of the good woman, that he had it not in his heart to seize upon her husband's arms, and he left this wild scene of rustic hospitality without supplies, and without the means of procuring them. Arriving once more at the water's edge, at the lower end of Lake Champlain, he came upon a hut, within which, on cautiously approaching it for reconnoisance, he discovered a party of soldiers all soundly asleep. Their canoe was moored by the shore, into which he sprang, and paddled himself up the lake, under the most encouraging prospect of a speedy and comparatively easy voyage to its head, whence his return home would be unattended with either difficulty or danger. But his pleasing anticipations were extinguished on the night following, as he approached the Isle au Noix, where he descried a fortification, and the glitter of bayonets bristling in the air, as the moonbeams played upon the burnished arms of the sentinels, who were pacing their tedious rounds. The lake being very narrow at this point, and perceiving that both sides were fortified, he thought the attempt to shoot his canoe between them, rather too hazardous an experiment. His only course, therefore was to run ashore and resume his travels on foot. Nor on landing, was his case in any respect enviable. Without shoes, without food, and without the means of obtaining either—a long journey before him, through a deep and trackless wilderness—it may well be imagined, that his mind was not cheered by the most agreeable anticipations. But without pausing to indulge unnecessarily his 'thick coming fancies,' he commenced his solitary journey, directing his course along the eastern lake shore, toward Albany. During the first four days of his progress, he subsisted entirely upon the bark of the birch—chewing the twigs as he went. On the fourth day, while resting by a brook, he heard a rippling of the water caused by the fish as they were stemming its current. He succeeded in catching a few of these, but having no means of striking a fire, after devouring one of them raw, the others were thrown away.

"His feet, by this time, were cruelly cut, brusied, and torn by thorns, briars, and stones; and while he could scarcely proceed by reason of their soreness, hunger and fatigue united to retard his cheerless march. On the fifth day, his miseries were augmented by the hungry swarms of musquetoes, which settled upon him in clouds, while traversing a swamp. On the same day, he fell upon the nest of a black duck—the duck sitting quietly upon her eggs until he came up and caught her. The bird was no sooner deprived of her life, and her feathers, than he devoured the whole, including its head and feet. The eggs were nine in number, which Sammons took with him; but on opening one, he found a little half-made duckling, already alive. Against such food his stomach revolted, and he was obliged to throw the eggs away.

"On the tenth day, he came to a small lake. His feet were now in such a horrible state, that he could scarcely crawl along Finding a mitigation of pain, by bathing them in water, he plunged his feet into the lake, and lay down upon its margin For a time it seemed as though he could never rise upon his feet again. Worn down by hunger and fatigue—bruised in body and wounded in spirit—in a lone wilderness, with no eye to pity and no human act to protect—he felt as though he must remain in that spot until it should please God, in his goodness, to quench the dim spark of life that remained. Still he was comforted in some measure, by the thought that he was in the hands of a Being without whose knowledge, not a sparrow falls to the ground.

"Refreshed at length, though to a trifling degree, he resumed his weary way, when on raising his right leg on the trunk of a fallen tree he was bitten in the calf by a rattlesnake. Quick as a flash, with his pocket knife, he made an inscision in his leg, removing the wounded flesh to a greater depth than the fangs of the serpent had penetrated. His next business was to kill the venemous reptile, and dress it for eating; thus appropriating the enemy that had sought to take his life, to its prolongation. His first meal was made from the heart and fat of the serpent. Feeling somewhat strengthened by the repast, and finding, moreover that he could not travel farther in his present condition, he determined to remain where he was for a few days, and by repose, and feeding on the body of the snake, recruit his strength. Discovering also, a dry fungus upon the trunk of a maple tree, he succeeded in striking a fire, by which his comforts were essentially increased. Still he was obliged to creep upon his hands and knees to gather food, and gather fuel, and on the third day, he was in such a state of exhaustion, as to be utterly unable to proceed. Supposing that death was inevitable and very near, he crawled to the foot of a tree, upon the bark of which he commenced inscribing his name—in the expectation that he should leave his bones there, and in the hopes that, in some way, by the aid of the inscription, his family might ultimately be apprised of his fate. While engaged in this sad work, a cloud of painful thoughts crowded upon his mind; the tears involuntary stole down his cheeks, and before he had completed the melancholy task, he fell asleep.

"On the fourth day of his residence at this place, he began to gain strength, and as a part of the serpent yet remained, he determined upon another effort to resume his journey. But he could not do so without devising some substitute for shoes. For this purpose he cut up his hat and waistcoat, binding them upon his feet—and thus he hobbled along. On the following night, while lying in the woods, he became strongly impressed with a belief that he was not far distant from a human habitation. He had seen no indications of proximity to the abode of man; but nevertheless, he was so confident of the fact, that he wept with joy. Buoyed up and strengthened by this impression, he resumed his journey on the following morning; and in the afternoon, it being the 28th of June, he reached a house in the town of Pittsford, in the New Hampshire Grants—now forming the state of Vermont. He remained there for several days, both to recruit his health, and if possible, to gain intelligence of his brother. But no tidings came; and as he knew Frederick to be a capital woodsman, he, of course, concluded that sickness, death, or recapture, must have interrupted his journey. Procuring a conveyance, Jacob traveled to Albany, and thence to Schenectady, where he had the happiness of finding his wife and family."

NARRATIVE OF FREDERICK SAMMONS.

"NOT less interesting, nor marked by fewer vicissitudes were the adventures of Frederick Sammons. The flight from the fort at Chamblee, was made just before sunset, which accounts for the chase having been abandoned so soon. On entering the edge of the woods, Frederick encountered a party of Indians, returning to the fort, from fatigue duty. Perceiving that he was a fugitive, they fired, and called out—'we have got him!' In this opinion, however, they were mistaken; for, although he had run close upon before perceiving them, yet being like Ashael of old, swift of foot, by turning a short corner, and increasing his speed, in ten minutes he was entirely cleared of the party. He then sat down to rest, the blood gushing from his nose, in consequence of the extent to which his physical powers had been taxed. At the time appointed, he also had repaired to the point, which, at his separation from Jacob, had been agreed upon as the place of meeting. The moon shone brightly, and he called loud and often for his brother—so loud indeed, that the guard was turned out in consequence. His anxiety was very great for his brother's safety; but in ignorance of *his* situation, he was obliged to attend to his own. He determined, however, to approach the fort—so near it, at least, as he could venture—and in the event of meeting any one, disguise his own character by inquiring whether the rebels had been taken. But a flash from the sentinel's musket, the report, and the noise of a second pursuit, compelled him to change the direction of his march, and proceed again with all possible speed. It had been determined by the brothers to cross the Sorel, and return on the east side of the river and lake; but there was a misunderstanding between them, as to the point of crossing the river—whether above or below the fort. Frederick repaired to what he supposed to be the designated place of crossing, below the fort, where he lingered for his brother until near morning. At length, having found a boat, he crossed over to the eastern shore, and landed just at the cock crowing. He proceeded directly to the barn where the supposed chanticleer had raised his voice, but found not a fowl on the premises. The sheep looked too poor by the dim twilight, to serve his purpose of food, but a bullock presenting a more favorable appearance, Frederick succeeded in cutting the unsuspecting animal's throat, and severing one of the hind quarters from the carcass, he shouldered and marched off with it directly into the forest. Having proceeded to a safe and convenient distance, he stopped to dress his beef, cutting off what he supposed would be sufficient for the journey, and forming a knapsack from the skin, by the aid of bark pulled from a tree.

"Resuming his journey, he arrived at the house of a French family, within the distance of five or six miles. Here he made bold to enter, for the purpose of procuring bread and salt, and in the hope also of obtaining a gun and ammunition. But he could neither obtain provisions, nor make the people understand a word he uttered. He found means, however, to prepare some tinder, with which he re-entered the woods, and hastened forward in a southern direction, until he ascertained, by the firing of the evening guns, that he had passed St. John's. Halting for the night, he struck a light; and having kindled a fire, occupied himself till morning in drying and smoking his beef, cutting it into slices for that purpose. His knapsack of raw hide was cured by the same process. Thus prepared, he proceeded onward without interruption or adventure, until the third day, when he killed a fawn and secured the venison. He crossed the Mirooski, or Onion river, on the next day; and having discovered a man's name carved upon a tree, together with the distance from the lake, (Champlain) eight miles, he bent his course for its shores, when he found a canoe with paddles. There was now a prospect of lessening the fatigue of his journey; but his canoe had scarce begun to dance upon the waters, ere it parted asunder, and he was compelled to hasten ashore and continue his march by land.

"At the close of the seventh day, and when, as he supposed, he was within two day's travel of settlement, he kindled his fire, and lay down to rest in health and spirits. But ere the dawn of day, he awoke with racking pains, which proved to be an attack of pleurisy. A drenching rain came on, continuing three days; during which time he lay helpless, in dreadful agony, without fire or shelter, or sustenance of any kind. On the fourth day, his pain having abated, he attempted to eat a morsel, but his provisions had become too offensive to be swallowed. His thirst being intense, he fortunately discovered a pond of water near by, to which he crawled. It was a stagnant pool, swarming with frogs—another providential circumstance, inasmuch as the latter served him for food. Too weak, however, to strike a light, he was compelled to devour them raw, and without dressing of any kind. Unable to proceed, he lay in this wretched condition fourteen days. Supposing that he should die there, he succeeded in hanging his hat upon a pole, with a few papers, in order that, if discovered, his fate might be known. He was lying upon a high bluff, in full view of the lake, and at no great distance therefrom. The hat, thus elevated, served as a signal, which saved his life. A vessel sailing past, descried the hat, and sent a boat ashore to ascertain the cause. The boatmen discovered the body of a man yet living, but senseless and speechless, and transferred him to the vessel. By the aid of medical attendance, he was slowly restored to his reason, and having informed the captain who he was, had the rather uncomfortable satisfaction of learning that he was on board of an enemy's ship, and at that moment lying at Crown Point. Here he remained sixteen days, in the course of which time he had the gratification to hear, from a party of Tories coming from the settlements, that his brother Jacob had arrived safe at Schenectady, and joined his family. He was also apprised of Jacob's sufferings, and the bite of the serpent, which took place near Otter Creek, close by the place where he had himself been so long sick. The brothers were, therefore, near together at the time of the greatest peril and endurance of both.

"Frederick's recovery was very slow. Before he was able to walk, he was taken to St. John's, and thence, partly on a wheelbarrow and partly in a calash, carried back to his old quarters, at Chamblee—experiencing much rough usage by the way. On arriving at the fortress, the guards saluted him by the title of Captain Lightfoot; and there was great joy at his re-capture. It was now about the 1st of August. As soon as his health was sufficiently recovered to bear it, he was heavily ironed, and kept in close confinement at that place, until October, 1782—fourteen months, without once beholding the light of the sun. Between St. John's nd Chamblee he had met a British officer with whom he was acquainted, and by whom he was informed that severe treatment would be his portion. Compassioning his situation, however the officer slipped a guinea and a couple of dollars into his hand, and they moved on.

"No other prisoners were in irons at Chamblee, and all but Sammons were taken upon the parade ground, twice a week for the benefit of fresh air. The irons were so heavy and so tight, as to wear into the flesh of his legs; and so incensed was Captain Steele, the officer of the 32 regiment, yet commanding the garrison at Chamblee, at the escape of his prisoner, that he would not allow the surgeon to remove the irons to dress the wounds, of which they were the cause, until a peremptory order was procured for that purpose, from General St. Leger, who was then at St. John's. The humanity of the surgeon prompted this application of his own accord. Even then, however, Steele would only allow the leg bolts to be knocked off—still keeping on the handcuffs. The dressing of his legs was a severe operation. The iron had eaten to the bone, and the grangrened flesh was of course to be removed. One of the legs ultimately healed up, but the other never became entirely well.

"In the month of November, 1781, the prisoners were transferred from Chamblee, to an island in the St. Lawrence, called, at that time, Prison Island—situated in the rapids, some distance above Montreal. Sammons was compelled to travel in his handcuffs, but the other prisoners were not thus encumbered. There were about two hundred prisoners on the island, all of whom were very closely guarded. In the spring of 1782, Sammons organized a conspiracy with nine of his fellow prisoners, to make their escape, by seizing a provision boat, and had well nigh effected their object. Being discovered, however, their purpose was defeated, and Sammons, as the ringleader, once more placed in irons. But at the end of five weeks, the irons were removed, and he was allowed to return to his hut.

"Impatient of such protracted captivity, Frederick was still bent on escaping, for which purpose he induced a fellow prisoner, by the name of M'Mullen, to join him in the daring exploit of seeking an opportunity to plunge into the river, and taking their chance of swimming to the shore. A favorable moment for attempting the bold adventure, was afforded on the 17th of August. The prisoners having, to the number of fifty, been allowed to walk to the foot of the island, but around the whole of which a chain of sentinels was extended, Sammons and M'Mullen, without having conferred with any one else, watching an opportunity when the nearest sentinel turned his back upon them, quietly glided down beneath a shelving rock, and plunged into the stream—each holding up and waving a hand, in token of farewell to their fellow prisoners, as the surge swept them rapidly down the stream. The sentinel was distant about six rods when they threw themselves into the river, and did not discover their escape until they were beyond the reach of any molestation he could offer them. Three quarters of a mile below the island, the rapids were such as to heave the river into swell, too large for boats to encounter. This was a frightful part of their voyage. Both, however, were expert swimmers, and by diving as they approached each successive surge, both succeeded in making the perilous passage—the distance of this rapid being about one hundred and fifty rods. As they plunged successively into these rapids, they had little expectation of meeting each other again in this world. But a protecting Providence ordered it otherwise and they emerged from the frightful billows quite near each other.

I am glad to see you,' said Sammons to his friend; 'I feared we should not meet again.' 'We have had a merry ride of it,' replied the other; 'but we could not have stood it much longer.

"The adventurous fellows attempted to land about two miles below the island, but the current was so violent as to baffle their purpose, and they were driven two miles farther, when they happily succeeded in reaching the land, at a place on the north side of the St. Lawrence, called by the Canadians 'The Devil's Point. A cluster of houses stood near the river, into some of which it was necessary the fugitives should go to procure provisions. They had preserved each a knife and tinder-box in their waistcoat pockets, and one of the first objects, after arming themselves with substantial clubs, was to procure a supply of tinder. This was effected by boldly entering a house and rummaging an old lady's work-basket. The good woman, frightened at the appearance of the visitors, ran out and alarmed the village—the inhabitants of which were French. In the meantime, they searched the house for provisions, fire-arms, and ammunition, but found none of the latter, and only a single loaf of bread. They also plundered the house of a blanket, blanket-coat, and a few other articles of clothing. By this time, the people began to collect in such numbers, that a precipitate retreat was deemed advisable. M'Mullen, being seized by two Canadians, was only released from their grasp by the well-directed blows of Frederick's club. They both then commenced running for the woods, when Sammons, encumbered with his luggage, unluckily fell, and the loaf rolled way from him. The peasants now rushed upon them, and their only course was to give battle, which they prepared to do in earnest; whereupon, seeing their resolution, the pursuers retreated almost as rapidly as they advanced. This demonstration gave the fugitives time to collect and arrange their plunder, and commence their travels anew. Taking to the woods, they found a resting place, where they halted until nightfall. They then sallied forth once more in search of provisions, with which it was necessary to provide themselves, before coming to the south side of the river, where, at that day, there were no settlements. The cattle fled at their approach; but they at length came upon a calf in a farmyard, which they captured, and appropriating to their own use and behoof a canoe moored in the river, they embarked with their prize, to cross over to the southern shore, but alas! when in the middle of the stream, their paddle broke, and they were in a measure left to the mercy of the flood, which was hurrying them onward, as they well knew, toward the rapids or falls of the Cedars. There was an island above the rapids, from the bank of which a tree had fallen into the river. Fortunately, the canoe was swept by the current into the branches of this tree top, among which it became entangled. While struggling in this predicament, the canoe was upset. Being near shore, however, the navigators got to land without losing the calf. Striking a fire, they now dressed their veal, and on the following morning, by towing their canoe along shore, to the south edge of the island, succeeded in crossing to their own side of the river. They then plunged directly into the unbroken forest, extending from the St. Lawrence to the Sacondaga, and after a journey of twelve days of excessive hardship, emerged from the woods within six miles of the point for which without chart or compass, Sammons had laid his course. Their provisions lasted but a few days, and their only subsequent food consisted of roots and herbs. The whole journey was made almost in a state of nudity—both being destitute of pantaloons, Having worn out their hats upon their feet, the last three days they were compelled to travel bare-footed. Long before their journey was ended, therefore, their feet were dreadfully lacerated and swollen. On arriving at Schenectady the inhabitants were alarmed at their wild and savage appearance—half naked, with lengthened beards and matted hair. The people at length gathered round them with strange curiosity; but when they made themselves known, a lady named Ellis, rushed through the crowd to grasp the hand of Frederick, and was so much affected at his altered appearance that she fainted and fell. The welcome fugitives were forthwith supplied with whatever food and raiment was necessary; and young Sammons soon joined his family, who had long given him up as lost, and who now received him with unspeakable joy, as one who had arisen from the dead."

Jacob Sammons died in 1810. Frederick and Thomas Sammons have since figured in the affairs of their country. Thomas for several years, represented his native county, Montgomery, in Congress; and in 1836, Frederick was chosen as elector for President and Vice President. A few years since, they were both alive, and were highly respected, and "prosperous gentlemen."

DEBORAH SAMSON.

It is not generally known that in the war of Independence there figured a character of scarcely less romantic interest than the maid of old whose name so abounds in song and history.

Deborah Samson was the daughter of obscure parents in Plymouth, Massachusetts. Poverty and evil example accompanied her childhood, but charity interfered, and the young girl was rescued from a position that threatened her with misery and placed with those from whom she received kindly treatment and every physical comfort. But her education was neglected. She, however, began to feel her inferiority in this point, and made every exertion in acquiring knowledge. By her own unaided exertions she succeeded in learning to read tolerably well. When her term of apprenticeship expired, she went into service, but as her main object was to acquire an education, she made an arrangement whereby she was to devote but half of her time in return for her board and clothing, and the remainder to an attendance upon the common district school. Here she progressed in her studies with great rapidity, and evinced a superior mind in her appetite for knowledge, and her determination to procure it in the face of all obstacles.

"Meantime the Revolutionary struggle had commenced. The gloom that had accompanied the outburst of the storm, hung over the whole land; the news of the carnage on the plains of Lexington; the sound of the cannon at Bunker's Hill, had reached every dwelling and vibrated on the heart of every patriot in New England. The zeal which had urged the men to quit their homes for the battle field, found its way to a female bosom; Deborah felt as if she would shrink from no effort or sacrifice in the cause which awakened all her enthusiasm. She entered with the most lively interest into every plan for the relief of the army, and bitterly regretted that, as a woman, she could do no more, and that she had not the privilege of a man, of shedding her blood for he country.

"There is no reason to believe that any consideration foreign to the purest patriotism, impelled her to the resolution of assuming male attire and enlisting in the army. She could have been actuated by no desire of gaining applause; for the private manner in which she quitted her home and associates, entrusting no one with her design, subjected her to surmises of a painful nature; and the careful preservation of her secret during the period of her military service, exonerates her from the least suspicion of having been urged to the step by an imprudent attachment. It is very likely that her youthful imagination was kindled by the rumor of brave deeds, and that her visions of 'the camp's stir and crowd and ceaseless 'larum' were colored richly by the hue of fancy. Curiosity to see and partake of this varied war-life, the restlessness of 'a heart unsouled and solitary'—the consuming of energies which had no object to work upon, may have contributed to the forming of her determinatian. It must be borne in mind, too, that she was restrained by no consideration that could interfere with the project. Alone in the world, there were few to inquire what had become of her, and still fewer to care for her fate. She felt herself accountable to no human being.

"By keeping the district school for a summer term, she had amassed the sum of twelve dollars. She purchased a quantity of coarse fustian, and working at intervals when she could be secure from observation, made up a suit of men's clothing; each article, as it was finished, being hid in a stack of hay. Having completed her preparations, she announced her intention of going where she could obtain better wages for her labor. Her new clothes, and such articles as she wished to take with her, were tied in a bundle. The lonely girl departed; but went not far, probably only to the shelter of the nearest wood, before putting on the disguise she was so eager to assume. Although not beautiful, her features were animated and pleasing, and her figure, tall for a woman, was finely proportioned. As a man, she might have been called handsome; but her general appearance was extremely prepossessing and her manner calculated to inspire confidence.

"She now pursued her way to the American army, where she presented herself in October, 1778, as a young man anxious to join his efforts to those of his countrymen in their endeavors to oppose the common enemy. She was received and enrolled in the army under the name of Robert Shirtliffe.

"For three years our heroine appeared in the character of a soldier. During this time, her exemplary conduct, and the fidelity with which her duties were performed, gained the approbation and confidence of the officers. She was a volunteer in several hazardous enterprises, and was twice wounded, the first time by a sword cut on the left side of the head. Many were the adventures she passed through; as she herself would often say, volumes might be filled with them. Sometimes placed unavoidably in circumstances in which she feared detection, she nevertheless escaped without the least suspicion being awakened among her comrades. The soldiers were in the habit of calling her 'Molly,' in playful allusion to her want of a beard; but not one of them ever dreamed that the gallant youth fighting by their side was in reality a female.

"About four months after her first wound she received another severe one, being shot through the shoulder. Her emotion when the ball entered she described to be a sickening terror at the probability that her sex would be discovered. She felt that death on the battle-field were preferable to the shame that would overwhelm her, and ardently prayed that the wound might close her earthly campaign. But, strange as it may seem, she escaped this time also unsuspected; and soon recovering her strength, was able again to take her place at the post of duty and in the deadly conflict. Her immunity was not, however, destined long to continue—she was seized with a brain fever, then prevalent among the soldiers. For the few days that reason struggled against the disease, her sufferings were indescribable; and most terrible of all was the dread least consciousness should desert her, and the secret she had guarded so carefully, be revealed to those around her She was carried to the hospital, and there could only ascribe her escape to the number of patients, and the negligent manner in which they were attended. Her case was considered a hopeless one, and she perhaps received less attention on that account. One day the physician of the hospital, inquiring—'How is Robert ?" received from the nurse in attendance the answer—'Poor Bob is gone.' The doctor went to the bed, and taking the hand of the youth supposed dead, found that the pulse was still feebly beating; attempting to place his hand on the heart, he perceived that a bandage was fastened tightly round the heart. This was removed, and to his utter astonishment he discovered a female patient, where he had least expected one!

'This gentleman was Dr. Birney, of Philadelphia. With a prudence, delicacy and generosity ever afterwards warmly appreciated by the unfortunate sufferer, he said not a word of his discovery, but paid her every attention, and provided every comfort her perilous condition required. As soon as she could be removed with safety, he had her taken to his own house, where she could receive better care. His family wondered not a little at the unusual interest manifested for the poor invalid soldier.

"Here occurred one of those romances in real life, which in strangeness surpass fiction. The doctor had a young and lovely niece, an heiress to considerable property, whose compassionate feelings led her to join her uncle in bestowing kindness on the friendless youth. Many censured the uncle's imprudence, in permitting them to be so much in each other's society, and to take drives so frequent together. The doctor laughed to himself, at the warnings and hints he received, and thought how foolish the censorious would feel, when the truth should come out. His knowledge, meanwhile, was buried in his own bosom, nor shared even with the members of his family. The niece was allowed to be as much with the invalid as suited her pleasure. Her gentle heart was touched, by the misfortunes she had contributed to alleviate; the pale and melancholy soldier, for whose fate no one seemed to care, who had no possession in the world save his sword, who had suffered so much in the cause of liberty, became dear to her. She saw his gratitude for the benefits and kindness received, yet knew by intuition, that he would never dare to aspire to the hand of one so gifted in fortune. In the confiding abandonment of woman's love, the fair girl made known her attachment, and offered to provide for the education of its object, before marriage. Deborah often declared, that the moment in which she learned that she had unwillingly gained the love of a being so guileless, was fraught with the keenest anguish she ever experienced. In return for the hospitality and tender care, that had been lavished upon her, she had inflicted pain upon one she would have died to shield. No way of amends seemed open, except confession of her real character, and to that, though impelled by remorse and self-reproach, she could not bring herself. She merely said to the generous girl that they would meet again; and though ardently desiring the possession of an education, that she could not avail herself of the noble offer. Before her departure, the young lady pressed on her acquaintance, several articles of clothing, such as in those times, many of the soldiers received from fair hands. All these were afterwards lost, by the upsetting of a boat, except the shirt and vest Robert had on at the time, which are still preserved as relics in the family.

"Her health being now restored, the physician had a long conference with the commanding officer of the company in which Robert had served, and this was followed by an order to the youth to carry a letter to General Washington.

"Her worst fears were now confirmed. From the time of her removal into the doctor's family, she had cherished a misgiving; which sometimes amounted almost to a certainty, that he had discovered her deception. In conversation with him, she anxiously watched his countenance, but not a word or look indicated suspicion, and she had again flattered herself that she was safe from detection. When the order came for her to deliver a letter into the hands of the commander-in-chief, she could no longer deceive herself.

"There remained no course but simple obedience. When she presented herself for admission at the head-quarters of Washington, she trembled as she had never done before the enemy's fire. Her heart sank within her; she strove in vain to collect and compose herself, and overpowered with dread and uncertainty, was usherd into the presence of the Chief. He noticed her extreme agitation, and supposing it to proceed from diffidence, kindly endeavored to re-assure her. He then bade her retire with an attendant, who was directed to offer her some refreshment, while he read the communication of which she had been the bearer.

"Within a short time, she was again summoned into the presence of Washington. He said not a word, but handed her in silence a discharge from the service, putting into her hand at the same time, a note containing a few brief words of advice, and a um of money sufficient to bear her expenses to some place where she might find a home. The delicacy and forbearance thus observed, affected her sensibly. 'How thankful'—she has often said, 'was I to that great and good man, who so kindly spared my feelings! He saw me ready to sink with shame; one word from him at that moment, would have crushed me to the earth But he spoke no word—and I blessed him.'

"After the war, she married Benjamin Gannett of Sharon.—It is but a few years since, she passed from the stage of human life. Her career to which her patriotism urged her, cannot be commended as an example: but her exemplary conduct after the first step, will go far to plead her excuse."*

JOSEPH BETTYS.

Joseph, or "Joe Bettys," was a remarkable character, who figured in the border wars of the revolution. He was a renegade from the American army, and for a long while was the scourge of the New York frontier; his deeds were marked by an equal boldness and cruelty, that made him the terror of all who had the misfortune to be ranked as his enemies. His principal employment, was the abduction of citizens to be conveyed into Canada, for each of whom he received a bounty; and in his expeditions for this purpose, he was always accompanied by small bodies of Indians. His hour for executing his projects, was at night, and it frequently happened that his conduct was not confined to the

---

* Mrs. Ellett

securing of prisoners, but he often revelled in the destruction of property and the infliction of cruelty, and his victims were often tormented by every means his savage ingenuity could devise. Cold blooded murder, and reckless barbarities of every kind, continually stained his soul. The section of country which suffered from his marauding expiditions, to this day is rife with stories of his daring and ferocity.

In the year 1776, he entered as sergeant in the New York forces, in which capacity he served his country faithfully, until being exasperated at the treatment, which he received from one of his superior officers, and retorting with threats and menances, he was reduced to the position of a common sentinel. This was more than he could bear, and he would have deserted, had not Lieutenant Ball, who had before befriended him, anticipating such a step, applied and procured for him, appointment as sergeant on board on one of the vessels on Lake Champlain, commanded by Arnold, which he accepted. In an action that ensued, Bettys displayed a wonderful daring and gallantry, which receiving no other notice than the thanks of his General, he conceived himself slighted, and determined to retaliate. In the spring of 1777, he deserted, and went over to the British forces, where he was soon elevated to the position of a spy, in which character he carried on the depredations we have spoken of.

Among the prisoners that he secretly seized and carried off in the early part of his career, was Samuel Patchim, afterwards a captain in the army. The account of his captivity and subsequent hardships, as here given, is as it was related by himself:—

"I was captured by Bettys, taken into Canada, and confined in Chamblee prison, in irons. I was the only prisoner whom he had on this occasion brought into Canada. There were six or seven more of my neighbors, when we started, to whom he gave the oath of allegiance, and sent them back. As for myself, he said I had served Congress long enough, and that I should now serve the king. He wished me to enlist in his company, but soon ound that this was not agreeable to my feelings. He then swore, that if I would not serve the king, I should remain in irons. I was confined in Chamblee prison four months; then I was removed to Montreal, and thence to an island, forty-five miles up the St. Lawrence, opposite Cadalake Fort. There I remained about one year. There were five prisoners in all, and we were guarded by sixty soldiers! seven sentinels at night.

"They had left no boats on the island by which we might make our escape, yet we all crawled out of the barracks at night, and went to the river side, there we made a raft by means of two or three logs and our suspenders, on which we sailed down the river five miles, when we landed on the Canada shore. There we appropriated to our own use, a boat belonging to the British, and crossed over to the American shore. While going down the rapids, we had lost our little stock of provisions, and for eight days out of twelve which we spent in the woods, we had nothing to eat save frogs, and rattlesnakes, and not half enough of them. We were chased eight days by the Indians, and slept every night on the boughs of some hemlock trees. At length we arrived at Northwest Bay, on Lake Champlain, when my companions, unable longer to travel, utterly gave out. I then constructed a raft on which to cross the lake, and having stripped my companions of their clothing, in order to make myself comfortable, left them to die of hunger and fatigue, and committed myself to the wintry waves. When in about the centre of the lake, I was taken by the crew of a British ship, and conveyed to St. John's, from thence to Quebec, and finally to Boston, where I was exchanged and sent home."

Bettys seemed to have a particular delight in taking prisoners among his own townsmen, and especially those against whom he held any grudge. On one occasion, having taken one whom he supposed to be the object he sought, and his prisoner managing to escape, he deliberately shot him dead, and then discovered that he had made a fatal mistake, and killed one of his best friends.

But his bloody career was destined to find a retributive end. One day, in the winter of 1781–2, a suspicious looking person was seen to pass over the farm of one John Fulmer, situated near Ballston Lake, in Albany county. A son of the farmer, Jacob, immediately obtained the aid of three of his neighbors, James and John Cory, and Francis Perkins, and started in pursuit of the suspicious stranger. There was a light fall of snow on the ground, by which means his course was easily tracked. But we will give an account of the enterprise in the words, of Jacob Fulmer, one of the party :—

"The morning had been foggy, and it appeared by the track, that the man had made a circuitous route, as if lost or bewildered. After making several turns, we came at length in sight of a log house, where one Hawkins, a noted tory, lived, toward which it appeared, he had laid a regular line. We followed the track and found that it went into the house. We approached undiscovered, for the snow was soft, and our footsteps were not heard. We went up to the door, and found it was unfastened, but heard people talking within.

"John Cory, who was the strongest of the party, now went forward, we following closely behind, and burst open the door. The man, who was the object of our suspicions and search, sat at the table eating his breakfast, with the muzzle of his gun leaning upon his shoulder, and the breech upon the floor between his legs. He grasped his musket and presented it to fire at us, but was hindered for a moment to remove the deer skin covering from the lock, and that moment lost his life. We seized him, took possession of his gun, and also two pistols, which he had in his coat pockets, and a common jack-knife. We then bound his arms behind him, with a pocket handkerchief, and conveyed him to my father's house. As yet, we knew not the name of our prisoner, but having asked him, he said. 'my name is Smith.'

"My mother knew him, and said, 'It is Joe Bettys.' He hung his head, and said, 'No, my name is Smith.' My sister Polly then came to the door and said, 'This is Joe Bettys—I know him well.' She had known him before he went to Canada, as he had boarded at Lawrence Van Epps, in Schenectady Patent, while she lived in the same house.

"We then conveyed him to John Cory's house, about a quarter of a mile distant, where we pinioned him more firmly. He sat down in a chair by the fire, and asked permission to smoke which was granted, and he then took out his tobacco box, and seemed to be engaged in filling his pipe, but as he stooped down, under pretence of lighting it, he threw something toward the fire which bounded from the forestick and fell upon the hearth. He then seized it, and threw it into the fire, before any one could prevent. John Cory then snatched it from the fire, with a handful of live coals. It was not injured. It was a piece of lead about three inches long, and one and a quarter inches wide, pressed together, and contained within it, a small piece of paper, on which were twenty-six figures, which none of our company could understand. It also contained an order, drawn on the mayor of New York, for thirty pounds sterling, payable on the delivery of the sheet-lead and paper enclosed. Bettys showed much uneasiness at the loss of the lead, and offered one hundred guineas to allow him to burn the paper. This we refused, for, though we did not understand the figures, we well knew the character of Bettys, as I had heard that he had killed two men at Shenesborough, near Whitehall, for fear of being betrayed in regard to the burning and plundering of a house in Chaughnawaga, and that he was generally known as a spy."

The narrative goes on to give the particulars of the journey to Albany, and the precautions taken to convey their prisoner safely through a district, abounding with tories who were affected to Bettys, but no rescue was attempted.

Much rejoicing was expressed, at the capture of the notorious Bettys, and when he was marched through Albany, the people gathered in maases to look upon him. In a short time, he was brought to trial, on the charge of being a spy, found guilty, condemned, and accordingly executed in the month of April, 1782.*

MR. AND MRS. FISHER.

In the town of North Castle, Westchester Co., N. Y., resided during the war of Independence, Mr. and Mrs. Fisher, a young married couple, who were both heart and soul enlisted in the patriotic cause, and whose best services were devoted to their coun-

---

* Prepared from a Paper by Joseph L. Chester, Esq.

try. Mr. Fisher was an efficient and active member of a partisan band, under Major Paulding, whose confidence and esteem he always enjoyed to an eminent degree, and who by his unflinching patriotism, and the energy and skill with which he thwarted the plans and designs of the tories, made himself particularly obnoxious to them. His active duties as a scout, sometimes kept him for months from his home, where his young wife had nothing but her heroism of spirit to oppose to the marauding bands that traversed the "Neutral Ground," and whose creed it was, to make war upon women and children indiscriminately. While the high minded whig, therefore, was serving his country, in the swamp and on the mountain, the wife had to undergo scenes, requiring an equal courage and fortitude, with those of his.

She was one of those women of the revolution, by whose indomitable spirit and active benevolence our armies were often held together, and our soldiers encouraged to persevere in the glorious course they had begun. She was without fear, and was always ready to serve her country, or defend herself, upon any emergency. The American soldier, too, often found relief from suffering, through her benevolence. She was one of those, who attended upon the wounded of White Plains, and administered comfort to the dying, and relief to the wounded. After this battle, when Washington's army was encamped near her residence, the commander-in-chief's table was often indebted for many of its delicacies, to the prudent attention and care of Mrs. Fisher Washington often expressed his obligations to her in person.

Many anecdotes are related of her daring. On one occasion, a favorite colt was stolen, when she mounted a horse and rode down to Morrissania, where the loyalists were encamped, and demanded of the English officer in command, the restoration of her property. The Englishman courteously assented, and the coat being found, it was restored to her. This was considered at the time, a most daring expedition. Her route, which was a long one, was through a section of country beset with marauders, who were never in the habit of hesitating to make war on a woman.

We remarked that the danger from the marauding tory bands prevented Mr. Fisher from visiting his home, but at long intervals There was one band of tories notorious for its cruelty, headed by one Blindberry, a most blood-thirsty wretch, whose memory to this day, is only preserved to be execrated. This fellow was the terror of the whole community. On one occasion, after having been absent for six months, Mr. Fisher's anxiety to see his family, became so great, that one evening he cautiously approached the house, and was admitted unseen. Late that night, after he had retired, steps were heard without, and presently there was a loud knocking at the door, with a peremptory summons for it to be opened. This not being heeded, it was repeated, with a threat to break open the door, if it was not complied with. The house was a simple, old-fashioned cottage, the door opening directly into a room, which was used by Mr. Fisher and his wife as a sleeping room. The party now discharged their pistols three or four times through the window, but the balls lodged harmlessly in the walls. This proceeding effecting nothing, they began at once to demolish the door, and in a few moments they burst roughly into the room. Mr. Fisher sprang from the bed, prepared to defend his wife and himself to the last. But the only object of this band was plunder. In those times, the country people were compelled to convert their effects into money, as everything moveable, would be sure to be captured, and having no means of investing their wealth, it was generally concealed in secure places. But these concealments rarely availed them anything, if their persons should fall into the hands of the tories, as every means of torture that ingenuity could suggest, was availed of to force the hapless victims to betray the hiding place of their wealth. Hanging, roasting over slow fires, or a pistol at the head, were the usual modes adopted.

The tory leader who was no other than this same Blindberry demanded of Mr. Fisher his gold. The stern patriot, who was a man of unconquerable will, calmly refused. The mauraders became enraged, and he was threatened with death if he persisted in his denial. But neither the flashing swords that gleamed around him, the musket at his breast, nor the furious aspects of the wretches, could move him a jot from his determined purpose. The word was given to try hanging. In an instant a rope was thrown over the branch of a tree, that stood by the door, and their victim was drawn beneath it, and the rope adjusted to his neck. Once more he was asked to give up his money. Without the tremor of a muscle he refused. The next moment he was dangling high up in the air. He was allowed to suspend for a few seconds, and lowered to the ground. His reply to the same question was given, in an undaunted refusal. Again did his tormentors run him up into the air; but when they again lowered him, he had fainted. In a few moments, however, he revived, and as the knowledge of the affair gradually broke upon his mind, he hundered out, "No, not a farthing!" Once more did the wretches swing him off, and this time he was kept suspended until they thought he was dead, when they lowered him, and seeing now no chance of obtaining the coveted gold, they departed.

The agony of the wife during this scene, can only be imagined. A tory was stationed by her side, and with a pistol at her head, enjoined silence on the penalty of her life. In those few minutes were crowded a life of torture and suffering. When they had gone, she tremblingly stole out to the side of her husband, and with what little strength she possessed, dragged his lifeless form into the house. With the vague hope that he might not be dead, she applied restoratives, and soon had the unspeakable joy of detecting signs of life. Ere morning, he was entirely restored, and that very day joined his scout.

Continuing their route, the tories fell upon several other of the neighbors, all of whom suffered some cruelty at their hands. At one house they placed its master in a chair, tied him down, and built a fire under him, by which means he was at last compelled by his unsupportable agony, to reveal the hiding place of his gold. But a terrible retribution was preparing for them. Major Paulding had gathered a party of his men, and were in hot pursuit of them. As the Major was following up their track, he stopped at the residence of Mr. Wright, an old Quaker, who felt a strong sympathy for the American cause, but whose principles prevented him from taking an active part in the contest. To the inquiry if such a party of tories as has been described, was seen, the Quaker replied in the affirmative, pointing out the course they had taken.

"What do you say, my men," said the Major to his followers, shall we follow them up?" A unanimous assent was given.

"Jonathan, if thee wishes to see those men," said Mr. Wright approaching Major Paulding, with a knowing look, "if thee wishes to see them particular, would it not be better for thee to go to "Brundage's Corner," as they are most likely from the north, and will return that way. There thee cau'st see them without doubt."

The shrewd insinuation of the Quaker, was caught in an instant The place referred to, afforded a most admirable place for an ambuscade, and by secreting themselves there, the enemy was certain to fall into their hands.

The whigs had not been concealed long, ere the party was heard approaching. At the signal, the patriots sprang forward and discharged their weapons. At the very first fire, the blood thirsty tory leader fell, some said from a bullet discharged by the hand of Major Paulding himself.

The intense hatred felt by the people toward Blindberry, and the universal joy manifested at his fall, prompted some to make a public rejoicing on the event, and in order to express their uncompromising hostility to their foe, his body was hung before the assembled patriots of the district, amid their jeers and expressions of pleasure. Among the assembly was Mr. Fisher, who but a few hours before had so nearly fallen a victim to his cruelty.

Some little time after the preceding events, while Mr. Fisher was on another visit to his family, sudden word was brought, that the tories were approaching. This, as before, was during the night. Mr. Fisher had reason to suppose, that the object of this party, was to secure his person, and it became necessary to obtain a place of concealment. The most advantageous one that offered, was beneath the flooring, which was loose, where was ample room for him, and where it was hoped, the tories would not think of looking for their enemy. Scarcely had he secreted himself, when the tories appeared. They burst into the presence of Mrs Fisher, in a boisterous manner, and with brutal jests and extravagant threats, demanded to be informed, where her husband was. To these inquiries, the undaunted woman deigned no reply.

"Come, give us a light," said the leader, "that we may ferret out your rebel husband's hiding place. I'll swear, that you've got him stowed away somewhere nere."

"I have no light," was the calm reply. The difficulties of prouring stores, sometimes left whig families for weeks without the common necessities.

"Come my woman, none of that!" broke in the tory; " a light we want, and a light we must have, so bring out your candles!"

"I have none," reiterated Mrs. Fisher.

The tory, with an oath, drew a pistol, cocked it, and coming up to her, placed the muzzle in her face. "Look here, my lady," said he, "we know that you've got your d——d rebel of a husband somewhere about here, and if you don't at once give us a candle, so that we may hunt out his hiding place, I'll blow your brains out."

"I have told you," replied the lady, "that I have no candle; I cannot give you one, so you may blow my brains out the moment you please." The heroic spirit that breathed in her words, and the firm look from her undauuted eye, convinced the tory that she was not to be intimidated. They were compelled to make their search in the dark. After rummaging into every nook and corner in vain, they gave up their object. On several other occasions, Mr. Fisher had similar narrow escapes.

We cannot refrain from referring to one enterprise in which Mr. Fisher was engaged, by which means fifteen whigs put to flight, over three hundred Hessians. The news of their approach was spread abroad, and the utmost consternation prevailed. The Hessians were always held in great terror by the country people. On this occasion, they fled at their approach into the forests and other secure fastnesses. Coney Hill, was the usual place of retreat on these alarms. This was a hill somewhat off from the main roads, and which was surrounded by narrow defiles, and reached only through dense thickets, while its rocky and irregular surface, afforded a means of defence impregnable. No fortress could have been more secure. All the inhabitants, therefore, retreated to this fastness, Mrs. Fisher alone of all neighbors, venturing to remain within her own house.

The usual road traveled by the armies, that led north from White Plains, in one place described a wide circuit, but there was a narrow, irregular road, sometimes used, that shortened the distance considerably. But this road was very dangerous to any large body of men. It led by the Coney Hill, which we have mentioned, and its whole length was through a rocky region, overgrown with tangled thickets of laurel, that would have afforded effectual protection and concealment to a body of assailants, and have made a small force formidable to a large one.

At a point on this road, therefore, Major Paulding and fifteen followers stationed themselves, with a belief, that from the irregular and incautious manner the Hessians were marching, they would be induced to lessen their route, by taking the shorter cut. The belief proved to be well founded. The spot where Major Paulding posted his ambuscade, was one remarkably well adapted to that kind of warfare. It was, where the road passing through a defile, made a sudden turn around a huge rock, and where it was so narrow, that six men could not pass abreast, while the whole rising ground on either side was irregular, with rough, jagged rocks, and covered with a dense growth of laurel.

Stationed at different points, and protected by rocky battlements, the little band quietly awaited the coming of their enemy. At last they appeared, approaching carelessly, and with an utter want of military prudence. Not a sound, nor a breath betrayed to them, the presence of a foe. The rocks, and laurel bushes, gave forth no sign of the deadly messengers to be launched from their bosoms. Part of the Hessians had already passed the turn of the road, when suddenly, like a clap of thunder from an azure sky, an explosion burst from the flinty rocks that surrounded them, and several of their number, pitched headlong to the earth Those in front, panic struck, fell back upon those in the rear while those in the rear pressed forward, uncertain of the danger, and discharged their muskets into the thickets, but the bullets rebounded harmlessly from the rocky walls, that enclosed their enemy. Another volley completed their panic. Terrified at the presence of an enemy, that seemed to fight from the bowels of the earth, and unable to estimate the full extent of their danger, which their imagination greatly magnified, they gave a wild cry, and fled precipitately.

This event afforded the whigs for a long time, much merriment, particularly as it was accompanied with no loss to the little party, who had given the Hessians their terrible fright. Mrs. Fisher was accustomed to give an amusing relation of the manner they appeared, as they flew by her house, each running at his utmost speed, with the tin cannisters and other numerous accoutrements with which the Hessian soldiers were always so plentifully provided—flying out in a straight line behind them.

The following incident, admirably illustrates the presence of mind, and the many resources of this courageous lady. One day, a whig neighbor burst hastily into her presence, saying, that he was pursued by a body of tories, and if not concealed immediately he was lost. It did not take a moment for Mrs. Fisher to decide upon her course. There was a large ash heap just out of the back door, some four or five feet in height, and as many long

Seizing a shovel, she hastened to the spot, and in a moment a sufficient excavation was made, into which the fugitive crawled, and Mrs. Fisher covered him with the ashes, first taking the precaution to procure a quantity of quills, which she placed one into the other, so as to form a continuous tube, through which the man could breathe, while remaining in his novel situation. Scarcely was all this accomplished, when the pursuers appeared, and questioned Mrs. Fisher sharply, at the same time examining the house and grounds. Several times during the search, Mrs. Fisher thought the hiding place was about to be discovered; and when one of the party walked directly over the ash heap, she gave up all for lost. But finding no clue to their enemy, they departed, leaving him in safety, and overcome with gratitude to his preserver.

Mr. Fisher survived the war several years, and Mrs. Fisher lived until quite recently. She often entertained her descendants with stories of the olden time, to one of whom the editor is indebted for the above particulars.

THRILLING ADVENTURE OF
LIEUTENANT SLOCUMB.

From Mrs. Ellet's "Women of the Revolution," we draw the following interesting sketch:

"When Lord Cornwallis set out from Wilmington, with the avowed purpose of conquering Virginia, he encamped, on the march from Halifax on the Neuse, in what is now called Wayne Co., North Carolina. His head-quarters were at Springbank while Colonel Tarleton, with his renowned legion, encamped the plantation of Lieutenant Slocumb. This consisted of leve and extensive fields, which at that season presented a most inviting view of fresh verdure from the mansion house. Lord Cornwallis himself gave it the name of "Pleasant Green," which it ever afterwards retained. The owner of this fine estate, held a subaltern's commission in the state line under Colonel Washington, and was in command of a troop of light horse, raised in his own neighborhood, whose general duty it was to act as rangers, scouring the country for many miles around, watching the movements of the enemy, and punishing the loyalists when detected in their vocation of pillage and murder. These excursions had been frequent, for two or three years, and were often of several weeks duration. At the present time, Slocumb had returned to the vicinity, and had been sent with twelve or fifteen recruits to act as scouts in the neighborhood of the British General. The morning of the day, on which Tarleton took possession of his plantation, he was near Springbank, and reconnoitered the encampment of Cornwallis, which he supposed to be his whole force. He then with his party, pursued his way slowly back in the direction of his own house, little dreaming that his beautiful and peaceful home, where, sometime before, he had left his wife and child, was then in possession of the terrible Tarleton.

"During these frequent excursions of the rangers, and the necessary absence of her husband, the superintendence of the plantation had always devolved upon Mrs. Slocumb. She depended for protection upon her slaves, whose fidelity she had proved, and from her own fearless and intrepid spirit. The scene of the occupation of her house, and Tarleton's residence with her, are drawn from her own relation.

"It was about ten o'clock, on a beautiful spring morning, that a splendidly dressed officer, accompanied by two aids, and followed at a short distance, by a guard of some twenty troopers, dashed up to the piazza in front of the ancient-looking mansion. Mrs. Slocumb was sitting there, with her child and a near relative young lady, who afterwards became the wife of Major Williams. A few house servants were also on the piazza.

"The officer raised his cap, and bowing to his horse's neck, addressed the lady with the question—

"'Have I the pleasure of seeing the mistress of this house and plantation?'

"'It belongs to my husband.'

"'Is he at home?' 'He is not.' 'Is he a rebel?'

"'No sir. He is in the army of his country, and fighting against our invaders; therefore not a rebel.' It is not a little singular, that although the people of that period gloried in their rebellion, they always took offence at being called rebels

"'I fear madam,' said the officer, 'that we differ in opinion. A friend to his country, will be a friend of the king, our master.'

"'Slaves only acknowledge a master in this country,' replied the lady.

"A deep flush crossed the florid cheeks of Tarleton, for he was the speaker; and turning to one of his aids, he ordered him to pitch the tents, and form the encampment in the orchard and field on the right. To the other aid, his orders were to detach a quarter guard, and station piquets on each road. Then bowing very low, he added, 'Madam, the service of his Majesty requires the temporary occupation of your property; and if it will not be too great an inconvenience, I will take up my quarters in your house.'

"The tone admitted no controversy. Mrs. Slocumb answered

"'My family consists of only myself, my sister and child, and : f⸺ negroes. We are your prisoners.'

"From the piazza where he seated himself, Tarleton commanded a view of the ground, on which his troops were arranging their camp. The mansion fronted the east, and an avenue one hundred and fifty feet wide, and about half a mile in length stretched to the eastern side of the plantation, where was a high way, with open grounds beyond it, partly dry meadow and partly sand barren. This avenue was lined on the south side by a high fence, and a thick hedge row of forest trees. These are now removed, and replaced by the 'Pride of India,' and other ornamental trees. On the north side, extended the common rail fence, seven or eight feet high, such as is usually seen on plantations in the low country. The encampment of the British troops being on that part of the plantation lying south of the avenue, it was completely screened by the fences and hedge row, from the view of any one approaching from down the counrtry.

"While the men were busied, different officers came up at intervals, making their reports and receiving orders. Among others, a tory captain, whom Mrs. Slocumb immediately recognised—for before joining the royal army, he had lived fifteen or twenty miles below—received orders in her hearing, to take his troop nd scour the country for two or three miles round.

"In an hour, every thing was quiet, and the plantation presented the romantic spectacle of a regular encampment, of some ten or eleven hundred of the choicest cavalry of the British Monarch.

"Mrs. Slocumb now addressed herself to the duty of preparing for her uninvited guests. A dinner was prepared, consisting of turkey, ham, beef, fowls, with vegetables, fruits, and some excel ent peach brandy, prepared under Lieutenant Slocumb's own supervision. This latter beverage received the unqualified praise of the party; and its merits were fully discussed. A Scotch officer, praising it by the name of whiskey, protested that he had never drank as good out of Scotland. An officer speaking with a slight brogue, insisted it was not whiskey, and that no Scotch drink ever equalled it. 'To my mind,' said he, 'it tastes as yonder orchard smells.'

"'Allow me, madam,' said Tarleton, 'to inquire, where the spirits we are drinking is procured?'

"'From the orchard where your tents stand,' answered Mrs. Slocumb.

"'Colonel,' said the Irish captain, 'when we conquer this country, is it not to be divided out amongst us?'

"'The officers of this army,' replied the Colonel, 'will undoubtedly receive large possessions of the conquered American provinces.'

"Mrs. Slocumb here interposed. 'Allow me to observe, and prophecy,' said she, 'the only land in the United States, which will ever remain in possession of a British officer, will measure but six feet by two.'

"'Excuse me, madam,' remarked Tarleton, 'for your sake, I regret to say—this beautiful plantation will be the ducal seat of some of us.'

"'Don't trouble yourself about me,' retorted the spirited lady. 'My husband is not a man who will allow a duke, or even a king, to have a quiet seat upon his ground.'

"At this point, the conversation was interrupted by rapid volleys of fire-arms, appearing to proceed from the wood, a short distance to the eastward. One of the aids pronounced it some straggling scout, running from the picket-guard; but the experience of Colonel Tarleton, could not be easily deceived.

"'There are rifles and muskets,' said he, 'as well as pistols and too many to pass unnoticed. Order boots and saddles, and you—captain, take your troop in the direction of the firing.'

"The officer rushed out to execute his orders, while the Colonel walked into the piazza, whither he was immediately followed by the anxious ladies. Mrs. Slocumb's agitation and alarm, may be imagined; for she guessed but too well the cause of the interruption. On the first arrival of the officers, she had been importuned even with harsh threats—not, however, by Tarleton—to tell where her husband when absent on duty, was likely to be found; but after her repeated and peremptory refusals, had escaped further molestation on the subject. She feared now that he had returned unexpectedly, and might fall into the enemy's hands, before he was aware of their presence.

"Her sole hope, was in a precaution she had adopted soon after the coming of her unwelcome guests. Having heard Tarleton give the order to the tory captain as before-mentioned, to patrol the county, she immediately sent for an old negro, and gave him directions to take a bag of corn to the mill, about four miles distant, on the road she knew her husband must travel, if he returned that day. 'Big George' was instructed to warn his master of the danger of approaching his home. With the indolence and curiosity natural to his race, however, the old fellow remained loitering about the premises, and was at this time lurking under the hedge row, admiring the red coats, dashing plumes, and shining helmets of the British troops.

"The colonel and the ladies continued on the look out from the piazza. 'May I be allowed, madam,' at length said Tarleton, 'without offence, to inquire if any part of Washington's army is in this neighborhood?'

"'I presume it is known to you,' said Mrs. Slocumb, 'that the Marquis and Greene are in this State. And you would not of course,' she added, after a slight pause, 'be surprised at a call from Lee, or your old friend Colonel Washington, who although a perfect gentleman, it is said, shook your hand, (pointing to the scar left by Washington' sabre,) very rudely when last you met.'*

"This spirited answer inspired Tarleton with apprehensions that the skirmish in the woods was only the prelude to a concerted attack on his camp. His only reply was a loud order to form the troops on the right; and springing on his charger, he dashed down the avenue a few hundred feet, to a breach in the hedge-row, escaped the fence, and in a moment was at the head of his regiment, which was already in line.

"Meanwhile, Lieutenant Slocumb, with John Howell, a private in his band, Henry Williams, and the brother of Mrs. Slocumb, Charles Hook, a boy of about thirteen years of age, were leading a hot pursuit of the tory captain who had been sent to reconnoitre the country, and some of his routed troop. These were first discerned in the open grounds east and northeast of the plantation, closely pursued by a body of American mounted militia; while a running fight was kept up with different weapons, in which four or five broadswords gleamed conspicuous. The foremost of the pursuing party appeared too busy with the tories to see anything else; and they entered the avenue at the same moment with the party pursued. With what horror and consternation did Mrs.

---

* It is said, that in a close encounter between Tarleton and Col. Washington, at the battle of the Cowpens, the former was wounded by a sabre cut in the hand.

Slocumb recognize her husband, her brother, and two of her neighbors, in chase of the tory captain and four of his band, already half way down the avenue, and unconscious that they were rushing into the enemy's midst.

"About the middle of the avenue one of the tories fell; and the course of the brave and imprudent young officers was suddenly arrested by 'Big George,' who sprang directly in front of heir horses, crying, 'Hold on Massa! de debbil here! Look yon!' A glance to the left showed the young men their danger; they were within pistol shot of a thousand men drawn up in order of battle. Wheeling their horses they discovered a troop already leaping the fence into the avenue in their rear. Quick as thought they again whirled their horses, and dashed down the avenue, directly towards the house, where stood the quarter-guard to receive them. On reaching the garden fence—a rude structure formed of a kind of lath, and called a wattled fence—they leaped that and the next, amid a shower of balls from the guard, cleared the canal at one tremendous leap, and, scouring across the open field to the northwest, were in the shelter of the wood before their pursuers could clear the fence of the enclosure. The whole ground of this adventure may be seen as a traveller passes over the Wilmington railroad, a mile and a half south of Dudley depot.

"A platoon had commenced the pursuit; but the trumpets sounded the recall before the flying Americans had crossed the canal. The presence of mind and lofty language of the eroic wife, had convinced the British colonel that the daring men who so fearlessly dashed into his camp were supported by a formidable force close at hand. Had the truth been known, and the fugitives pursued, nothing could have prevented the destruction not only of the four who fled, but of the rest of the company on the east side of the plantation.

"Tarleton had rode back to the front of the house, where he remained eagerly looking after the fugitives till they disappeared in the wood. He called for the tory captain, who presently came forward, questioned him about the attack, asked the names of the American officers, and dismissed him to have his wounds dressed, and see after his men. The last part of the order was needless; for nearly one half of his men had fallen.

"The British officers now returned to their peach brandy and coffee, and closed the day with a merry night.

"Slocumb and his companions passed rapidly around the plantation and returned to the ground where the encounter had taken place, collecting on the way the stragglers of their troop.

"Slocumb raised a company of two hundred men, and with them thoroughly harassed the rear of the royal army on its march until it crossed the Roanoke, when he hastened to join Lafayette at Warrenton."

THE EXECUTION OF COL. ISAAC HAYNE.

AFTER Charleston had fallen into the hands of the British, many of the Whigs of South Carolina were induced to take the protections which were offered by Cornwallis. They were led to this step by the belief that the cause was hopeless in the South, and were promised by virtue of these protections to be allowed to remain quietly at their homes and take no part in the contest. But what was their surprise when soon after they were called upon to take up arms under the British commanders and against their countrymen. Conceiving that faith had been broken with them, and their promises of neutrality no longer binding, they destroyed their protections and at once ranked themselves under the Continental leaders. Among these was Col. Isaac Hayne, a man of unblemished reputation, fine talents, and lofty patriotism. Indignant at the course pursued by the British, and being summoned to appear at Charleston to take up arms against his country, he hastened to the American army and began to take an active part in the contest. But unfortunately he fell into the enemy's hands, was conveyed to Charleston, submitted by the order of Rawdon to a mock trial, and to the horror of all, condemned to death. He received his sentence with calmness, but the whole country was horrified. Both English and Americans interceded for his life, and the ladies of Charleston immortalized themselves by the spirited address they framed and delivered to his captors in his behalf. But all was of no avail. The cruel heart of Rawdon could not be moved; not even the captive's motherless children with bended knees and tearful prayers could move his obdurate nature.

His eldest child was a boy of thirteen, and he was permitted to remain with his father in prison up to the time of the execution. This boy was actuated by an affection for his father of the most romantic earnestness and fervor. Beholding him loaded with irons and condemned to die, he was overwhelmed with consternation and sorrow; nothing could assuage his grief nor allay his sorrow. In vain did his father endeavor to console him by reminding him that his unavailing grief only tended to increase his own misery; that he was only to leave this world to be admitted into a better; that it was glorious to die for liberty, and that he himself was calm and prepared for the event. The boy would not be comforted. "To-morrow," said the unhappy father, "I set out for immortality; you will accompany me to the place of my execution, and when I am dead, take my body and bury it by the side of your poor mother." In an agony of grief the wretched youth fell weeping on his father's neck, crying, "Oh, my father, my father, I die with you!" The chains that bound the father prevented him from returning the embrace of his son, but he said, in reply, "Live, my son; live, to honor God by a good life, live to take care of your brothers and sisters."

The next morning the son walked beside the father to the place of execution. The history of the war does not afford a more heart-rending incident. There was not a citizen of Charleston whose bosom did not beat with anguish and swell with suppressed indignation. There was sorrow in every countenance, and when men spoke with each other it was in accents of horror.

When the parent and child came in sight of the gallows, the father strengthened himself, and said to the weeping boy by his side, "Tom, my son, show yourself a man! that tree is the boundary of my life and all my life's sorrow. Beyond that the wicked cease from troubling, and the weary are at rest. Don't lay too much at heart our separation, it will be short. 'Twas but lately your mother died—to-day, I die. And you, my son, though but young, must shortly follow."

"Yes, my father," replied the heart-broken youth, "I shal' hortly follow you, for indeed I feel that I cannot live long."

And this melancholy anticipation was fulfilled in a manner far more dreadful than is implied in the mere extinction of life. When his father was torn from his side his tears flowed incessantly, and his bosom was convulsed with heart-rending sobs, but when he saw his beloved parent in the hands of the executioner, the halter adjusted to his neck, and then his form convulsively struggling in the air, the fountain of his tears was suddenly staunched, and he stood transfixed and motionless with horror. He never wept again. When all was over he was led from the scene, but there was a strange wildness in his look, and a palor in his cheek, that alarmed and terrified all who looked upon him. The terrible truth soon became known. His reason had fled forever. It was not long ere he followed his father to the grave, but his death was even more terrible than that of his parent's. In his last moments he often called upon his father, and in accents of such thrilling anguish that the sternest hearted wept to hear him. We know of no incident in history, no passage in romance, more truly touching than this melancholy history.

ADVENTURES OF MAJOR GENERAL CLINTON.

MAJOR GENERAL JAMES CLINTON commanded at Fort Clinton on the occasion of its assault by Sir Henry Clinton. Here he was joined by his brother George Clinton. The attack of Sir Henry was resisted with a devoted heroism, but overcome by superior numbers, and attacked by English ships of war in the stream, they were gradually overcome. But the battle was desperately contested, and when at last all hope was gone, Clinton, disdaining to surrender, gathered a body of men around him, and with his brother at his side, attempted to force his way through the enemy's ranks.

"Fleeing to the river shore he came upon a small boat, in which he urged his brother George to embark, and make his escape. The latter firmly refused to go, unless he accompanied him. But this was impossible; and to end the dispute, James pushed his brother into the boat, and shoved it from the shore, before he had any time to offer any resistance, then springing on a horse near by, galloped away. It was dark; and as he came to a bridge, which he must cross, he saw it occupied with English soldiers. They challenged him; but ordering them to clear the way, he drove the spurs in his horse, and dashed through the bayonets, one of which pierced his leg. Knowing that his safety lay in reaching the mountains, he flung himself from his horse, and snatching the bridle from his head, plunged into the woods. His remarkable presence of mind did not forsake him in this critical moment. He knew that unless he could catch another horse, he must perish amid the mountains with his wound, before he could reach any settlement; and remembering that there were many half-wild horses roving about the shores, he suddenly bethought himself that he might possibly take one of these next morning and escape. So, preserving the bridle he had taken, he limped away; and sliding down a precipice a hundred feet high into a ravine, was out of the reach of his pursuers. Creeping along the steep and rocky sides, with the blood oozing rapidly from his wound, he slipped and fell into the stream. The cold plunge helped him, for it stayed the effusion of blood; and drenched and faint, he made his way to the mountains, where he remained all night, racked with pain, covered with blood, and burned with fever When daylight dawned he began to look about him, and finally came upon a horse, which he caught. Placing the bridle, which he still retained, upon him, he mounted bare-back and rode sixteen miles—every step driving a dagger into the wounded leg before he came to a house. He presented a frightful spectacle the astonished inmates—his regimentals were covered with blood, his cheeks flushed with fever, and his voice hollow and husky."

After his recovery Clinton joined Sullivan's expedition against the Indians, in which he won new laurels. On his return he was stationed at Albany, where he remained until near the close of the war.

"While here an incident occurred which illustrated in a striking manner his character. A mutiny had broken out in a regiment, and it refused to obey the orders to march. When word was brought to Clinton a fearful expression passed over his countenance, and snatching up his pistols, he walked to the head of the refractory regiment. Casting his eye along it for a moment, he thundered out 'March!' but not a soldier stirred. Turning to the ringleader, he presented his pistol to his breast, and told him to advance, or he would shoot him dead on the spot. The dastardly sergeant knew well what kind of a man he had to deal with, and pale with rage and fear, moved on. Clinton then passed along to the second and third officer, in the same way, till he traversed the whole line and put it in motion. Thus, by his resolution and energy, he quelled a dangerous mutiny, and reduced the disobedient ranks to subordination."

ADVENTURES OF LIEUT. RICHARD DALE.

LIEUTENANT RICHARD DALE, afterwards Commodore, served in our youthful navy during the Revolutionary contest. Four several times he was taken a prisoner. On one occasion being captured by a frigate, the prisoners were placed on board the prize, under a small crew, but during the night becoming separated from the English vessel, the captors rose upon their conquerors, retook the brig, and carried her into Baltimore. He put out to sea in the same vessel, but encountering an English man-of-war, he was again captured, and this time carried into Plymouth. The prisoners were examined and thrown into Mill prison on a charge of treason. Here they were doomed to a rigorous and painful confinement. "So severe," says Cooper, "were the privations of the Americans on this occasion, that, in pure hunger, they caught a stray dog one day, skinned, cooked and ate him to satisfy their cravings for food." But their situation eventually attracted the attention of the humane, and their sufferings were relieved. But time passing on, and despairing of ever being freed by exchange, they resolved to attempt an escape. We quote from his life by Cooper.

"A suitable place was selected, and a hole under a wall was commenced. The work required secrecy and time. The earth was removed, little by little in the pockets of the captives, care being had to conceal the place, until a hole of sufficient size was made to permit the body of a man to pass through. It was a tedious process, for the only opportunity which occurred to empty their pockets, was while the Americans were exercising in the halls of their prison for a short period each day. By patience and perseverance they accomplished their purpose, however, every hour dreading exposure and defeat.

"When all was ready, they passed through the hole and escaped. This was in February 1778. The party wandered about the country in company, and by night, for more than a week, suffering all sorts of privations, until it was resolved to take the wiser course of separating. Dale, accompanied by one other, found his way to London, hotly pursued. At one time, the two lay under some straw in an out-house, while the premises were searched by those who were in ques of them. On reaching London, Dale and his companion immediately got on board a vessel about to sail for Dunkirk. A press gang unluckily took this craft in its rounds and suspecting the true object of the fugitives, they were arrested, and their characters being ascertained, they were sent back to Mill Prison in disgrace.

"This was the commencement of a captivity far more tedious than the former. In the first place, they were condemned to forty days imprisonment in the black hole, as a punishment for the late escape; and released from this durance, they were deprived of many of their former indulgences. Dale himself took his revenge in singing "rebel songs," and paid a second visit to the black hole as the penalty. This state of things, with alternations of favor and punishment, continued quite a year, when Dale, singly succeeded in again effecting his great object of getting free.

"The mode in which this second escape was made is known, but the manner by which he procured the means, he refused to his dying day to disclose. At all events, he obtained a full suit of British uniform, attired in which, and seizing a favorable opportunity, he boldly walked past all the sentinels, and got off. That some one was connected with this escape, who might suffer by his revelations is almost certain; and it is a trait in his character worthy of notice, that he kept this secret, with scrupulous fidelity, for forty-seven years. It is not known that he ever divulged it even to any individual in his own family.

"Rendered wary by experience, Dale now proceeded with great address and caution. He probably had money as well as clothes. At all events, he went to London, found means to pro cure a passport, and left the country for France unsuspected and undetected. On reaching a friendly soil, he hastened to L'Orient, and joined the force then equipping under Paul Jones. This commander obtained a commission for Dale, and made him the first lieutenant of his own ship."

When Dale effected this last escape, he was but twenty-three years of age, having been made four times a prisoner, and effecting his escape three different times, each under very different circumstances. So much variety of adventure at so early an age, gives a peculiar charm to his history.

MISS MONCRIEFFE.

During the early part of the war, a gentleman named Wood was residing about seven miles from Peekskill. He was a zealous whig, but the associations and tastes of his English wife, caused her prejudices to decide in favor of the loyalists. Among the inmates of the family, was Miss Moncrieffe, a visitor from New York, and the daughter of Major Moncrieffe of the English army. This lady was young, of surpassing beauty, fascinating manners, and possessed of rare accomplishments, with intellectual gifts of a high order. Her beauty, the care and richness lavished upon her dress, combined with her pleasing attainments, dazzled all those who came within the range of her influence, and Mr. Wood's house soon became the resort of all those who could obtain the acquaintance of this beautiful and spirited girl. Among the visitors who thronged around the brilliant lady, were several officers of the American army. It was not in the power of these to resist the enslaving charms of their beautiful countrywomen, and they were delighted to find, that her sentiments sympathized with the patriotic cause, and listened with unqualified pleasure to the words of patriotism from lips so fair, and to the approbation of one to whom it was not in their power to resist doing homage. She encouraged conversation, upon the state of the country and its prospects and so unrestrained became their connection, that confidential disclosures were made to her from time to time, and by insinuating questions, she would often learn of all the plans and movements in contemplation, to circumvent the enemy.

Miss Moncrieffe was an excellent equestrian. She rode out every day, sometimes accompanied, but oftener alone. She could ride any horse, however spirited, and usually went abroad in a magnificent costume, that from its exceeding beauty, and singular style, received much comment. One morning as she was taking her accustomed ride, alone, on passing a farm-house, the barking of a dog, that suddenly sprang into the road, frightened the horse. The animal started aside; she was thrown to the ground, and so severely stunned, as to be entirely insensible. The people ran out from the house, lifted her up, and carried her in and laid her on the bed. While endeavoring to restore her, they unbuttoned the vest of her riding habit, to allow her to breathe more freely, when a letter fell out, which was picked up and lain on the table. It was not long before she began to recover consciousness, and in a few moments was fully restored to her senses. Suddenly observing the open flaps of her vest, she started up in great agitation exclaiming, "Who unbuttoned my waist-coat? Where is the letter? ah, I am lost—lost!" A woman at her side took up the letter, and was about to hand it to her, when a man standing by, whose suspicions were aroused by the strangeness of her manner, sprang forward and seized it. With the greatest alarm and anxiety, she begged him to restore it, but as he observed it was addressed to New York, and more and more suspicious from the over anxiety of her manner, he positively refused to deliver it up, until its contents should be known. Finding her efforts to obtain the letter in vain, and having received no injury from her fall, she was obliged to mount her horse and depart without it.

There was now but one course for her to pursue. An exposure of the contents of the letter would prove her ruin. She immediately began to prepare for returning to New York, but before she could get ready to depart, a party of soldiers rode up and entered the house, and the officer informed her that she must be considered as a prisoner, and be conducted to the destination pointed out by his orders.

It was ascertained, that the letter thus opportunely discovered, contained information relative to an intended movement of the American army. It was proved in the examination, that the young lady was in the habit, repeatedly of sending her British friends the information reposed in her by the young American officers, who supposing her to be actuated by a strong interest in the cause they espoused, had confided in her the secrets of the army. When she wrote a letter, she concealed it in the vest of her riding habit, and riding by an appointed spot, contrived to drop it upon the ground unseen, when it was immediately picked up by an accomplice hid in the bushes, and then conveyed from hand to hand until it reached New York. All this came to ligh by the confession of the accomplice himself.

Miss Moncrieffe was retained as a prisoner. Her countrymen not disposed to deal harshly with one so young, beautiful and accomplished, her trial was postponed from time to time, until at last she was given up to her friends.*

AN EXTRAORDINARY ADVENTURE.†

The American authorities found much difficulty in disposing of their prisoners. They had no posts regularly fitted for the purpose, and they could suggest no better means for securing them, than to place them under guard in a thickly settled part of the country, where the inhabitants were most decidedly hostile to the English. The town of Lancaster, in Pennsylvania, was one of those selected for this purpose. The prisoners were confined in barracks, enclosed with a stockade, and vigilantly guarded. But in spite of all precautions, they often disappeared in an unaccountable manner, and nothing was heard of them till they had resumed their places in the English army. Many and various were the conjectures as to the means of their escape; the officers inquired and investigated in vain; the country was explored to no purpose; the soldiers shook their heads, and told of fortune-tellers, pedlars, and such characters who had been seen at intervals; and sundry of the more credulous could think of nothing but supernatural agency; but whether man or spirit, was the conspirator, the mystery was unbroken.

When this became known to Washington, he sent General Hazen to take this responsible charge. This energetic officer

---

* Mrs. Ellett.

† From the first volume of the " New England Magazine"

after exhausting all resources, resorted to stratagem. He was convinced that, as the nearest British post was more than a hundred miles distant, the prisoners must be aided by Americans, but where the suspicion should fall, he could not even conjecture, the eproach of toryism being almost unknown in that region. Having been trained to meet exigencies of this kind in a distinguished career, as colonel in the British army, his plan was formed at once, and communicated to an officer of his own, upon whose talent he relied for its successful execution. This was Captain Lee, whose courage and ability fully justified the selection.

The secret plan concocted between them, was this. It was to be given out that Lee was absent on furlough or command. He, meanwhile, was to assume the dress of a British prisoner, and, having provided himself with information and a story of his capture, was to be thrown into the barracks where he might gain the confidence of the soldiers, and join them in a plan of escape. How well Captain Lee sustained his part, may be inferred from the fact that when he had disappeared and placed himself among the prisoners, his own officers and soldiers saw him every day without the least suspicion. The person to whom the author of this sketch is indebted for these particulars, was the intendant of the prisoners, and familiar with Lee; but, though compelled to see him often in the discharge of his duty, he never penetrated the disguise. Well it was for Lee, that his disguise was so complete. Had his associates suspected his purpose to betray them, his history would have been embraced in the proverb, "dead men tell no tales."

For many days he remained in this situation, making no discoveries whatever. He thought he perceived at times, signs of intelligence between the prisoners and an old woman, who was allowed to bring fruit for sale, within the enclosure. She was known to be deaf and half-witted, and was therefore no object of suspicion. It was known that her son had been disgraced and punished in the American army, but she had never betrayed any malice on that account, and no one dreamed that she could have had the power to do injury if she possessed the will. Lee watched her closely, but saw nothing to confirm his suspicions. Her dwelling was about a mile distant, a wild retreat where she shared her miserable quarters, with a dog and cat, the former of which mounted guard over her mansion, while the latter encouraged superstitious fears that were equally effectual in keeping visitors away.

One dark, stormy night, in autumn, he was lying awake at midnight, meditating on the enterprise he had undertaken, which though in the beginning it had reccommended itself to his romantic disposition, had now lost all its charms. It was one of those tempests, which in our climate so often hang upon the path of the departing year. His companions slept soundly, but the wind, which shook the building to its foundation, and threw heavy splashes of rain against the window; conspired with the state of his mind to keep him wakeful. All at once, the door was gently opened, and a figure moved silently into the room. It was too dark to observe its motions narrowly, but he could see that it stooped towards one of the sleepers who immediately rose; next it approached and touched him on the shoulder. Lee immediately started up; the figure then allowed a slight gleam from a dark lantern to pass over his face, and as it did so, whispered impatiently, "not the man—but come!" It then occurred to Lee, that this was the opportunity he then desired. The unknown then whispered to him, to keep his place till another man was called; but just at that moment, some noise disturbed him, and making a sign to Lee to follow, he moved silently out of the room.

They found the door of the house unbarred, and a small part of the fence removed, where they passed out without molestation; the sentry had retired to a shelter where he thought he could guard his post without suffering from the rain; but Lee saw that his conductors put themselves in preparation to silence him if he should happen to address them. Just without the fence, appeared a stooping figure, wrapped in a red cloak, and supporting itself with a large stick, which Lee at once perceived could be no other than the old fruit woman. But the most profound silence was observed; a man came out of a thicket at a little distance, and joined them, and the whole party moved onward under the guidance of the old woman. At first, they frequently stopped to listen, but having heard the sentinels cry, "all's well," they seemed reassured, and moved with more confidence than before.

They soon came near to her cottage, under an overhanging bank, where a bright light was shining out from a little window upon the wet and drooping boughs that hung near it. The dog received them graciously, and they entered. A table was spread with some coarse provisions upon it, and a large jug, which one of the soldiers was about to seize, when the man who conducted them, withheld him.

"No," said he, "we must first proceed to business." He then went to a small closet, from which he returned with what seemed to have been originally a bible, though now it was worn to a mahogany color, and a spherical form. While they were doing this, Lee had time to examine his companions; one of whom was a large, quite good-looking soldier, the other a short, stout man, with much the aspect of a villain. They examined him in turn, and as Lee had formerly been obliged to punish the shorter soldier severely, he felt some misgivings when the fellow's eye rested upon him. Their conductor was a middle-aged, harsh-looking man, whom Lee had never seen before.

As no time was to be lost, their guide explained to them in a few words, that, before he should undertake his dangerous enterprise, he should require of them to swear upon the scriptures, not to make the least attempt to escape, and never to reveal the circumstances or agents in the proceeding, whatever might befal them. The soldiers, however, insisted on deferring this measure, till they had formed some slight acquaintance with the contents of the jug, and expressed their sentiments on the subject, rather by actions than words. In this they were joined by Lee, who by this time had begun to contemplate the danger of the enterprise, in a new and unpleasant point of view. If he were to be compelled to accompany his party to New York, his disguise would at once be detected, and it was certain that he would be hanged as a spy. He had supposed, beforehand, that he should find no difficulty in escaping at any moment; but he saw that their conductor had prepared arms for them, which they were to use in taking the life of any one who should attempt to leave them—and then the oath. He might possibly have released himself from its obligations, when it became necessary for the interests of his country; but no honorable man can well bear to be driven to an emergency, in which he must violate an oath, however reluctantly taken. He felt that there was no retreating, when there came a heavy shock, as if something falling against the sides of the house; their practiced ears at once detected the alarm gun; and their conductor, throwing down the old bible, which he had held all the while impatiently in his hand, directed the party to follow him in close order, and immediately quitted the house, taking with him his dark lantern.

They went on with great dispatch, but not without difficulty. Sometimes their footing would give way on some sandy bank or slippery field; and when their path led through the woods, the wet boughs dashed heavily in their faces. Lee felt that he might have deserted his precious companions while they were in this hurry and alarm; but he felt, that, as yet, he had made no discoveries; and however dangerous his situation was, he could not bear to confess that he had not nerve to carry it through. On he went, therefore, for two or three hours, and was beginning to sink with fatigue, when the barking of a dog brought the party to a stand. Their conductor gave a low whistle, which was answered at no great distance, and a figure came forward in the darkness who whispered to their guide, and then led the way up to a building, which seemed, by the shadowy outline, to be a large stone barn. They entered it, and were severally placed in small nooks where they could feel that the hay was all around them, except on the side of the wall. Shortly after, some provisions were brought to them with the same silence, and it was signified to them that they were to remain concealed through the whole of the coming day.

Through a crevice in the wall Lee could discover, as the day came on, that the barn was attached to a small house. He was so near the house that he could overhear the conversation which was carried on about the door. The morning rose clear, and it was evident from the inquiries of horsemen, who occasionally galloped up to the door, that the country was alarmed. The farmer gave short and surly replies, as if unwilling to be taken off from his labor; but the other inmates were eager in their questions. and, from the answers, Lee gathered that the means by which he and his companions had escaped were as mysterious as ever.

The next night, when all was quiet, they resumed their march, and explained to Lee, that, as he was not with them in their conspiracy and was accidentally associated with them in their escape, they should take the precaution to keep him before them, just behind the guide. He submitted without opposition, though the arrangement considerably lessened the chances in favor of his escape. He observed, from the direction of the stars, that they did not move in a direct line toward the Delaware, but they changed their course so often that he could not conjecture at what point they intended to strike the river. He endeavored, whenever any peculiar object appeared, to fix it in his memory as well as the darkness would permit, and succeeded better than could have been expected, considering the agitated state in which he traveled.

For several nights they went on in this manner, being delivered over to different persons from time to time; and as Lee could gather from their whispering conversation, they were regularly employed on occasions like the present, and well rewarded by the British for their services. Their employment was full of danger; and though they seemed like desperate men, he could observe that they never remitted their precautions. They were concealed by day in barns—cellars—caves made for the purpose, and similar retreats, and one day was passed in a tomb, the dimensions of which had been enlarged, and the inmates, if there had been any, banished to make room for the living. The burying grounds were a favorite retreat, and on more occasions than one they were obliged to resort to superstitious alarms to remove intruders upon their path; their success fully justified the experiment, and, unpleasantly situated as he was, in the prospect of soon being a ghost himself, he could not avoid laughing at the expedition with which old and young fled from the fancied apparitions under clouds of night, wishing to meet such enemies, like Ajax, in the face of day.

Though the distance to the Delaware was not great, they had now been twelve days on the road, and such was the vigilance and suspicion prevailing throughout the country, that they almost despaired of effecting their object. The conductor grew impatient; and Lee's companions, at least one of them, became ferocious. There was, as we have said, something unpleasant to him in the glance of this fellow toward him, which became more and more fierce as they went on; but it did not appear whether it were owing to circumstances or actual suspicion. It so happened that, on the twelfth night, Lee was placed in a barn, while the rest of the party sheltered themselves in the cellar of a little stone church, where they could talk and act with more freedom, both because the solitude of the place was not often disturbed even on the Sabbath—and because even the proprietors did not know that illegal hands had added a cellar to the conveniences of the building.

The party were seated here as the day broke, and the light, which struggled in through crevices opened for the purpose howed a low room about twelve feet square, with a damp floor and large patches of white mould upon the walls. Finding, probably, that the pavement afforded no accommodations for sleeping, the worthies were seated each upon a little cask, which seemed like those used for gunpowder. Here they were smoking pipes with great diligence, and, at intervals not distant, applying a huge canteen to their mouths, from which they drank with upturned faces, expressive of solemn satisfaction. While they were thus engaged, the short soldier asked them in a careless way, if they knew whom they had in the party. The others started, and took their pipes from their mouths to ask him what he meant.

"I mean," said he, "that we are honored with the company of Captain Lee, of the rebel army. The rascal once punished me, and I never mistook my man when I had a debt of that kind to pay. Now I shall have my revenge."

The others hastened to express their disgust at his ferocity, saying, that if, as he said, their companion was an American officer, all they had to do was to watch him closely. They said that, as he had came among them uninvited, he must go with them to New York and take the consequences; but, meantime, it was their interest not to seem to suspect him, otherwise he might give an alarm, whereas it was evidently his intention to go with them till they were ready to embark for New York. The other persisted in saying that he would have his revenge with his own hand, upon which the conductor, drawing a pistol declared to him that if he saw the least attempt to injure Captain Lee, or any conduct which would lead him to suspect that his disguise was discovered, he would that moment shoot him through the head. The soldier put his hand upon his knife with an ominous scowl upon the conductor, but seeing that he had to do with one who was likely to be as good as his word, he restrained himself, and began to arrange some rubbish to serve him for a bed. The other soldiers followed his example, and their guide withdrew, locking the door after him.

The next night they went on as usual, but the manner of their conductor showed there was more danger than before; in fact, he explained to the party, that they were now not far from the Delaware, and hoped to reach it before midnight. They occasionally heard the report of a musket, which seemed to indicate that some movement was going on in the country. Thus warned, they quickened their steps, and it was not long before they saw a gleam of broad clear light before them, such as is reflected from calm waters even in the darkest nights. They moved up to i with deep silence; there were various emotions in their breasts; Lee was hoping for an opportunity to escape from an enterprize, which was growing too serious, and the principal objects of which were already answered; the others were anxious lest some accident might have happened to the boat on which they depended for crossing the stream.

When they came to the bank there were no traces of a boat on the waters. Their conductor stood still for a moment in dismay; but, recollecting himself, he said it was possible it might have been secured lower down the stream, and, forgetting everything else, he directed the larger soldier to accompany him, and, giving a pistol to the other, he whispered, " if the rebel officer attempt to betray us, shoot him; if not, you will not, for your own sake, make any noise to show where we are." In the same instant they departed, and Lee was left alone with the ruffian.

He had before suspected the fellow knew him, and now doubts were changed to certainty at once. Dark as it was, it seemed as if fire flashed from his eye, now that he felt revenge was in his power. Lee was as brave as any officer in the army; but he was unarmed, and though he was strong, his adversary was still more powerful. While he stood, uncertain what to do, the fellow seemed to be enjoying the prospect of revenge, as he looked upon him with a steady eye. Though the officer stood in appearance unmoved, the sweat rolled in heavy drops from his brow. He soon took his resolution, and sprang upon his adversary with the intention of wresting the pistol from his hand; but the other was upon his guard, and aimed with such precision, that, had the pistol been charged with a bullet, that moment would have been his last. But it seemed that the conductor had trusted to the sight of his weapons to render the use of them unnecessary, and had therefore loaded them only with powder; as it was, the shock threw Lee to the ground; but fortunately as the fellow dropped the pistol, it fell where Lee could reach it, and as his adversary stooped, and was drawing his knife from his bosom, Lee was able to give him a stunning blow. He immediately threw himself upon the assassin, and a long and bloody struggle began; they were so nearly matched in strength and advantage, that neither dared unclench his hold for the sake of grasping the knife; the blood gushed from their mouths, and the combat would have probably ended in favor of the assassin, when steps and voices were heard advancing, and they found themselves in the hands of a party of countrymen, who were armed for the occasion, and were scouring the banks of the river. They were forcibly torn apart, but so exhausted and breathless, that neither could make any explanation, and they submitted quietly to the disposal of their captors.

The party of armed countrymen though they had succeeded in their attempt, and were sufficiently triumphant on the occasion, were sorely perplexed to determine how to dispose of their prisoners. After some discussion, one of them proposed to obtain the decision of the wisdom of the nearest magistrate. They accordingly proceeded with their prisoners to his mansion, about two miles distant, and called on him to rise and attend to business. A window was hastily thrown up, and the justice put forth his night-capped head, and, with more wrath than became his dignity, ordered them off; and, in requital for their calling him out of bed in the cold, generously wished them to the warmest place which then occurred to his imagination. However, resistance was vain; he was compelled to rise; and, as soon as the prisoners were brought before him, he ordered them to be taken in irons to the city of Philadelphia. Lee improved the opportunity to take the old gentleman aside, and told him who he was, and why he was thus disguised; the justice only interrupted him with the occasional inquiry, "Most done?" When he had finished, the magistrate told him that his story was very well made, and told in a manner very creditable to his address, and that he should give it all the weight it seemed to require. All Lee's remonstrance were unavailing.

As soon as they were fairly lodged in prison, Lee prevailed on the jailor to carry a note to Gen. Lincoln, informing him of his condition. The general received it as he was dressing in the morning, and immediately sent one of his aids to the jail. That officer could not believe his eyes when he saw Captain Lee. His uniform, worn out when he assumed it, was now hanging in rags about him, and he had not been shaved for a fortnight; he wished, very naturally, to improve his appearance before presenting himself before the Secretary of War; but the orders were peremptory to bring him as he was. The general loved a joke full well; his laughter was hardly exceeded by the report of his own cannon and long and loud did he laugh that day.

When Captain Lee returned to Lancaster, he immediately attempted to retrace the ground; and so accurate, under all the unfavorable circumstances, had been his investigation, that he brought to justice fifteen persons, who had aided the escape of

British prisoners. It is scarcely necessary to say to those who know the fate of revolutionary officers, that he received, for this hazardous and effectual service, no reward whatever.

MISS MOORE.

Miss Behethland Moore, the daughter of Captain Moore, who was present at Braddock's defeat, and who died in 1770, resided with her mother and step-father, Captain Samuel Savage, in Edgefield District, South Carolina. Her youth was passed among the eventful scenes of our revolution, and a number of incidents are related, that go to prove her calm courage, and her inflexibility of purpose. She was born in 1764, and therefore, in the earlier part of the contest was nothing more than a child.

The terrors of the war were often enacted before the very door of her step-father's residence. On one occasion, a most sanguinary skirmish took place just before the house, between a a body of Col. Washington's cavalry, and some of Rawdon's men. Shortly after a party of the British in search of plunder, broke into the house. But the family had been forewarned, and concealed their treasures. In searching for plunder they discovered a quantity of apples, and began to roll them down the stairs. while the soldiers below picked them up. Miss Moore, nothing fearing, commanded them to desist, with an air so determined and resolute, that an officer standing by, admiring so courageous a spirit in a girl so young, ordered the soldiers to obey her.

On another occasion, a party of tories in pillaging the house. commanded one of the servants to bring them the horses. Miss

Moore commanded him not to obey. The tories repeated the order, accompanied with a threat to beat him if he refused. The command of the young girl was reiterated, and just as the tory was about putting his threat into execution, she threw herself between them, and preserved the slave from the intended violence

At one time, great danger was threatening Captain Wallace, who commanded a small force, a few miles distant. It was of the utmost importance that this intelligence should be conveyed to him, but there was no male whose services could be commanded, and, therefore, Miss Moore volunteered to convey the message herself. This was when she was but fifteen. Midnight was chosen as the hour, and accompanied by her little brother, and a female friend, she set out in a canoe up the river towards the encampment of the whigs. Silently and swiftly they propelled their frail vessel up the dark current, through forests buried in darkness, and a profound silence that awed them ; with the calm stars above, and the deep river gloomily rolling by, and no human sounds to relieve the oppressive solemnity of the hour. It was the hour too, when the enemy usually set out on their marauding expeditions, and the young girls knew that neither their sex, nor innocence would preserve them from ruthless foes, who were more relentless and cruel, than the swarthy savages of the forest. But the fate of many of their countrymen depended on their exertions, and, as it proved, the future destiny of our heroine, was involved in the successful issue of their enterprise. Undismayed by the perils of the journey, the young girls bent their energies to the task before them, and at last saw lights glimmering in the distance, that pointed out their destination. They soon reached the encampment, a picturesque scene, with the ruddy glow from the camp fires, casting the surrounding scene in still greater shadow and motley groups of figures gathered around the fires, sleeping, talking, eating, &c. After delivering the warning to Captain Wallace, the girls embarked in their canoe to return, and soon left the encampment behind, winding their way through dense forests, and reached their home in safety.

The next morning, a handsome and gallant looking American officer, rode up to the door of Captain Savage's residence, and requested to make a few inquiries of the young lady, by whose energy and zeal her countrymen had been saved from an impending danger. Miss Moore appeared, and when her youthful and blooming beauty greeted the eyes of the young officer, an exclamation of pleasure burst from his lips. He almost forgot to make his inquiries, until reminded by the blushing damsel, but her voice rather increased than relieved his embarrassment. All his questions having been at last answered, and having no excuse by which to prolong the interview, he was reluctantly compelled to depart, but his eyes to the last rested on the fair girl's form. It is said that the young lady was no less struck with the handsome dragoon's figure, and that his face came often to her in her dreams that night.

It was not long before the young officer made an excuse for again visiting the house where resided the beauty who had bound him captive to her charms, and as these impressions were reciprocal, he soon discovered welcome in her manner, and drew happy auguries therefrom. He became an accepted suitor. But their love in a measure verified the old adage. The step-father opposed the union; at first strenuously, but the perseverance of the lover, gradually broke down his opposition, and he eventually yielded consent.

It was not till 1784, that Miss Moore became united to Captain William Butler, afterwards General Butler, member of Congress, from 1801 till 1814, and commander of the southern forces, as Major General, during the last war with Great Britain.

Mrs. Butler filled a distinguished place in society, and was celebrated for her lofty virtues, high intelligence, and graceful refinement. Her distinguished husband died in 1821, but not until quite recently was she called upon to close her mortal career.

ADVENTURES OF MR. FERRIS.

At early morn, of a day in September, 1776, a long line of boats put off from the enemy's fleet, which for some days had been lying nearly opposite Throg's Neck, on Long Island sound, and approached in an imposing manner to the shore. The gay regimentals of the soldiers, and the glittering bayonets that threw back the sun's rays in floods of brilliant and dazzling light, with the sounds of martial music, and the occasional solemn booming of a gun, presented a beautiful and inspiriting scene. But to the residents of the country, who were tremblingly watching the disembarkation, the pageant was only one of terror, and as with heavy hearts they watched the invaders land upon their soil, their bosoms sunk in hopeless despair, and a long era of oppression, suffering, and imprisonment was opened to them, of which this was the first scene in the drama.

In the house of James Ferris, a large land holder, and wealthy farmer, residing on the Neck, a cheerful and happy family group were gathered at the morning meal. But as they arose from the table, the appalling sight burst upon their view, and in an instant peace and contentment were changed into dismay and terror. Part of the troops had already landed, and their danger was imminent. Mr. Ferris was aged and crippled, and thus escape to him was impossible, but his son, Thomas Ferris, a young man of twenty, he determined to save for future services to his country The trembling hands of the whole family group, were immediately engaged in preparing him for departure; his clothes were hastily tied up in a handkerchief, and with his musket thrown over his shoulder, he sprang upon the horse ready saddled at the door, and galloped off toward the head of the Neck. But he was observed by the British, and a party sent to prevent his escape. He succeeded, however, in reaching the head of the Neck before his enemies, but as he crossed the bridge, a volley of musketry was discharged after him by the disappointed soldiery. Not a bullet touched him, however, and he hurried forward to join the American ranks.

The members of the family, whose peace had been thus suddenly disturbed, meanwhile, remained in the most keen anxiety as to the fate of the fugitive. The discharges which they heard did not serve to allay their fears, but the approach of the enemy to the door, turned their thoughts to their own danger. Mr. Ferris had hoped that his age, and his inaction in the contest, would preserve him from molestation. · But he was mistaken. When, indeed, in the course of the war, was a dependence on British mercy justified! He was ruthlessly seized, and torn from his family, despite their entreaties, and sent to New York as a prisoner We are all aware of the terrible sufferings of the American captives confined in New York, and of the attrocities practiced upon them by their inhuman keepers. Mr. Ferris was thrown into the old sugar house prison, where, subjected to every exposure, half starved, and compelled to eat the unwholesome food placed before him, he contracted a disease which then prevailed among the prisoners. His strength became utterly prostrated, and he was brought to an extremity of suffering, difficult to realize. But during the term of his confinement, Mrs. Ferris, who was a determined and resolute woman, went into the city for the purpose of attempting to procure his liberation. Undaunted by the innumerable obstacles in such an attempt, and undismayed by the almost utter hopelessness, she persevered to the last, and eventually procured his release. But it was at an hour when disease had wasted his strength, and death was hovering so close upon him that his captors considered him of no more danger to the cause of his majesty. The devoted wife bore him to her home, only to see him die. It was but a few days after he was borne out from his pestilential dungeon, that he was carried to his last earthly abode; and the soil that rested upon his bosom, covered one of the many martyrs who purchased the liberty of their country, not in the wild excitement of the battle field, but in the silent, slow, and unanimated agonies of the dungeon; by the cancker of suffering that eat into their souls and consumed their heart-strings.

Thomas Ferris, young and active, with a vigorous and powerful frame, now became one of the deadliest and most dangerous enemies to the invader. We can readily imagine that the horrors which surrounded his father's untimely end, gave an edge to his animosity, and often nerved his arm in the contest. He was generally employed in collecting information of the movements of the British forces, and this duty brought him into frequent connection with Luther Kennicut, one of those persons employed by the commander-in-chief to frequent the camp of the enemy in the capacities of spies, and who have been immortalized in the character of Harvey Birch.* This class of men in doing signal service to their country, were placed in situations most trying to their patriotism. They were usually suspected to be refugees, and as such were frequently exposed to the honest indignation of their whig neighbors, and indignities thus heaped upon them by those whom they served, could only have been allayed by the consciousness of the great benefits their services were conferring upon the patriotic cause. They usually went about as pedlars, and would pass through the enemy's lines, and even penetrate into the very presence of the British leaders, by means of their pursuit, with unsuspected impunity. This Kennicut was one of the most active men thus employed. Whenever any movement was in contemplation by the British army, he would adroitly manage to become possessed of all the particulars, and then pass through the line under the pretence of selling his articles, and meeting his accomplices in secret places, at night, in the depths of the wood, convey his intelligence to the American officers. Young Ferris was of those employed in receiving the intelligence thus gained by Kennicut; and he declared after the war that many serious consequences were averted from the American army, by means of the faithful services of the despised, but patriotic pedlar.

In one of the many interviews between Ferris and Kennicut, a bold plan was conceived by them for the surprise and capture of one of the principal British officers while in his own camp. The British army were encamped on Throg's Neck, and the quarters of the officer, whom they designed to capture, were in the house of Mr. Ferris. Two other enterprising patriots were engaged in

---

* Kennicut was the original of this celebrated character of Cooper's.

the attempt. On the evening fixed upon, Ferris and his two companions, Kennicut appointing to meet them on the Neck, cautiously approached the sentinels. Their manner of passing the guard, was ingenious and bold. It was done by crawling along the shore through the sedge, cautiously advancing as the sentinel's back was turned toward them, and when he advanced, they would lie close and still in the sedge. By this slow and critical means, they at last passed the sentinel, and got on to the Neck, and soon joined Kennicut at the place of meeting. A place of concealment was now found for them, and the plan for the capture arranged, which was to take place at midnight of the next evening. Young Ferris who was acquainted with the house, was to conduct the party to the apartment of the officer, whom they were to seize, gag, and muffle, and escape with him from the Neck as expeditiously and silently as possible. It was a daring plan, but its success would crown them with lasting honor. After the completion of all the arrangements, Kennicut left them. Some little time after his departure, Ferris becoming very thirsty, incautiously ventured to the well, near to the house, for the purpose of procuring water, when he was observed and recognized by one of the negro slaves belonging to the house. In a few minutes after this incident, Kennicut came to them hurriedly, and informed them that their presence on the Neck was known, that the guard was doubled all round the Neck, and that a thorough search was ordered to be made for them, at the first approach of daylight. They were now in a critical situation. To escape from the Neck in the same manner they reached it, was impossible, as at this point a vigilant watch would doubtless be stationed. Ferris proposed to escape by swimming, but his two companions could not swim, and they begged most earnestly not to be abandoned

But the resources of men inured to danger, and familiar with stratagem, were not exhausted. Towards the lower end of the Neck there was an old stone wall, which had been built double, and which was surrounded by a thick and tangled mass of plumb bushes. The plan was to remove one side of the wall, and rebuild it in such a manner so as to afford hollow places for their concealment. Ferris and Kennicut first built in their two companions, and lastly, Ferris took his place, and Kennicut alone completed the entombment. These singular and ingenious cages having been finished, Kennicut surveyed them closely, and with scrutiny on all sides. The form of the wall was but little altered from its original shape, while the screen work of bushes effectually curtained it from observation. Assured of the completeness of the concealment, Kennicut, with a few words of caution, left Ferris and his companions in their voluntary imprisonment, with a promise to return to them whenever he might do so with prudence.

The situation of our heroes, must indeed have been trying. It was not long before daylight appeared, and then they could hear the search that was going on all around them. Presently the tramp of soldiers was heard, which grew nearer and nearer, and their hearts sank desparingly within them, as they could detect their approach directly to the spot where they were concealed. Two files of soldiers, one on each side of the wall, came along close by the side of the wall, and so near to them, that with a switch two feet long, the prisoners could have touched them. Suddenly, and to the great terror of the adventurers, the word of halt was given; and our heroes believed their discovery certain. The grass which had been trampled down by them in the process of erecting their prisons, arrested the attention of the soldiers, and a brief conference as to its cause, was held within hearing of the captives. One remarked, that "there the d——d rebels must have lain last night,"—but another was of opinion, that it was where the deserters, who had escaped the day previous, had lain during the night. Satisfied with this solution of the cause, the party resumed their march, much to the relief and delight of our incarcerated friends. They remained in their concealment the entire day, and much of the ensuing night, without food, and in a state of unceasing anxiety. Towards morning, Kennicut came and released them. They now abandoned their intention of securing the officer, and set about escaping from the Neck in the same manner they had come upon it.

Mr. Ferris was frequently engaged in enterprizes of a similar nature to this, during the period of the war. On one occasion, he accompanied an expedition in two whale boats, eastward, and approaching Stonington they resolved to cut out two vessels, a sloop and a schooner belonging to the British, which were lying at anchor in the harbor. At the hour of midnight, when all was hushed and still, they cautiously rowed towards the vessels, the one to which Mr. Ferris belonged approaching the schooner. But one man walked its deck, the others being asleep below, and he seemed to be unconscious of the danger which threatened the vessel. Not a sound denoted their approach, and the boat was by the vessel's side, and the assailants already pouring upon the deck, ere the sentinel was aware of the attack. A pistol at his head commanded immediate silence, or death the penalty, and in a moment the hatches and companion-way were secured, the cables cut, the sails hoisted, and they slowly moved from the shore. But at this juncture they were saluted by cannon from the battery on shore, the alarm having been given by the hoisting of the sails, and with balls ploughing the sea about them and occasionally whistling through the rigging, they stood out to sea, but were soon out of sight and beyond the reach of the enemy.

Numerous adventures and "hair-breadth 'scapes" occurred to Mr. Ferris during the eventful period of the war, but the foregoing, from their daring and ingenuity particularly commend themselves to the admiration of the reader. The author is indebted to a son of Mr. Ferris, now residing in Westchester County, in this State, for the particulars of the above sketch.

EXPLOITS OF SERGEANT JASPER.

Every reader of American history is acquainted with the name of Sergeant Jasper. He served in "Marion's Brigade," and by his heroism and talents he won a reputation rarely acquired by one in so obscure a position. At the celebrated battle of Fort Moultrie, in the hottest fire of the battle, the flag of the fort was shot away, and fell without the fort. Jasper instantly leapt over the ramparts on to the beach, where he was fully exposed to a most terrific fire, and seizing the flag, bound it to a sponge staff, and stuck it on the rampart in the sand. This act was performed with the most undisturbed coolness, and received the acclamations of the soldiers. After the battle, Gen. Rutledge presented him with a sword as a token of esteem for his chivalrous bravery.

"Jasper possessed remarkable talents for a scout. He could wear all diguises with admirable ease and dexterity. He was a perfect Proteus, in ability to alter his appearance; perpetually entering the camp of the enemy, without detection, and invariably returning to his own with soldiers he had seduced, or prisoners he had captured. Such was the confidence in his fidelity and skill, that a roving commission was granted him, with Lberty to pick his associates from the brigade. Of these he seldom chose more than six. He would often go off and return with a prisoner before his absence was known. He was known to catch a party that was looking for him. On one occasion he went into the British lines at Savannah, as a deserter, and was gladly received After a stay of eight days in which time he learned of the strength, situation and intentions of the enemy, he returned to his companions.

"While in the exercise of his roving privileges he, on one occasion, visited the post of the enemy at Ebenezer. At this post he had a brother, who held the same rank in the British service, that he held in the American. This instance was quite too common in the history of the period and country, to occasion much surprise, or cause any suspicion of the integrity of either party. William Jasper loved his brother and wished to see him: it is very certain, at the same time, that he did not deny himself the privilege of seeing all around him. The Tory was alarmed at William's appearance in the British camp, but the other quieted his fears, by representing himself as no longer an American soldier. He checked the joy which this declaration excited in his brother's mind, by assuring him that, though he found little encouragement in fighting for his country, "he had not the heart to fight against her." Our scout lingered for two or three days in the British camp, and then, by a *detour*, regained that of the American's; reporting to his Commander all that he had seen. He was encouraged to repeat his visit a few weeks after, but this time he took with him a comrade, one Sergeant Newton, a fellow quite as brave in spirit, and strong in body as himself. Here he was again well received by his brother, who entertained the guests kindly for several days. Meanwhile, a small party of Americans were brought into Ebenezer as captives, over whom hung the danger of "short shrift and sudden cord." They were on their way to Savannah for trial. They had taken arms with the British, as hundreds more had done, when the country was deemed reconquered; but, on the approach of the American army, had rejoined their countrymen, and were now once more at the mercy of the power with which they had broken faith. 'It will go hard with them,' said the Tory Jasper to his Whig brother; but the secret comment of the other was, 'it shall go hard with me first.' There was a woman, the wife of one of the prisoners, who, with her child, kept them company. William Jasper and his friend were touched by the spectacle of their distress; and they conferred together, as soon as they were alone, as to the possibility of rescuing them. Their plan was soon adopted. It was a simple one, such as naturally suggests itself to a hardy and magnanimous character. The prisoners had scarcely left the post for Savannah, under a guard of eight men, a sergeant and corporal, when they took leave of their host, and set forth also, though in a different direction from the guard. Changing their course when secure from observation, they stretched across the country and followed the footsteps of the unhappy captives. But it was only in the pursuit that they became truly conscious of the difficulty, nay, seeming impossibility, of effecting their object. The guard was armed, and ten in number; they but two, and weaponless. Hopeless, they nevertheless followed on. Two miles from Savannah there is a famous spring, the waters of which are well known to travelers. The conjecture that the guard might stop there, with the prisoners, for refreshment, suggested itself to our companions; here, opportunities might occur for the rescue, which had nowhere before presented themselves. Taking an obscure path with which they were familiar, which led them to the spot before the enemy could arrive, they placed themselves in ambush in the immediate neighborhood of the spring. They had not long to wait. Their conjecture proved correct. Th guard was halted on the road opposite the spring. The corporal with four men conducted the captives to the water, while the sergeant, with the remainder of his force, having made them ground their arms near the road, brought up the rear. The prisoners threw themselves upon the earth—the woman and her child, near its father. Little did any of them dream that deliverance was at hand. The child fell asleep in the mother's lap. Two of the armed men kept guard, but we may suppose with little caution. What had they to apprehend, within sight of a walled town in the possession of their friends? Two others approached the spring, in order to bring water to the prisoners. Resting their muskets against a tree they proceeded to fill their canteens. At this moment Jasper gave the signal to his comrade. In an instant the muskets were in their hands. In another, they had shot down the two soldiers upon duty; then clubbing their weapons, they rushed out upon the astonished enemy, and felling their first opponents each at a blow, they succeeded in obtaining possession of the loaded muskets. This decided the conflict, which was over in a few minutes. The surviving guard yielded themselves to mercy before the presented weapons. Such an achievement could only be successful from its audacity and the operation of circumstances. The very proximity of Savannah increased the chances of success. But for this the guard would have taken better precautions. None were taken. The prompt valor, the bold decision the cool calculation of the instant, were the essential elements which secured success. The work of our young heroes was not done imperfectly. The prisoners were quickly released, the arms of the captured British put into their hands, and, hurrying away from the spot which they have crowned with a local celebrity not soon to be forgotten, they crossed the Savannah in safety with their friends and foes."

Soon after this Jasper lost his life in a manner that has immortalized him. After the celebrated victory achieved by Moultrie at the fort which bears his name, the citizens of Charleston vied with each other in doing honor to the conquerors. A lady, named Mrs. Elliot, presented a pair of colors to the regiment, and in a speech that accompanied the presentation she invoked its courage to defend them "as long as they can wave in the air of liberty." Subsequently, in the attack upon Savannah, the ensign bearers, Lieutenants Bush and Hume, in planting them on the British lines, were shot down. Lieutenant Gay, in endeavoring to carry them forward, also fell; and Jasper in seizing one of the flags, as it fell from Hume, was mortally wounded, but he succeeded in bearing it away in safety.

AN ACT OF MERCY REWARDED.

AT the time when the cause of the patriots looked so dark in the south, and when the few whigs who refused to receive the offered protections of the British commander, were beginning to gather in partizan bands with the determination to resist the foe unto the last, Col. Bratton assumed an important influence in furthering the plans of the whigs, and gathering them together to resist the enemy. The active energy he manifested in the cause, made him particularly obnoxious to the British, who at last resolved to crush him. Captain Huck, with a command of four hundred men, was dispatched with instructions to hunt him down.

Col. Bratton resided near Brattonsville, South Carolina, and his grounds became the scene of a victory, known in the history of the war, as Huck's defeat. To this spot, Captain Huck proceeded, and entered the house, on the evening of the day which preceded the victory, roughly demanding of Mrs. Bratton, where her husband was. She calmly replied that he was in Sumter's army. This reply enraged the British officer, but he controlled his anger, while he endeavored to persuade her to confess her knowledge of his retreat, and promising that if she would induce him to join the royalists, he should receive a commission in the army. The officer eloquently pictured the hopelessness of the "rebel" cause, and stated truly that the whigs themselves generally despaired of success. But to these specious arguments, and tempting promises, the heroic lady yielded nothing, and declared that she would rather see her husband perish at once, in the cause he had assumed to defend, than to wear lofty honors in the armies of her country's enemy. This reply broke down the officer's command of his temper, and one of the soldiers, actuated by that spirit of deadly hatred, and unrelenting cruelty, that so pervaded the breasts of our country's invaders, seized a reaping hook near at hand, and bringing it into contact with her throat, would in an instant have ruthlessly murdered her, had not the officer second in command, sprang forward and rescued her from his hands.

The troops, after partaking of a supper in Mrs. Bratton's resi dence, proceeded to another house at a short distance, and en camped for the night. Colonel Bratton having received information of their whereabouts, meanwhile, was rapidly approaching their position, with the hope of surprising and defeating them. His own command numbered only fifty, while that of the enemy was four hundred. But they kept negligent watch, and the little band of patriots falling suddenly upon them, in their sleep, a short and bloody conflict ensued, which resulted in the total defeat and rout of the enemy. Captain Huck was killed in the contest, and the command devolved upon the second officer, whose valor and exertions to retrieve the disaster, were in vain. The conflict had changed ground, so as to be directly around Mrs. Bratton's house, and when it was ceased, Mrs. Bratton appeared upon the ground, administering relief to the wounded and dying.

Among the prisoners was the officer by whose interposition the life of Mrs. Bratton had been saved. Actuated by a spirit of retaliation, for the many enormities that had been inflicted by the British on their whig prisoners, the conquerors expressed a determination to condemn this officer to death. The more humane remonstrated, but the majority were blinded to justice by a thirst for vengeance. When the officer learned the doom to which he was condemned, he disdained to plead for his life, but requested to be conducted to the presence of Mrs. Bratton. He seemed to be one of finer spirit than most of the officers in the British army, in the southern country. When brought before Mrs. Bratton, she instantly recognized him as the officer who had saved her life. Prompted by gratitude as well as mercy, she pleaded with his captors for his life. At first they turned a deaf ear to her intercession; but when in a simple and touching eloquence, she related the noble part he had taken in her deliverance, the stern purpose of the conquerors relaxed, and he was spared. He resided with her in mutual friendship until he was exchanged. This romantic incident is well attested.

Another anecdote is told of Mrs. Bratton. On one occasion her husband had secretly stored a large quantity of ammunition near the house, but the royalists getting wind of it, a party was despatched to obtain it. Mrs. Bratton heard of their approach, and seeing no chance to preserve the much valued treasure from their conquest, resolved that if the whigs must lose, the royalists should not gain it. She therefore laid a train from the depot of the ammunition, and just as the royalists came in sight, she fired it. The explosion that suddenly broke upon the ears of the foe, told them that their purpose was frustrated, and disappointed, they retraced their steps.

CAPTAIN NATHAN HALE.

THE impartial reader will question the justice of history, which has done so much for the memory of Andre, and left that of Hale in comparative oblivion. And yet we can discover but little difference in their cases. Both were possessors of genius and taste, both were endowed with all excellent qualities and attainments, and both were impelled by a desire to serve the cause they respectively espoused, and both suffered a similar death, but under vastly different circumstances. And yet a magnificiently sculptured monument in Westminister Abbey, perpetuates the name of the English officer, while none know where sleeps the ashes of Hale, and neither stone nor epitaph tells us of the services ren dered by him; while the first is honored in every quarter where the English language is spoken, the name of the latter is unknown to many of his countrymen. "There is something more than natural in this, if philosophy could find it out."

Nathan Hale was not twenty years of age, when the first gun of the revolution broke upon the ears of the colonists. The patriotic cause at once aroused his enthusiastic love for liberty and justice, and without pausing for a moment to consider the prudence of such a step, his ardent nature prompted him at once, to throw himself into the ranks of his country's defenders. Distinguished as a scholar, and respected, by all who knew him, for his brilliant talents, he was at once tendered a captain's commission in the light infantry. He served in the regiment commanded by Col. Knowlton, and was with the army in its retreat after the disastrous battle of Long Island.

After the army had retreated from New York, and while it was posted on the heights at Harlem, the commander-in-chief earnestly desired to be made acquainted with the force and contemplated movements of the enemy, and for this purpose, applied to Col. Knowlton to select some individual capable of performing the hazardous and delicate service. Knowlton applied to Hale, who, on becoming acquainted with the wishes of Washington, immediately volunteered his services. He stated, that his object in joining the army, was not merely for fame, but to serve the country; that as yet, no opportunity had offered for him to render any signal aid to her cause, and when a duty so imperative and so important as this was demanded of him, he was ready to sacrifice not only life, but all hope of glory, and to suffer the ignomy which its failure would cast upon his name. His friends endeavored to dissuade him from the undertaking, but lofty considerations of duty impelled him to the step.

Having disguised himself as a schoolmaster, he crossed the sound at Fairfield, to Huntingdon, and proceeded thence to Brooklyn. This was in September, 1776. When he arrived at Brooklyn, the enemy had already taken possession of New York He crossed over to the city, his disguise unsuspected, and pursued the objects of his mission. He examined all their fortifications with care, and obtained every possible information relative to the number of the enemy, their intentions, &c. Having accomplished all that he could, he left the city, and retraced his steps to Huntington. While here, waiting for a boat to convey him across the sound, his apprehension was effected. There are great discrepancies in the various accounts which are given of his arrest, but all agree that it was through the means of a refugee cousin, who detected his disguise. According to one account, while he was at Huntingdon, a boat came to the shore, which he at first supposed to be one from Connecticut, but which proved to be from an English vessel lying in the sound. He incautiously approached the boat and was recognised by his tory relative, who was in the boat at the time. He was arrested, and sent to New York.

There cannot be a more striking proof of the different value set upon the services of Andre and Hale by their respective nations, than the fact afforded by the different manner of their arrest. There was not a single circumstance connected with the captur of Andre, but what is known to every reader of history, but in th. case of Hale, who stands Andre's equal in every particular, it is not even known with certainty how he was apprehended. We have a few uncertain legends relative to it, but these are widely different some making him arrested on the sound, some on the island, and others on the outskirts of the city. But there was one circumstance connected with Hale's capture, which should enhance our sympathy for him. Andre fell into the American hands by means of the sagacity, watchfulness, and fidelity of our own soldiers; but Hale was betrayed by the base perfidy and treason of a renegade relative. And what two opposite phases of human nature does the contrast between these two incidents afford! In the first, we find three men, three poor men, so fixed in principle and determined in right, that the most tempting offers—offers when an assent would have given them wealth, ease, and luxury—were refused. Strong honesty overcame temptation, and they were content to struggle on in poverty, oblivion, and privation, with unsullied hearts, rather than feast and riot in luxury. But in the latter incident, we find one of the most execrable acts recorded in history. The betrayal of Hale by his relative, contrasted with the stern integrity of Andre's captures, affords a most striking picture between virtue and vice, between lofty honor, and degraded baseness.

We are all aware of what followed the capture of Andre. He was tried before an honorable court, and while strict justice demanded his life, the necessity was deplored by his judges, and his fate aroused in every heart the keenest sympathy and the deepest sorrow. But how widely different was the unhappy end of the noble Hale! He was surrendered to the incarnate fiend, Cunningham, the provost-marshal, and ordered to immediate execution, without even the formality of a trial. On the twenty-first of September, 1776, he was dragged to the spot designed for th purpose, and there accompanied by only a few privates, his sentence was brutally executed. His manner was undaunted, and his soul never flinched in the moment of trial. Previous to the execution, he had, by permission, addressed a few lines to his family, but these, after his death, were destroyed by Cunningham, and the reason assigned for this was, " that the rebels should never know they had a man in their army, who could die with such firmness." The use of a bible, and the attendance of a minister were denied him; and thus surrounded by mocking lips and un pitying hearts, his noble soul took flight.

It must be remembered, in measuring the character of Hale, tha it was not hope of promotion, nor promise of pecuniary reward that induced him to take the step he did. Nothing but an earnest wish to serve his country, impelled him to the course, and this circumstance removes every stigma that would otherwise hang upon him as a spy, and elevates him to the rank of a martyr.

It is absurd to argue, that there is any difference between the cases of Andre and Hale. Both were apprehended within the enemy's, lines, disguised in assumed characters, and this made them amenable to the stern construction of military law. There is not a shadow of reason for elevating the character of Andre above that of Hale. Indeed, when we remember the last words of each, the American officer appears as the grandest hero of the two. " Bear witness," said Andre, " that I die like a brave man." His last thoughts were selfish, and he wished only for the preservation of his own unstained honor. But the thoughts of Hale were upon his native land, "*he only lamented that he had but one life to lose for his country.*"

Several efforts have been made, at different times, to erect a monument to Hale. But it has not yet been done. In 1835, congress voted a thousand dollars towards this object, but no action has since been taken upon it. It is a trite and often quoted saying, "that republics are ungrateful." Is not this history a shameful evidence of its truth?

The late Dr. Dwight penned the following tribute to the memory of Hale:—

> "Thus, while fond virtue wished in vain to save,
> Hale, bright and generous, found a hapless grave;
> While *Genius'* living flame his bosom glow'd,
> And *science* charmed him to her sweet abode;
> In *worth's* fair path, adventured far,
> The *pride* of peace, and rising *grace* of war"

CAPTURE OF CAPTAIN HARPER.

In the month of April in 1780 it was the intention of Captain Brant, the Indian chieftain, to make a descent upon the upper fort of Schoharie, but which was prevented by an unlooked for circumstance. Col. Vrooman had sent out a party of scouts to pass over to the head waters of the Charlotte river, where resided certain suspected persons, whose movements it was their duty to watch. "It being the proper season for the manufacture of maple sugar, the men were directed to make a quantity of that article, of which the garrison were greatly in want. On the 2d of April this party, under the command of Capt. Harper, commenced their labors, which they did cheerfully, and entirely unapprehensive of danger, as a fall of snow, some three feet deep, would prevent, they supposed, the moving of any considerable body of the enemy, while in fact they were not aware of any body of the armed foe hort of Niagara. But on the 7th of April they were suddenly surrounded by a party of about forty Iudians and Tories, the first knowledge of whose presence was the death of three of their party

The leader was instantly discovered in the person of the Mohawk chief, who rushed up to Capt. Harper, tomahawk in hand, and observed; 'Harper, I am sorry to find you here!'

"'Why are you sorry Captain Brant?' replied the other.

"'Because' replied the chief, 'I *must* kill you, although we were schoolmates in our youth*'—at the same time raising his natchet, and suiting the action to the word. Suddenly his arm fell, and with a piercing scrutiny, looking Harper full in the face, he inquired—'Are there any regular troops in the fort in Schoharie?' Harper caught the idea in an instant. To answer truly, and admit there were none, as was the fact, would but hasten Brant and his warriors forward to fall upon the settlements at once, and their destruction would have been swift and sure. He therefore informed him that a reinforcement of three hundred Continental troops had arrived to garrison the forts only two or three days before. This information appeared very much to disconcert the chieftain. He prevented the farther shedding of blood, and held a consultation with his subordinate chiefs. Night coming on, the prisoners were shut up in a pen of logs, and guarded by the Tories, while among the Indians controversy ran high whether the prisoners should be put to death or carried to Niagara. The captives were bound hand and foot, and were so near the council that Harper, who understood something of the Indian tongue, could hear the dispute. The Indians were for putting them to death, but Brant exercised his authority to effectually prevent the massacre.

"On the following morning Harper was brought before the Indians for examination. The chief commenced by saying that

---

* Brant received an English education.

he was suspicious he had not told him the truth. Harper, however, although Brant was eyeing him like a basilisk, repeated his former statements, without the improper movement of a muscle, or any betrayal that he was deceiving. Brant satisfied of the truth of the story, resolved to retrace his steps to Niagara. Bu his warriors were disappointed in their hopes of spoils and victory and it was only with the greatest difficulty that they were prevented from putting the captives to death.

"Their march was forthwith commenced, and was full of pain, peril, and adventure. They met on the succeeding day with two loyalists who both disproved Harper's story of troops being at Schoharie, and the Captain was again subjected to a piercing scrutiny; but he succeeded so well in maintaining the appearance of truth and sincerity as to arrest the upraised and glittering tomahawk. On the same day an aged man, named Brown, was accidentally fallen in with and taken prisoner, with two youthful grandsons; the day following being unable to travel with sufficient speed, and sinking under the weight of the burden imposed upon him, the old man was put out of the way with the hatchet. The victim was dragging behind, and when he saw preparations making for his doom, took an affectionate farewell of his little grandsons, and the Indians moved on, leaving one of their number, with his face painted black—the mark of the executioner—behind with him. In a few moments afterward, the Indian came up, with the old man's scalp dangling from between the ramrod and the muzzle of his gun.

"They constructed floats, and sailed down the Susquehana to the confluence of the Chemung, at which place their land-travelling commenced. Soon after this, a severe trial and narrow escape befel the prisoners. During his march from Niagara on this expedition, Brant had detached eleven of his warriors, to fall once more upon the Minisink settlement, for prisoners. This detachment, as it subsequently appeared, had succeeded in taking captive five athletic men, whom they secured and brought with them as far as Tioga Point. The Indians slept very soundly, and th five prisoners had resolved, on the first opportunity, to make their escape. While encamped at this place during the night, one of the Minisink men succeeded in extricating his hands from the binding cords, and with the utmost caution, unloosed his four companions. The Indians were locked in the arms of deep sleep around them. Silently, without causing a leaf to rustle, they each snatched a tomahawk from the girdles of their unconscious enemies, and in a moment nine of them were quivering in the agonies of death. The two others were awakened, and springing upon their feet, attempted to escape. One of them was struck with a hatchet between the shoulders, but the other fled. The prisoners immediately made good their own retreat, and the only Indian who escaped unhurt, returned to take care of his wounded companion. As Brant and his warriors approached this point of their journey, some of his Indians having raised a whoop, it was returned by a single voice, with the *death yell!* Startled at this unexpected signal, Brant's warriors rushed forward to ascertain the cause. But they were not long in doubt. The lone warrior met them, and soon related to his brethren the melancholy fate of his companions. The effect upon the warriors, who gathered in a group to hear the recital, was unexpressibly fearful. Rage, and a desire of revenge, seemed to kindle every bosom, and light every eye as with burning coals. They gathered around the prisoners in a circle, and began to make unequivocal preparations for hacking them to pieces. Harper and his men, of course gave themselves up for lost. While their knives were unsheathing, and their hatchets glittering, as they were flourished in the sunbeams the only survivor of the murdered party rushed into the circle and interposed in their favor. With a wave of the hand, as of a warrior entitled to be heard—for he was himself, a chief—silence was restored, and the prisoners were surprised by the utterance of an earnest appeal in their behalf. He eloquently and impressively declaimed in their favor, upon the ground that it was not they who murdered their brothers; and to take the lives of the innocent, would not be right in the eyes of the Great Spirit. His appeal was effective. The passions of the incensed warriors were hushed, their eyes no longer shot forth the burning glances of revenge, and their gesticulations ceased to menace immediate and bloody vengeance.

"True, it so happened, that this chief knew all the prisoners—he having resided in the Schoharie canton of the Mohawks, during the war. He doubtless felt a deeper interest in their behalf on that account. Still, it was a noble action, worthy of the proudest era of chivalry, and in the balmy days of Greece and Rome, would have crowned him almost with ' an apotheosis and rights divine.' The interposition of Pochohantas, in favor of Captain Smith, before the rude court of Powhaltan, was, perhaps, more romantic; but when the motive which prompted the generous action of the princess, is considered, the transaction now under review, exhibits the most of genuine benevolence. Pochohantas was moved by the tender passion—the Mohawk Sachem, by the feelings of magnanimity, and the eternal principles of justice. It is a matter of regret, that the name of this high souled warrior is lost, as, alas! have been too many that might serve to relieve the dark and vengeful portraiture of Indian character, which it has so well pleased the white man to draw! The prisoners themselves were so impressed with the manner of their signal deliverance, that they justly attributed it to a direct interposition of Providence."*

After the most acute sufferings from hunger and exhaustion the party at last arrived at Niagara. The last night of their journey, they encamped a short distance from the fort. In the morning the prisoners were informed that they were to run the gauntlet, and were brought out, where two parallel lines of Indians were drawn out, between which the prisoners were to pass, exposed to the whips and blows of the savages. The course to be ran, was towards the fort. Harper was the first one selected, and at the signal, sprang from the mark with extraordinary swiftness. An Indian near the end of the line, fearing he might escape without injury, sprang before him, but a blow from Harper's fist felled him; the Indians enraged, broke their ranks and rushed after him, as he fled with the utmost speed towards the fort. The garrison, when they saw Harper approaching, opened the gates, and he rushed in, only affording sufficient time for the garrison to close the gates, ere the Indians rushed upon it, clamoring for the possession of their victim. The other prisoners taking advantage of the breaking up of the Indian ranks, took different routes, and all succeeded in reaching the fort without passing through the terrible ordeal, which was intended for them.

* Stone's Life of Brant.

A DESPERATE ENCOUNTER.

"Col. Allen McLane, who died at Wilmington, Del., in 1820, at the patriarchial age of 83, was distinguished for his personal courage, and for his activity as a partisan officer. He was long attached to Major Lee's famous legion of horse. While the British occupied Philadelphia, McLane was constantly scouring the upper end of Bucks and Montgomery counties, to cut off the scouting parties of the enemy, and intercept their supplies of provisions. Having agreed for some purpose, to rendesvouz near Shoemakertown, Col. McLane ordered his little band of troopers to follow at some distance, and commanded two of them to precede the main body, but also to keep in his rear; and if they discovered an enemy, to ride up to his side and inform him of it, without speaking aloud. While leisurely approaching the place of rendesvouz in this order, in the early gray of the morning, the two men directly in the rear, forgetting their orders, suddenly called out, " Colonel, the British !" faced about, and putting spurs to their horses, were soon out of sight. The colonel looking around, discovered that he was in the centre of a powerful ambuscade, into which the enemy had silently allowed him to pass without his observing them. They lined both sides of the road, and had been stationed there to pick up any straggling party of the Americans that might chance to pass. Immediately on finding they were discovered, a file of soldiers rose from the side of the highway, and fired at the colonel, but without effect; and as he put spurs to his horse, and mounted the road-side into the woods, the other part of the detachment also fired. The colonel miraculously escaped; but a shot striking his horse upon the flank, he dashed through the woods, and in a few minutes reached a parallel road upon the opposite side of the forest. Being familiar with the country, he feared to turn to the left, as that course led to the city, and he might be intercepted by another ambuscade. Turning therefore, to the right, his frightened horse carried him swiftly beyond the reach of those who had fired upon him. All at once however, on emerging from a piece of woods, he observed several British troops stationed near the road-side, and directly in sight ahead, a farm house, around which he observed a whole troop of the enemy's cavalry drawn up. He dashed by the troops near him without being molested, they believing he was on his way to the main body to surrender himself. The farm-house was situated at the intersection of two roads, presenting but two avenues by which he could escape. Nothing daunted by the formidable array before him, he galloped up to the cross roads, on reaching which, he spurred his active horse, turned suddenly to the right, and was soon fairly out of reach of their pistols, though as he turned, he heard them call loudly to surrender or die! A dozen were instantly in pursuit; but in a short time they all gave up the chase except two. Col. Mc Lane's horse, scared by the first wound he had ever received, and being a chosen animal, kept ahead for several miles, while his two pursuers followed with unwearied eagerness. The pursuit at length waxed so hot, that, as the colonel's horse stepped out of a small brook which crossed the road, his pursuers entered it at the opposite margin. In ascendng a little hill, the horses of the three were greatly exhausted, sc nuch so, that neither could be urged faster than a walk. Occaionally, as one of the troopers pursued on, a little in advance of his companion, the colonel slackened his pace, anxious to be attacked by one of the two; but no sooner was his willingness discovered, than the other fell back to his station. They at length approached so near, that a conversation took place between them; the troopers calling out, 'surrender you d——d rebel, or we'll cut you in pieces.' Suddenly one of them rode up on the right side of the colonel, and, without drawing his sword, laid hold of the colonel's collar. The latter, to use his own words, " had pistols *which he knew he could depend on.*' Drawing one from the holster, he placed it to the heart of his antagonist, fired, and tumbled him dead on the ground. Instantly the other came upon his left, with his sword drawn, and also seized the colonel by the collar of his coat. A fierce and deadly struggle here ensued, in the course of which Col. Mc Lane was desperately wounded in the back of his left hand, the sword of his antagonist cutting asunder the veins and tendons of that member. Seeing a favorable opportunity, he drew his other pistol, and with a steadiness of purpose, which appeared even in his recital of the incident, placed it directly between the eyes of his adversary, pulled the trigger, and scattered his brains on every side of the road! Fearing that others were in pursuit, he abandoned his horse in the highway; and apprehensive, from his extreme weakness, that he might die from loss of blood, he crawled into an adjacent mill-pond, entirely naked, and at length succeeded in stopping the profuse flow of blood occasioned by his wound."

ANECDOTES OF COL. HORRY.

Col. Horry served under General Marion. His adventures were numerous, and some of them very amusing. He has left a MS. Memoir from which Mr. Simms draws the particulars of several of his exploits. From Mr. Simms we quote :*

"He was brave, and ambitious of distinction. This ambition led him to desire a command of cavalry rather than of infantry. But he was no rider—was several times unhorsed in combat, and was indebted to the fidelity of his soldiers for his safety. On one occasion his escape was more narrow from a different cause. Crossing the swamp at Lynch's Creek, to join Marion, in the dark, and the swamp, swimming, he encountered the bough of a tree to which he clung, while his horse passed from under him. He was no swimmer, and but for timely assistance from his followers, would have been drowned. Another story is told of him which places him in a scarcely less ludicrous attitude. He was ordered by Marion to wait, in ambush, the approach of a British detachment. The duty was executed with skill; the enemy was completely in his power. But he labored under an impediment in his speech, which, we may readily suppose, was greatly increased by anxiety and excitement. The word 'fire' stuck in his throat, as 'Amen' did in that of Macbeth. The emergency was pressing, but this only increased the difficulty. In vain did he make the attempt. He could say 'fi–fi—fi!' but he could get no further—the 'or' was incorrigible. At length, irritated almost to madness, he exclaimed, '*shoot*, d—n you, *shoot!* you know what I would say! Shoot, and be d——d to you!'

---

* Life of Marion, by W. Gilmore Simms

"He was present, and acted bravely, in almost every affair of consequence, in the brigade of Marion. At Quimly, Capt. Baxter a man distinguished by his great strength and courage, as well as size, and by equally great simplicity of character, cried out, I am wounded, colonel!' 'T' .nk no more of it, Baxter,' was the answer of Horry, 'but stand to your post.' 'But I can' stand' says Baxter, 'I am wounded a second time.' 'Lie down then, Baxter, but quit not your post.' 'They have shot me again colonel,' said the wounded man, 'and if I stay any longer here, I shall be shot to pieces.' 'Be it so, Baxter, but stir not,' was the order, which the brave fellow obeyed, receiving a fourth wound before the engagement was over."

Another adventure is thus related by Horry himself. "I was sent" he writes, "by Gen. Marion to reconnoitre Georgetown. I proceeded with a guide through the woods all night. At the dawn of day, I drew near the town. I laid an ambuscade, with thirty men and three officers, near the road. About sunrise a chair appeared with two ladies escorted by two British officers. I was ready in advance with an officer to cut them off, but reflecting that they might escape, and alarm the town, which would prevent my taking greater numbers, I desisted. The officers and chair halted very near me, but soon the chair went on, and the officers gallopped in retrogade into the town. Our party continued in ambush, until 10 o'clock A. M.

"Nothing appearing, and men and horses having eaten nothing for thirty-six hours, we were hungered, and retired to a plantation of my quarter-master's, a Mr. White, not far distant. There a curious scene took place. As soon as I entered the house . . . . four ladies appeared, two of whom where Mrs. White and her daughter. I was asked what I wanted. I answered, food, re freshment. The other two ladies were those whom I had seen escorted by the British officers. They seemed greatly agitated, and begged most earnestly that I would go away, for the family was very poor, had no provisions of any sort,—that I knew that they were Whigs, and surely would not add to their distress. So pressing were they for my immediately leaving the plantation, that I thought they had more in view than they pretended. I kept my eye on Mrs. White, and saw she had a smiling countenance, but said nothing. Soon she left the room, and I left it also and went into the piazza, laid my cap, sword and pistols on the long bench, and walked the piazza;—when I discovered Mrs. White behind the house chimney beckoning me. I got to her undiscovered by the young ladies, when she said: 'Colonel Horry, be on your guard; these two young ladies, Miss F— and M—, are just from Georgetown; they are much frightened, and I believe the British are leaving it and may soon attack you. As to provisions, which they make such a rout about, I have plenty for your men and horses in yonder barn, but you must affect to take them by force. Hams, bacon, rice, and fodder, are there. You must insist on the key of the barn, and threaten to split the door with an axe if not immediately opened.' I begged her to say no more, for I was well acquainted with all such matters—to leave the ladies and everything else to my management. She said 'Yes; but do not ruin us: be artful and cunning, or Mr. White may be hanged and all our houses burnt over our heads.' We both secretly returned, she to the room where the young ladies were, and I to the piazza I had just left." "This little narrative will give some idea of the straits to which the good whig matrons of Carolina were sometimes reduced in those days. But no time was allowed Horry to extort the provisions as suggested. He had scarcely got to the piazza when his videttes gave the alarm. Two shots warned him of the approach of the foe, and forgetting that his cap, sabre and pistols, lay on the long bench on the piazza, Horry mounted his horse, left the enclosure, and rushed into the melée. The British were seventeen in number, well mounted, and commanded by a brave fellow named Merritt. The dragoons taken by surprise, turned in flight, and, smiting at every step, the partisans pursued them with fatal earnestness. But two men are reported to have escaped death or captivity, and they were their captain and a sergeant. It was in approaching to encounter Merritt that Horry discovered that he was weaponless. 'My officers,' says he, 'in succession, came up with Captain Merritt, who was in the rear of his party, urging them forward. They engaged him. He was a brave fellow. Baxter, with pistols, fired at his breast, and missing him, retired; Postelle and Greene, with swords, engaged him; both were beaten off. Greene nearly lost his head. His buckskin breeches were cut through several inches . . . . I almost blush to say that this one British officer beat off three Americans." The honor of the day was decidedly with Merritt, though he was beaten. He was no doubt a far better swordsman than our self-taught cavalry, with broadswords wrought out of mill saws. Merritt abandoned his horse, and escaped to a neighboring swamp, from whence, at midnight, he got into Georgetown.*

---

* Weems speaking for Horry, tells us that he met with Captain Merritt after the war in New York, who recognized him, and told him that he had never had such a fright in all his life as upon that occasion. "Will you believe me, sir," said he, "when I assure you that I went out that morning with my locks of as bright an auburn as ever curled upon the forehead of youth, and by the time I had crawled out of the swamp into Georgetown that night, they were as gray as a badger!"

In one of his numerous encounters, while his men were individually engaged and scattered through the woods around him, he suddenly found himself alone, and assailed by a tory captain, named Lewis, at the head of a small party. "Lewis was armed with a musket, and in the act of firing, when a sudden shot from the woods tumbled him from his horse, in the very moment when his own gun was discharged. The bullet of Lewis took effect on Horry's horse. The shot which so seasonably slew the tory, had been sent by the hands of a boy named Given.

A HIGH SPIRITED FAMILY.

JUST after the defeat of Col. Ferguson at King's Mountain, General Cornwallis in retreating towards Winnsboro' halted for the night at Wilson's plantation, near Steel creek. The British general, with his staff, and the infamous Tarleton occupied the house of Mrs. Wilson. Supper was ordered and prepared for the British officers. Cornwallis in order to obtain a knowledge of his hostess, entered into conversation with her, and soon found that he was occupying the house of a noted whig leader, Robert Wilson, who at that time with his son John, was a prisoner in the Camden jail, and who was the father and brother of more than a dozen active whig soldiers. The British general upon this, attempted to enlist the sympathies of his hostess with the royal cause. He observed, that it was a matter of sincere regret with him, to be compelled to wage a war, the worst calamities of which fell upon women. He was inclined to believe, that there were many worthy men in the rebel army, who had been induced to take up arms by the delusive promises of unprincipled leaders. "Madam," he continued, "your husband and your son are my prisoners; the fortunes of war may soon place others of your sons—perhaps all your kinsmen, in my power. Your sons are young, aspiring and brave. In a good cause, fighting for a generous and powerful king, such as George III., they might hope for rank, honor and wealth. If you could but induce your husband and sons to leave the rebels, and take up arms for their lawful sovereign, I would almost pledge myself, that they shall have rank and consideration in the British army. If you, madam, will pledge yourself to induce them to do so, I will immediately order their discharge."

To this appeal, Mrs. Wilson replied, that her husband and sons were indeed dear to her, and that she would do anything her conscience would uphold to advance their interests. For five years, they had been engaged in the struggle for liberty, and had never faltered nor fled from the contest. "I have seven sons who are now, or have been, bearing arms," she continued,—"indeed my seventh son, Zaccheus, who is only fifteen years old, I yesterday assisted to get ready, to go and join his brothers in Sumpter's army. Now, sooner than see one of my family turn back from the glorious enterprise, I would take those boys, (pointing to three or four small sons) and with them would myself enlist under Sumter's standard, and show my husband and sons how to fight, and if necessary, to die for their country!" "Ah! General!" broke in Tarleton,—"I think you've got into a hornet' nest! Never mind, when we get to Camden, I'll take good care that old Robert Wilson never comes back again!"

"On the next day's march, a party of scouts captured Zaccheus, who was found on the flank of the British army, with his gun, endeavoring to diminish his Majesty's forces. He was immediately taken to the head of the column, and catechised by Cornwallis, who took the boy along with him on the march, telling him that he must act as his guide to the Catawba, and show him the best ford. Arriving at the river, the head of the army entered at the point designated by the lad, but the soldiers had scarcely gone half across, before they found themselves in deep water—and drawn by a rapid current down the stream. Believeing that the boy, on whom he had relied, to show him the best ford, had purposely brought him to a deep one, in order to embarrass his march, the general drew his sword, and flourishing it over him swore he would cut off his head for his treachery. Zaccheus replied, that he had the power to do so, as he had no arms, and was his prisoner; 'but sir,' said he, 'don't you think it would be a cowardly act for you to strike an unarmed boy with your sword? If I had but the half of your weapon, it would not be so cowardly; but then you know it would not be so safe!'

"Struck by the lad's cool courage, the general became calmer—told him he was a fine fellow, and that he would not hurt a hair of his head. Having discovered that the ford was shallow enough by bearing up stream, the British army crossed over in safety, and proceeded towards Winnsboro'. On this march, Cornwallis dismissed Zaccheus, telling him to go home and take care of his mother, and to tell her, to keep her boys at home. After h reached Winnsboro', Cornwallis dispatched an order to Rawdon to send Robert Wilson and his son John, with several others, to Charleston, carefully guarded. Accordingly in November, abou the 20th., Wilson, his son and ten others, set off under the escort of an officer and fifteen or twenty men. Below Camden, on the Charleston route, parties of British soldiers and trains of waggons were continually passing, so that the officer had no fear of the

Americans, and never dreamed of the prisoners attempting an escape. Wilson formed plans, and arranged everything several times, but owing to the presence of large parties of the enemy, they could not be executed. At length, being near Fort Watson they encamped before night, the prisoners being placed in the yard, and the guard in the portico and house. A sentinel was posted in the portico over the stock of arms, and all hands went to providing for their evening repast.

"Having bribed a soldier to buy some whiskey, for it had been a rainy day, the prisoners pretended to drink freely, and one of them seemingly more intoxicated than the rest, insisted upon treating the sentinel. Wilson followed him as if to prevent him from giving him the whiskey, it being a breach of military order. Watching a favorable opportunity, he seized the sentinel's musket, and the drunken man, suddenly becoming sober, seized the sentinel. At this signal the prisoners rushed to the guns in the portico, while the guard taking the alarm, rushed out of the house. In the scramble for arms, the prisoners succeeded—drove the soldiers into the house, at the point of the bayonet, and the whole guard surrendered at discretion. Unable to take off their prisoners, Wilson made them all hold up their right hands and swear never again to bear arms against the cause of 'liberty and the continental congress,' and then told them that they might go to Charleston on parole; but if he ever caught one of them in arms again, he would 'hang him up to a tree like a dog.'

"Scarcely were they rid of their prisoners, before a party of British dragoons came in sight. As the only means of escape, they separated and took to the woods. Some of them reached Marion's camp at Snow Island, and Wilson, with two or three others, arrived safely at Mecklenburg—a distance of over two hundred miles, through a country overrun by British troops."*

ESCAPE OF CAPTAIN PLUNKETT.

"CAPTAIN PLUNKETT, a high-spirited Irishman, whose attachment to the cause of liberty had led him to seek a commission in the continental army, had, by the chances of war, been compelled to give up his sword, and to surrender himself a prisoner to the enemy. Previously to this untoward event, by the suavity of his manners, and uniformly correct conduct, he had rendered himself an acceptable guest in many families in Philadelphia, and particularly so, to one of the society of Friends, who, however averse to warfare, were not insensible of the claims of those to their regard, who, by the exercise of manly and generous feelings, delighted to soften its asperities. There was among them, a female, mild and gentle as a dove, yet, in firmness of mind, a heroine, in personal charms, an angel. She saw the sufferings of the captive soldier, and under the influences of pity, or perhaps a more powerful passion, resolved, at all hazards, to relieve him. It accidentally happened that the uniform of Captain Plunkett's regiment, bore a striking resemblance to that of a British corps, which was frequently set as a guard over the prison in which he was confined. A new suit of regimentals was, in consequence, procured and conveyed, without suspicion of sinister design, to the captain. On the judicious use of them rested the hopes of his fair friend to give

---

* "Women of the Revolution."

him freedom. It frequently happened that officers of inferior grade, while their superiors affected to shun all intercourse with the rebels, would enter the apartments of the prisoners, and converse with them with kindness and familiarity, and then at their pleasure, retire. Two sentinels constantly walked the round without, and the practice of seeing their officers walking in and out of the interior prison, became so familiar, as scarcely to attract notice, and constantly caused them to give way without hesitation, as often as an officer showed a disposition to retire. Captain Plunkett took the advantage of this circumstance, and putting on his new coat, at the moment that the relief of the guard was taking place, sallied forth, twitching a switch carelessly about, and ordering the exterior door of the prison to be opened, walked without opposition into the street. Repairing without delay, to the habitation of his fair friend, he was received with kindness, and for some days secreted and cherished with every manifestation of affectionate regard.

"To elude the vigilance of the British Guards, if he attempted to pass into the country in his present dress, was deemed impossible. Woman's wit, however, is never at a loss for contrivances, while swayed by the influence of love or benevolence. Both, in this instance may have aided invention. Plunkett had three strong claims in his favor; he was a handsome man—a soldier—and an Irishman. The general conduct of the Quakers, exempted the sect in a great measure from suspicion, in so great a degree, indeed, that the barriers of the city were generally entrusted to the care of their members, as the best judges of the characters of those persons who might be allowed to pass them. A female Friend from a farm near the city, was in the family, on a visit to a relative. A pretext was formed to present her with a new suit of clothes, in order to possess that which she wore when she entered the city. Captain Plunkett was immediately disguised as a woman, and appeared at the barrier, accompanied by his anxious deliverer.

"'Friend Roberts,' said the enterprising enthusiast, 'may this damsel and myself pass to visit a friend at a neighboring farm?'

"'Certainly,' said Roberts, 'go forward.' The city was speedily left behind, and Captain Plunkett found himself safe, under the protection of Colonel Allen M'Lane, his particular friend."

ATTEMPTED ABDUCTION OF GEN. SCHUYLER.

THE scouting parties of the enemy, emboldened by the feeble state of the country, and encouraged by the high rewards offered them, were exceedingly active in the securing of influential Americans, and conveying them to Canada as prisoners. By stratagems, and sometimes by force, they fell upon those persons, marked as their victims, and by rapid marches would manage to escape beyond pursuit almost before their outrages would be known. Many of these attempts were successful, but others signally failed. The latter was the case with one of their most audacious attempts, in the securing of Gen. Schuyler; they, also, failed in their object with Gen. Gansevoort.

Gen. Schuyler's residence was in the suburbs of Albany. He had retired from the army, but still was of vast consequence and influence to the American cause. The importance that he assumed in the control of affairs, made it an especial object with Haldimand, the British commander in Canada, to secure his person.

A desperate plot was, therefore, set on foot. John Waltermeyer a notorious Tory partizan, was entrusted with the execution of the design, and with a company of whites and Indians, he proceeded to Albany, and prepared to entrap his anticipated victim. The General had been cautioned often of the danger to which he was subjected by such attempts; and the frequency with which influential citizens were entrapped, and captured, was sufficient cause for him to exercise every vigilance and caution. He had, therefore, added to his usual household, a guard of six men, who were, by turns, on duty day and night.

The evening of a sultry day in August, was selected as the occasion to make the attempt. The general and his family were all gathered in the front hall of his house, and the doors were all thrown wide open, in order to admit all the cooling air possible, when a servant announced that a stranger at the back gate required the presence of the general, on a matter of business. A message so singular, at once excited suspicion. Unfortunately, the evening was so very warm, that the servants had dispersed. The three sentinels just relieved from duty, had retired, and the others, who should have been at their post, were stretched on the grass in the garden. The doors were hastily closed and fastened, while the family hurried to the upper rooms, the general to arm himself, and the others for security. They presently discovered the house surrounded by a body of armed men, and almost immediately was heard the crash of heavy blows against the doors be 'ow. The general threw up a window to arouse the guard, and with the hope that it might alarm the town, or bring assistance from some quarter. A violent struggle was now heard below. The three guards who were within the house, had been aroused, and were endeavoring to drive the assailants back. But by an unfortunate incident, they were without their weapons, and had only the weight of their persons to oppose in resistance. Mrs. Church, a daughter of the general, had perceived, some hours before, her little son playing with the muskets, and not supposing they would be wanted, while she feared the consequences of their being within reach of the child, had caused them to be removed, while she neglected to inform the guard of the circumstance. But the brave fellows, nothing daunted, opposed, themselves, unarmed, to the besieging troop, and by dealing blows as soundly as they could with their fists, they managed for a few moments to keep them at bay, but their overwhelming force soon overcome the resistance, and they rushed into the house. While this struggle was going on, the alarmed and terrified ladies above, were in an agony of fear at the remembrance that in their bustle of escaping, an infant had been left in the nursery, which was situated on the first floor. Mrs. Schuyler was about flying to its rescue, but the general prevented her, when Margaret, the third daughter, rushed forth, and hastily descending a private stairway, reached the room, and snatched the babe from the cradle, where it was lying in undisturbed repose. But as she was hurrying from the room with her valued burthen, a tomahawk, hurled by an unseen hand, glanced by her side, and buried itself in the wall, carrying with it a remnant of her dress. Undismayed by this circumstance, or by the violent commotion in the hall, she hastened to the same private way by which she had descended, when in rapid flight to the rooms above, to her terror, she was confronted by Waltermeyer, the leader of the gang, who exclaimed—" Wench, where is your master ?" With admirable presence of mind, she replied— " Gone to arouse the town." Alarmed at this, he hurried by, permitting her to escape to the room where the family was gathered, who, in dreadful apprehension, were awaiting the issue of her daring and heroic exploit.

Waltermeyer hastily summoned his followers from the drawing room, where they were engaged in plundering the plate, and who reluctantly desisted from their work, to listen to the orders of their leader. At this moment the general threw up a window and called out—"Come on my brave fellows, surround the hous and secure the villains who are plundering." The party terrified at this, and supposing that they were surrounded, made a precipitate retreat from the house, carrying with them the three men who had so heroically defended the house, one of whom was wounded. Waltermeyer himself had received a bullet from one of the general's pistols, but was only slightly wounded. By this time the city was alarmed, and the citizens came hurrying to the spot, but not before the entire body of assailants had fled.

The three guard were conveyed into Canada, and were restored after the war. To each the general bequeathed a farm in reward for his services.

ADVENTURES OF DR. CALDWELL.

The Rev. David Caldwell, a Presbyterian minister in North Carolina, was very much subjected to the persecutions of the loyalists. At one time, while he was absent, a party of British cam to his house and occupied it, turning Mrs. Caldwell out of doors who was obliged to seek refuge in the smoke house, where she remained for two days with no other food than a little dried fruit after remaining for two days on the plantation, during which time they had destroyed everything, they prepared to leave, but before doing so, in order that nothing should be left undone which their hatred could suggest to do, the valuable library of Dr. Caldwell, containing books it was impossible to replace, and manuscripts that had cost years of study and labor, was wantonly burned. A large fire was built for the purpose, and the books brought in armsfull and cast upon the flames.

"The persecution of Dr. Caldwell continued while the British occupied that portion of the state. His property was destroyed, and he was hunted as a felon; snares were laid for him, and pretences used to draw him from his hiding places; he was compelled to pass nights in the woods, and ventured only at the most imminent peril to see his family. Often he escaped captivity or death, as it were, by a miracle. At one time when he had ventured home on a stolen visit, the house was suddenly surrounded by armed men, who seized him before he could escape, designing to carry him to the British camp. One or two were set to guard him, while the others went to gather such articles of provisions and clothing as could be found worth taking away. When they were nearly ready to depart, the plunder collected being piled in the middle of the floor, and the prisoner standing beside it with his guard, Mrs. Dunlap, who with Mrs. Caldwell had remained in an adjoining apartment, came forward. With the promptitude and presence of mind for which women are often remarkable in sudden emergencies, she stepped behind Dr. Caldwell, leaned over his shoulder, and whispered to him as if intending the question for his ear alone, asking if it was not time for Gillespie and his men to be there. One of the soldiers who stood near caught the words, and with evident alarm demanded what men were meant. The lady replied that she was merely speaking to her brother. In a moment all was confusion; the whole party was panic-struck; exclamations and hurried questions followed; and in the consternation produced by this ingenious, though simple manœuvre, the tories fled precipitately, leaving their prisoner and their plunder. The name of Gillespie was a scourge and terror to the loyalists, and this party knew themselves to be within the limits of one of the strongest whig neighborhoods in the state."

The plantations of Dr. Caldwell and his brother Alexander, were near each other. One evening, during Alexander's absence from home, two soldiers entered his house, and began rudely to seize upon everything they saw worth carrying off, having ordered his wife to prepare supper for them. They were supposed to belong to the army of Cornwallis, at that time foraging in the neighborhood. Not knowing what to do, Mrs. Caldwell sent to her brother-in-law for advice. He sent word in answer, that she must treat the men civilly, and have supper ready as soon as practicable; but that she must observe where they placed their guns, and set the table at the other end of the house. He promised to come over in the meantime, and conceal himself in a haystack close by; and she was to inform him as soon as the men had set down to supper. These directions were implicitly followed. The house was a double cabin, containing two rooms on the same floor. While the men were leisurely discussing their repast, Dr. Caldwell quietly entered the other apartment, took up one of the guns and stepping to the door of the room where they were so comfortably occupied, presented the weapon, and informed them they were his prisoners, and their lives would be the forfeit, should they make the least attempt to escape. They surrendered immediately, and Dr. Caldwell marched them to his own house, where he kept them till morning, and then suffered them to depart on their parole."*

COLONEL WILLETT.

Colonel Willett, possesses an enviable reputation for the skill and courage he manifested in the border wars of New York, during the revolution. He was engaged in many successful enterprises, two of which won for him especial honor. During the siege of Fort Stanwix, General Herkimer made an attempt to relieve it. He was approaching with a large body of militia, when it was resolved to make a diversion in his favor. Two hundred men were placed on parade for the purpose, and Col. Willett entrusted with the command. But meanwhile, Gen. Herkimer fell into an ambuscade of the enemy, when ensued the fearful battle of Oriskany. The sally, however, was made by Col. Willett, which was most successful. The camp of the enemy was attacked, they were routed, and large quantities of stores fell into the hands of the conqueror. With so much skill was this attack made, that although two camps, one of the British, the other of the Indians, fell successively into the hands of Willett, and in returning to the ort with the conquered stores, he encountered some opposition by Colonel St. Leger, yet the enterprise was accomplished without the loss of a single man.

But the relief of the fort still being an object of the utmost importance, and the failure of General Herkimer, to come to their id, convincing them that he had met with some misfortune, it

---

* " Women of the Revolution."

was thought advisable to make another effort to secure the assistance so much needed. The militia of Tyron county, having formerly expressed a strong attachment to Col. Willett, it was supposed that if he could appear among them, it might have the effect of inspiriting them with fresh resolution, and induce them a second time to attempt the raising of the seige. Actuated by these considerations, Col. Willett resolved to make the hazardou attempt of reaching the settlements down the river. From th memoirs of Col. Willett, by his son, we draw the particulars of this perilous enterprise:

"About 10 o'clock, on the night of the 10th of August, [1777], Col. Willett left the fort, accompanied by Major Stockwell, whom he selected for this purpose, as he was a good hunter, and was well acquainted with the Indian method of travelling in the wilderness. They passed privately through the sally-port of the fort, and proceeding silently along the marsh, they reached the river, which they crossed by crawling over a log, unperceived by the enemy's sentinels, who were not many yards from them. Having thus happily succeeded in crossing the river without being discovered, they advanced cautiously into a swampy wood, where they soon found themselves so enveloped in darkness, as to be unable to keep a straight course. While in a state of uncertainty as to the safest step for them to take, they were alarmed by the barking of a dog, at no great distance from them. Knowing that the Indians, after their camp had been broken up on the other side of the river, had removed to this side, they thought it most advisable to remain where they were, until they should have light sufficient to direct their course. Placing themselves therefore agains a large tree, they stood perfectly quiet for several hours. At ength, perceiving the morning-star, they again set out, but in stead of proceeding in a direct line to reach the settlement, they took nearly a northern direction, which after a few miles brought them again to the river. With the intention of concealing their route, in case their tracks should be discovered, they stepped in and out of the river several times, crossing occasionally to the opposite side, until reaching a spot where they could completely conceal their track by stepping on stones, they left the river, took a north course for a few hours, and then travelled east until night, without making a single stop. As it was necessary for them to be encumbered as little as possible, they had left the fort with no other weapon, but a spear for each, eight feet in length, which was intended to serve as a staff as well as a weapon of defence. They had taken no baggage nor blanket; and all the provision they had with them, consisted of a few crackers and cheese, which they had put in their pockets, together with a quart of canteen spirits. Having halted for the night, they refreshed themselves with such provision as they had; after which, their situation being too perilous to think of kindling a fire, they lay down to sleep wrapped in each other's arms. Though it was then the height of summer, yet the night was so cold, as, together with hard travelling the day before, and sleeping on the ground without any covering, made them feel very stiff when they arose the next morning. Colonel Willett had so severe a rheumatic attack in one of his knees, as to cause a limp in his walk for several hours. Setting out once more, they directed their course farther to the south, and about 9 o'clock came to an opening in the woods, occasioned by a windfall. In this opening, among the fallen trees, they found a forest of raspberries and blackberries, quite ripe, which afforded them a most delicious and refreshing repast. Though the day was very warm, yet, deriving new vigor from their banquet of berries, they proceeded expiditously towards the settlement, where they arrived at three o'clock, having travelled in this time about fifty miles. On arriving at Fort Dayton, a small stockade fort at the German Flats, they received a hearty welcome from Colonel Weston, who was stationed there with his regiment."

Proceeding from Fort Dayton, Colonel Willett soon joined a detachment of troops under Gen. Leamand, marching to the relief of the fort. The British General Register for 1777, speaking of this enterprise, says:—"They passed by night through the besieger's works, and in contempt of the danger and cruelty of the savages, made their way fifty miles through pathless and unexplored morasses, in order to raise the country and bring relief to the fort. Such an action demands the praise even of an enemy."

INTREPID CONDUCT OF MAJOR JAMES.

AFTER the fall of Charleston, the British commander in South Carolina issued a proclamation, granting protection to all those of the rebels, who would lay down their arms, and refrain from the further levying of war on his majesty. The apparently hopeess condition of the cause and the entire want of an organized force for resistance, induced many worthy citizens to avail themelves of England's offered protection. But scarcely had they done so, when another proclamation appeared, to the effect that they were not only to submit to English authority, but be compelled to take up arms in support of the royal cause. This proceeding, looked upon, by the people, as an infamous trap, aroused their indignation. The residents of one district when about to avail themselves of the offers in the first proclamation, had the second placed before them. At a loss to understand such conflicting offers, they despatched a delegate to the nearest British authority in order that the matter should be explained, and their doubts satisfied. Major John James was chosen as this delegate.

"Under this appointment, Major James repaired to Georgetown, the nearest British post, which was then under the command of one Captain Ardesoif. Attired as a plain backwoodsman, James obtained an interview with Ardesoif, and, in prompt and plain terms, entered at once upon the business for which he came. But when he demanded the meaning of the British protection, and asked upon what terms the submission of the citizens was to be made, he was peremptorily informed that 'the submission must be unconditional.' To an inquiry, whether the inhabitants were to be allowed to remain upon their plantations, he was answered in the negative. 'His Majesty,' said Ardesoif, 'offers you a free pardon, of which you are undeserving, for you all ought to be hanged; but it is only on condition that you take up arms in his cause.' James, whom we may suppose to have been very far from relishing the tone and language in which he was addressed, very coolly replied, that 'the people whom he came to *represent*, would scarcely submit on such conditions.' The republican language of the worthy Major provoked the representative of royalty. The word 'represent,' in particular, smote harshly on his ears something, too, in the cool, contemptuous manner of the Major, may have contributed to his vexation. '*Represent!*' he exclaimed in a fury—'You d——d rebel, if you dare speak in such language, I will have you hung up at the yard arm!' Ardesoif, it must be known was a sea-captain. The ship which he commanded lay in the neighboring river. He used only an habitual form of speech when he threatened the 'yard-arm,' instead of the tree. Major James gave him no time to make the correction. He was entirely weaponless, and Ardesoif wore a sword; but the inequality, in the moment of his anger, was unfelt by the high-spirited citizen. Suddenly rising, he seized upon the chair on which he had been sitting, and floored the insolent subordinate at a blow then hurrying forth without giving his enemy time to recover, he mounted his horse, and made his escape to the woods before pursuit could be attempted.

"His people were soon assembled to hear his story. The exactions of the British, and the spirit which James had displayed, in resenting the insolence of Ardesoif, at once aroused their own. Required to take the field, it did not need a moment to decide 'under which king.'

A NOVEL SITUATION.

In the fall of 1781 a man was captured in the vicinity of Fort Plain, by seven Indians and hurried off into the wilderness. At night the party halted at a deserted log tenement. The Indians built a fire, and after supper gathered around it discussing the misfortunes of their expedition which thus far had resulted in but a few scalps, and only one prisoner. They therefore resolved to kill and scalp their captive in the morning, and return toward the Mohawk with the hope of better success. Upon this conclusion they stretched themselves upon the floor for sleep, with their prisoner between two of them, who was bound by cords which were also fastened to the bodies of his keepers. The whole of the dis cussion carried on by the savages was understood by the captive, who, in the greatest alarm at his approaching fate, began to tax his ingenuity for some way to escape. The Indians were soon in a sound slumber, but their white companion kept wide awake, vainly striving to devise a plan for his escape, and beginning to despair and to yield himself to his doom, when, as he accidentally moved his hand upon the floor, it rested upon a fragment of broken window glass.

"No sooner did the prisoner seize the glass, than a ray of hope entered his bosom, and with this frail assistant he instantly set about regaining his liberty. He commenced severing the rope across his breast, and soon it was stranded. The moment was one of intense excitement; he knew that it was the usual custom for one or more of an Indian party to keep watch and prevent the escape of their prisoners. Was he then watched? Should he go on, with the possibility of hastening his own doom, or wait and see if some remarkable interposition of Providence might save him? A monitor within whispered, "Faith without works is dead," and after a little pause in his efforts, he resumed them, and soon had parted another strand; and as no movement was made, he tremblingly cut another; it was the last, and as it yielded he sat up. He was then enabled to take a midnight view of the group around him, in the feeble light reflected from the moon through a small window of a single sash. The enemy appeared to sleep, and he soon separated the cords across his limbs. He then advanced to the fire and raked open the coals, which relected their partial rays upon the painted visages of those misguided heathen, whom British gold had bribed to deeds of damning darkness; and being fully satisfied that all were sound asleep, he approached the door.

The Indians had a large watch-dog outside the house. He cautiously opened the door, sprang out and ran, and as he had anticipated, the dog was yelling at his heels. He had about twenty rods to run across a cleared field before he could reach the woods: and as he neared them, he looked back, and in the clear light of the moon, saw the Indians all in pursuit. As he neared the forest, they all drew up their rifles and fired upon him, at which instant a strong vine caught his foot and he fell to the ground. The volley of balls passed over him, and bounding to his feet, he gained the beechen shade. Not far from where he entered, he had noticed the preceding evening, a large hollow log, and on coming to it, he sought safety within it. The dog, at first ran several rods past the log, which served to mislead the party, but soon returned near it, and ceased barking, without a visit to the entrance of the captive's retreat.

' The Indians sat down over him, and talked about their prisoner's escape. They finally came to the conclusion, that he had either ascended a tree near, or that the *devil* had aided him in his escape, which to them appeared the most reasonable conclusion. As morning was approaching, they determined on taking an early breakfast, and returning to the river settlements, leaving one of their number to keep a vigilant watch in that neighborhood, for their captive, until afternoon of the following day, when he was to join his fellows at a designated place. This plan settled, an Indian proceeded to an adjoining field, where a small flock of sheep had not escaped their notice, and shot one of them. While enough of the mutton was dressing to satisfy their immediate wants, others of the party struck up a fire, which they chanced, most unfortunately for his comfort, to build against the log *directly opposite their lost prisoner.* The heat became almost intolerable to the tenant of the fallen basswood, before the meat was cooked —besides, the smoke and steam which found their way through the small worm-holes and cracks, had nearly suffocated him, ere he could sufficiently stop their ingress, which was done by thrusting a quantity of leaves and part of his own clothing into the crannies. A cough, which he knew would insure his death, he found it most difficult to avoid: to back out of his hiding place would also seal his fate, while to remain in it much longer, he felt conscious, would render his situation, to say the least, not enviable.

"After suffering most acutely in body and mind for a time, the prisoner (who was again such by accident), found his miseries alleviated when the Indians began to eat, as they then let the fire burn down, and did not again replenish it. After they had dispatched their breakfast of mutton, the prisoner heard the leader caution the one left to watch in that vicinity, to be wary, and soon heard the retiring footsteps of the rest of the party. Often during the morning, the watchman was seated or standing over him. Not having heard the Indian for some time, and believing the hour of his espionage past, he cautiously crept out of the log; and finding himself alone, being prepared by fasting and steaming for a good race, he drew a bee-line for Fort Plain, which he reached in safety, believing, as he afterwards stated, that all the Indians in the state could not have overtaken him in his flight."*

---

* Simms' "History of Schoharie Co"

THE DEATH OF MAJOR HENLEY.

AFTER the retreat from Long Island, and while the American army was stationed at Harlem Heights, the English had possession of a small island at the mouth of the Harlem river, near Hurl Gate in the East river, which was covered by one of their ships of war. From this ship, on the twenty-second day of September 1776, two seamen deserted and went to the quarters of General Heath. Upon being examined, they stated that the cannon had been removed from the island to the frigate, and that but a few men, with a number of officers, and a large quantity of provisions and stores, remained there at this time. On receiving this information a surprise of the island was determined upon, and three flat-bottomed boats were at once prepared for the purpose, each boat to carry two hundred and forty men. They were under the command of Colonel Jackson, Major Logan, and a Major whose name is not known. At the favorable opportunity, they floated down the Harlem river, at night, and with the tide, with the hope of arriving to their destination about the break of day.

Major Henly who was mortified at being excluded from the enterprise, applied to General Heath for the privilege of accompanying the expedition as a volunteer, which with some reluctance was granted. Says the biographer of Major Henley, "Perhaps of the many young and gallant spirits, who then crowded to fight beneath the banners of liberty, none were more ardent in her cause, or more amiable and better loved by his cotemporaries than was Major Henley. Young, courageous, aspiring and sanguine n the cause of his native country, he considered no duty too arduous, no deprivation too great, no suffering too severe, in assisting her advancement to independence."

"A couple of hours after midnight, the boats received their complement of men, and were proceeding slowly down the narrow and winding creek. There was no light to guide them on their way, save that which issued from the bright stars of heaven, shining from its broad spread canopy. There was no voice nor whispering to break the perfect silence of that hour; and the ripplings caused by the prows of the boats passing through the water, was all the indication of their making any progress. They had nearly gained the scene of their operations, when lo! as they considered themselves secure from any annoyance, and all things promising the best success to the undertaking, they were hailed from the shore by one of the American sentinels.

"'Stop!' cried he, 'or I will fire!'

"This faithful sentinel had not, unfortunately, been informed of the expedition. They replied from the boats:

"'We are friends!'

"He repeated his challenge and said:

"'You must stop and come to the shore.'

"'Hush we are friends,' said they from the boats, 'keep silence.'

"This interruption occurred opposite the point where General Heath was to stand a spectator of the attack upon the island. Major Henly seeing the general and several officers there, leaped from the boat into the water, which was some feet deep, and waded to the shore, and in an instant was before him.

"'Sir, will it do?' said he, taking the general by the hand.

"'I see nothing to the contrary.'

"'Then sir, it shall do,' answered the major in an emphatic manner, at the same time shaking the general smartly by the hand; in a moment he was on board the boat again. He had no sooner seated himself than a command was given to the oarsmen to proceed.

"'Pull away for your lives.'

"The sentinel heard the order, presented his piece and fired but without doing any injury. Early dawn was just lighting u he horizon when they reached the island; the precise momen they had intended. The boat in which the officers were, landed The two seconds in command were to spring from the boat, one on each side, and lead on the troops from the other two boats, which were to land each side of the first. The enemy's guard charged them on their gaining the shore, having been apprised of the attack by the discharge of the sentinel's musket, but were instantly driven back. Owing to some unaccountable misunderstanding, or something that deserves a less honorable designation, the men in the other two boats, instead of joining them, lay at a distance from the shore irresolute and inactive. The British, observing that the Americans were not supported, returned warmly to the charge; while the latter finding themselves deserted, and Colonel Jackson having received a shot in his leg, returned to their boat.

"They lost fourteen of their number; and painful to relate, Major Henly, who had proved himself most active in this unfortunate affair, while getting over the side of the boat, was sho through the heart by a musket ball. He gave one shrill cry, and leaping some two or three feet from where he stood, fell dead among his comrades, covering them with his blood.

"Thus fell a brave and gallant soldier. He had just entered into manhood, with a robust health and strong arm, and had it pleased the Great Disposer for him to have continued for a longer period upon the stage of life, he would probably, from his early promise, have been a theme of eulogy and admiration. His body was consigned to the dust with military honors, and the soldiers who gathered around the remains of their much loved companion, wept at his untimely fall.

"The success of the expedition in which he was engaged would have been very probable had only one of the other boats landed but, in the opinion of all concerned, the two would have insured the full execution of the whole plan. The delinquents were arrested and tried by a court-martial. One of the captains was cashiered."

ADVENTURES OF COL. HARPER.

In the year 1778 a notorious Tory leader, McDonald, at the head of three hundred Indians and Tories, were committing great ravages on the frontiers, and audaciously carrying on their depredations in the vicinity of the forts of Schoharie, which were all so weakly garrisoned, that they could offer no resistance to them. Col. Harper, stationed at one of the forts, perceiving the wanton barbarities of the enemy, resolved to undertake a journey to Albany, in order to procure sufficient aid to arrest them in their career. It was an expedition full of peril, but he sallied boldly orth, and although the enemy lined his entire route, he undauntedly resolved to secure help for the perishing inhabitants, or sacrifice his own life in the attempt. His first day's journey was uninterrupted, and at evening he rode up to a tory tavern, coolly demanded a room, and without apparent fear or apprehension retired for the night. But he was not unprepared. Presently there was a loud rapping at the door. He demanded what was wanted? "We want to see Col. Harper," was the reply. He deliberately arose, unlocked the door, and taking his sword and pistols, seated himself on the bed to receive his visitors. They were four, and entered blusteringly, and with threatening aspects. The colonel raised his pistols and said, "step one inch over that mark, and you are dead men." There was something in his determined and resolute aspect that arrested their progress. Their boldness fled before his unflinching eye, and irresolute they looked from one to the other at a loss how to proceed. In vain did they look for a sign of weakness in his manner; the least show of such a thing would have proved his destruction. Overawed, and abashed, they retreated from his presence with what grace they could, and left him master of the field. Still, however, feeling himself insecure, he did not sleep again that night, but kept a wary watch. In the morning he boldly mounted his horse, and although the enemy were concealed in the vicinity of the house, for some reason he was allowed to pass unmolested. But an Indian followed him almost the entire rest of the way; whenever the colonel would turn and present a pistol he would run with all his might, but again steal cautiously in his rear. Uninjured the colonel reached Albany, procured aid, hastened back to Schoharie, and wreaked a sudden retribution on the marauders.

The following account of another succesful enterprise of Col. Harper, we find in Campbell's "Annals of Tryon County."

"In the year 1777, he had command of one of the forts in Schoharie county, and of all the frontier stations in that region. He left the fort in Schoharie, and came out through the woods to Harpersfield, in the time of making sugar, and thence laid his course for Cherry Valley, to investigate the state of things there and as he was pursuing a blind kind of Indian trail, and was ascending what are now called Decatur Hills, he cast his eye forward, and saw a company of men coming directly towards him who had the appearance of Indians. He knew that if he attempted to flee from them, they would shoot him down; he resolved to advance right up to them, and make the best shift fo himself he could. As soon as he came near enough to discern the white of their eyes, he knew the head man and several others; the head man's name was Peter, an Indian with whom Col. Harper had often traded, at Oquago before the revolution began. The colonel had his great-coat on, so that his regimentals were concealed, and he was not recognised; the first words of address of Col. Harper's was, ' How do you do, brothers ?'

"' Well—how do you do, brother ?' was the reply.

"' On a secret expedition: and which way are you bound brothers ?'

"' Down the Susquehannah, to cut off the Johnstown settlement.'

"' Where do you lodge to night ?' inquired the colonel.

"' At the mouth of Schenevas creek,' was the reply. Then shaking hands with them, he bid them good speed and proceeded on his journey.

"He had gone but little way from them, before he took a circuit through the woods, a distance of eight or ten miles, on to the head of Charlotte river, where were a number of men making sugar; ordered them to take their arms, two days provisions, a canteen of rum, and a rope, and meet him down the Charlotte, at a small clearing called Evan's Place, at a certain hour that afternoon; then rode with all speed through the woods to Harpers field; collected all the men there making sugar, and being armed and victualed, each man with his rope, laid his course for Charlotte. When he arrived at Evan's Place, he found the Charlotte men in good spirits, and when he mustered his men, there were fifteen, including himself, exactly the same number as there were of the enemy; then the colonel made his men acquainted with the enterprise.

"They marched down the river a little distance, and then bent their course accross the hill to the mouth of Schenevas creek; when they arrived at the brow of the hill, where they could overlook the valley where the Schenevas flows, they cast their eyes down upon the flats, and discovered the fire around which the enemy lay encamped.

"'There they are,' said Col. Harper. They descended with great stillness, forded the creek, which was breast high to a man; after advancing a few hundred yards, they took some refreshment, and then prepared for the contest. Daylight was just beginning to appear in the east. When they came to the enemy, they lay in a circle with their feet towards the fire, in a deep sleep; their arms and all their implements of death, were all stocked up according to the Indian custom, when they lay themselves down for the night; these the colonel secured by carrying them off a distance, and laying them down. Then each man taking his rope in his hand, placed himself by his fellow; the colonel rapped his man softly, and said, 'Come, it is time for men of business to be on their way,' and then each one sprang upon his man, and after a most severe struggle they secured the whole of the enemy.

"After they were all safely bound, and the morning had so far advanced, that they could discover objects distinctly, says the Indian Peter, 'Ha! Col. Harper! now I know thee—why did I not know thee yesterday?'

"'Some policy in war, Peter.'

"'Ah, me find em so now.'

"The colonel marched the men to Albany, delivered them up to the commanding officer, and by this well executed feat of valor, he saved the Johnstown settlement from a wanton destruction."

NARROW ESCAPE OF COLONEL SNIPES.

During the revolutionary contest in South Carolina, the most malignant enmity existed between the whigs and tories, which often occasioned scenes and incidents of the most ferocious and terrible nature. One of these which occurred to Col. Snipes of Marion's brigade, we extract from the "Life of Marion," by Simms.

"Col. Snipes was a Carolinian, of remarkable strength and courage. He was equally distinguished for his vindictive hatred of the tories. He had suffered some domestic injuries at their hands, and he was one who never permitted himself to forgive. His temper was sanguinary in the extreme, and led him, in his treatment of the loyalists, to such ferocities as subjected him, on more than one occasion, to the harshest rebuke of his commander. It is not certain at what period in the war the following occurrence took place, but it was on one of those occasions when the partisan militia claimed a sort of periodical privilege of abandoning their general to look after their families and domestic interests. Availing himself of this privilege, Snipes pursued his way to his plantation. His route was a circuitous one, but it is probable that he pursued it with little caution. He was more distinguished for au dacity than prudence. The Tories fell upon his trail, which they followed with the keen avidity of the sleuth-hound. Snipes reached his plantation in safety, unconscious of pursuit. Having examined the homestead and received an account of all things done in his absence, from a faithful driver, and lulled into security by the seeming quiet and silence of the neighborhood, he retired to rest, and, after the fatigues of the day, soon fell into a profound sleep. From this he was awakened by the abrupt entrance and cries of his driver. The faithful negro apprised him, in terror, of the approach of the Tories. They were already on the plantation. His vigilance alone prevented them from taking his master in bed. Snipes, starting up, proposed to take shelter in the barn, but the driver pointed to the flames already bursting from that building. He had barely time to leave the house, covered only by his night shirt, and by the counsel of the negro, to fly to the cover of a thick copse of briars and brambles, within fifty yards of the dwelling, when the Tories surrounded it. The very task of penetrating this copse, so as to screen himself from sight, effectually removed the thin garment which concealed his nakedness. The shirt was torn from his back by the briars, and the skin shared in its injuries. But, once there, he lay effectually concealed from sight. Ordinary conjecture would scarcely have supposed that any animal larger than a rabbit would have sought or found shelter in such a region. The Tories immediately seized upon the negro and demanded his master, at the peril of his life. Knowing and fearing the courage and the arm of Snipes, they did not enter the dwelling, but adopted the less valorous mode of setting it on fire, and, with pointed muskets, surrounded it, in waiting for the moment when their victim should emerge. He, within a few steps of them, heard their threats and expectations, and be-field all their proceedings. The house was consumed, and the intense heat of the fire subjected our partisan, in his place of retreat, to such torture, as none but the most dogged hardihood could have endured without complaint. The skin was peeled from his body in many places, and the blisters were shown long after, to person who are still living. But Snipes too well knew his enemies, and what he had to expect at their hands, to make any confession. He bore patiently the torture, which was terribly increased, when finding themselves at fault, the Tories brought forward the faithful negro who had thus far saved his master, and determined to extort from him, in the halter, the secret of his hiding-place. But the courage and fidelity of the negro proved superior to the terrors of death. Thrice was he run up the tree, and choked nearly to strangulation, but in vain. His capability to endure proved superior to the will of the Tories to inflict, and he was at length let down, half dead,—as, in truth, ignorant of the secret which they desired to extort. What were the terrors of Snipes in all this trial? What his feelings of equal gratitude and apprehension? How noble was the fidelity of the slave—based upon what gentle and affectionate relationship between himself and master—probably from boyhood! Yet this is but one of a thousand such attachments, all equally pure and elevated, and maintained through not dissimilar perils."

A SCENE IN THE FOREST.

"In the early part of the war, a sergeant and twelve armed men undertook a journey through the wilderness, in the state of New Hampshire. Their route was remote from any settlements, and they were under the necessity of encamping over night in the woods. Nothing material happened the first day of their excursion; but early in the afternoon of the second, they, from an emminence discovered a body of armed Indians advancing towards them, whose number rather exceeded their own. As soon as the whites were perceived by their red brethren, the latter made signals, and the two parties approached each other in an amicable manner. The Indians appeared to be much gratified with meeting the sergeant and his men, whom they observed they considered as their protectors; said they belonged to a tribe which had raised the hatchet with zeal in the cause of liberty, and were determined to do all in their power to repel the common enemy They shook hands in friendship, and it was, 'How d'ye do *pro*, how d'ye do *pro*,' that being their pronunciation of the word brother. When they had conversed with each other, for some time, and exchanged mutual good wishes, they at length separated, and each party travelled in a different direction. After proceeding to the distance of a mi'e or more, the sergeant, who was acquainted with all the different tribes, and knew on which side of the contest they were respectively ranked, halted his men and addressed them in the following words:

"'My brave companions, we must use the utmost caution, or this night may be our last. Should we not make some extraordinary exertions to defend ourselves, to-morrow's sun may find us sleeping never to wake. You are surprised comrades, at my words, and your anxiety will not be lessened, when I inform you, that we have just passed our most inveterate foe, who, under the mask of pretended friendship you have witnessed, would lull us to security, and by such means, in the unguarded moments of our midnight slumber, without resistance, seal our fate.'

"The men with astonishment listened to this short harrangue; and their surprise was greater, as not one of them had entertained the suspicion but they had just encountered friends. They all immediately resolved to enter into some scheme, for their mutual preservation and destruction of their enemies. By the proposal of their leader, the following plan was adopted and executed:

"The spot selected for their night's encampment, was near a stream of water, which served to cover their rear. They felled a large tree, before which on the approach of night, a brilliant fire was lighted. Each individual cut a log of wood about the size of his body, rolled it nicely in his blanket, placed his hat upon the extremity, and laid it before the fire; that the enemy might be deceived, and mistake it for a man. After logs equal in number to the sergeant's party were thus fitted out, and so artfully arranged, that they might be easily mistaken for so many soldiers, the men with loaded muskets placed themselves behind the fallen tree, by which time the shades of evening began to close around. The fire was supplied in fuel, and kept burning brilliantly until late in the evening, when it was suffered to decline. The critical time was now approaching, when an attack might be expected from the Indians; but the sergeant's men rested in their place of concealment with great anxiety, till near midnight, without perceiving any movement of the enemy.

"At length a tall Indian was discovered through the glimmering of the fire, cautiously moving towards them, making no noise, and apparantly using every means in his power to conceal himself from any one about the camp. For a time his actions showed him to be suspicious, that a guard might be stationed to watch any unusual appearance, who would give the alarm in case of danger; but all appearing quiet, he ventured forward more boldly rested upon his toes, and was distinctly seen to move his finger as he numbered each log of wood, or what he supposed to be a human being quietly enjoying repose. To satisfy himself more fully, as to the number, he counted them over a second time, and cautiously retired. He was succeeded by another Indian, who went through the same movements, and retired in the same manner. Soon after the whole party, sixteen in number, were discovered, approaching, and greedily eyeing their supposed victims. The feelings of the sergeant's men can better be imagined than described, when they saw the base and cruel purpose of their enemies, who were now so near, that they could scarcely be restrained from firing upon them. The plan however, of the sergeant was to have his men remain silent in their places of concealment till the muskets of the savages were discharged, that their own fire might be more effectual, and opposition less formidable.

"Their suspense was not of long duration. The Indians, in a body, cautiously approached, till within a short distance, they then halted, took deliberate aim, discharged their pieces upon inanimate *logs*, gave the dreadful warwhoop, and instantly rushed forward, with tomahawk and scalping knife in hand, to despatch the living, and obtain the scalps of the dead. As soon as they had collected ir close order, more effectually to execute their horrid intentions, the party of the sergeant, with unerring aim, discharged their pieces, not on logs of wood, but perfidious savages, not one of whom escaped destruction by the snare into which their cowardly and blood-thirsty dispositions had led them."

A GALLANT COMBAT.

Soon after the capture of Charleston, Capt. Watson, at the head of a party of mounted Rangers, conceived the idea of surprising a party of Tories encamped near Orangeburgh. He was joined by William Butler, who commanded a small body of cavalry, some fifteen in number. Butler was burning with the desire to avenge the most brutal and atrocious murder of his father, which had occurred a short time before. He had been surrounded in a house by a large body of Tories, and in view of the superior numbers, himself and party had capitulated, when they were marched out of the house one by one, and deliberately cut to pieces. The elder Butler, was singled out by the blood-thirsty leader of the party, who slew him with his own hand. Fired by this remembrance, young Butler, afterward so distinguished in the annals of the south, let no opportunity pass for wreaking his vengeance on the enemy. On this occasion the whole party, under Watson, set out, at near sundown, and rode rapidly towards heir destination. On their route they captured a Tory, who unfortunately afterwards escaped, and thus their hope of meeting their adversaries unprepared, was destroyed. Watson prudently advocated for return, but the fiery Butler, still mourning his murdered parent's memory, earnestly urged an advance, and avowed his determination to proceed with his own command, whether as sisted by Watson or not. Watson was of too chivalrous a nature to turn his back upon his friend, and they, therefore, hurried forward upon their enterprise. It was after daylight when they arrived near the place where they expected to find the Tory encampment. They descried two men standing alone, and Butler, Watson, and Varney, a sergeant of renowned courage, rode up to arrest them. Suddenly Watson cried out, "Beware! the whole body of the enemy are at hand!" The whole party were close at his heels, when suddenly the Tories, sprang from their ambuscade, and poured into the devoted body of patriots, a destructive and terrible fire. The heroic Watson, and the intrepid Varney, with several others, tumbled wounded from their horses. Butler, alone of all the officers, was unwounded. "Suffer me not," exclaimed Watson, to him, "to fall into their hands." Butler sprang forward, and seizing the bodies of his friends, unmindful of the fire poured in by the enemy, he triumphantly bore them into the midst of his own party.

It was seen that the Tories doubled the Whigs, while to give them a greater preponderance, a part of the Whigs took flight and fled. But those that remained, were every one a hero, and prepared to conquer or fall. To add to the desperation of their situation, their ammunition, in the conflict that ensued, soon gave out, and the Royalists began to advance upon them. Butler however, was equal to the emergency. He formed his men in compact order, and placing himself at their head, charged impetuously on the enemy. With nothing but their swords and their nigh courage to support them, the heroic band hurled themselves upon their adversaries, and with so much violence and impetuous fury was the crash, that the enemy were staggered, and began to fall into confusion. Butler's sword swept everything before him, and fell upon his opponent like a thunderbolt, each blow nerved by the recollection of his murdered father. The little band bore their antagonists along, who, in vain, though far superior in number, endeavored to bear up against their assailants. They began o yield, and to seek safety in flight; their resistance grew weak, and Butler following up his charge with still greater resolution, they were driven into the swamp in their rear, and the whigs remained master of the field. It had been a hard fought conflict against a superior number, and the victory was gallantly and heroically achieved. But alas! it was attained by a fearful price. Those gallant heroes, Watson and Varney, lay weltering in their blood. As the party passed the place where they lay, Varney, by an effort, raised himself on one arm—waved his hand, while a gleam of triumph passed athwart his countenance—fell back, and his book of life was closed. They dug with their swords, soldier's graves, and buried them on the field of victory.[*]

A GALLANT ENTERPRISE.

"On the river Ogechee, in the state of Georgia, was stationed Captain French, with a detachment of about forty British regulars. At the same place, lay five British vessels; of these, four were armed, the largest mounting fourteen guns.

"Col. John White, of the Georgia line, meditating the capture of this station, was able to call to his assistance but four individuals, Captain Etholen, and three privates. Resolute in their

---

[*] Garden.

purpose, notwithstanding the disparity of force they would be obliged to encounter, these five soldiers of fortune boldly advanced to the enemy's post.

"Having arrived in the neighborhood of it at night, they kindled numerous fires, the light of which reached their adversaries, so arranging them, as to represent, by them, the lines of a considerable camp. To render their stratagem the more imposing, they then rode hastily about, in various directions, in imitation of the staff of an army, disposing their sentinels, and issuing their orders in a loud voice.

"The artifice succeeded, and Captain French supposed that he was menaced by a large body of Americans. Accordingly, on being summoned by Col. White, he surrendered his detachment, the crews of the five vessels, amounting to nearly fifty in number, with the vessels themselves, and one hundred and fifty stand of arms.

"But the difficulty of the enterprising captors was not yet terminated. The British soldiers and sailors might discover the imposition that had been practised on them, and attempt a rescue; and five armed men were not sufficient to restrain, by force, near a hundred without arms. The same genius, however, hat had planned the first part of the adventure, was competent o the completion of it.

"With great seriousness, and some emotion in his manner, Col. White told Capt. French, that in consequence of certain ecent enormities, perpetrated by a detachment of British and royalists, his troops were so deeply exasperated, that he was afraid they would advance on the captured party, and in violation of his commands put them to death: that he had, already, experienced great difficulty in restraining them; and should they be placed as a guard over the prisoners, he was convinced their rage would become ungovernable. He, therefore, directed the British Captain to follow, with his whole party, Capt. Etholen, and two of the soldiers as guides, who would conduct them, without delay, to a place of safety, and good quarters. For his kindness and humanity, Col. White received the thanks of his prisoners, who immediately marched off, in a body, with their small escort, anxious to hasten their pace, lest the enraged Americans should advance on them, and cut them to pieces.

"The Colonel and one soldier remained behind, with a view, as he informed Captain French, to restrain by his presence any improper violence his troops might be inclined to offer, and to conduct their march at some distance in the rear. Meanwhile, he collected as expeditiously as possible, a body of militia from the neighboring district. Placing himself at the head of these, who were mostly mounted on good horses, he soon overtook his prisoners, whom he found safe under their guides, and rejoicing in the generous treatment they had experienced.

"This affair of partisan gallantry, though not very momentous in its consequences, was, notwithstanding, so extraordinary in its nature, conducted with so much address, marked with such a chivalrous spirit of enterprise, and so honorable to the officers who conceived and executed it, that it should be much more generally known and admired than it is."

NARRATIVE OF THE BARONESS REIDESEL.

EVERY American reader is familiar with this lady's name. She was the lady of one of Burgoyne's Major-Generals, a distinguished German officer, and with two infant children, accompanied her husband in the disastrous campaign of Burgoyne. She was a beautiful and accomplished woman, and the devotion which prompted her to follow her lord to the camp and tented field, and the sufferings and privations she there was compelled to undergo, have always excited the admiration and sympathy of the world. The sufferings which beset the English army on their retreat, after the battle of Saratoga, exceeds the power of words to describe. But no history gives so vivid and powerful a picture of the retreat, as the simple and unaffected narrative of Baroness Reidesel. General Wilkinson, who introduces her account into his memoirs, remarks, that she suffered more than the horrors of the grave, in their most frightful aspect; and he adds, that he had " more than once seen her charming blue eyes bedewed with tears at the recital of her sufferings."

"As we had to march still further, I ordered a large calash to be built, capable of holding my three children, myself and two female servants; and in this manner we moved with the army in the midst of the soldiery, who were very merry, singing songs, and panting for action. We had to travel through almost impassable woods, and a most picturesque and beautiful country, which was abandoned by its inhabitants, who had repaired to the standard of General Gates: they added much to his strength, as they were all good marksmen, and fitted by habit for the species of warfare the contending parties were then engaged in; and the love of their country inspired them with more than ord.nary courage. The army had shortly to encamp. I generally remained about an hour's march in the rear, where I received daily visits from my husband. The army was frequently engaged in small affairs, but nothing of importance took place; and as the season was getting cold, Major Williams, of the artillery, proposed to have a house built for me, with a chimney, observing that it would not cost more than five or six guineas, and that the frequent change of quarters was very inconvenient to me: it was accordingly built, and was called the Block-house, from its square form, and the resemblance it bore to those buildings.

"On the 19th of September, an affair happened, which, though it turned out to our advantage, yet obliged us to halt at a place called Freeman's Farm; I was an eye-witness to the whole affair, and as my husband was engaged in it, I was full of anxiety, and trembled at every shot I heard. I saw a great number of the wounded, and, what added to the distress of the scene, three of them were brought into the house in which I took shelter. One was a Major Harnage, of the sixty-second British regiment, the husband of a lady of my acquaintance; another was a lieutenant, married to a lady with whom I had the honor to be on terms of intimacy; and the third was an officer of the name of Young.

"In a short time afterwards I heard groans proceeding from a room near mine, and knew they must have been occasioned by he sufferings of the last mentioned officer, who lay writhing with his wounds.

"His mournful situation interested me much; and the more so, because the recollection of many polite attentions, received from a family of that name during my visit to Englund, was still forcibly impressed on my mind. I sent to him, and begged him to accept my best services, and afterwards furnished him with food and refreshments; he expressed a great desire to see me, politely calling me his benefactress. I accordingly visited him, and found him lying on a little straw, as he had lost his equipage. He was a young man eighteen or nineteen years of age and really the beloved nephew of the Mr. Young, the head of th family I have mentioned, and the only son of his parents. This last circumstance was what he lamented most; as to his pain, he thought lightly of it. He had lost much blood, and it was thought necessary to amputate the leg, but this he would not consent to, and of course a mortification took place. I sent him cushions and coverings, and my female friends sent him a mattress. I redoubled my attention to him, and visited him every day, for which I received a thousand wishes for my happiness. At last his limb was amputated, but it was too late, and he died the following day. As he lay in the next room to me, and the partition was very thin, I distinctly heard his last sigh, when his immortal part quitted its frail tenement.

"But severer trials awaited us, and on the 7th of October, our misfortunes began. I was at breakfast with my husband, and heard that something was intended. On the same day I expected Generals Burgoyne, Phillips, and Frazer, to dine with us. I saw a great movement among the troops; my husband told me it was merely a reconnoisance, which gave me no concern, as it often happened. I walked out of the house, and met several Indians in their war dresses, with guns in their hands. When I asked them where they were going, they cried out, "*war! war!*" meaning that they were going to battle. This filled me with apprehension, and I had scarcely got home before I heard re ports of cannon and musketry, which grew louder by degrees, till at last the noise became excessive.

About four o'clock in the afternoon, instead of the guests whom I expected, General Frazer was brought on a litter, mortally wounded. The table, which was already set, was instantly removed, and a bed placed in its stead for the wounded general. I sat trembling in a corner; the noise grew louder, and the alarm increased; the thought that my husband might perhaps be brought in, wounded in the same manner, was terrible to me, and distressed me exceedingly. General Frazer said to the surgeon, '*Tell me if my wound is mortal; do not flatter me.*' The ball had passed through his body, and, unhappily for the general, he had eaten a very hearty breakfast, by which the stomach was distended, and the ball, as the surgeon said, had passed through it. I heard him often exclaim with a sigh, " *O fatal ambition! Poor General Burgoyne! Oh! my poor wife!*" He was asked if he had any request to make, to which he replied, that, '*If General Burgoyne would permit it, he should like to be buried, at six o'clock in the evening, on the top of a mountain, in a redoubt which had been built there.*'

"I did not know which way to turn; all the other rooms were full of sick. Towards evening I saw my husband coming; then I forgot all my sorrows, and thanked God that he was spared to me. He ate in great haste, with me and his aid-de-camp, behind the house. We had been told that we had the advantage over the enemy, but the sorrowful faces I beheld told a different tale; and before my husband went away he took me aside, and said everything was going very badly, and that I must keep myself in readiness to leave the place, but not to mention it to any one.

I made the pretence that I would move the next morning into my new house, and had everything packed up ready.

"Lady Ackland had a tent not far from our house; in this she slept, and the rest of the day she was in the camp. All of a sudden a man came in to tell her that her husband was mortally wounded, and taken prisoner. On hearing this she became very miserable.—We comforted her by telling her that the wound was very slight, and advised her to go over to her husband, to do which she would certainly obtain permission, and then she could attend him herself. She was a charming woman, and very fond of him. I spent much of the night in comforting her, and then went again to my children, whom I had put to bed.

"I could not go to sleep, as I had General Frazer and all the other wounded gentlemen in my room, and I was sadly afraid my children would wake, and by their crying disturb the dying man in his last moments, who often addressed me and apologized '*for the trouble he gave me.*' About three o'clock in the morning, I was told that he could not hold out much longer; I had desired to be informed of the near approach of this sad crisis, and I then wrapped up my children in their clothes, and went with them into the room below. About eight o'clock in the morning *he died.*

"After he was laid out, and his corpse wrapped up in a sheet, we came again into the room, and had this sorrowful sight before us the whole day; and, to add to the melancholy scene, almost every moment some officer of my acquaintance was brought in wounded. The cannonade commenced again; a retreat was spoken of, but not the smallest motion was made towards it. About four o'clock in the afternoon, I saw the house, which had just been built for me, in flames, and the enemy was now not far off. We knew that General Burgoyne would not refuse the last request of General Frazer, though, by his acceding to it, an unnecessary delay was occasioned, by which the inconvenience of the army was much increased. At six o'clock the corpse was brought out, and we saw all the generals attend it to the mountain. The chaplain, Mr. Brudenell, performed the funeral service rendered unusually solemn and awful from its being accompanied by constant peals from the enemy's artillery. Many cannon-balls flew close by me, but I had my eyes directed towards the mountain,* where my husband was standing, amidst the fire of the enemy; and, of course, I could not think of my own danger.

"General Gates afterwards said, that, if he had known it had been a funeral, he would not have permitted it to be fired on.

"As soon as the funeral service was finished, and the grave of General Frazer closed, an order was issued that the army should retreat. My calash was prepared, but I would not consent to go before the troops. Major Harnage, though suffering from his wounds, crept from his bed, as he did not wish to remain in the hospital, which was left with a flag of truce. When General Reidesel saw me in the midst of danger, he ordered my women and children to be brought into the calash, and intimated to me to depart without delay. I still prayed to remain, but my husband, knowing my weak side, said, 'well then, your children must go, that at least they may be safe from danger.' I *then* agreed to enter the calash with them, and we set off at eigh o'clock.

"The retreat was ordered to be conducted with the greatest

---

* The height occupied by Burgoyne on the 18th, which ran parallel with the river till it approached General Gate's camp.

silence, many fires were lighted, and several tents left standing; we travelled continually during the night. At six o'clock in the morning we halted, which excited the surprise of all; General Burgoyne had the cannon ranged and counted; this delay seemed to displease everybody, for if we could only have made another good march, we should have been in safety. My husband, quite exhausted with fatigue, came into my calash, and slept for three hours. During that time, Capt. Willoe brought me a bag full of bank notes, and Captain Grismar his elegant watch, a ring, and a purse full of money, which they requested me to take care of, and which I promised to do, to the utmost of my power. We again marched, but had scarcely proceeded an hour, before we halted, as the enemy was in sight; it proved to be only a reconnoitering party of two hundred men, who might easily have been made prisoners, if General Burgoyne had given proper orders on the occasion.

"The Indians had now lost their courage, and were departing for their homes; these people appeared to droop much under adversity, and especially when they had no prospect of plunder. One of my waiting-women was in a state of despair, which approached to madness; she cursed and tore her hair, and when I attempted to reason with her, and to pacify her, she asked me if I was not grieved at our situation, and on my saying I was, she tore her cap off her head and let her hair fall over her face, saying to me 'it is very easy for you to be composed and talk; you have your husband with you; I have none, and what remains to me but the prospect of perishing or losing all I have?' I again bade her take comfort, and assured her I would make good whatever she might happen to lose; and I made the same promise to Ellen, my other waiting-woman, who, though filled with apprehensions, made no complaints.

"About evening we arrived at Saratoga; my dress was wet through and through with rain, and in this state I had to remain the whole night, having no place to change it; I however got close to a large fire, and at last lay down on some straw. At this moment General Phillips came up to me, and I asked him why he had not continued our retreat, as my husband had promised to cover it, and bring the army through? 'Poor, dear woman,' said he, 'I wonder how, drenched as you are, you have the courage still to persevere, and venture further in this kind of weather; I wish,' continued he, 'you was our commanding general; General Burgoyne is tired, and means to halt here to-night and give us our supper.'

"On the morning of the 7th, at 10 o'clock, General Burgoyne ordered the retreat to be continued, and caused the handsome houses and mills of General Schuyler to be burnt; we marched, however, but a short distance, and then halted. The greatest misery at this time prevailed in the army, and more than thirty officers came to me, for whom tea and coffee was prepared, and with whom I shared all my provisions, with which my calash was in general well supplied, for I had a cook who was an excellent caterer, and who often in the night crossed small rivers, and foraged on the inhabitants, bringing in with him, sheep, small pigs, and poultry, for which he very often forgot to pay, though he received good pay from me so long as I had any, and was ultimately handsomely rewarded. Our provisions now failed us, for want of proper conduct in the commissary's department, and I began to despair.

"About two o'clock in the afternoon, we again heard a firing of cannon and small arms; instantly all was alarm, and every thing in motion. My husband told me to go to a house not far off. I immediately seated myself in my calash, with my children, and drove off; but scarcely had we reached it before I discovered five or six armed men on the other side of the Hudson. Instinctively I threw my children down in the calash, and then concealed myself with them. At this moment the fellows fired, and wounded an already wounded English soldier, who was behind me. Poor fellow! I pitied him exceedingly, but at this moment had no means or power to relieve him.

"A terrible cannonade was commenced by the enemy, against the house in which I sought to obtain shelter for myself and children, under the mistaken idea that all the generals were in it. Alas! it contained none but wounded and women. We were at last obliged to resort to the cellar for refuge, and in one corner of this I remained the whole day, my children sleeping on the earth with their heads in my lap; and in the same situation I passed a sleepless night. Eleven cannon balls passed through the house, and we could distinctly hear them roll away. One poor soldier who was lying on a table, for the purpose of having his leg amputated, was struck by a shot, which carried away his other; his comrades had left him, and when we went to his assistance, we found him in the corner of a room, into which he had crept, more dead than alive, scarcely breathing. My reflections on the danger to which my husband was exposed now agonized me exceedingly, and the thoughts of my children, and the necessity of struggling for their preservation, alone sustained me.

"The ladies of the army who were with me, were Mrs. Harnage, a Mrs. Kennels, the widow of a lieutenant who was killed, and the lady of the commissary. Major Harnage, his wife, and

Mrs. Kennels, made a little room in a corner with curtains to it, and wished to do the same for me, but I preferred being near the door, in case of fire. Not far off my women slept, and opposite to us three English officers, who, though wounded, were determined not to be left behind; one of them was Captain Green, an aid-de-camp to Major General Phillips, a very valuable officer and most agreeable man. They each made me a most sacred promise not to leave me behind, and, in case of sudden retreat, that they would each of them take one of my children on his horse; and for myself, one of my husband's was in constant readiness.

"Our cook, whom I have before mentioned, procured us our meals, but we were in want of water, and I was often obliged to drink wine, and to give it to my children. It was the only thing my husband took, which made our faithful hunter, Rockel, express one day his apprehensions, that, 'the general was weary of his life, or fearful of being taken, as he drank so much wine.' The constant danger which my husband was in, kept me in a state of wretchedness; and I asked myself, if it was possible, I should be the only happy one, and have my husband spared to me unhurt, exposed as he was to so many perils. He never entered his tent, but lay down whole nights by the watch fires; this alone was enough to have killed him, the cold was so intense.

"The want of water distressed us much; at length we found a soldier's wife, who had courage enough to fetch us some from the river, an office nobody else would undertake, as the American shot at every person who approached it; but out of respect for her sex, they never molested *her*.

"I now occupied myself through the day in attending the wounded; I made them tea and coffee, and often shared my dinner with them for which they offered me a thousand expressions of gratitude. One day a Canadian officer came to our cellar, who had scarcely the power of holding himself upright, and we concluded he was dying for want of nourishment; I was happy in offering him my dinner, which strengthened him, and procured me his friendship. I now undertook the care of Major Bloomfield, another aid-de-camp of General Phillips; he had received a musket ball through both cheeks, which in its course had knocked out several of his teeth, and cut his tongue; he could hold nothing in his mouth, the matter which ran from his wound almost choked him, and he was not able to take any nourishment except a little soup, or something liquid. We had some Rhenish wine, and in the hope that the acidity of it would cleanse his wound, I gave him a bottle of it. He took a little now and then, and with such effect, that his cure soon followed; thus I added another to my stock of friends, and derived a satisfaction which in the midst of suffering, served to tranquilize me and diminish their acuteness.

"One day, General Phillips accompanied my husband, at the risk of their lives, on a visit to us. The General, after having witnessed our situation, said to him, 'I would not for ten thousand guineas come again to this place, my heart is almost broken.'

"In this horrid situation we remained six days; a cessation of hostilities was now spoken of, and eventually took place. A convention was afterwards agreed on; but one day a message was sent to my husband who had visited me, and was reposing in my bed, to attend, a council of war, where it was proposed to break the convention; but, to my great joy, the majority were for adhering to it. On the 16th, however, my husband had to repair to his post, and I to my cellar. This day fresh beef was served out to the officers, who till now had only had salt provisions, which was very bad for their wounds. The good woman who brought us water, made us an excellent soup of the meat, but I had lost my appetite, and took nothing but crusts of bread dipped in wine. The wounded officers, my unfortunate companions, cut off the best bit, and presented it to me on a plate. I declined eating anything, but they contended that it was necessary for me to take nourishment, and declared they would not touch a morsel till I afforded them the pleasure of seeing me partake. I could no longer withstand their pressing invitations, accompanied as they were by assurances of happiness they had in offering me the first good thing they had in their power, and I partook of a repast rendered palatable by the kindness and good will of my fellow-sufferers, forgetting for the moment the misery of our apartment, and the absence of almost every comfort.

"On the 17th of October, the convention was completed. General Burgoyne and the other generals waited on the American General Gates; the troops laid down their arms, and gave themselves up prisoners of war! And now the good woman who had supplied us with water at the hazard of her life, received the reward of her services; each of us threw a handful of money into her apron and she got altogether about twenty guineas. At such a moment as this, how susceptible is the heart, of feelings of gratitude!

"My husband sent a message to me, to come over to him with my children. I seated myself once more in my dear calash, and then rode through the American camp. As I passed on, I observed, and this was a great consolation to me, that no one eyed me with looks of resentment, but that they all greeted us, and even showed compassion in their countenances at the sight of a woman with small children. I was, I confess, afraid to go over to the enemy, as it was quite a new situation to me. When I drew near the tents, a handsome man approached and met me, took my children from the calash, and hugged and kissed them, which affected me almost to tears. 'You tremble,' said he, addressing himself to me, 'be not afraid.' 'No,' I answered, 'you seem so kind and tender to my children, it inspires me with courage.' He now led me to the tent of General Gates, where I found Generals Burgoyne and Phillips, who were on a friendly footing with the former. Burgoyne said to me, 'Never mind; your sorrows have now an end.' I answered him, 'that I should be reprehensible to have any cares, as he had none; and I was pleased to see him on such friendly footing with General Gates.' All the Generals remained to dine with General Gates.

"The same gentleman who received me so kindly, now came and said to me, "You will be very much embarrassed to eat with all these gentlemen; *come with your children to my tent, where I will prepare for you a frugal dinner, and give it with a free will.*' I said '*You are, certainly a husband and a father, you have shown me so much kindness.*' I now found that he was GENERAL SCHUYLER. He treated me with excellent smoked tongue, beefsteaks, potatoes, and good bread and butter! Never could I have wished to eat a better dinner; I was content; I saw all around me were so likewise; and, what was better than all, my husband was out of danger.

"When we had dined, he told me his residence was at Albany, and that General Burgoyne intended to honor him as his guest, and invited myself and children to do so likewise. I asked my husband how I should act; he told me to accept the invitation. As it was two days' journey there, he advised me to go to a place which was about three hour's ride distant. General Schuyler had the politeness to send with me a French officer, a very agreeable man, who commanded the reconnoitering party, of which I have before spoken; and when he had escorted me to the house where I was to remain, he turned back again.

"Some days after this we arrived at Albany, where we so often wished ourselves; but we did not enter it as we expected we should —victors! We were received by the good General Schuyler, his wife, and daughters, not as enemies, but kind friends; and they treated us with the most marked attention and politeness, as they did General Burgoyne, who had caused General Schuyler's beautifully finished house to be burnt. In fact, they behaved like persons of exalted minds, who determined to bury all reccollections of their own injuries in the contemplation of our misfortunes. General Burgoyne was struck with General Schuyler's generosity, and said to him, 'You show me great kindness, though I have done you much injury.' 'That was the fate of war;' replied the brave man, 'let us say no more about it.'"

LYDIA DARRAH.

THE following account of the signal service rendered to our cause by a heroine quakeress, Lydia Darrah, first appeared in the American Quarterly Review:

When the British army held possession of Philadelphia, General Harris' head-quarters were in Second street, the fourth door below Spruce, in a house which was before occupied by General Cadwallader. Directly opposite, resided William and Lydia Darrah, members of the Society of Friends. A superior officer of the British army, believed to be the Adjutant General, fixed upon one of their chambers, a back room, for private conference; and two of them frequently met there, with fire and candles, in close consultation. About the second of December, the Adjutant General told Lydia that they would be in the room at seven o'clock, and remain late; and that they wished the family to retire early to bed; adding, that when they were going away, they would call her to let them out, and extinguish their fire and candles She accordingly sent all the family to bed; but, as the officer had been so particular, her curiosity was excited. She took off her shoes, and put her ear to the key-hole of the conclave. She overheard an order read for all the British troops to march out, late in the evening of the fourth, and attack General Washington's army, then encamped at White Marsh. On hearing this, she returned to her chamber and laid herself down. Soon after, the officers knocked at her door, but she rose only at the third summons, having feigned to be asleep. Her mind was so much agitated that, from this moment, she could neither eat nor sleep; supposing it to be in her power to save the lives of thousands of her countrymen; but not knowing how she was to convey the necessary information to General Washington, nor daring to confide it even to her husband. The time left, was, however, short; she quickly determined to make her way, as soon as possible, to the American outposts. She informed her family, that, as they were in want of flour, she would go to Frankfort for some; her husband insisted that she should take with her the servant maid; but, to his surprise, she positively refused. She got access to General Howe, and solicited—what he readily granted,—a pass through the British troops on the lines. Leaving her bag at the mill, she hastened towards the American lines, and encountered on her way an American, Lieutenant Colonel Craig, of the light horse, who, with some of his men, was on the look-out for information. He knew her, and inquired whither she was going. She answered, in quest of her son, an officer in the American army; and prayed the Colonel to alight and walk with her. He did so, ordering his troops to keep in sight. To him she disclosed her momentous secret, after having obtained from him the most solemn promise never to betray her individually, since her life might be at stake, with the British. He conducted her to a house near at hand, directed a female in it to give her something to eat, and he speeded for head-quarters, where he brought General Washington acquainted with what he had heard. Washington made, of course, all preparation for baffling the meditated surprise. Lydia returned home with her flour; sat up alone to watch the movement of the British troops; heard their footsteps; but when they returned, in a few days after, did not dare to ask a question, though solicitous to learn the event. The next evening, the Adjutant General came in, and requested her to walk up to his room, as he wished to put some questions. She followed him in terror; and when he locked the door, and begged her, with an air of mystery to be seated, she was sure that she was either suspected, or had been betrayed. He inquired earnestly whether any of her family were up the last night he and the other officer met:—she told him that they all retired at eight o'clock. He observed—'I know *you* were asleep, for I knocked at your chamber door three times before you heard me; I am entirely at a loss to imagine who gave Washington information of our intended attack, unless the walls of the house could speak. When we arrived near White Marsh, we found all their cannon mounted, and the troop prepared to receive us; and we have marched back like a parcel of fools."

CAPTURE OF PRESIDENT DAGGETT.

On the occasion of the invasion of New Haven, the Rev. Dr Daggett, at that time president of Yale College, armed himself with a musket, and went out with his fellow citizens to oppos the enemy. He was wounded and taken prisoner. Whilst ir the hands of the British he was asked, whether if released, he would again take up arms against them?—to which he answered, "I rather believe I shall, if I get an opportunity." We subjoin an account of his captivity, as given by himself.

"An account of the cruelties and barbarities which I received from the British soldiers, after I had surrendered myself a prisoner into their hands. It is needless to relate all the leading circum stances which threw me in their way. It may be sufficient just to observe, that on Monday morning, the 5th inst., (July 1779,) the town of New Haven was justly alarmed, with very threatening appearances of a speedy invasion from the enemy. Numbers went out armed to oppose them; I among the rest, took the station assigned me, upon Milford Hill, but was soon directed to quit it, and retire further north, as the motions of the enemy required. Having gone as far as I supposed was sufficient, I turned down he hill to gain a little covert of bushes, which I had in my eye; but to my great surprise, I saw the enemy much nearer than I expected, their advanced guards being little more than twenty rods distant, plain, open ground between us. They instantly fired upon me, which they continued until I had run a dozen rods, discharging not less than fifteen or twenty balls at me alone; however, through the preserving providence of God, I escaped them all unhurt, and gained the little covert at which I aimed, which concealed me from their view, while I could plainly see them through the weeds and bushes, advancing towards me within about twelve rods. I singled out one of them, took aim, and fired upon him; I loaded my musket again, but determined not to discharge any more, and as I saw I could not escape from them, I determined to surrender myself a prisoner. I begged for quarter, and that they would spare my life. They drew near to me I think two only in number, one on my right hand, the other on my left, the fury of infernals glaring in their faces. They called me a damned old rebel, and swore they would kill me instantly. They demanded, what did you fire upon us for? I replied, because it is the exercise of war. Then one made a pass at me with his bayonet, as if he designed to thrust it through my body. With my hand I tossed it up from its direction, and sprang in so near to him that he could not hurt me with his bayonet. I still continued pleading and begging for my life, with the utmost importunity, using every argument in my power to mollify them, and induce them to desist from their murderous purposes. One of them gave me four gashes on my head with the edge of his bayonet, to the skull bone, which caused a plentiful effusion of blood. The other gave me three slight pricks with the point of his bayonet, on the trunk of my body, but they were no more than kin deep. But what is a thousand times worse than all that has been related, is the blows and bruises they gave me with the heavy barrels of their guns on my bowels, by which I was knocked down once, or more, and almost deprived of life; by which bruises, I have been almost confined to my bed ever since. These scenes might take up about two minutes of time. They seemed to desist a little from their design of murder, after which they stript me of my shoes and knee buckles, and also my stock buckle. Their avarice further led them to rob me of my pocket-handkerchief, and a little old tobacco box. They then bade me march towards the main body, which was about twelve rods distant; when some officers inquired of me who I was, I gave them my name, station and character, and begged their protection, that I might not be any more abused or hurt by the soldiers. They promised m their protection. But I was robbed of my shoes, and was com mitted to one of the most unfeeling savages that ever breathed They then drove me with the main body, a hasty march of five miles or more. I was insulted in the most shocking manner, by the ruffian soldiers, many of which came at me with fixed bayonets, and swore that they would kill me on the spot. They damned me, those that took me, because they spared my life. Thus, amidst a thousand insults, my infernal driver hastened me along faster than my strength would admit, in the extreme heat of the day, weakened as I was by my wounds, and the loss of blood, which at a moderate computation could not be less than one quart. And when I failed in some degree, through faintness, he would strike me on the back with a heavy walking staff, and kick me behind with his foot. At length, by the supporting power of God, I arrived at the green, in New Haven. But my life was almost spent, the world around me several times appearing as dark as midnight. I obtained leave of an officer to be carried into the widow Lyman's, and laid upon a bed, where I lay the rest of the day and succeeding night, in such acute and excruciating pain as I never felt before."

THE MURDER OF MR. AND MRS. CALDWELL.

THE Rev. James Caldwell, pastor of the First Presbyterian Church in Elizabethtown, N. J., acted as Chaplain of the American army while in New Jersey, and by his zealous patriotism, and patriotic appeals, often contributed to arouse the spirits of the soldiers, and to inspire them with a greater energy in the performance of their trying duties. He was very popular in the community, and received the unlimited confidence of Washington.

But his lofty patriotism, and unflinching zeal in the American cause, made him hated by the enemy, who sought every means to get him into their power, and a price was set upon his head. When preaching, he frequently was compelled to lay his loaded pistols by his side in the pulpit. At one time he resided in Springfield, but afterwards removed to "Connecticut Farms," about four miles from Elizabethtown. Here was enacted the first part of the tragedy we are about to relate.

A company of British troop from New York, under command of the Hessian General, Knyphausen, landed in Elizabethtown in June of 1780, and marching directly into the interior, proceeded to wreak their cruelty upon every living thing that fell in their way. Houses were fired, cattle destroyed, helpless people murdered, or left without shelter, clothing, or food. Mr. Caldwell heard of their approach, and immediately prepared to escape. He put his elder children in a wagon, and sent them on to some of his friends for protection. He then desired his wife, with the younger children, to take means of flight, but she announced her determination of remaining, as none would have cause to offer injury to her. Finding she would not yield to his persuasion, and believing it impossible that their resentment could extend to an unprotected mother, with her babe clasped to her heart, Mr. Caldwell resolved to leave them, and seek his own safety alone. He was mounted, and receiving the last assurance of her resolve to stay, when the gleam of arms announced the approach of the enemy, and he rode rapidly off.

Mrs. Caldwell having concealed what things were of value, took her infant in her arms, and retired to her chamber, the window of which commanded the road. Here, with her three little ones around, she awaited the approach of the enemy, feeling conscious that her unprotected state would secure respect and safety. One little girl was standing by the window watching the approach of the troops, when one of the soldiers left the road, and came to the window, which he had no sooner reached, than he placed the muzzle of his gun against it, and deliberately fired, when Mrs. Caldwell fell suddenly back, and almost instantly expired.

Not content with depriving her of life, the inhuman monsters wreaked their cruelty on her senseless body. Her clothes were nearly torn off, and her body removed to the road side, where it was subjected to every indignity, while the torch was applied to the dwelling, and then the work of destruction was done.

The effect of this terrible blow upon the husband can only be imagined. He was that morning standing upon the heights of Springfield, and by the aid of a spy-glass could see the smoke from the burning houses. "Thank God," he exclaimed, "the fire s not in the direction of my house." He was too soon to learn the sad mistake.

The royalists attempted to throw off the responsibility of this act, by asserting that Mrs. Caldwell was killed by a chance shot. But all the evidence goes to show that it was deliberately planned, and that the soldier by whose hand the bloody deed was committed, only acted in accordance with his orders. The fact that her body was allowed to be so rudely treated, while many of the officers felt their abhorrence for the deed, proves that although they felt respect for her remains, they knew the will of their superiors, and therefore dared not show it.

The following anecdote, connected with this invasion, shows pretty clearly who were the murderers of Mrs. Caldwell. The flames from the burning dwelling could be seen from "Liberty Hall," the residence of Gov. Livingston, who was at that time absent from home. Parties of soldiers were continually passing the house, but for some reason it was spared. But about midnight a party of soldiers, partially intoxicated, rushed into the house. The maid-servant—all the males in the establishment having taken refuge in the woods early in the day, to avoid being made prisoners—fastened herself in the kitchen; and the ladies, (Mrs. Livingston and her daughters) crowded together like frightened deer, locked themselves in another apartment. Their place of retreat was soon discovered by the ruffians; and afraid to exasperate them by refusing to come out, one of Governor Livingston's daughters opened the door. A drunken soldier seized her by the arm; she grasped the villain's collar, and, at the very moment, a flash of lightning illuminated the hall, and falling upon her white dress—he staggered back, exclaiming, with an oath, 'It's Mrs. Caldwell, that we killed to-day.' One of the party was at length recognized, and by his intervention, the house was finally cleared of the assailants."*

But the vengeance of Mr. Caldwell's enemies was not yet sa-

---

* Life of Livingston.

tiated; the tragedy so far was incomplete. It was on the 24th of November, 1781, that he himself fell beneath the ruthless murderer's hand, and the blow this time came from a source where he thought himself secure. On the day above mentioned, he went to Elizabethtown Point, for a Miss Murray, who had come from New York, under a flag of truce. After conducting her to his gig, he returned to the boat, to obtain a bundle which had been left behind. As he came on shore, the American sentinel challenged him, and demanded what "contraband goods" he had there. Mr. Caldwell stepped forward to tender the bundle to the proper officer, not wishing to enter into a dispute about it then, when the report of a musket was heard, and he fell dead, pierced by two balls. He had been shot by a man named Morgan, who had just been relieved from duty as a sentinel. He was arrested, tried, condemned, and was executed. There can be no doubt but that he was bribed to the deed by British gold, as there was no shadow of a cause to suppose that enmity existed between Mr. Caldwell and him.

Viewed from any point, these two murders were among the most atrocious acts perpetrated by the invaders of our country, and in a history full of atrocities, they will always rank as bloody fiendish and treacherous.

CAPTAIN CUNNINGHAM.

"At the beginning of the war of the revolution, Captain Cunningham enlisted in one of the minute companies, and continued in that service until Virginia armed a few fast sailing pilot boat schooners. Thus was the navy of that state commenced. It, however, varied materially; sometimes amounting to as many as fifty vessels, and occassionally to only one. Among them was the schooner Liberty, which was never captured, although several times sunk in the rivers to conceal her from the enemy. Captain Cunningham embarked and remained in the Liberty, as her first lieutenant, until the war assumed a more regular form. Captain Cunningham purchased a small schooner, and engaged in traffic to the West Indies. Sea officers were encouraged to engage in commerce as the only means of procuring the munitions of war.

"On these occasions he encountered great risk from the enemy's fleets. Once, in the month of June, he suddenly came upon an English frigate, off Cape Henry, in a dense fog. The English commander ordered him to strike his colors, and haul down his light sails, or he would sink him. By a judicious and skilful stratagem, he made the enemy believe he intended to surrender. He, therefore suspended his threatened firing. At the moment they discovered that Cunningham intended to escape, the jib-boom of the frigate caught in the topping-lift of the schooner's main-boom. Captain Cunningham sprang up to the stern, with a knife, to free his vessel. While in the act of cutting the rope, a British marine shot him through the arm. Nothing daunted, he deliberately effected his object, and amid a shower of grape, his vessel shot away from the frigate, and in a few moments was out of sight.

"Some time after, Captain Cunningham joined the army, on the south side of James river, and had the misfortune, while on a foraging expedition, to be taken by the enemy, and carried into Portsmouth. He had then been recently married.

"One day he said to an uncle of his, (also a prisoner) that he would see his wife the next evening, or perish in the attempt. 'My dear Will, are you mad?' was the reply.

"The prison in which he was confined, was a large sugar-house, at the extreme end of the town. enclosed by a strong stockade fence. At sunset every evening, the guard, composed of forty or fifty men, were relieved by fresh troops, and on their arrival, the two guards, with their officers, were paraded in front of the prison, on each side of the pathway to the gate. At this hour, the ceremony observed on the occasion was in progress; the relieved guard had stacked their arms, and were looking at their baggage; the fresh guard were relieving sentinels, and, in a degree, at their ease. This was the time selected by Captain Cunningham. The sentinel had just begun to pace his ground, and awful, indeed, was the moment. Captain Cunningham was justly a great favorite with the prisoners, who all, in silent terror, expected to see their beloved companion pinned to the earth by many bayonets, for expostulation had been exhausted. '*My wife, or death!*' was his watchword.

"The sentinel's motions had been sagaciously calculated upon, and as he turned from the prison, Captain Cunningham darted out, and butted him over at his full length, and ran past him through the gate. It was now nearly dark. All was uproar and confusion. Cunningham soon reached a marsh near the house, and was nowhere to be found. Volley after volley was fired after him, and some of the balls whistled over his head. Ere long, he arrived at the southern branch of Elizabeth River, which he swam over a little below the navy yard at Gosport, and finally reached the place whither his wife had fled.

Lieut. Church, who had served as Captain Cunningham's first lieutenant, was determined that his master should not alone encounter the danger of an escape. He, therefore, followed him and strange as it may appear, he was never heard of, or accounted for."

ADVENTURE OF A SOLDIER.

"PETER FRANCISCO, of Virginia, early enlisted in the continental service, and was a man of wonderful personal prowess. He was over six feet in height, and his weight was two hundred and sixty pounds. He usually carried a sword, having a blade five feet in length and of great weight, and this he wielded with so much skill and force, that every swordsman who came in contact with him paid the forfeit of his life. Such was his personal strength, that he could easily shoulder a cannon weighing 1100 pounds. This wonderful strength induced in him so much confidence, that he was utterly fearless, and never was daunted at any danger, no matter how formidable. The following anecdote is related of him :—

"While the British army was spreading havoc and desolation all around them, by their plunderings and burnings in Virginia, in 1781, Francisco had been reconnoitering, and while stopping at a house of Mr. Wand, nine of Tarleton's cavalry came up, with three negroes, and told him he was their prisoner. Seeing he was overpowered by numbers, he made no resistance. Believing him to be very peacable, they all went into the house, leaving him and the paymaster together.

"'Give up instantly all that you possess of value,' said the latter 'or prepare to die.'

"'I have nothing to give up,' said Francisco, 'so use your pleasure.' 'Deliver instantly,' rejoined the soldet, 'those massy silver buckles which you wear in your shoes.'

"'They were a present from a valued friend,' replied Francisco, 'and it would grieve me to part with them. Give them into your hands I never will. You have the power; take them, if you think fit.' The soldier put his sabre under his arm, and bent down to take them. Francisco, finding so favorable an opportunity to recover his liberty, stepped one pace in his rear, drew the sword from under the arm of his enemy, and instantly gave him a blow across the scull.

"'My enemy,' observed Francisco, 'was brave, and though severely wounded, drew a pistol, and in the same moment that he pulled the trigger, I cut his hand nearly off. The bullet grazed my side. Ben Wand, (the man of the house) very ungenerously brought out a musket, and gave it to one of the British soldiers, and told him to make use of that. He mounted the only horse he could get, and presented it at my breast. It missed fire. I rushed on the muzzle of the gun. A desperate struggle ensued. I disarmed and wounded him. Tarleton's troop of *four hundred men* were in sight. All was hurry and confusion, which I increased by repeatedly hallooing, as loud as I could, '*come on, my brave boys; now's your time; we will soon despatch these few, and then attack the main body!*' The wounded man flew to the troop; the others were panic-struck and fled. I seized Wand.

and would have despatched him, but the poor wretch begged for his life, he was not only an object of my contempt, but pity. The eight horses that were left behind, I gave him to conceal for me. Discovering Tarleton had despatched ten more in pursuit of me, I made off. I eluded their vigilance. They stopped to refresh themselves, I, like an old fox, doubled and fell on their rear."

He succeeded in escaping from his pursuers. He was engaged in numerous encounters with the enemy, in all of which he displayed the same fearlessness and great strength.

ADVENTURES OF GENERAL PUTNAM.

At one time, when General Putnam had command of the army in New York, he was visiting his out posts at West Greenwich, when Gov. Tryon, with a corps of fifteen hundred men, was on a march against it. Putnam had with him only one hundred and fifty men, with two pieces of artillery; with them he took his station on the brow of a steep declivity, near the meeting house. The road turned to the north, just before it reached the edge of the steep; after proceeding in this direction for a considerable distance, it inclined to the south, rendering the descent gradually and tolerably safe. As the British advanced, they were received with a sharp fire from the artillery; but perceiving the dragoons about to charge, Putnam ordered his men to retire to a swamp, naccessible to cavalry while he himself dashed directly down the precipice, in a spot where one hundred stone steps had been cut out in the solid rock, for the accommodation of foot passengers.

His pursuers who were close upon him, paused with astonishment as they reached the edge, and saw him accomplish his perilous descent, and not one of them daring to follow, they discharged their pistols after him, one bullet of which passed through his hat, This wonderful feat has done more for the name of Putnam, than almost any other one act. The declivity, from this circumstance has since borne the name of " Putnam's Hill."

Somewhere, near the time the above exploit took place, the following adventure was performed by General Putnam: The stronghold of Horse Neck, was in the possession of the British, and Putnam with a few followers, were lurking in its vicinity, bent on driving them from the place. Tired of lying in ambush, the men became impatient, and importuned the general with questions, as to when they were going to have a 'bout with the foe. One morning he made a speech, something to the following effect, which convinced them that something was in the wind:—

"Fellows! you've been idle too long, and so have I. I'm going to Bush's at Horse Neck, in an hour, with an ox-team, and a load of corn. If I come back, I will let you know the particulars; if I should not, let them have it!"

"Within an hour he was mounted in his ox-cart, dressed as one of the commonest Yankee farmers, and was soon at the Bush's tavern, which was in possession of the British troops. No sooner did the officers espy him, than they began to question him as to his whereabouts, and finding him a complete simpleton, (as they thought) they began to quiz him, and threatened to seize his corn and fodder.

"How much do you ask for your whole concern?" asked they.

"In marcy sake, gentlemen," replied the mock clod-hopper, with the most deplorable look of entreaty, " only let me off, and you shall have my bull team and load for nothing; and if that wont dew, I'll give you my word, I'll return to morrow, and pay you heartily for your kindness and condescension."

"Well," said they, "we'll take you at your word, leave the team and provender with us, and we wont require any bail for your appearance.'

Putnam gave up the team, and sauntered about an hour or so gaining all the information that he wished; he then returned to his men, and told them of the foe, and his plan of attack.

The morning came, and with it sallied out the gallant band. The British were handled with rough hands, and when they surrendered to General Putnam, the clod-hopper sarcastically remarked, "Gentlemen, I have only kept my word. I told you I would call, and pay you for your kindness and condescension."

INCIDENTS AT THE BATTLE OF ORISKANY.

In the midst of the battle, while it raged hottest, and when the combatants were engaged hand to hand, in a conflict more ferocious and bloody, perhaps, than any other of the revolutionary struggle, a welcome sound burst upon the provincials, which was greeted by hearty cheers of welcome from them, while it dismayed the enemy. The sound that broke upon those engaged in their bloody work, was that of firing in the direction of Fort Stanwix which was hailed as a reinforcement of American troops. But this circumstance had well nigh proved fatal. Col. Butler of the English troops, availing himself of a suggestion, despatched a company of his troop in the disguise of American soldiers, with directions to approach the battle-field, from the direction of the fort, in such a manner so as to deceive the Americans into the belief that they were the earnestly wished for reinforcement. But as they approached, the quick eye of Captain Gardinier, detected the cheat, and to the exclamations of those around him, that they were friends, he replied, "Not so; they are enemies! don't you see their green coats." The disguised troops continued to advance until they were hailed by Gardinier, "at which moment one of his own soldiers, observing an acquaintance, and supposing him a friend, ran to meet him, and presented his hand. It was grasped but with no friendly grip, as the credulous fellow was dragged into the opposing line, and told that he was a prisoner, He did not yield without a struggle; during which Gardinier, watching the action and the result, sprang forward, and with a blow from his spear, levelled the captor to the dust, and liberated his man. Others of the foe instantly set upon him, of whom he slew the second, and wounded a third. Three of the disguised enemy now sprang upon him, and one of his spurs becoming entangled in their clothes, he was thrown to the ground. Still contending, however, with almost super-human strength, both of his thighs were transfixed to the earth by the bayonets of two of his assailants, while the third presented a bayonet to his breast, as if to thrust him through. Seizing this bayonet with his left hand, by a sudden wrench he brought its owner down upon himself, where he held him as a shield against the arms of the others until one of his own men, observing the struggle, flew to his rescue. As the assailants turned upon their new adversary, Gardinier rose upon his seat; and although his hand was severely lacerated by grasping the bayonet which had been drawn through it, he seized his spear, lying by his side, and quick as lightning planted it to the barb in the side of the assailant, with whom he had been clenched. The man fell and expired. While engaged in the struggle, some of his own men called out to Gardinier—for God's sake, Captain, you are killing your own men !' He replied—' they are not our men—they are the enemy—fire away !' A deadly fire from the provincials answered, and then the parties once more rushed with bayonet and spear, grappling and fighting with terrible fury; while the shattering of shafts and the clashing of steel, mingled with every dread sound of war and death, and the savage yells, more hideous than all, presented a scene which can be more easily imagined than described. The unparalleled fortitude and bravery of Captain Gardinier, inspired fresh spirit into his men, some of whom enacted wonders of valor likewise.

"It happened during the melee, in which the contending parties were mingled in great confusion, that three of Johnson's Greens' rushed within the circle of the provincials, and attempted to make prisoner of a Captain Dilenback. This officer had declared he would never be taken alive, and he was not. One of his three assailants seized his gun, but he suddenly wrenched it from him, and felled him with the butt. He shot the second dead, and thrust the third through with his bayonet. But in the moment of his triumph, at an exploit of which the mighty Hector, or either of the sons of Zerniah might have been proud, a ball laid this brave man low in the dust."

General Herkimer, who commanded the American forces, in the early part of the contest, had been struck by a ball, which shattered his leg, at the same moment killing his horse. Undaunted by this accident, and indifferent to the severity of the pain, the brave old general continued in the battle, seated on his saddle which was placed on a little hillock by a tree, against which he leaned for support, and gave his orders with undisturbed coolness, while his men fell in scores around him, and the exposure of his situation made him a mark for the enemy. Amid the clashing of weapons, the report of artillery, and the yells of the combatants, all mingled in one wild, fearful outburst, as if man had been turned into a fiend, and a love of blood had assumed the mastery of every other passion, General Herkimer, deliberately took his pipe from his pocket, lit it, and cooly continued to smoke, amid all the horrors that surrounded him. It is said, that old Blucher, in the battle of Leipsic, in a similar manner, sitting upon a hillock, smoked and gave his orders; but Blucher was not wounded. General Herkimer's leg was amputated, but it was done so unskillfully, that the flow of blood could not be stopped, and the consequence was fatal. During the operation, he smoked, and chatted in excellent spirits; and when his departure grew nigh, he called for a bible, and read aloud until his fading strength compelled him to desist.

ADVENTURE OF COL. COCHRAN.

"COLONEL COCHRAN having been sent to Canada as a spy, hi mission was suspected, and a large bounty offered for his head While there he was taken sick, and hearing that he was suspect ed, concealed himself for a few days in a brush heap, unable to make his escape, or even walk. Having suffered much from his sickness and want of nourishment, and having discoveied a log cabin at a considerable distance from the spot where he was concealed, the only one in sight, he crept to it on his hands and knees, for the purpose of soliciting assistance. On his approach to the rear of the cabin, he heard three men in earnest conversation, and it happened that he was the subject of their discourse. Having heard of the heavy bounty offered for the Colonel, and having seen a man in the vicinity a few days before, answering the description of him, they were forming their plans, and expressing their determination to find his whereabouts, and take him for the sake of the bounty. One of the men was the owner of the cabin. His wife was also present; and the others were his brother and brother-in-law. Soon after this conversation, the three men started in pursuit. He crept into the cabin, and frankly told the woman, who seemed favorably impressed towards him on account of his almost helpless condition, that he had overheard the conversation; that he was the man of whom they were in search; and that he should throw himself entirely upon her mercy, trusting to her fidelity for protection. This she very kindly promised him, to the utmost of her ability. Having received some restoratives, which seemed to give relief, and taken suitable nourishment, he lay down on a bed in the room, for the purpose of taking some repose. After the men had been absent about three hours, they returned; when she concealed him in a closet by the side of the fire-place, taking good care, while the men were in the house, to keep near it, that if anything should be wanted from within, she might be ready to get it herself. During the time the men were in the house, they expressed much confidence in the belief that the Colonel was concealed somewhere in the vicinity, and named many places in which they intended to look for him. Having taken some food, and otherwise prepared themselves, the men departed to renew their search.

"Soon after they retired, the woman, not considering the Colonel's present situation safe, proposed that he should conceal himself at some distance from the cabin, where she might secretly bring him food, and render such other assistance as he needed. She accordingly directed him to take post on a certain hill, about half a mile distant, where he might be able to discover any person's approach, and to flee, if he was able, should it become necessary. He manifested an inclination to resume his former position in the brush heap, which was in the midst of a patch of ground that had been cut over for a fallow; but she told him her husband intended to burn it the next day, and in that case he would be certainly discovered, or perish in the conflagration. He then submitted entirely to her directions, and crept along to the hill in the best way he could. He remained some time in this place of concealment, undiscovered by any one except this faithful Rahab of the forest, who, like the good Samaritan, poured in the oil and wine, until his strength was in a measure restored, and he was enabled to return to his country and his home.

"Some years after the close of the war, and while the Colonel lived at Ticonderoga, he accidentally met with this kind-hearted woman, and rewarded her handsomely for her fidelity."

ANECDOTES OF SERGEANT McDONALD.

SERGEANT McDONALD was another of those daring spirits whose exploits have been so intimately connected with the name of Marion. He was distinguished for his wonderful coolness and daring, for a keen sagacity, and for great strength and agility.

In one of Marion's numerous encounters with the enemy, when commanded by Major Gainey, he was victorious, and his enemies put to flight. "Great expectations," says Simms, "were formed of Gainey's ability to cope with Marion. On this occasion, though he made his escape, his mode of doing so was characterized by a peculiar circumstance, which rendered it particularly amusing to one side, and annoying to the other. He was singled out in the chase by McDonald, who was admirably mounted. Gainey was fortunate in being well mounted, also. McDonald, regarding but the one enemy, passed all others. He himself said that he could have slain several in the chase. But he wished for no meaner object than their leader. One man alone, who threw himself in the way of pursuit, became its victim. Him he shot down, and, as they went at full speed down the Black river road, at the corner of Richmond fence, the sergeant had gained so far upon his enemy, as to be able to plunge his bayonet into his back. The steel separated from his gun, and, with no time to extricate it, Gainey rushed into Georgetown, with the weapon still conspicuously showing how close and eager had been the chase, and how narrow the escape. The wound was not fatal."

In Col. Watson's expedition against Marion, while pressing hard upon the partisan chief, among the captures of the British commander, was the entire wardrobe of McDonald. The sergeant felt that it was a point of honor that he should recover his clothes. He despatched a messenger, with a flag, to Watson, demanding his property, and at the same time gravely assuring him that if his clothes were not returned, he would kill eight of his men. Watson, irritated by a late defeat, was furious at the absurd and audacious message. He contemptuously ordered the messenger to return; but some of his officers, aware of the character of McDonald, urged that the clothes might be returned to the partisan, as he would be sure to keep his word if they were not. Watson yielded, and when the messenger returned to McDonald, he said, "You may now tell Col. Watson that I will kill but *four* of his men."

A ROMANTIC INCIDENT.

In the British station at Georgetown, South Carolina, was an English adjutant, by the name of Crookshanks—not a poetical name certainly, but, as the reader will see, his name did not prevent him from being placed in a very romantic situation, and which only ought to have happened a few centuries ago, to have secured for all the parties concerned, a lasting fame in poetry, and made them the envied of all romance worshippers.

There lived in Georgetown, a fair daughter of a rebel publican, whose bright eye proved a strong attraction to the English officers, who crowded her father's inn, and rivalled each other in their efforts to win the smiles of the rebel maid. But to one alone did she incline, and it soon became noted how the happy adjutant frequented the presence of his mistress, and with what delight he sought out her society. Love sprang up between them, and after time they became solemnly affianced. But their future was unpromising; the war gave no promise of a rapid end, and their opposition in principles, which the prejudices of their education could not remove, threatened them continually with a painful separation. In the peaceful enjoyment, however, of the present, they drowned all dread of evil in the future.

One night the adjutant, and several of his comrades slept under the rebel inn keeper's roof. It chanced to be the very occasion when Georgetown was surprised by the whigs. At early morn the young lady was suddenly awakened by the reports of muskets, the clashing of swords, and the shouts of combatants, among which she recognized her lover's voice. In the greatest alarm, she sprang from her bed, and rushed, half dressed, out upon the piazza, where, to her terror, she saw her lover surrounded by a body of her countrymen, whose swords already hung suspended above his head, and threatening him with instant destruction. With a quick cry she sprang forward, rushed before the swords of his assailants, and threw herself upon his neck, exclaiming, "O save! save Major Crookshanks!" The sudden appearance of such a protector, coupled with admiration for her heroism, completely disarmed his opponents. He was taken prisoner, but released on his parole, and suffered to remain with his betrothed. The possession of so brave and true-hearted a woman, and the remembrance of this signal deliverance, no doubt, contributed in after years to the worthy adjutant's happiness.

HEROISM OF A YOUNG GIRL.

Mr. Robert Gibbes, a gentleman earnestly devoted to the patriotic cause, was the owner of a plantation on the Stono, a few miles from Charleston, on which, on a certain occasion, a Hessian battalion encamped, compelling the family to surrender to their use the lower part of the mansion, and to confine themselves in the upper story. While here on one dark and stormy evening, two gallies appeared, ascending the river, which forthwith began a most destructive fire upon the Hessian encampment. The house ppeared particularly exposed, although the vessels had been commanded to avoid firing upon it, and to confine their attack to the enemy's encampment. Of this Mr. Gibbes was not aware, and with the permission of the English commander, he set out, although suffering acutely from an infirmity, and with his numerous family, hastened to the protection of a neighboring planta tion. The balls were falling thick and fast, sometimes scattering dirt and sand over the party, while their loud whizzing, mingled with the fury of the distant affray, rendered the scene one of danger and terror. But scarcely had they proceeded so far as to bo out of danger from the balls, when to their unutterable agony they discovered, that in the confusion and hurry of departure, an infant had been left behind. To leave the child alone in his danger was impossible, and to return for him was an attempt of imminent peril. Mr. Gibbes was suffering under an infirmity that made his movements exceedingly slow and painful, and therefore it was impracticable for him to return. The frightened and chattering servants, stood trembling around, looking from one to the other in bewildering despair. Of all the rest of the party, saving Mrs. Gibbes, who was severely indisposed, none were above the age of childhood. While thus undecided, Miss Mary Ann Gibbes, but thirteen years of age, sprang forward and heroically offered to go for the lad, who was a son of Mrs. Fenwick, Mrs Gibbes' sister-in-law. The night was dark and stormy, the distance considerable, and the whole space swept by the cannon of the assailant. But without fear she retraced the way, and reached the house without injury, where the scene was one of unmingled terror. Undismayed by the thundering of the cannon, the crashing of the balls, the shrieks, shouts and imprecations of the combatants, she sprang to the door with the intention of entering when she was brutally refused by the sentinel. But tears, entreaties, and the natural eloquence prompted by her heroism, an the high purpose on which she was bent, overcame his opposition, and she was permitted to enter. With rapid steps she ascended to the third story, and finding the child there in safety she clasped it to her bosom, and hastened to overtake her retreating family, her course, as before, full of danger, and often the ploughing balls would scatter clouds of dust over her person. Uninjured, her perilous journey was performed, and when she reached her friends, she was welcomed by shouts of enthusiasm and admiration. This intrepid action, worthy of an adult, and all glorious in a child, borrows a fair share of romance by the reflection that the child thus saved, afterwards became Lieutenant Colonel Fenwick, so highly distinguished by his services in the last war with Great Britain.

A SPY IN BURGOYNE'S CAMP.

CHRISTOPHER FISHER, was selected by General Gates, to go into Burgoyne's army as a spy, whose mission was to circulate letter among the Hessian soldiers, to induce them to desert, and to bring on an engagement in such a manner as Gates desired. Fisher' mode of proceeding was related by himself, to an American officer, by whom it was communicated to the author of the "History of Schoharie County." Fisher stated, that on the day appointed, he approached the enemy's picket, with a sheep upon his back which had been killed for the occasion. Upon being hailed by the guard, and demanded his business, Fisher replied, " that the Yankees had destroyed all his property but one sheep, which he had killed, and was then taking to his freinds." Upon this report, he was delivered over by the sentinel into the keeping of an officer. When asked what proof he could give, that he was not deceiving, Fisher replied that, " the rebel's are preparing to give you battle, and if you will go with me, I will convince you of it's truth." The officer accompanied Fisher to a certain place in view, of which was a wood. Here had been stationed, agreeable to the order of Gates, a company of Morgan's riflemen, who were to exhibit themselves in a stealthy manner. The riflemen wore frocks, and were easily distinguished. "There—there," says Fisher, "don't you see them devils of Morgan's dodging about among the trees ?" The movements of the American riflemen, were indeed visible enough to the English officer. When urged to enlist in the British service, Fisher pleaded an aversion to a war, and declared it necessary to return home to protect his family against the rebels. He was allowed to depart for the army on his pleasure, and soon embraced an opportunity. A company of British troops was sent to dislodge the riflemen, which brought on a general engagement, and thus the spy succeeded to the wishes of Gates. Another object of Fisher's mission was also effected. The letters circulated among the Hessians, had a good effect, and many of them deserted from the British army, either ntering the American service, or settling down as good citizens

CAPTURE OF A TORY.

George Cuck, a notorious tory, who was engaged with the enemy at Oriskany, and in their attack upon Cherry Valley, entered the valley of the Mohawk, in the spring of 1779, to secur the scalps of Captain James Gardinier, and Lieut. Quackenboss, two efficient whigs, for which the enemy had offered a large bounty. He was concealed in the house of one Van Zuyler, a tory friend, who lived in the town of Glen. This Van Zuyler had three daughters, of whom certain whigs became enamoured. One of these, James Cromwell, on one occasion, went over to pay his devotion to the charms of his Dulcinea, and accompanied her to the sugar bush, to assist her in the annual labor of boiling the sap of the maple for sugar. While here a mutual interchange of confidence took place, and among other things, the young lady confided to her lover, the secret, that the tory Cuck, was concealed in her father's house, and was always secreted under the floor when there were any visitors. Cromwell received this information with astonishment, and in a very little while made an excuse for departing. He hurried to Captain Gardinier and communicated this intelligence. That very night a dozen of whigs were assembled, and the charge of capturing the tory entrusted to Lieut. Quackenboss. As Cuck was a desperado, and a terror to the whole neighborhood, Quackenboss was instructed to capture or kill him at all hazards.

The party set forward with alacrity. When they were within a quarter of a mile of the house, they halted, and Quackenboss in a brief and spirited speech, informed them of the object of the expedition, and he concluded by stating, that as Cuck was a bold and desperate fellow, and doubtless well armed, some of them would probably fall beneath his hand. He, therefore, only wanted volunteers to accompany him, and all who did not wish to engage in so desperate and enterprise were at liberty to return. The whole party without exception, declared their readiness to accompany their leader. The plan for proceeding was now determined on. It was agreed the party should separate and approach the house in different directions, so as not to excite suspicion. Quackenboss and three others approached the house from the front, and as they did so, they were greeted with the yelping of the watch-dog, which caused the opening of a little slide for observation, by a member of the family; but seeing only four persons, the inmates supposed they were sugar makers. On reaching the door, and finding it fastened, the soldiers burst it open, and rushed into the house, much to the surprise and confusion of the family. "What do you want here?" demanded Van Zuyler. "The tory George Cuck," was the reply. Van Zuyler said he was not in the house, but the assailants proceeded to the search. The other parties had now entered. There was a dark stairway leading to an upper room in which it was thought the object of their search might be concealed. As one of the party was about ascending the stairs, Quackenboss drew a large chest from the wall, when suddenly out sprang Cuck, from a hole in the floor, discharging a pistol at the party, but at the same moment a bullet from the wary lieutenant entered his head, and he pitched forward upon the floor. The suddenness of his appearance had completely paralised most of the party, and the one who was ascending the stairs, was so startled by the sudden and rapid firing, that he came near tumbling back to the ground. Cuck was not yet dead, and one of the party placed the muzzle of his gun to his head, and blew his brains out. Thus fell the man who had imbrued his hands in the blood of his neighbors and countrymen. Had not the party divided into separate squads and obtained entrance into the house before their object was known, his capture would doubtless have been only obtained at a great loss, for he was thoroughly prepared for a desperate resistance. As it was the rapidity only with which the work was done saved many valuable lives.*

CAPTAIN HUDDY.

Among those whose active zeal, and daring deeds made them objects of terror to the enemy, was Captain Joshua Huddy, who figured conspicuously in various encounters in Monmouth county, and other parts of New Jersey. His dwelling was situated at Colt's Neck, about five miles from Freehold. Here in the summer of 1780, he was attacked by a party of about sixty refugees commanded by one Tye, or Col. Tye as he was commonly called, who was a mulatto, and a daring fellow. He usually commanded a mongrel crew of negroes and tories, and was much feared through that section of the country. He is represented to have been a brave and an honorable man, and was far more respected as an enemy, than many of his brethren of a fairer complexion. On the occasion of this attack, Huddy had no other assistance but a young servant girl, but with his weak aid, he managed to defend the house for some length of time against the assailants.

---

* "History of Schoharie County.

Several muskets had fortunately been left in the house by the guard, generally stationed there, but at this time absent. These the girl loaded, while Huddy, by appearing at different windows, and discharging them, gave the impression that there were many defenders. He wounded several, and while Tye, their leader, was setting fire to the house, he shot him in the neck. Tye afterwards died of lockjaw occasioned by this wound. The flames now began to increase so rapidly, that all hopes of maintaining the building against the foes were at an end, and Huddy agreed to surrender, provided they would extinguish the fire.

When the enemy entered the building, they were much exasperated at the feebleness of its defenders, and were only restrained by their leader from butchering them on the spot. The militia now collecting, they were obliged to retreat, carrying Huddy with them. Their boats were stationed near Black Point, between Shrewsbury and Nivisink rivers, which they reached with all possible speed. As they pushed off from the shore, Huddy jumped overboard, and was shot in the thigh, as was supposed by the militia, then in close pursuit. He held up one of his hands toward them, exclaiming, "*I am Huddy! I am Huddy!*" swam to the shore, and escaped.

In March, 1782, about two years after the above incident, Huddy commanded a block house at Tom's river, which was attacked by a party of refugees from New York, and taken, after the ammunition was expended, and no alternative but surrender left. After the little brave garrison was in the power of the enemy, they deliberately murdered five men, even while they were asking for quarters. The prisoners were carried to New York, from which place Huddy was taken on board of a guard ship, heavily ironed, and thrown into the hold of the vessel.

While confined, he was informed by one of the refugees that he was to be hanged, " for he had taken a certain Phillip White, a refugee in Monmouth Co., cut off both his arms, broke his legs, pulled out one of his eyes, damned him, and then bid him run." He answered, " it is impossible I could have taken Phillip White I being a prisoner in New York at the time, closely confined, and for many days before he was made prisoner." Some of his comrades confirmed this statement. Notwithstanding this, four days after (April 12th) he was dragged from his prison, and conveyed by Captain Lippencott, commanding a company of sixteen refugees, to Gravelly Point, on the sea shore, at the foot of Neversink hills, when he was deliberately and barbarously executed. He made his will beneath the gallows with quiet composure, then mounted the barrel, and met his fate with an admirable and undisturbed firmness.

For this deliberate murder, Washington resolved upon retaliation, and a correspondence to this effect was opened with Sir Henry Clinton. Capt. Lippencott was court-martialed, but was acquitted, as it appeared that he acted under orders. The speedy termination of the war, prevented Washington's plan of retaliation from being carried out.

COLONEL FISHER.

A PARTY of Indians, some twenty in number, attacked, on on of their incursions into the Mohawk Valley, the homestead of Col. Fisher. They attempted to gain admittance into the house by cutting in the door, but being fired upon from a window, they retreated around the corner of the house, where they were less exposed, and were soon after joined by the main body of the enemy, some three hundred in number. An entrance was soon effected, but Col. Fisher and his brothers still defended the house, and a melee followed on the stairway. On their attempting to ascend, several balls were fired up through the floor, but without effect. At this period the sisters escaped from the cellar kitchen and fled to the woods. Mrs. Fisher in attempting to follow them, was struck down by a blow from the butt of a musket. The ammunition of the brothers was now exhausted, and their castle no longer tenable. Harman Fisher jumped from a back window, with the hope of escaping by flight, but just as he was about leaping a garden fence, the fatal bullet overtook him, and in a moment more the tomahawk had finished the work, and his scalp was seized upon as a trophy. As the enemy ascended the stairs, Col. Fisher discharged a pistol he held in his hand, and calling for quarters, threw it behind him, in token of submission. An Indian ran up, and struck him down with a tomahawk. He fell upon his face, and the Indian after scalping him, inflicted with his knife a gash in the back of the neck, and then turned him over with the intention of cutting his throat, but his cravat prevented it, the knife only entering just through the skin. His brother, Capt. Fisher, as the enemy ascended the stairs retreated to one corner of the room, but an Indian hurled a tomahawk at him, which brought him down, and he was then killed and scalped. The house was then plundered and fired, and the savages departed. In a short time the consciousness of Col Fisher returned. He soon discovered the dead body of his brother and also that the house was on fire. With great difficulty he succeeded in dragging his brother's body from the building. At the door he found his mother, faint from the blow dealt on her head, and too weak to render him any assistance. With almost incredible exertions, weak as he was from his numerous wounds, he succeeded in getting the body and his mother from the building, and securing a bed, he dragged it from the flames to a little distance from the house, and threw himself upon it in an utter state of exhaustion. A negro slave belonging to one of the neighbors, soon after arrived at the spot. He inquired of the Colonel what he should do for him. Fisher, too weak to speak, signified by signs his desire for water. Tom, for that was the negro's name, hastened to procure water for the wounded man, and while engaged in this act of kindness, a tory neighbor approaching, was applied to for assistance, but who only replied, "let the cursed rebel die." As soon as the Colonel could speak, he directed Tom to harness a span of colts then in pasture, which, from the fogginess of the morning, had escaped the notice of the enemy. Tom harnessed them to a wagon, in which the bodies of the murdered brothers, and the Colonel and his mother were placed, and they were driven to a place of safety. Singular to state, the severe wounds of Col. Fisher all healed, and he lived until 1809, when he died of a complaint in the head, caused, no doubt, by the loss of his scalp.

AN ESCAPE FROM THE PRISON SHIP.

I was one of eight hundred and fifty souls confined in th Jersey, in the summer of '81, and witnessed several daring attempts to escape. They generally ended tragically. They wer always undertaken in the night, after wrenching or filing the bar off the port-holes. Having been on board several weeks, and goaded to death in various ways, four of us concluded to run the hazard. We set to work and got the bars off, and waited impatiently for a dark night; we lay in front of Mr. Remsen's door inside of the pier head, and not more than twenty yards distant. There were two guard sloops, one on our bow and the other off our quarter, a short distance from us. The dark night came—the first two were lowered quietly into the water—the third made some rumbling. I was the fourth that descended, but had not struck off from the vessel before the guards were alarmed, and fired upon us. The alarm became general, and I was immediately hauled on board. They manned their boats, and with their lights and implements of death, were quick in pursuit of the unfortunates, cursing and swearing, and bellowing and firing. It was awful to witness this scene of blood. It lasted about one hour—all on board trembling for our shipmates. These desperadoes returned to their different vessels rejoicing that they killed hree d——d rebels.

"About three years after this I saw a gentleman in John street, near Nassau, who accosted me thus:—'Manley, how do you do?' I could not recollect him. 'Is it possible you do not know me? recollect the old Jersey,' and he opened his vest and bared his breast I immediately said to him, 'You are James M'Clean.'

I am,' he replied. We both stepped into Marrener's public house, at the corner, and he related his marvelous escape to me.

"'They pursued me—I frequently dived to evade them, and when I came up, they fired on me. I caught my breath, and immediately dove again, and held my breath, till I crawled along the mud. They no doubt thought they killed me. I, however, with much exertion, though weak and wounded, made out to reach the shore, and got into a barn, not far from the ship, a little north from Mr. Remsen's house. The farmer, the next morning, came into his barn—saw me lying on the floor, and ran out in a fright. I begged him to come to me, and he did. I gave an account of myself—where I was from—how I was pursued, with several others. He saw my wounds; took pity on me; sent for his wife, and bound up my wounds, and kept me in the barn till nightfall—took me into his house—nursed me secretly, and then furnished me with clothing, &c.; and when I was restored, he took me with him, into his market boat, to this city, and went with me to the west part of the city—procured me a passage over to Bergen, and I landed somewhere in Communipaw. Some friends helped me across Newark bay, and then I worked my way, until I reached Baltimore, to the great joy of all my friends.'"*

---

* Revolutionary Incidents of Long Island.

A DARING YOUTH.

The annexed incident which occured in Freehold, N. J., evinces an act of bravery in a mere youth, that renders it worthy of record.

"On a fine morning in May, 1780, as the family of Mr. David Firman, sheriff of the county, were at breakfast, a soldier almost out of breath suddenly burst into the room, and stated, that as he and another soldier were conducting to the court-house two men, taken up on suspicion at Colt's Neck, they had knocked down his comrade, seized his musket, and escaped. The sheriff, on hearing this relation, immediately mounted his horse, and galloped to the court-house to alarm the guard. His son Tunis, a lad of about seventeen, and small of his age, seized a musket, loaded only with small shot to kill blackbirds in the cornfields, and putting on a cartridge-box, despatched his brother Samuel up stairs for the bayonet, and then, without waiting for it, hurried off alone in the pursuit.

"After running in a westerly direction about a mile, he discovered the men sitting on a fence, who, on perceiving him, ran into a swamp. As the morning was warm, he hastily pulled off his coat and shoes, and darted in after them, keeping close upon them for over a mile, when they got out of the swamp, and each climbed into separate trees. As he came up, they discharged at him the musket taken from the guard. The ball whistled over his head. He felt for his bayonet, and, at that moment, perceived that, in his haste, it was left behind. He then pointed his gun at the man with the musket, but deemed it imprudent to fire, reflecting, even if he killed him, his comrade could easily master such a stripling as himself. He compelled the man to throw down the musket, by threatening him with death if he did not instantly comply. Then, loading the fuzee from his cartridge-box, he forced his prisoners down from the trees, and, armed with his two loaded muskets, he drove them toward the court-house, care ful, however, to keep them far apart, to prevent conversation. Passing by a spring, they requested permission to drink.

"'No!' replied the unterrified boy, understanding their design. 'You can do as well without it as myself; you shall have some by-and-by.'

"Soon after, his father, at the head of a party of soldiers in the pursuit, galloped past in the road within a short distance. Tunis hallooed, but the clattering of their horse's hoofs drowned his voice. At length he reached the village, and lodged his prisoners in the county prison.

"It was subsequently discovered that these men were brothers, from near Philadelphia, that they had robbed and murdered a Mr. Boyd, a collector of taxes in Chester county, and, when taken, were on their way to join the British. As they had been apprehended on suspicions merely of beng refugees, no definite charge could be brought against them. A few days after, sheriff Firman saw an advertisement in a Philadelphia paper, describing them, with the facts above mentioned, and a reward of $20,000 (*Continental* money) offered for their apprehension. He, accompanied by his son, took them on there, where they were tried and executed. On entering Philadelphia, young Tunis was carried through the streets in triumph upon the shoulders of the military In the latter part of the war, this young man became very active, and was the particular favorite of Gen. David Forman."

CRUELTY OF THE TORIES.

MANY stories are told of the comparative kindness and cruelty of the Indians and Tories in the Border Wars of the Revolution The following incidents, from "Stone's Border Warfare of New York," will show that the white man often excelled in cruelty, his Indian ally. The Captain Brant spoken of, was the renowned Joseph Brant, or Thayendanega, the great leader of the Six Nations, and an object of terror to the western frontier of the State of New York. He frequently was called " a monster."

"A lad in Schoharie county, named William M'Kown, while engaged in raking hay alone in a meadow, happening to turr round, perceived an Indian very near him. Startled at his perilous situation, he raised his rake for defence, but his fears were instantly dissipated by the savage, who said, 'Do not be afraid, young man; I shall not hurt you.' He then inquired of the youth for the residence of a loyalist named Foster. The lad gave him the proper direction, and inquired of the Indian whether he knew Mr. Foster? 'I am partially acquainted with him,' was the reply, 'having once seen him at the Half-way Creek.' The Indian then inquired the lad's name, and having been informed, he added—'You are a son of Captain M'Kown, who lives in the northeast part of the town, I suppose: I know your father very well: he lives neighbor to Captain M'Kean: I know M'Kean very well, and a very fine fellow he is, too.' Emboldened by the familiar discourse of the Indian, the lad ventured to ask his name in turn. Hesitating for a moment, his rather unwelcome visitor replied:—'My name is Brant!' 'What! Captain Brant!' eagerly demanded the youth. 'No: I am a cousin of his,' was the rejoinder; but accompanied by a smile and a look that plainly disclosed the transparent deception. It was none other than the terrible Thayendanegea himself."

On the other hand, the following tragic circumstance sustains the assertion that the Tories were oftentimes more cruel than their savage associates. While parties of Indians and Tories were prowling about the borders of Schoharie, the Indians killed and scalped a mother, and a large family of children.

"They had just completed the work of death, when some loyalists of the party came up, and discovered an infant breathing sweetly in its cradle. An Indian warrior, noted for his barbarity, approached the cradle with his uplifted hatchet. The babe looked up in his face, and smiled; the feelings of nature triumphed over the ferocity of the savage; the hatchet fell with his arm, and he was about stooping down to take the innocent in his arms, when one of the loyalists, cursing him for his humanity, thrust it through with his bayonet, and, thus transfixed, held it up, struggling in the agonies of death, as he exclaimed—'*this, too, is a rebel!*'"

Here is another instance which proves that the Indian was often superior to his white companion in warfare, in magnanimity and generosity. Just after the invasion of Schoharie county by Brant, when the enemy had departed, a crowd of inhabitants were gathered about Fort Hunter, each with a tale of sorrow and grief. Among them was a young woman whose grief was of the most poignant kind. She had lost her husband, an infant, and several other members of the family were dead, or prisoners. Presently a young Indian came upon the scene, with a letter in his hand, addressed "to the commanding officer of the rebel army," and bearing an infant in his arms. The letter was opened and read as follows :—

"Sir—I send you by one of my runners, the child which he will deliver, that you may know that whatever others may do, *I* do not make war upon innocent children, I am sorry to say I have those engaged with me in the service, who are more savage than the savages themselves."

This was signed by Brant. The infant was found to belong to the disconsolate mother, and to her overwhelmning joy was restored to her bosom.

AFFECTING SCENES.

In the massacre of Cherry Valley, a Mr. Mitchell, while at work in a field, beheld a party of Indians approaching his house. He sprang forward in order to reach it, and protect his family, but the Indians reached it before him, and he was obliged to flee to the wood. Although pursued, he evaded his enemies and escaped. Upon returning, a terrible spectacle presented itself—it was the charred and burnt timbers of his house, and in the midst of the ruin, the bodies of his wife and four children. He flew to their sides, and upon examination, found life remaining in one of his children, a little girl of twelve years of age. He raised her up with the hope of restoring her, when he beheld another party of the enemy approaching. He scarcely had time to hide himself behind a log fence, before they were at the house. From his hiding place he had the inexpressible anguish to witness an infamous Tory, by the name of Newbury, extinguish the little spark of life remaining in his child, by a brutal blow from his hatchet. The next day unaided, he carried their bodies on a sled to the fort, and there the soldiers assisted him in the melancholy task of their burial. All that was left of those but a day before gathered around him in happiness and peace, were consigned to one common grave, and he stood alone, bereft of every joy for which he had lived and hoped. But retributive justice is not always silent. Newbury, who had so fiendishly robbed him of his only living child, was afterwards arrested as a spy, and by the evidence of Mr. Mitchell, was condemned and executed.

About the same time of the murder of Mr. Mitchell's family, Mrs. Clyde, wife of Col. Clyde, on the approach of the Indians, collected together her children, and fled to the woods. That entire day, and all the succeeding night, she lay concealed under a log, with her children, and one of them an infant, gathered around her, with a pitiless storm of snow and rain chilling them to the bones, and the frightful yells of the savages, and the shrieks of the murdered inhabitants, falling fearfully upon their ears. Parties of the savages passed by where she lay, and one so near that the butt of his gun trailed upon the log as he passed. At last a party from the fort, at the intercession of her husband, sallied out to her rescue, and brought them into the fort drenched with rain, and stiffened with cold. Mrs. Clyde had been unaccompanied by her eldest daughter, about ten years of age, and she supposed her to be safe in the fort, but when she arrived there, she learned that the little girl had not been seen. She was afterwards discovered. When fleeing from the house, she had escaped to the woods alone, and had remained concealed all this while, thinly clad, and thus greatly exposed to the severity of the weather, and racked with momentary apprehensions of death.*

A STORY OF A DOG.

In 1778, just after the raising of the siege of Fort Stanwix, in the Mohawk Valley, the following occurrence took place. Captain Gregg, and a corporal were out shooting during the day, when as evening drew near, they prepared to return to the fort, as parties of Indians were sometimes prowling about. But a flock of pigeons alighting near them, they were about to fire upon them, when two shots were heard, and Gregg saw his companion fall dead, while he felt a wound in his side, which so weakened him that he speedily fell. Two Indians immediately appeared from a thicket and approached them. Gregg at once saw that his only hope was to feign death. One of the savages struck him in the head with his hatchet, and then with his knife cut a circle around his crown, and with his teeth drew off his scalp. The Indians now withdrew, and soon as they were fairly gone, Gregg, although suffering terribly from his wounds in his side and head, resolved to endeavor to reach his companion, from a belief that if he could place his head on the corporal's body, his anguish from the wound in his head would be essayed. He, therefore, made an effort to rise, but he had no sooner got to his feet, than he fell heavily. Not despairing, he essayed again, but with the same result. The third time he so far succeeded, as to be enabled to

---

Campbell's Annals of Tyron County.

stagger slowly to the spot where the corporal lay. He found his companion lifeless and scalped. He placed his head upon his bloody body, and as he had hoped, this position afforded him some relief.

But the comfort of this position was destroyed by the annoyances of a small dog, which had accompanied him in his expedition, who now came up to him in great agony, leaping, yelping, and whining around his master, whom he annoyed by his great distress. Wearied with his efforts to force the dog from him, he exclaimed involuntarily, "if you wish so much to help me, go and call some one to my relief." To his surprise, the dog immediately bounded off through the forest at his utmost speed.

The dog made his way to where three men were fishing, about a mile from the scene where the tragedy was enacted, and as he came up to them, began to cry and whine, and endeavoring to attract their attention by bounding off into the woods, returning, and urging them to follow him. These extraordinary actions of the dog convinced the men that there was some unusual cause, and they resolved to follow him. They proceeded for some distance, and finding nothing, while darkness was already settled around, making the forest exceedingly dangerous, they determined to return. But no sooner did they attempt to retrace their steps, than the dog began to cry out with his utmost violence, caught hold of their coats with his teeth, and endeavored to force them to follow. As they continued to return, the violence of the dog increased, until the men astonished at the pertinacity of his manner, concluded to go with him. Presently, they came to where Gregg was lying, whom they found still living. They buried the corporal, and carried the captain into the fort. Astonishing as it may seem, the wounds of Gregg, severe as they were, healed up, and he recovered his perfect health.

DICEY LANGSTON.

"DICEY LANGSTON, was the daughter of Solomon Langston, of Laurens district, South Carolina. She possessed an intrepid spirit, which is highly serviceable in times of a nergency, and which, as she lived in the days of the Revolution, she had more than one opportunity to display. Situated in the midst of tories, and being patriotically inquisitive, she often learned by accident, or discovered by strategy, the plottings so common in those days, against the whigs. Such intelligence she was accustomed to communicate to the friends of freedom on the opposite side of the Ennoree river.

"Learning one time that a band of loyalists—known in those parts as the 'Bloody scout'—were about to fall upon the 'Elder settlement,' a place where a brother of hers and other friends were residing, she resolved to warn them of their danger. To do this, she must hazard her own life. But off she started, alone, in the darkness of the night; travelled several miles through the woods, and over marshes and across creeks, through a country where foot-logs and bridges were then unknown; came to the Tyger, a rapid and deep stream, into which she plunged and waded till the water was up to her neck; she then became bewildered, and zigzagged the channel for some time; reached the opposite shore at length—for a helping Hand was beneath, a kind Providence guiding her:—hastened on; reached the settlement, and her brother and the whole community were safe!

"She was returning one day from another settlement of whigs—in the Spartanburg district, when a company of tories met her and questioned her in regard to the neighborhood she had just left; but she refused to communicate the desired information. The leader of the band then held a pistol to her breast, and threatened to shoot her if she did not make the wished for disclosure.

"'Shoot me if you dare! I will not tell you!' was her dauntless reply, as she opened a long handkerchief that covered her neck and bosom, thus manifesting a willingness to receive the contents of the pistol, if the officer insisted on disclosures or life. The dastard, enraged at her defying movement, was in the act of firing, at which moment one of the soldiers threw up the hand holding the weapon, and the cowerless heart of the girl was permitted to beat on. .

"The brothers of Dicey were no less patriotic than she; and they having, by their active services on the side of freedom, greatly displeased the loyalists, these latter were determined to be revenged. A desperate band accordingly went to the house of their father, and finding the sons absent, they were about to wreak their vengeance on the old man, whom they hated for the sons' sake. With this intent one of the party drew a pistol; but just as it was aimed at the breast of her aged and infirm father, Dicey rushed between the two, and though the ruffian bade her get out of his way or receive in her own breast the contents of the pistol, she regarded not his threats, but flung her arms around her father's neck and declared she would receive the ball first, if the weapon must be discharged. Such fearlessness and willingness to offer her own life for the sake of her parent, softened the heart of the 'bloody scout,' and Mr. Langston lived to see his noble daughter perform other heroic deeds.

"One time her brother James, in his absence, sent to the house for a gun which he had left in her care, with orders for her to deliver it to no one except by his direction. On reaching the house one of the company who were directed to call for it, made known their errand, whereupon she brought and was about to deliver the weapon. At this moment it occurred to her that she had not demanded the countersign agreed on between herself and brother. With the gun still in her hand, she looked the company sternly in the face, and remarking that they wore a suspicious look, called for the countersign. Hereupon one of them, in jest, told her she was too tardy in her requirements; that both the gun and its holder were in their possession.

"'Do you think so,' she boldly asked, as she cocked the disputed weapon and aimed it at the speaker. 'If the gun is in your possession,' she added, 'take charge of it!' Her appearance indicated that she was in earnest, and the countersign was given without further delay. A hearty laugh on the part of the 'liberty men,' ended the ceremony."

WONDERFUL ESCAPE FROM INDIANS.

JAMES MORGAN, a native of Maryland, married at an early age and soon after settled himself near Bryant's station, in the wilds of Kentucky. Like most pioneers of the west, he had cut down the cane, built a cabin, deadened the timber, enclosed a field with a worm fence, and planted some corn.

It was on the fifteenth day of August, 1782;—the sun had descended; a pleasant breeze was playing through the surrounding wood; the tall cane bowed under its influence, and the broad green leaves of the corn waved in the air; Morgan had seated himself in the door of his cabin, with his infant on his knee; his young and happy wife had laid aside her spinning-wheel, and was busily engaged in preparing the frugal meal. That afternoon Morgan had accidentally found a bundle of letters, which he had finished reading to his wife before he had taken his seat in the door. It was a correspondence in which they had acknowledged an early and ardent attachment for each other, and the perusal left evident traces of joy on the countenance of both; the little infant, too, seemed to partake of its parents' feelings by its cherub smiles, its playful humor, and infantile caresses. While thus agreeably employed, the report of a rifle was heard, another, and another, followed in quick succession. Morgan sprang to his feet, his wife ran to the door, and they simultaneously exclaimed " IN DIANS!"

The door was immediately barred, and the next moment all their fears were realized, by a bold and spirited attack of a small party of Indians. The cabin could not be successfully defended, and time was precious. Morgan, cool, brave, and prompt, soon decided. While he was in the act of concealing his wife under the floor, a mother's feelings overcame her—she arose—seized her infant, but was afraid that its cries would betray her place of concealment. She hesitated—gazed silently upon it—a momentary struggle between affection and duty took place. She once more pressed her child to her agitated bosom; again and again kissed t with impassioned tenderness. The infant, alarmed at the profusion of tears that fell upon its cheek, looked up in its mother's face, threw its little arms around her neck, and wept aloud. "In the name of Heaven, Eliza, release the child, or we shall be lost," said the distracted husband, in a soft imploring tone of voice, as he forced the infant from his wife; hastily took up his gun, knife and hatchet; ran up the ladder that led to the garret, and drew it after him. In a moment the door was burst open, and the savages entered.

By this time, Morgan had secured his child in a bag, and lashed it to his back; then throwing off some clapboards from the roof of his cabin, resolutely leaped to the ground. He was instantly assailed by two Indians. As the first approached, he knocked him down with the butt end of his gun. The other advanced with uplifted tomahawk; Morgan let fall his gun and "closed in." The savage made a blow—missed aim, but severed the cord that bound the infant on his back, and it fell. The contest over the child now became warm and fierce, and was carried on with knives only. The robust and athletic Morgan, at length got the ascendancy. Both were badly cut, and bled freely, but the stabs of the white man were better aimed, and deeper, and the savage soon sunk to the earth in death. Morgan hastily took up his child and gun, and hurried off.

The Indians in the house, busily engaged in drinking and plundering, were not apprized of the contest in the yard, until the one that had been knocked down gave signs of returning life, and called them to the scene of action. Morgan was discovered, immediately pursued, and a dog put on his trail. Operated upon by all the feelings of a husband and a father, he moved on with the speed of a hunted stag, and soon outstripped the Indians, but the dog kept in close pursuit. Finding it impossible to outrun or elude the cunning animal, trained to hunts of this kind, he halted and waited until it came within a few yards of him, fired and brought him down—reloaded his gun, and again pushed forward.

In a short time he reached the house of his brother, who resided between Bryant's station and Lexington, where he left the child, and the two brothers immediately set out for his dwelling. As they approached the clearing, a light broke upon his view—his speed quickened, his fears increased, and the most agonizing apprehensions crowded upon his mind. He emerged from the cane-brake—beheld his house in flames, and almost burnt to the ground. "My Wife!" he exclaimed, as he pressed one hand to his forehead, and grasped the fence with the other, to support his tottering frame. He gazed for some time on the ruin and desolation before him, advanced a few steps, and sunk exhausted to the earth.

Morning came—the bright luminary of Heaven arose—and still found him seated near the almost expiring embers. In his right hand he held a small stick, with which he was tracing the name of "ELIZA," on the ground—his left was thrown over his favorite dog, that lay by his side, looking first on the ruin, and then on his master, with evident signs of grief. Morgan arose. The two brothers now made a search, and found some bones almost burned to ashes, which they carefully gathered, and silently consigned to their mother earth, beneath the wide-spread branches of a venerable oak, consecrated by the purest and holiest recollections.

Several days after this, Morgan was engaged in a desperate battle at the lower Blue Licks. The Indians came off victors, and the surviving whites retreated across the Licking, but were pursued by the enemy for a distance of six-and-thirty miles.

James Morgan was among the last that crossed the river, and was in the rear until the hill was descended. As soon as he beheld the Indians re-appear on the ridge, he felt anew his wrongs.

and recollected the lovely object of his early affections. He urged on his horse and pressed to the front. While in the act of leaping from his saddle, he received a rifle ball in his thigh, and fell; an Indian sprang upon him, seized him by the hair, and pplied the scalping-knife. At this moment Morgan cast his eyes upward and recognized the handkerchief that bound the head of the savage, and which he knew to be his wife's. This added renewed strength to his body, and increased activity to his fury. He quickly threw his left arm around the Indian, and with a death-like grasp, hugged him to his bosom, plunged his knife into his side, and he expired in his arms. Releasing himself from the savage, Morgan crawled under a small oak, on an elevated piece of ground, a short distance from him. The scene of action shifted, and he remained undiscovered and unscalped, an anxious spectator of the battle.

It was now midnight. The savage band after taking all the scalps they could find, left the battle-ground. Morgan was seated at the foot of the oak, its trunk supported his head. The rugged and uneven ground that surrounded him was covered with the slain; the once white and projecting rocks, bleached with the rain and sun of centuries, were crimsoned with the blood that had warmed the heart and animated the bosom of the patriot and the soldier. The pale glimmering of the moon, occasionally threw a faint light upon the mangled bodies of the dead, then a passing cloud enveloped all in darkness, and gave additional horror to the feeble cries of a few still lingering in the last agonies of protracted death, rendered doubly appalling the coarse growl of the bear, the oud howl of the wolf, the shrill and varied notes of the wild cat, and the panther, feeding on the dead and dying. Morgan beheld the scene with heart-rending sensations, and looked forward with the apathy of despair, to his own end.

A large and ferocious looking bear, covered with blood, now approached him; he threw himself on the ground—silently commended his soul to Heaven and in breathless anxiety awaited his fate. The satiated animal slowly passed on without noticing him. Morgan raised his head—was about offering thanks for his unexpected preservation, when the cry of a pack of wolves opened upon him, and again awakened him to a sense of his danger. He placed his hands over his eyes—fell on his face, and in silent agony awaited his fate. He now heard a rustling in the bushes —steps approached—a cold chill ran over him.—Imagination—creative, busy imagination, was actively employed; death—the most horrible death, awaited him—his limbs would, in all probability, be torn from his body, and he be devoured alive. He felt a touch—the vital spark was almost extinguished—another touch more violent than the first, and he was turned over—the cold sweat ran down in torrents—his hands were violently forced from his face—the moon passed from under a cloud—a faint ray beamed upon him—his eyes involuntarily opened and he beheld his *wife*, who, in scarce audible voice, exclaimed, "*My husband!— my husband!*" and fell upon his bosom.

Morgan now learned from his wife, that after the Indians had entered the house, they found some spirits and drank freely; an altercation soon took place—one of them received a mortal stab and fell; his blood ran through the floor on her. Believing it to be the blood of her husband, she shrieked aloud, and betrayed her place of concealment. She was immediately taken and bound. The party, after setting fire to the house, proceeded to Bryant's station. On the day of the battle of the Blue Licks, a horse, with saddle and bridle, rushed by her, which she knew to be her husband's. During the action, the prisoners were left unguarded—made their escape, and lay concealed beneath some bushes under the bank of the river. After the Indians had returned from the pursuit, and left the battle-ground, she, with some other persons that had escaped with her, determined to make a search for their friends, and if on the field, and living, to save them if possible from the beasts of prey. After searching for some time, and almost despairing of success, she fortunately discovered him.

The party of Colonel Logan found Morgan and his wife, and restored them to their FRIENDS, their INFANT, and their HOME.

A PATRIOTIC GIRL.

WE find the following incident in the first volume of American Anecdotes, "original and select." The young heroine of the adventure, afterwards married a rich planter, named Therwits, who lived on the Congaree.

"At the time General Greene retreated before Lord Rawdon from Ninety-Six, when he had passed Broad river, he was very desirous to send an order to General Sumter, who was on the Wateree, to join him, that they might attack Rawdon, who had divided his force. But the General could find no man in tha part of the state who was bold enough to undertake so dangerous a mission. The country to be passed through for many miles was full of blood-thirsty tories, who on every occasion that offered imbrued their hands in the blood of the whigs. At length Emily Geiger presented herself to General Greene, and proposed to act as his messenger : and the General, both surprised and delighted, closed with her proposal. He accordingly wrote a letter and delivered it, and at the same time communicated the contents of it verbally, to be told to Sumter in case of accidents.

"Emily was young, but as to her person or adventures on th way, we have no further information, except that she was mounted on horseback, upon a side-saddle, and on the second day of her journey she was intercepted by Lord Rawdon's scouts. Coming from the direction of Greene's army, and not being able to tell an untruth without blushing, Emily was suspected and confined to a room; and as the officer in command had the modesty not to search her at the time, he sent for an old tory matron as more fitting for that purpose. Emily was not wanting in expedient, and as soon as the door was closed and the bustle a little subsided, she *ate up the letter*, piece by piece. After a while the matron arrived, and upon searching carefully, nothing was to be found of a suspicious nature about the prisoner, and she would disclose nothing. Suspicion being thus allayed, the officer commanding the scouts, suffered Emily to depart wither she said she was bound; but she took a route somewhat circuitous to avoid further detention, and soon after struck into the road, to Sumter's camp, where she arrived in safety. Emily told her adventure, and delivered Greene's verbal message to Sumter, who, in consequence, soon after joined the main army at Orangeburg."

TRIALS OF A PATRIOT.

THOMAS MCCALLA, lived in Chester district, South Carolina during the latter part of the revolution. He was frequently in engagements, and in 1780, he fell into the hands of the enemy, was thrown into the jail at Camden, and threatened daily with hanging. The efforts of his wife to obtain his release, are detailed in the following manner, by Mrs. Ellett.

While this brave man was languishing in prison, expecting death from day to day, his wife remained in the most unhappy state of suspense. For about a month she was unable to obtain any tidings of him. The rumor of Sumter's surprise, and that of Steel, came to her ears; she visited the places where those disasters had occurred, and sought for some trace of him, but without success. She inquired, in an agony of anxiety, of the women who had been to Charlotte, for the purpose of carrying clothes or provisions to their husbands, brothers, or fathers, not knowing but that he had gone thither with the soldiers; but none could give her the least information. Imagination may depict the harrowing scenes that must have passed, when females returning to their homes and children after carrying aid to the soldiers, were met by such inquiries from those who were uncertain as to the fate of their kindred. To these hapless sufferers no consolation availed, and too often was their suspense terminated by more afflicting certainty.

In the midst of Mrs. McCalla's distress, and before she had gained any information, she was called to another claim on her anxiety; her children took the small-pox. John was very ill for nine days with the disease, and his mother thought every day would be his last. During this terrible season of alarm, while her mind was distracted by cares, she had to depend altogether upon herself, for she saw but one among her neighbors. All the families in the vicinity were visited with the disease, and to many it proved fatal. As soon as her child was so far recovered as to be considered out of danger, Mrs. McCalla made preparations to go to Camden. She felt convinced that it was her duty to do so, for she clung to the hope that she might there learn something of her husband, or even find him among the prisoners.

With her to resolve was to act, and having set her house in order, she was in the saddle long before day, taking the old Charleston road leading down on the west side of the Catawba river. The mountain gap on Wateree creek was passed ere the sun rose, and by two o'clock she had crossed the river, passing the guard there stationed, and entered Camden. Pressing on with fearless determination, she passed the guard, and desiring to be conducted to the presence of Lord Rawdon, was escorted by Major Doyle to the head-quarters of that commander. His Lordship then occupied a large, ancient looking house on the east side of the main street. The old site of the town is now in part deserted, and that building left standing alone some four hundred yards from any other, as if the memories associated with it had rendered the neighborhood undesirable. It was here that haughty and luxurious nobleman fixed his temporary residence, "sitting as a monarch," while so many true unfortunates, whose fate hung on his will, were languishing out their lives in prison, or atoning for their patriotism on the scaffold.

Into the presence of this august personage, Mrs. McCalla was conducted by the British major. Her impression at first sight was favorable; he was a fine looking young man, with a countenance not unpreposessing, which we may suppose was eagerly searched for the traces of human sympathy by one who felt that all her hopes depended on him. His aspect gave her some encouragement, and being desired to explain the object of her visit, she pleaded her cause with the eloquence of nature and feeling; making known the distressed situation of her family at home, the fearful anxiety of mind she had suffered on account of the prolonged absence of her husband and the ignorance of his fate, and her children's urgent need of his care and protection. From Major Doyle she had at length learned that he was held a prisoner by his lordship's orders. She had come, therefore, to entreat mercy for him; to pray that he might be released and permitted to go home with her. This appeal to compassion she made with all the address in her power, nor was the untaught language of distress wanting in power to excite pity in any feeling heart.

Lord Rawdon heard her to the end. His reply was characteristic. "I would rather hang such ——rebels than eat my breakfast." This insulting speech was addressed to his suppliant while her eyes were fixed on him in the agony of her entreaty, and the tears were streaming down her cheeks. His words dried up the fountain at once, and the spirit of the American matron was roused.

"Would you?" was her answer, while she turned on him a look of the deepest scorn. A moment after, with a struggle to control her feelings, for she well knew how much depended on that—she said, "I crave of your lordship permission to see my husband."

The haughty chief felt the look of scorn his cruel language had called up in her face, for his own conscience bore testimony against him, but pride forbade his yielding to the dictates of better feel ing "You should consider madam," he answered, "in whose presence you now stand. Your husband is a rebel——"

Mrs. McCalla was about to reply—but her companion, the Major, gave her a look warning her to be silent, and in truth the words that sprang to her lips would have ill pleased the Briton. Doyle now interposed, and requested his lordship to step aside with him for a moment. They left the apartment, and shortly afterwards returned. Rawdon then said to his visitor, with a stately coldness that precluded all hope of softening his determination: "Major Doyle, madam, has my permission to let you go into the prison. You may continue in the prison *ten minutes only*, Major, you have my orders." So saying, he bowed politely both to her and the officer, as intimating that the business was ended, and they were dismissed. They accordingly quitted the room.

The sight of the prison-pen almost overcame the fortitude of the resolute wife. An enclosure like that constructed for animals, guarded by soldiers, was the habitation of the unfortunate prisoners, who sate within on the bare earth, many of them suffering with the prevalent distemper, and stretched helpless on the ground, with no shelter from the burning sun of September. "Is it possible," cried the matron, turning to Doyle, "that you shut up men in this manner, as you would a parcel of hogs!" She was then admitted into the jail, and welcome indeed was the sight of her familiar face to McCalla. The time allotted for the interview was too short to be wasted in condolement or complaint; she told him she must depart in a few minutes, informed him of the state of his family—inquired carefully what were his wants, and promised speedy relief. When the ten minutes had expired, she again shook hands with him, assuring him she would shortly return with clothes for his use, and what provisions she could bring, then turning walked away with a firm step, stopping to shake hands with young John Adair and the other captives with whom she was acquainted. The word of encouragement was not wanting, and as she bade the prisoners adieu, she said: "Have no fear; the women are doing their part of the service." "I admire your spirit, madam," Doyle observed to her, "but must request you to be a little more cautious."

Mrs. McCalla was furnished by the Major with a pass, which she showed to the officer on duty as she passed the guard on her return, and to the officer at the ferry. She rode with all speed and was at home before midnight; having had less than twenty-four hours for the accomplishment of her whole enterprise; in that time riding one hundred miles, crossing the river twice, and passing the guard four times—visiting her husband, and having the interview with Lord Rawdon, in which probably for the first time in his life he felt uneasiness from a woman's rebuke. It convinced him that even in the breast of woman a spirit of independence might dwell, which no oppression could subdue, and before which brute force must quail, as something of superior nature. How must the unexpected outbreaking of this spirit, from time to time, have dismayed those who imagined it was crushed forever throughout the conquered province!

It is proper to say that Mrs. McCalla met with kinder treatment from the other British officers to whom she had occasion to apply at this time, for they were favorably impressed by the courage and strength of affection evinced by her. Even the soldiers, as she passed them, paid her marks of respect. The tories alone showed no sympathy nor pity for her trials; it being constantly observed that there was deeper hostility towards the whigs on the part of their countrymen of different politics, than those of English birth.

Mrs. McCalla began her work immediately after her arrival at home; making new clothes, altering and mending others, and preparing provisions. Her preparations being completed, she again set out for Camden. This time she had the company of one of her neighbors, Mrs. Mary Nixon. Each of the women drove before her a pack-horse, laden with the articles provided for the use of their suffering friends. They were again admitted to the presence of Lord Rawdon to petition for leave to visit the prisoners, but nothing particular occurred at the interview. His lordship treated the matron who had offended him with much haughtiness, and she on her part felt for him a contempt not the less strong that it was not openly expressed. From this time she made her journeys about once a month to Camden, carrying clean clothes and provisions; being often accompanied by other women bound on similar errands, and conveying articles of food and clothing to their captive fathers, husbands, or brothers. They rode without escort, fearless of peril by the way, and regardless of fatigue, though the journey was usually performed in haste, and under the pressure of anxiety for those at home as well as those to whose relief they were going. On one occasion, when Mrs. McCalla was just about setting off alone upon her journey, news of a glorious event was brought to her; the news of the battle of King's Mountain, which took place on the seventh of October She did not stop to rejoice in the victory of her countrymen, bu went on with a lightened heart, longing, no doubt, to share the joy with him who might hope, from the changed aspect of affairs, some mitigation of his imprisonment.

. . . About the first of December, Mrs. McCalla went

again to Camden. On the preceding trip she had met with Lord Cornwallis, by whom she was treated with kindness. Whatever hopes she had grounded on this, however, were doomed to disappointment; he was this time reserved and silent. She was afterwards informed by the Major that a considerable reverse had be fallen his majesty's troops at Clermont, and the annoyance felt on this account—Doyle said—was the cause of his not showing as much courtesy as he usually did to ladies. "You must excuse him," observed the good-natured officer, who seems to have always acted the part of a peace-maker on these occasions; and he added that Cornwallis had never approved of the cruelties heretofore practised.

Towards the last of December the indefatigable wife again performed the weary journey to Camden. McCalla's health had been impaired for some months, and was now declining; it was therefore necessary to make a strenuous effort to move the compassion of his enemies, and procure his release. Rawdon was in command, and she once more applied to him to obtain permission for her husband to go home with her. As might have been anticipated, her petition was refused: his lordship informed her that he could do nothing in the premises; but that if she would go to Winnsboro' and present her request to Lord Cornwallis, he might possibly be induced to give her an order for the liberation of the prisoner.

To Winnsboro', accordingly, she made her way, determined to lose no time in presenting her application. It was on New Year's morning that she entered the village. The troops were under parade, and his lordship was engaged in reviewing them; there could be no admission, therefore, to his presence for some time, and she had nothing to do but remain a silent spectator of the imposing scene. A woman less energetic, and less desirous of improving every opportunity for the good of others, might have sought rest after the fatigues of her journey, during the hours her business had to wait; Sarah McCalla was one of heroic stamp, whose private troubles never caused her to forget what she might do for her country. She passed the time in noticing particularly everything she saw, not knowing but that her report might do service. After the lapse of several hours, the interview she craved with Cornwallis was granted. He received her with courtesy and kindness, listened attentively to all she had to say, and appeared to feel pity for her distresses. But his polished expression of sympathy, to which her hopes clung with desperation, was accompanied with regret that he could not, consistently with the duties of his Majesty's service, comply unconditionally with her request. He expressed, nevertheless, entire willingness to enter into an exchange with General Sumter, releasing McCalla for any prisoner he had in his possession. Or he would accept the pledge of General Sumter that McCalla should not again serve until exchanged, and would liberate him on that security. "But, madam," he added, "it is Sumter himself who must stand pledged for the keeping of the parole. We have been too lenient heretofore, and have let men go who immediately made use of their liberty to take up arms against us."

With this the long-tried wife was forced to be content, and she now saw the way clear to the accomplishment of her enterprise. She lost no time in returning home, and immediately set out for Charlotte to seek aid from the American general. She found Sumter at this place, nearly recovered of the wounds he had received in the action at Blackstock's, in November. Her appeal to him was at once favorably received. He gave her a few lines, stating that he would stand pledged for McCalla's continuance at home peaceably until he should be regularly exchanged. This paper was more precious than gold to the matron whose perseverance had obtained it; but it was destined to do her little good. She now made the best of her way homeward. After crossing the Catawba, she encountered the army of General Morgan, was stopped, being suspected to be a tory, and taken into his presence for examination. The idea that she could be thus suspected afforded her no little amusement, and she permitted the mistake to continue for some time, before she produced the paper in Sumter's hand-writing which she well knew would remove every difficulty. She then informed the general of her visit to Winnsboro' on the first of January, and her sight of the review of the troops. Morgan thanked her for the information and dismissed her, and without further adventure she arrived at her own house.

A few days after her return, the British army, being on its march from Winnsboro', encamped on the plantation of John Service, in Chester district, and afterwards at Turkey creek. Mrs. McCalla went to one of those camps in the hope of seeing Lord Cornwallis. She succeeded in obtaining this privilege; his lordship recognised her as soon as she entered the camp, and greeted her courteously, questioning her as to her movements, and making many inquiries about Sumter and Morgan. On this last point she was on her guard, communicating no more information than she felt certain could give the enemy no manner of advantage, nor subject her friends to inconvenience. At length she presented to the noble Briton the paper which she imagined would secure her husband's freedom. What was her disappointment when he referred her to Lord Rawdon, as the proper person to take cognizance of the affair! The very name was a death-blow to her hopes, for she well knew she could expect nothing from his clemency. Remonstrance and entreaty were alike in vain; Cornwallis was a courteous man, but he knew how, with a bland smile and well-turned phrase of compliment, to refuse compliance even with a request that appealed so strongly to every feeling of humanity, as that of an anxious wife pleading for the suffering and imprisoned father of her children. She must submit, however, to the will of those in power; there was no resource but another journey to Camden, in worse than doubt of the success she had fancied just within her reach.

It was a day or two after the battle of the Cowpens, that she crossed the ferry on her way to Camden. She had not yet heard of that bloody action, but, observing that the guard was doubled at the ferry, concluded that something unusual had occurred. As she entered the village, she met her old friend Major Doyle, who stopped to speak to her. His first inquiry was if she had heard the news; and when she answered in the negative, he told her of the " melancholy affair" that had occurred at Cowpens. The time, he observed, was most inauspicious for the business on which he knew she had come. " I fear, madam," he said, " that his lordship will not treat you well."

" I have no hope," was her answer, " that he will let Thomas go home; but, sir, it is my duty to make efforts to save my husband. I will thank you to go with me to Lord Rawdon' quarters."

Her reception was such as she had expected. As soon as Rawdon saw her, he cried angrily, " You here again, madam Well—you want your husband—I dare say! Do you not know what the ———— rebels have been doing ?"

"I do not, sir," replied the dejected matron, for she saw that his mood was one of fury.

"If we had hung them," he continued, "we should have been saved this. Madam! I order you most positively never to come into my presence again!"

It was useless, Mrs. McCalla knew, to attempt to stem the tide; she did not therefore produce, nor even mention the paper given her by Sumter, nor apologise for the intrusion by saying that Lord Cornwallis had directed her to apply to him; but merely answered in a subdued and respectful tone by asking what she had done.

"Enough!" exclaimed the irritated noble. "You go from one army to another, and Heaven only knows what mischief you do! Begone."

She waited for no second dismissal, but could not refrain from saying, as she went out, in an audible voice, "My countrymen must right me." Lord Rawdon called her back and demanded what she was saying. She had learned by this time some lessons in policy, and answered, with a smile, "We are but simple country folk." His lordship probably saw through the deceit, for turning to his officer, he said, "Upon my life, Doyle, she is a wretch of a woman!" And thus she left him.

That great event—the battle of the Cowpens—revived the spirits of the patriots throughout the country. Everywhere, as the news spread, men who had before been discouraged flew to arms. The action took place on the seventeenth of January, 1781; on the twenty-second of the same month, six wagons were loaded with corn at Wade's island, sixty miles down the Catawba for the use of General Davison's division. The whole whig country of Chester, York and Lancaster may be said to have risen in mass, and was rall ing to arms. Mecklenburg, North Carolina, was again the scene of warlike preparations; for the whigs hoped to give the enemy another defeat at Cowans or Batisford on the Catawba. On the twenty-fourth of January, General Sumter crossed this river at Landsford, and received a supply of corn from Wade's island. His object was to cross the districts to the west in the rear of the advancing British army, to arouse the country and gather forces as he went, threaten the English posts at Ninety-Six and Granby, and go on to recover the State. While Cornwallis marched from his encampment on Service's plantation, the whigs of Chester, under the gallant Captain John Mills and James Johnston, were hovering near, watching the movements of the hostile army as keenly as the eagle watches his intended prey. Choosing a fit opportunity, as they followed in the rear, they pounced upon a couple of British officers, one of whom was Major McCarter, at a moment when they had not the least suspicion of danger, took them prisoners in sight of the enemy, and made good their retreat. By means of this bold exploit the liberation of McCalla was brought about, at a time when his wife was wholly disheartened by her repeated and grievous disappointments. When General Sumter passed through the country, a cartel of exchange was effected, giving the two British officers in xchange for the prisoners of Chester district in Camden and Charleston.

The person sent with the flag to accomplish this exchange in Camden, was Samuel Neely of Fishing creek. As he passed through the town to the quarters of Lord Rawdon, he was seen and recognized by the prisoners, and it may be supposed their hearts beat with joy at the prospect of speedy release. But in consequence of some mismanagement of the business, the unfor tunate men were detained in jail several weeks longer. Neely was in haste to proceed to Charleston, being anxious, in the accomplishment of his mission in that city, to get his son Thomas out of the prison-ship, and in his hurry probably neglected some necessary formalities. His countrymen in Camden were kept in confinement after his return from Charleston with his son. Captain Mills was informed of this, and indignant at the supposed disrespect shown by Lord Rawdon to the cartel of General Sumter, wrote a letter of remonstrance to Rawdon, which he entrusted to Mrs. McCalla to be conveyed to him.

Our heroine was accompanied on this journey by Mrs. Mary Dixon, for she judged it impolitic that the letter should be delivered by one so obnoxious to his lordship as herself. Still she deemed it her duty to be on the spot to welcome her liberated husband, supply all his wants, and conduct him home. The distance was traversed this time with lighter heart than before, for now she had no reason to fear disappointment. When they arrived at Camden, they went to the jail. John Adair was standing at a window; they saw and greeted each other, the women standing in the yard below. Perhaps in consequence of his advice, or prudential considerations on their part, they determined not to avail themselves of the good offices of Major Doyle on this occasion. Adair directed them to send the jailor up to him, and wrote a note introducing his sister to the acquaintance of Lord Rawdon. The two women then proceeded to the quarters of that nobleman. When they arrived at the gate, Mrs. McCalla stopped, saying she would wait there, and her companion proceeded by herself. She was admitted into the presence of Lord Rawdon, who read the note of introduction she handed to him, and observed, referring to the writer—that the small-pox had al most finished him; still he had come very near escaping from the jail; that he was "a grand 'scape-gallows." On reading the letter of Captain Mills, his color changed, and when he had finished it, turning to Mrs. Nixon, he said in an altered tone: "I am sorry these men have not been dismissed, as of right they ought." He immediately wrote a discharge for eleven of the prisoners, and put it into her hands, saying: "You can get them out, madam I am very sorry they have been confined so many weeks longer than they should have been." At the same time he gave Mrs. Nixon a guinea. "This," he said, "will bear your expenses."

His lordship accompanied her on her way out, and as she passed through the gate his eye fell on Mrs. McCalla, whom he instantly recognized. Walking to the spot where she stood near the gate, he said fiercely: "Did I not order you, madam, to keep out of my presence?" The matron's independent spirit flashed from her eyes, as she answered: "I had no wish, sir, to intrude myself on your presence; I stopped at the gate on purpose to avoid you." Unable to resist the temptation of speaking her mind for once, now that she had a last opportunity, she added: "I might turn the tables on you, sir, and ask, why did *you* come out to the gate to insult a woman? I have received from you nothing but abuse. My distresses you have made sport of, and I ceased long since to expect anything from you but ill treatment. I am now not your supplicant; I came to *demand*, as a right, the release of my husband!" So saying, she bowed to him contemptuously, wheeled about, and deliberately walked off, without stopping to see how her bold language was received. Mrs. Nixon hastened after her pale as death, and at first too much frightened to speak. As soon as she found voice, she exclaimed:

"Sally! you have ruined us, I am afraid! Why, he may put us both in jail!"

Mrs. McCalla laughed outright. "It is not the first time, Mary," she replied, "that I have given him to understand I thought him a villain!" The two made their way back to the prison, but even after they got there Mrs. Nixon had not recovered from her terror. She was informed that it would be some time before the prisoners could be released. The blacksmith was then sent for, and came with his tools. The sound of the hammering in the apartments of the jail, gave the first intimation to the women who waited to greet their friends, that the helpless captives were chained to the floor. This precaution had been adopted not long before, in consequence of some of the prisoners having attempted an escape. They were then put in handcuffs or chained by the ankle. These men left the place of their long imprisonment and suffering in company with the two women, and as they marched through the streets of Camden, passing the British guard, they sang at the top of their voices, the songs of the "liberty-men."

MRS. SHUBRICK.

The following anecdotes of Mrs. Richard Shubrick may be found in the First Series of Major Garden's Revolutionary Anecdotes. "There was," he writes, "an appearance of personal debility about her that rendered her peculiarly interesting: it seemed to solicit the interest of every heart, and the man would have felt himself degraded who would not have put his life at hazard to serve her. Yet, when firmness of character was requisite, when fortitude was called for to repel the encroachments of aggression there was not a more intrepid being in existence.

"An American soldier, flying from a party of the enemy sought her protection, and was promised it. The British, pressing close upon him, insisted that he should be delivered up, threatening immediate and universal destruction in case of refusal. The ladies, her friends and companions, who were in the house with her, shrunk from the contest, and were silent; but, undaunted by their threats, this intrepid lady placed herself before the chamber into which the unfortunate fugitive had been conducted, and resolutely said, 'To men of honor the chamber of a lady should be as sacred as the sanctuary! I will defend the passage to it though I perish. You may succeed, and enter it, but it shall be over my corpse.' 'By God,' said the officer, 'if muskets were only placed in the hands of a few such women, our only safety would be found in retreat. Your intrepidity, madam, gives you security; from me you shall meet no further annoyance.'

"At Brabant, the seat of the respectable and patriotic Bishop Smith, a sergeant of Tarleton's dragoons, eager for the acquisition of plunder, followed the overseer, a man advanced in years, into the apartment where the ladies of the family were assembled, and on his refusing to discover the spot in which the plate was concealed, struck him with violence, inflicting a severe sabre wound across the shoulders. Aroused by the infamy of the act, Mrs. Shubrick, starting from her seat, and placing herself betwixt the ruffian and his victim, resolutely said, 'Place yourself behind me, Murdoch; the interposition of my body shall give you protection, or I will die:' then, addressing herself to the sergeant, exclaimed,

'O what a degradation of manhood—what departure from that gallantry which was once the characteristic of British soldiers. Human nature is degraded by your barbarity;—but should you persist, then strike at *me*, for till I die, no further injury shall be done to *him*.' The sergeant, unable to resist such commanding eloquence, retired."*

THE PRIVATEER.

Gustavus Conyngham, who commanded one of the American Privateers, was an object of great terror to the British. His vessel was called the "Revenge," and the fear which that dreaded name inspired, was augmented by the exaggerated statements that were industriously circulated in reference to its commander. He was represented as a man of gigantic frame and ferocious countenance, and prints of him after this fashion were exhibited in London shop windows, and labelled, "The Arch Rebel." He was repeatedly captured by the enemy, treated with the most barbarous severity, and only saved from execution by the resolutions of Congress, which declared that his death should be avenged by that of certain royalist officers then in custody.

---

* "The hope, however, of attaining the object in view, very speedily subjected the unfortunate Murdoch to new persecution. He was tied up under the very tree where the plate was buried, and threatened with immediate execution unless he would make the discovery required. But although well acquainted with the unrelenting severity of his enemy, and earnestly solicited by his wife, to save his life by a speedy confession of the place of deposit, he persisted resolutely, that a sacred trust was not to be betrayed, and actually succeeded in preserving it."

During the early part of the war, when the terror of his name was shared by every Englishman on the sea, a vessel was cruising near the West India Islands, on board of which were three ladies, who suffered many apprehensions of meeting with the terrible privateer, whom story and tradition represented as a monster in human form. Suddenly one day, when the ladies were upon the deck, a cry came from aloft—"A sail! a sail!" In an instant all was confusion. The captain hastened up the shrouds to examine the appearance of the stranger. A few moments sufficed to make its character known. It was no other than the terrible privateer. The captain returned to the deck, and communicated the unpleasant news, which at once threw the ladies into an agony of fear. They retired to the cabin, in tears, and half fainting.

The strange sail gradually drew near. There was no chance of escape; and a gun from the vessel at once denoted its object. The pursued vessel lay-to, and a boat put off from the stranger, containing two officers and several men. They soon stood upon the Englishman's deck. The commanding officer was a young man of about twenty-five, of a light, elegant figure, and a face pleasing in the extreme, marked by a slight shade of melancholy. He made some inquiries concerning the vessel, and on being informed that there were ladies in the cabin, colored, and said to his lieutenant—that he would have to go and say to them, the passengers were not prisoners, but guests. The lieutenant excused himself by saying that he had not "confidence enough to speak to them," when the first speaker went into the cabin.

The terrified ladies, momentarily expecting the appearance of a gigantic monster, were surprised by the entrance into the cabin of a slightly formed and elegant figure, who greeted them with marked respect. The fears of the ladies were at once dispelled.

The youngest with much naiveté, asked if he was really a pirate.

"I am captain of an American privateer," he answered, "and he, I trust, cannot be a pirate."

"Are you the captain of the 'Revenge?'"

"I am."

"Is it possible you are the man represented to be a bloody and ferocious pirate, whose chief delight is in scenes of carnage?" inquired the ladies.

"I am that person of whom these nursery tales have been told; whose picture is hung up to frighten children. I have suffered much from British prisons and from British calumny; but my sufferings will never make me forget the courtesy due to ladies."

The ladies could not realize that these were the sentiments of a man common report had branded as ferocious and bloodthirsty.

The vessels lay together for several days. During this time Conyngham showed the most marked respect to the passengers, and succeeded in winning their esteem. The lieutenant's relation of his many gallant achievments awakened even a deeper interest with the ladies. It soon became evident that Conyngham was smitten with the charms of the younger of the party, who evinced great pleasure in the society of the captain. The gallant American had achieved a conquest not anticipated by his fair captive. After a few days, the ladies were placed on board a vessel bound to one of the islands. They parted with the captain with regret. But with one the separation was not of long duration. They met again, and not many months elapsed ere the American led a lovely and beautiful bride to the altar. The romantic manner of their meeting, and the marvellous stories told of the fiendish American pirate, served, no doubt, in after times to make them merry.

THE MAIDEN WARRIOR.

WE have recorded in an earlier part of this volume, the exploits of Sergeant Jasper, of Marion's brigade, but we did not give an account of an incident, connected with him, of a most romantic and touching nature.

Sometime just before, or about the beginning of the war, he had the good fortune to save the life of a young, beautiful, and dark-eyed creole girl, called Sally St. Clair. Her susceptible nature was overcome with gratitude to her preserver, and this soon ripened into a passion of love, of the most deep and fervent kind. She lavished upon him the whole wealth of her affections, and the whole depths of a passion nurtured by a southern sun. When he was called upon to join the ranks of his country's defenders, the prospect of their separation almost maddened her. Their parting came, but scarcely was she left alone, than her romantic nature prompted the means of a re-union. Once resolved, no consideration of danger could dampen her spirit, and no thought of consequences could move her purpose. She severed her long and jetty ringlets, and provided herself with male attire. In these she robed herself, and set forth to follow the fortunes of her lover.

A smooth faced, beautiful, and delicate stripling appeared among the hardy, rough, and giant frames, who composed the corps to which Jasper belonged. The contrast between the stripling and these men, in their uncouth garbs, their massive faces, embrowned and discolored by sun and rain, was indeed striking. But none were more eager for the battle, or so indifferent to fatigue, as the fair faced boy. It was found that his energy of character, resolution and courage, amply supplied his lack of physique. None ever suspected him to be a woman. Not even Jasper himself, although she was often by his side, penetrated her disguise.

The romance of her situation increased the fervor of her passion. It was her delight to reflect that, unknown to him, she was by his side, watching over him in the hour of danger. She fed her passion by gazing upon him in the hour of slumber, hovering near him, when stealing through the swamp and thicket, and being always ready to avert danger from his head.

But gradually there stole a melancholy presentment over the poor girl's mind. She had been tortured with hopes deferred; the war was prolonged, and the prospect of being restored to him grew more and more uncertain. But now she felt that her dream of happiness could never be realized. She became convinced that death was about to snatch her away from his side, but she prayed that she might die, and he never knew to what length the violence of her passion led her.

It was an eve before a battle. The camp had sunk into repose. The watchfires were burning low, and only the slow tread of sentinels fell upon the profound silence of the night air, as they moved through the dark shadows of the forest. Stretched upon the ground, with no other couch than a blanket, reposed the war like form of Jasper. Climbing vines trailed themselves into a canopy above his head, through which the stars shone down softly. The faint flicker from the expiring embers of a fire fell athwart his countenance, and tinged the cheek of one who bent above his couch. It was the smooth faced stripling. She bent low down as if to listen to his dreams, or to breathe into his soul pleasant visions of love and happiness. But tears trace themselves down the fair one's cheek, and fall silently, but rapidly upon the brow of her lover. A mysterious voice has told her that the hour of parting has come; that to-morrow her destiny is consummated There is one last, long, lingering look, and then the unhappy maid is seen to tear herself away from the spot, to weep out her sorrows in privacy.

Fierce and terrible is the conflict that on the morrow rages on that spot. Foremost in the battle is the intrepid Jasper, and ever by his side fights the stripling warrior. Often during the heat and the smoke, gleams suddenly upon the eyes of Jasper the melancholy face of the maiden. In the thickest of the fight, surrounded by enemies, the lovers fight side by side. Suddenly a lance is levelled at the breast of Jasper; but swifter than the lance is Sally St. Clair. There is a wild cry, and at the feet of Jasper sinks the maiden, with the life blood gushing from the white bosom, which had been thrown, as a shield, before his breast. He heeds not now the din, nor the danger of the conflict; but down by the side of the dying boy he kneels. Then for the first time does he learn that the stripling is his love; that often by the camp fire, and in the swamp, she had been by his side; that the dim visions, in his slumber, of an angel face hovering above him, had indeed been true. In the midst of the battle, with her lover by her side, and the barb still in her bosom, the heroic maiden dies!

Her name, her sex, and her noble devotion, soon became known through the corps. There was a tearful group gathered around her grave; there was not one of those hardy warriors, who did not bedew her grave with tears. They buried her near the river Santee, "in a green shady nook that looked as if it had been stolen out of Paradise."

MAJOR ISRAEL FEARING.

ON the 7th of September, 1778, the British troops made an attempt to destroy the village of Fairhaven, in Massachusetts, but were thwarted in their plans, by the bravery of Major Israel Fearing. Fairhaven is situated opposite New Bedford, on the Acushanet river, and is connected with the latter city by a long bridge. The following account of the enemy's attack, and their repulse, is from "Dwight's Travels:"

"They proceeded up the river with the intention of burning Fairhaven, but a critical attention to their movements, had convinced the inhabitants of their design, and induced them to prepare for their reception. The militia of the neighboring country were summoned to the defence. Their commander was a man far advanced in years. Under the influence of that languor which at this period enfeebles both the body and the mind, he determined that the place must be given up to the enemy, and that no opposition to their ravages, could be made with any hope of success. This decision of their officer necessarily spread its benumbing influence over the militia, and threatened an absolute prevention of all enterprise, and the destruction of this handsome village

" Among the officers, belonging to the brigade, was Israel Fearing, a major of one of the regiments. This gallant young man observing the torpor which was spreading among the troops, invi led as many as had sufficient spirit to follow him, and station themselves at the post of danger. Among those who accepted the invitation, was one of the colonels, who of course became the commandant; but after they had arrived at Fairhaven, and the night had come on, he proposed to march his troops back into the country. He was warmly opposed by Major Fearing, and finding that he could not prevail, prudently retired to a house three miles distant, where he passed the night in safety.

"After the colonel had withdrawn, Major Fearing now commander-in-chief, arranged his men with activity and skill; and soon perceived the British approaching. The militia, in the strictest sense, raw, already alarmed by the reluctance of their superior officers to meet the enemy, and naturally judging that men of years must understand the real state of the danger better than Major Fearing, a mere youth, were panic-struck at the approach of the enemy, and instantly withdrew from their post. At this critical moment, the major, with the decision which awes men into a strong sense of duty, rallied them; and placing himself in the rear, declared, in a tone which removed all doubt, that he would kill the first man whom he found retreating. The resolution of their chief recalled theirs. With the utmost expedition he led them to the scene of danger. The British had already set fire to several stores. Between these buildings and the rest of the village, he stationed his troops, and ordered them to lie close in profound silence, until the enemy, who were advancing, should have come so near, that no marksman could easily mistake his object. The orders were punctually obeyed. When the enemy had arrived within this distance, the Americans rose, and with a well directed fire gave them a warm and unexpected reception. The British fled instantly to their boats, and fell down the river with the utmost expedition. From the quantity of blood found the next day in their line of march, it was supposed that their loss was considerable. Thus did this heroic youth, in opposition to his superior officers, preserve Fairhaven, and merit a statue from its inhabitants.

CAPTIVITY OF ETHAN ALLEN.

SHORTLY after Ethan Allen's celebrated conquest of Ticonderoga, he joined the expedition into Canada, under Generals Schuyler and Montgomery. He had no commission from congress, but was induced by the commanding officers to follow the army, under a promise that he should, when occasion required, command certain detachments in the army. He was despatched into Canada with letters to the Canadians, explaining the object of the expedition, which was not aimed against the inhabitants of the country, their liberties or religion, but against the British possessors. The Canadians were invited to make common cause with the continentals, and expel the invader. His message was partly successful, and numbers of Canadians joined the congressional banner.

On a second expedition of a similiar nature, he was induced to undertake an enterprise against Montreal. Matters promised him success, but at a critical moment many of his Canadian allies abandoned him. The result was a total defeat, which ended in the surrender of himself and party.

When he was brought before General Prescott, the commanding English officer, he was asked his name and title. The reply cast the Briton into a towering passion. He could not forget the loss of Ticonderoga, and time had not softened the bitterness of hatred he felt against the hero of that glorious adventure. The Englishman so far forgot his position, as to threaten the person of Allen with his cane, and applied to him every offensive epithet he could command. Finding that Allen confronted him with an undaunted gaze, he looked around for something else on which to wreak his hatred. He ordered the Canadians who had been taken with Allen, to be brought forward, and executed. As they were brought forward, wringing their hands in consternation at the prospect of death, the heart of Allen was touched, as he could but feel their present position was brought about by his instrumentality. He, therefore flung himself between the executioners and the intended victims, opened his coat, and told General Prescott to let his vengeance fall on him alone, as he was the sole cause of the Canadians taking up arms.

The guard paused, and looked towards their General, and indeed it was a moment of suspense and interest to all present. The General stood quiet a moment or two in hesitation, and then said—"I will not execute you now; but you shall grace a halter at Tyburn," accompanying his speech with a series of emphatic oaths.

Allen was now removed on board the Gaspee schooner of war, loaded with irons of immense weight, and cast into the hold of the vessel. Here his sufferings were of the most acute nature. His only accommodations were a chest, on which he sat during the day, and which served him as a couch at night. The irons upon his ankles were so tight, that he could scarcely lie down, and then only in one position. Here he was visited by many officers of the English army, some of whom treated him civilly, but others were abusive and insulting.

At the expiration of six weeks, he was removed to a vessel off Quebec, where he received kind and courteous treatment. Here he remained until his removal on board of the vessel which was to carry him to England. Here all of the prisoners, thirty-four were thrust into a small apartment, each heavily ironed. They were compelled during the whole voyage to remain in their confinement, and were subjected to every indignity that cruelty could invent.

When first ordered to enter into their filthy apartment, Allen refused, and endeavored to argue their brutal keeper out of his inhuman purpose, but all in vain. The reply to his appeal was insults of the grossest kind, and an officer of the vessel insulting him by spitting in his face, hand-cuffed as he was, the intrepid American sprang upon the dastard, and knocked him at length upon the floor. The fellow hastily scrambled out of the reach of Allen, and placed himself under the protection of the guard. Allen challenged him to fight, offering to meet him even with irons upon his wrists, but the Briton, trembling with fear, contented himself with the protection afforded him by British bayonets, and did not venture to oppose the intrepid American. The prisoners were now forced into their den at the point of the bayonet.

The sufferings of the captives during the voyage were intense. Their privations soon brought on diarrhoea and fevers. But notwithstanding their sickness, they received no attention from their gaolers, and even those who were crazed with raging thirst, were denied the simple boon of fresh water.

On arriving at Falmouth, the prisoners were all marched through the town, to Pendennis Castle, about a mile distant. The fame of Allen had preceeded him, and multitudes o. people were gathered along the route to gaze upon him, and the other pris oners. The throng was so great, that the guard were compelled to force a passage through the crowd. Allen appeared conspicuous among his fellow prisoners, by his eccentric dress. When captured, he was taken in a Canadian dress, consisting of a red shirt, a red worsted cap, a short fawn-skin jacket, and breeches of sagathy; and in this dress he was escorted through the wondering crowd at Falmouth. Ticonderoga was a place of notoriety in England, and the hero who had so signally conquered it, was an object of interest and wonder to the people.

Allen was now visited by a great number of people, some of whom were attracted from great distances, in order to see and converse with the American celebrity. Discussion ran high as to his eventual disposal. Some declared that he would be hung and argued the justice of the act. But others defended and supported the Americans. Even in parliament the merits of the question were discussed.

From their prison in Pendennis Castle they were removed to the Solebay frigate, to be removed to America, stopping at Cork for provisions and water. The commanding officer was harsh and cruel, and on the first day, ordered the prisoners from the deck, declaring that it was a place for gentlemen only to walk. A few days after Allen shaved and dressed, and proceeded to the deck. The captain addressed him in great rage, and said, "Did not order you not to come on deck?" Allen replied that he had said that it was the place for gentlemen to walk, and that he was Col. Allen, a gentleman and soldier, who had not been properly introduced to him. His reply was characteristic of his bru tal disposition. "G—d d——n you, don't walk on the same side of the deck that I do."

The sufferings of the prisoners continued, but when at Cork, their situation received the attention of several benevolent gentlemen, who exerted themselves to allieve them. Ample stores and clothing were sent on board, but the captain refused privilege to the prisoners to enjoy them.

The vessel proceeded to America, first casting anchor in the harbor of Cape Fear, North Carolina. From this place Allen was removed to Halifax. Here his treatment continued of the same kind, that, from the first had characterized his captivity. He received here some kind attentions from Captain Smith, which he afterwards had occasion to return in a signal manner. After a confinement of two months he was removed to a man-of-war, to be conveyed to New York, for the purpose of effecting an exchange. When arrived on board of the vessel he was delighted to find that he was under the command of Captain Smith, who had before served him.

When Col. Allen met Captain Smith on board the vessel, he greeted him with thanks for his kindness. The noble captain disclaimed all merit, and said: "This is a mutable world, and one gentleman never knows but that it may be in his power to help another." This sentiment was strikingly verified in the course of the voyage.

One night, as they were sailing along the coast of Rhode Island, Captain Burk and a few other prisoners, came to Allen with a plan for destroying the British officers, seizing the vessel, and carrying her into some friendly port. A large quantity of cash on board was held up as an inducement for the enterprise. But Captain Smith had generously distinguished the prisoners, and for this reason Allen strongly condemned the plan. He declared that if the attempt was made, he would assist in the defence of the Briton with all his skill and strength. Finding the conspiracy so strenuously opposed by the most influential of the prisoners, it was abandoned, upon the assurance that they should not be betrayed.

Upon arriving in New York Col. Allen was released on parole, but restricted to the limits of New York. An attempt was made soon after to induce him to join the British ranks. He was offered a heavy sum of money, and large tracts of land, either in New Hampshire or Connecticut, when the country was conquered. The integrity of the man, however, was unassailable. His reply to the proposition was characteristic. He said that the offer reminded him of a certain incident in Scripture. The devil, he said, took Christ to a high hill, and showing him the kingdoms of earth, offered him their possession, if he would fall down and worship him, "when all the while the damned soul had not one foot of land upon earth!" It may be believed that those sent to negotiate with him did not fail to understand the illustration.

Col. Allen, in a narrative of his captivity, written by himself, gives a fearful account of the condition of the American prisoners in New York. Before his exchange he was arrested on the absurd charge of breaking his parole, and thrown into the provost jail. Here he remained from August to May, during which time he witnessed instances of suffering of the most agonizing kind, and was himself compelled again to feel the barbarous treatment of British officials. At the expiration of the above period he was excharged, and once more tasted of the sweets of freedom.

A FAIR EXCHANGE.

"In 1779, Major General Silliman was appointed Superintendant of the Coast of Fairfield, Connecticut. In the month of May, Sir Henry Clinton directed a small company to cross the sound from Lloyd's Neck, and, if possible, make him prisoner One of them was an inhabitant of Newtown, and he was well acquainted with the general's residence, and the best modes of access to it. The party consisted of eight, who reached the house about midnight. The family were awakened by a violent assault upon the door. The general sprang from bed, seized a musket, and approached the door. As he passed the window, he saw the men, and at once comprehended their design. He attempted to fire, but his musket only flashed. At that instant the assailants broke through the window, and seized him, exclaiming, that he was their prisoner, and that he must go with them. They permitted him to dress, but plundered him of pistols, gun and sword, and then hurried him away to the shore. As they approached the shore of Lloyd's Neck, Col. Simcoe, the commanding officer, who was waiting for them, exclaimed, 'Have you got him?' They answered, Yes. 'Have you lost any men?' No. 'That is well, replied Simcoe, 'your Sillimans are not worth a man, nor your Washingtons.' Gen. Silliman's eldest son was taken with him They were ordered to the guard house.

"At that time there was no prisoner in the hands of the Americans whom the British would accept for the general, and consequently it was determined to procure one. The person selected was the Hon. Thomas Jones, of Fort Neck, Long Island, and Captain Daniel Hawley undertook to secure his person. On the

4th of November, aided by twenty-five volunteers, he proceeded to Mr. Jones' residence at about nine in the evening. There was a ball in the house, and the noise of music and dancing prevented the approach of the adventurers being heard. Captain Hawley knocked at the door, and perceiving that nobody heard him forced it, and found Judge Jones standing in the entry. He instantly told him he was his prisoner, and immediately conducted him off noiselessly, together with a young gentleman whose name was Hewlett. A guard of soldiers was posted at a small distance from the road. When they came near the spot, Judge Jones hemmed very loud, and was forbidden by Capt. Hawley to repeat the sound. He, however, did repeat it; but being told by his conductor that another repetition would be followed by fatal consequences, he desisted. They reached their destination safely with their prisoner. Mr. Jones was hospitably entertained at the house of Mrs. Silliman, and when the exchange was effected, the vessels that contained them met mid way on the sound. The two gentlemen having dined together, parted, and proceeded immediately to their respective places of destination."

A PATRIOT'S SUFFERINGS.

"Soon after the battle of Long Island, an event occurred which exhibited in bold relief the intrepidity and patriotism of Captain Birdsall, a whig officer. An American vessel, laden with flour for the army, had been captured by the British, in the Sound; and Col. Birdsall believing she might be retaken, offered, if the undertaking was approved of by his superior officer, to superintend the enterprize himself. The proposal was accepted, when the captain with a few select men, made the experiment, and succeeded in sending the vessel to her original destination. But it so happened that himself and one of his men were taken prisoners by the enemy. It was his fate to be imprisoned in the jail, then called he Provost, under the surveillance of that monster in human shape, the infamous Cunningham. He requested the use of pen, ink, and paper, for the purpose of acquainting his family of his situation. On being refused, he made a reply, which drew from the keeper some opprobious epithets, accompanied by a thrust of his sword, which penetrated the shoulder of his victim, and caused the blood to flow freely. Being locked up alone in a filthy apartment, and denied any assistance whatever, he was obliged to dress the wound with his own linen; and then to endure, in solitude and misery, every indignity which the malice of the Provost-marshal urged him to inflict upon a *damned rebel*, who, he declared, *ought to be hung*.' After several miserable months of confinemen and starvation, he was exchanged."

COLONEL JOHN SMALL.

COLONEL JOHN SMALL was an officer in the British army, who had served in the French wars, and was the dearly valued friend of Israel Putnam. When the war broke out with the mother country, he obeyed the dictates of his prejudices, and supported the cause of the king, as he was undoubtedly bound to do by his birth and allegiance. The following incidents, which occurred at Bunker Hill, he has given to the world himself. They redound to the credit of Putnam, as well as confirm his own reputation for honor and courage. They were related to Mr. Turnbull, in London, in 1786, who at that time was engaged on a painting of the battle, and we give them in his own words. "When the British troops advanced the second time to the attack of the redoubt, I with other officers, was in front of the line to encourage the men we had advanced very near the works undisturbed, when an irregular fire, like a feu de joie was poured in upon us; it was cruelly fatal. The troops fell back, and when I looked to the right and the left, I saw not one officer standing; I glanced my eye to the enemy, and saw several young men levelling their pieces at me; I knew their excellence as marksmen, and considered myself gone. At this moment my old friend Putnam rushed forward, and striking up the muzzles of their pieces with his sword, cried out, 'For God's sake, my lads, don't fire at that man—I love him as I do my brother?' We were so near each other that I heard his words distinctly. He was obeyed; I bowed, thanked him, and walked away unmolested.

"The other anecdotes relate to the death of General Warren. At the moment when the troops succeeded in carrying the redoubt and the Americans were in full retreat, Gen. Howe, who had been hurt by a spent ball, which bruised his ancle, was leaning on my arm. He called suddenly to me: 'Do you see that elegant young man who has just fallen? do you know him?' I looked to the spot to which he pointed—'Good God, sir, I believe it is my friend Warren.' 'Leave me then instantly—run—keep off the troops, save him if possible.' I fled to the spot, 'My dear friend, said I to him, 'I hope you are not badly hurt:'—he looked up seemed to recollect me, smiled, and died! A musket ball had passed through the upper part of his head"

ADVENTURE BY TWO LADIES.

During the seige of Augusta, two ladies, Grace and Rachael Martin, residing in the Ninety-Six district, South Carolina, learning upon one occasion, that a courier, under the protection of two British soldiers, was to pass their residence, bearing important dispatches, resolved by a well planned stratagem to surprise the party, and deprive the courier of the papers. Disguising themselves in male attire, and provided with arms, they concealed themselves in a thicket on the road side, and patiently awaited the approach of the enemy. It was night, and the darkness favored their plan. They had not remained long in their concealment, before the courier and his escort made their appearance. They were riding carelessly along, without apprehension of danger, when suddenly two figures sprang from a bushy covert, and loudly demanded the dispatches, at the same time presenting their pistols in a threatening manner. Bewildered and alarmed, they yielded at once without any resistance. The ladies then placed them on parole, and hastened home by a near route through the woods, and had scarcely arrived and divested themselves of their male attire, when the same party came riding up to the door, requesting accommodations. The mother of the heroines admitted them, and asked why they had returned, after passing her house but a short time before. They replied by exhibiting their paroles, and stating that they had been taken prisoners by "two rebels." The young ladies, unsuspected by their guests, rallied them of their unfortunate adventure, and inquired "why they did not use their arms", to which they replied, "that they were fallen upon so sudden, they had not time." During their stay, they were as severely overcome by the malicious wit and ralliery of the ladies, as they had been before, by their superior bravery and cunning. The next day they rode away, little dreaming that their hosts had been their conquerors. The dispatches obtained in the heroic manner described, were sent to General Greene, and proved of importance.

CAPTURE OF GENERAL WOODHULL.

On August 28th, 1776, a party of British light horse, entered Jamaica, Long Island, in pursuit of General Woodhull, who had left that town but a short time before. He was pursued and overtaken at Carpenter's inn, two miles east of Jamaica, where he had sought shelter from the rain. He had dispatched his men, some ninety in number, on in advance, while he remained, expecting messengers from Congress. The general was just coming out of the house, and proceeding to the shed where his horse was tied, when the enemy appeared, dashing up to him, and shouting, "surrender, you d——d rebel!" The general delivered his sword, on the assurance from his captors, that he should be treated like an honorable prisoner, and a gentleman. But no sooner was the venerable soldier completely in their power, than they brutally commanded him to say "God save the King!" "God save us all!" was his sublime reply. "God save the king," they again shouted, and struck at him ferociously. His head, and uplifted arm received the sabre cuts aimed at him, and seven gashes let out the patriot's blood. All wounded and bleeding as he was, he was mounted behind one of the troopers, and hurried off to Jamaica, where the surgeon of the village was refused permission to dress his wounds. A British surgeon was called in, who bungingly did the work. The next day he was removed to the Prison ship, where, notwithstanding his mangled condition, he was obliged to sleep on the bare floor of the transport, until a lieutenant privately provided him with a mattrass. His arm mortified, and death ensued.

BRITISH BARBARITY.

On Arnold's expedition into Connecticut, it became necessary, in order to secure possession of New London, to capture Fort Griswold, situated on the opposite side of the river. Col. Eyre, with a large body of men, was dispatched against it; and although the Americans resisted spiritedly, the works were carried by the enemy. During the contest, one of the guns in the fort was becoming useless for the want of wadding, when a patriotic lady, who was in the fort, instantly loosed a flannel petticoat from her person, and threw it to the gunners, with the exclamation, "this will enable you to fire a few shots more."

The scene that ensued upon the surrender of the fort, is one of the blackest stains on the English flag. But few of the Americans were killed during the contest, but after the surrender, seventy of them were massacred in cold blood. When Major Montgomery entered the fort, (his superior, Col. Eyre, being wounded) he asked who commanded it. The brave Col. Ledyard, responded very civilly, "I once had that honor, the command is your's now;" at the same time offering his sword. The brutal Major instantly seized it, and plunged it into the breast of his unarmed foe. An American officer standing by, instantly revenged this treachery by cutting down Montgomery, but was in turn slaughtered. This example of the officer was instantly followed by a general slaughter of the prisoners. The British afterward loaded an ox-cart with wounded Americans, and started it down a hill with the intention of running it into the river, but just as it obtained considerable velocity, it struck a large tree, and the concussion was so great, that several were killed by it, and all put to the keenest torture. What are we to think of such wanton barbarity! But even this did not satisfy them. After removing their own dead and wounded, they laid a train of powder to the magazine, and left the fort, although there were several wounded Americans within it. But the explosion was prevented by a wounded soldier, who crawled upon the train, and saturated it with his life blood, so that the fire could not communicate with the magazine.

ADVENTURE OF CHARLES MORGAN.

CHARLES MORGAN, was a shrewd private of the Jersey brigade, a good soldier, and had attracted the notice of the Marquis de la Fayette. In the course of the movements on James river, the marquis was anxious to procure exact information of the force under Cornwallis, and if poss'ble, to penetrate his lordship's designs he considered Charles as a proper agent for the accomplishment of his purposes, and proposed to him to enter the British camp in the character of a deserter, but in reality as a spy. Charles undertook the perilous enterprise, merely stipulating that, if he were detected, the marquis should cause it to be inserted in the Jersey newspapers, that he was acting under the orders of his commanding officer.

The pretended deserter entered the British lines and was conducted into the presence of Cornwallis. On being questioned by that nobleman, concerning his motives for desertion, he replied, "that he had been with the American army from the beginning of the war and that while under General Washington, he was satisfied; but now that they had put them under a Frenchman, he did not like it, and therefore had deserted." Charles was received without suspicion, was punctual in discharging his duty as a soldier, and carefully observed everything that passed. One day while on duty with his comrades, Cornwallis, who was in close conversation with some of his officers, called him and asked, "How long will it take the marquis to cross James river?"

"Three hours, my lord," was the answer.

"Three hours!" exclaimed his lordship, "will it not take three days?"

"No, my lord," said Charles; "the marquis has so many boats, each boat will carry so many men; and if your lordship will take the trouble of calculating, you will find he can cross in three hours." Turning to his officers, the earl said, in the hearing of the American, "the scheme will not do."

Charles was now resolved to abandon his new friends: and for that purpose plied his comrades with grog, till they were all in high spirits with the liquor. He then began to complain of the wants in the British camp, extolled the plentiful provision enjoyed by the Americans, and concluded by proposing to them to desert: they agreed to accompany him, and left it to him to manage the sentinels. To the first he offered, in a very friendly manner, a draught of rum from his canteen; but, while the soldier was drinking, Charles seized his arms, and then proposed to him to desert with them, which he did through necessity. The second sentinel was served in the same way; and Charles hastened to the American camp at the head of seven British deserters On presenting himself before his employer, the marquis exclaimed "Ah, Charles! have you got back?"

"Yes sir," was the answer, "and have brought seven more with me." The marquis offered him money, but he declined accepting it, and only desired to have his gun again: the marquis then proposed to raise him to the rank of a corporal or sergeant, but Charles' reply was, "I will not have any promotion; I have abilities for a common soldier, and have a good character: should I be promoted, my abilities may not answer, and I may lose my character." He, however, generously requested for his fellow-soldiers, who were not so well supplied with stockings, shoes, and clothing, as himself, the marquis' interference to procure a supply of their wants.

EXPLOITS ON THE FRONTIERS.

The following daring exploits, which we draw from various sources, admirably illustrate the sagacity and coolness of our backwoodsmen. Had they been performed by mailed and gauntletted knights of old, and sung by minstrel chroniclers, they would to this day, be the favored themes of poets, and have become immortalized. Assuredly they are as well worthy a place in history, when enacted by those, whose unconquerable spirits helped to form and rear the independence of our country, as if performed by the half-robber hero of the middle ages. Heroism is heroism, and no more, whether it glows beneath a leather-jerkin or a steeled breast-plate.

DAVID ELERSON.

David Elerson was one of those bold spirits, who took an active part in the Border Wars of the Revolution, along the Mohawk Valley, and on the western frontiers of the State of New York. He followed Sullivan in his celebrated invasion of the Indian Territory in 1779, and while Morgan's rifle corps, to which he belonged, was stationed at the head of Otsego Lake, occurred the following adventure:

"He had rambled off to an old clearing, at the distance of a mile or more from the camp, to gather pulse for dinner. Having filled his knapsack, while adjusting it in order to return to camp, he was startled at the rustling of the tall and coarse herbage around him, and in the same instant beheld ten or a dozen Indians, who had crept upon him so cautiously as to be just on the point of springing to grasp him. Their object clearly was rather to make him a prisoner than to kill him, since he might easily have been shot down unperceived. Seizing his rifle, which was standing by his side, Elerson sprang forward to escape. A shower of tomahawks hurtled through the air after him; but as he plunged into a thicket of tall weeds and bushes, he was only struck on one of his hands, his middle finger being nearly severed. A brisk chase was immediately commenced. Scaling an old brush-wood fence, Elerson darted into the woods, and the Indians after him. He was as fleet as a stag, and perceiving that they were not likely soon to overtake, the pursuers discharged their rifles after him, but luckily without effect. The chase was then continued from eleven till three o'clock—Elerson using every device and stratagem to elude, or deceive the Indians, but they holding him close. At length, having gained a moment to breathe, an Indian started up in his front. Drawing up his rifle to clear the passage in that direction, the whizz of a bullet fleshing his side, and the crack of a rifle, from another point, taught him that delays were particularly dangerous at that spot. The Indian in front, however, had disappeared on his presenting his rifle, and Elerson again darted forward. His wounded side bled a little, though not enough to weaken him. Having crossed a ridge, he paused a moment in the valley beyond, to slake his thirst—his mouth being parched, and himself almost fainting. On rising from the brook, the head of one of his pursuers peeped over the crest of the hill. He raised his rifle, but such was his exhaustion he could not hold it steady. A minute more, and he would have been in the power of the savages. Raising his rifle again, and steadying it by the side of a tree, he brought the savage tumbling headlong down the hill. In the next moment his trusty rifle was re-loaded and primed, and in the next the whole group of his pursuers came rushing over the ridge. He again supposed his moments were numbered; but being partly sheltered by the trunk of a large hemlock, they saw not him, but only the body of their fallen comrade yet quivering in the agonies of death. Drawing in a circle about the body of their companion, they raised the death wail; and as they paused, Elerson made another effort to fly. Before they resumed the pursuit, he had succeeded in burying himself in a dark thicket of hemlocks, where he found the hollow trunk of a tree, into which he crept. Here he lay ensconced two full days, without food or dressings for his wound. On the third day he backed out of 'the loop-hole of his retreat,' but knew not which way to proceed—not discerning the points of the compass. In the course of two or three miles, however, he came to a clearing, and found himself at Cobleskill—having, during his recent chase, run over hill and dale, bog, brook, and fence, upward of twenty-five miles!"

ATTACK ON MR. SHANKLAND'S HOUSE.

"About the same time, and probably by the same party of Indians, the premises of a Mr. Shankland, lying in their tract, situated in the outskirts of Cherry Valley, were assaulted. Residing two or three miles from the village, his house had escaped the common destruction which had fallen upon his neighbors in the preceding autumn. But he had nevertheless removed his family to the valley of the Mohawk for safety, and had returned to his domicil accompanied only by his son.. They were awakened just before dawn by the assailants, who were endeavoring to cut away the door with their hatchets. Taking down his two guns, Mr. Shankland directed his son to load them, while he successively fired to the best advantage. But not being able to see the enemy, he determined upon a sortie. Having a spear, or espontoon, in the house, he armed himself therewith, and carefully unbarring the door, rushed forth upon the besiegers, who fled back at his sudden apparition. One of the Indians whom he was specially pursuing, tumbled over a log, and as Mr. Shankland struck at him, his spear entered the wood, and parted from the shaft. Wrenching the blade from the log, he darted back into the house, barred the door, and again commenced firing upon the assailants. They had been so much surprised by this rushing out upon them, that they neither fired a shot, nor hurled a tomahawk, until he had returned to his castle, and barred the sally port. During this part of the affray, his son, becoming frightened, escaped from the house, and ran for the woods. He was pursued, overtaken, and made captive. The father, however, continued the fight—the Indians firing through the casements at random, and he returning the shots as well as he could. At one time he thought of sallying forth again, and selling his life to the best advantage; but by thus doing, he very rightly judged that he should at once involve the life of his son. The Indians, growing wearied of fighting at such disadvantage, at last attempted to make sure of their victim by applying the torch, and the house was speedily in flames. But it so happened that between the rear of the house and the forest, a field of hemp interposed—into which Mr. Shankland contrived to throw himself, unperceived by the Indians. Concealed from observation by the hemp, he succeeded in reaching the woods and making good his retreat to the Mohawk. Meantime the Indians remained by the house until it was consumed, together, as they supposed, with the garrison. They then raised a shout of victory, and departed."

DARING ADVENTURE OF A CAPTIVE.

"Among the captives taken by the Indians on the Ohio in 1780 was a man named Alexander McConnell, of the Kentucky settlers. He found his captors, five in number, to be pleasant tempered and social, and he succeeded in winning their confidence, by degrees, until they essentially relaxed the rigors of his confinement at night. His determination was of course to escape. At length his fastenings were so slight, that while they were asleep he succeeded in the entire extrication of his limbs. Still he dared not to fly, lest escape from so many pursuers should be impracticable, and his life, should he be re-taken, would surely be required in payment for the rash attempt. To strike them successively with one of their own tomahawks would be impossible. His next plan was cautiously to remove three of their loaded rifles to a place of concealment, which should, nevertheless, be convenient for his own purpose. Then placing the other two at rest upon a log, the muzzle of one aimed at the head of one Indian, and the other at the heart of a second, with both hands he discharged the rifles together, by which process two of his enemies were killed outright. As the three others sprang up in amazement, McConnell ran to the rifles which he had concealed. The work was all but of a moment. Seizing another rifle, and bringing it in range of two of the three remaining savages, both fell with the discharge, one dead and the other wounded. The fifth took to his heels, with a yell of horror which made the forest ring."

A GALLANT DEFENCE.

In a German settlement in the upper section of the Mohawk Valley resided one John Christian Shell, who had built a block house of his own, which was large, substantial, and well calculated for defence. On one occasion when this district was threatened with an invasion by the Indians and Tories, the inhabitants had all taken refuge in Fort Dayton, except Shell, who resolved to remain and defend his own domicil. He and his sons were at work in a field, when a party of the enemy appeared, headed by one McDonald. Himself and four of his sons succeeded in reaching their castle, but the two younger, twins of but eight years old, fell prisoners into the hands of the assailants. Once within the house, and its ponderous door barricaded, Shell commenced the battle, his wife loading the pieces, while himself and sons discharged them. The besiegers, however, were determined and brave. An effort was made by them to set fire to the building, but the galling fire from the garrison drove them back. McDonald procured a crow-bar, and endeavored to break open the door, but a well-directed shot from Shell, struck him in the leg, and put him *hors du combat*. With the rapidity of lightning Shell sprang to the door, unbolted it, seized the wounded man, and dragged him into the fort, ere his followers could arrive to rescue him. This was a most fortunate circumstance. The ammunition of the besieged was running low, and the consequences of such an event were seriously apprehended. But their prisoner was amply provided with cartridges, and he was compelled to deliver them up under the threat of instant death should he refuse

Thus the leader of the enemy supplied the means for the defeat of his own party. They had been severely galled, and now drew off for a respite. The battle had commenced at two o'clock, and it was now nearly dark. The garrison also needed breathing time, and feeling assured that the building would not be fired while the enemy's leader was in his possession, Shell ceased firing But the enemy soon rallied to the fight, and while Shell was engaged in a hymn of thanksgiving, they marched up to the fort and thrust their rifles through the loop-holes, but Mrs. Shell seizing an axe, by rapid and sure blows, completely ruined every musket thrust through the walls, by bending the barrels. A few more shots from Shell, and the assailants were driven back. Shell then ran up to the second story, just at twilight, and called out in a loud voice, that Capt. Small was approaching, and added—"Capt. Small, march your company around upon this side of the house. Capt. Getman, you had better wheel your men off to the left, and come up on that side." The directions of Shell were given with so much apparent earnestness, that the enemy really believed troops were approaching, and they retreated, taking with them the two boy prisoners. They were restored after the war.

HEROISM OF A WOMAN.

During an attack by Tories and Indians on Fort Hunter, the females within the fortress displayed a heroism worthy of lasting praise and commendation. They were provided with arms, and were prepared to use them should occasion offer. The well of the fort was without the works, and a soldier was detached to bring water into the fort for the use of the garrison. The office was one of great danger, and the soldier showed signs of fear and trepidation in performing the duty required of him. This was observed by an interesting young lady, and she snatched the bucket and ran forth herself for the water. She was within the enemy's fire, but without change of color, or any evidence of fear she drew and brought bucket after bucket to the thirsty soldiers, and escaped entirely without injury.

STIRRING INCIDENTS.

In the spring of 1779, two men named Cowley and Sawyer, were captured near Harpersfield, by a party of Indians, and carried off prisoners towards Canada. One of the captives was an Irishman, the other Scotch. They were captives eleven days before a favorable opportunity was afforded them to escape. They had arrived at a deserted hut near Tioga Point, when they were set to work to cut wood a few rods distant. Cowley took this opportunity to take a newspaper from his pocket, and pretended to read its contents, while he recounted to him a plan for escape, and explained the part they were to take in the attempt. That night they lay down to rest in the hut, as usual, a prisoner between two Indians. When the captives were satisfied their foes were all sound in sleep, they cautiously arose and secured the savage's weapons, and shook the priming from them. They then armed themselves, one with a tomahawk, the other with an axe, and stationed themselves by two of the Indians who were considered the most formidable of the party. At the given signal the blows fell suddenly and surely upon their victims; but unfortunately Sawyer, in attempting to force his weapon from the skull of the Indian, drew the handle from it, and thus the rest of the work remained to be performed by Cowley. The noise in dispatching the first two Indians, awoke their companions, one of whom in attempting to rise received a blow from Cowley's axe upon his shoulder which caused him to fall back stunned. The fourth also received a heavy blow from the axe, but he escaped to a neighboring swamp, and when found by his pursuers was already dead Upon the return of Cowley and Sawyer to the hut, while they were engaged in discussing their next course, the Indian who had been stunned by the blow of the axe, suddenly sprang to his feet, rushed to the rifles at hand, snapped one at his foes, but finding the priming gone, he dashed into the woods and disappeared.

The next morning the two friends started on their return, but they soon discovered that they were pursued by a party of Indians, who, no doubt, were hot for their blood. Their vigilance and skill were now roused to the utmost. During one night and two days they remained concealed beneath a shelving rock, and one time a dog belonging to the enemy, scented out their retreat, but to the astonishment and great joy of the fugitives, he contented himself with smelling around them, and left without barking or otherwise alarming the pursuers. Although surrounded by the enemy, and on one night seeing the fires lit by the savages, literally enclosing them in on all sides, they had the good fortune to elude the vigilance of their foes, and to arrive at a frontier settlement, safe, but exhausted from fatigue and hunger.

A DARING FELLOW.

SAMUEL BRADY was a powerful, bold and vigorous backwoodsman, who from his many successful attacks on the Indians, was particularly obnoxious to them. He was also a very successful beaver hunter, and on one of his excursions to Beaver river, Mohoning, in pursuit of these animals, it so happened that he was surprised in his camp and taken prisoner by a party of Indians. To have slain him at once would have been small satisfaction, he was, therefore, taken alive to the encampment of the savages, for the purpose of being burned alive in the presence of all the Indians of the village, and by the exquisite sufferings of such a death obtain that revenge they so dearly prized.

"After tne usual exultations and rejoicings at the capture of a noted enemy, and causing him to run the gauntlet, a fire was prepared, near which Brady was placed, after being stripped naked, and with his arms unbound. Previously to tying him on the stake, a large circle was formed around him, consisting of Indian men, women, and children, dancing and yelling, and uttering all manner of threats and abuse that their small knowledge of the English language could afford. The prisoner looked on these preparations of death, and on his savage foes, with a firm countenance and a steady eye, meeting all their threats with a truly savage fortitude. In the midst of their dancing and rejoicing, a squaw of one of their chief's came near him with a child in her arms. Quick as thought, and with instinctive presence of mind, he snatched it from her and threw it into the midst of the flames. Horror-struck at the sudden outrage, the Indians simultaneously rushed to rescue the infant from the fire. In the midst of this confusion, Brady darted from the circle, overturning all that came in his way, and rushed into the adjacent thicket, with the Indians at his heels. He ascended the steep side of a hill, amidst a shower of bullets, and dashing down the opposite declivity, secreted himself in the deep ravine and laurel thicket that abounded for several miles beyond the hill. His knowledge of the country, and wonderful activity, enabled him to elude his enemies, and reach the settlement on the south of the Ohio river, which he crossed by swimming. The hill near whose base, this adventure is said to have happened, still goes by his name."

On one occasion, when pursued by a large body of savages, he approached the Cuyahoga, at a place where the river cut a deep chasm through the rocks, leaving a steep declivity on each bank. As they drew near this spot, the Indians fancied his capture certain, but they did not yet appreciate the powers and resources of their enemy. Knowing that life or death were in the effort, Brady, as he approached the chasm, prepared for a mighty effort, and with one bound cleared the wide space, to the utter and bewildering astonishment of his pursuers, who stopped short in admiration at the daring and wonderful feat. It so happened that in landing on the opposite cliff, he dropped into a low place, and seizing the bushes, he helped himself to ascend to the top of the cliff. Before the Indians could recover their astonishment, he was half way up the opposite hill, but still within reach of their rifles. They had forbore to use the rifle before, in the hope of taking his life, and glutting, by torture, their long-delayed revenge, but now seeing he was likely to escape, they sent a volley of bullets after him, one of which wounded him in the hip. The Indians having to make a circuit before they could cross the stream, Brady now gained considerably on them. But his limb began to grow stiff from his wound, which retarded his progress, and his pursuers in turn advanced rapidly upon him. He, therefore, made for a pond, swam under water some distance, and came up where the trunk of a large oak which had fallen into the water, concealed him from observation. The Indians traced him to the pond, and there his tracks of blood ceasing, and being unable to see any signs of him they came to the conclusion that in attempting to escape by swimming, he had drowned. They, therefore, departed, and then Brady, fatigued and lame, crawled out from the pond, and hurried towards his house. The chasm across which he performed his wonderful feat, to this day, is known by the name of "Brady's Leap."

A FEARFUL ENCOUNTER.

"In the summer of 1782, a party of seven Wyandots made an incursion into a settlement some distance below Fort Pitt, in Virginia. Here finding an old man alone in a cabin, they killed him, packed what plunder they could find, and commenced their retreat. Amongst their party was a celebrated Wyandot chief, who, in addition to his fame as a warrior and counsellor, was, as to his size and strength, a real giant.

"The news of the visit of the Indians soon spread through the neighborhood, and a party of eight good riflemen was selected in a few hours for the purpose of pursuing the Indians. In this party were two brothers, of the names of Adam and Andrew Poe. They were both famous for courage, skill, and activity. This little party commenced the pursuit of the Indians with a determination, if possible, not to suffer them to escape, as they usually did on such occasions, by making a speedy flight to the Ohio river, crossing it, and then dividing into small parties, to meet at a distant point in a given time. The pursuit was continued the greater part of the night, after the Indians had done the mischief. In the morning the party found themselves on the trail of the Indians, which led to the river. When arrived within a little distance of the river, Adam Poe, fearing an ambuscade, left the party, who followed directly on the trail, to creep along the brink of the river bank, under cover of the woods and bushes, to fall on the rear of the Indians, should he find them in ambuscade. He had not gone far before he saw the Indian rafts at the water's edge. Not seeing any Indians, he stepped softly down the bank, with his rifle cocked. When about half way down, he discovered the large Wyandot chief, and a small Indian, within a few steps of him. They were standing with their guns cocked, and looking in the direction of our party, who, by this time, had gone some distance lower down the bottom. Poe took aim at the large chief, but his rifle missed fire. The Indians hearing the snap of the gun lock, instantly turned round and discovered Poe, who being too near them to retreat, dropped his gun, and sprang from the bank upon them, and seizing the large Indian by his clothes on his breast, and at the same time embracing the neck of the small one, threw them both down on the ground, himself being uppermost. The small Indian soon extricated himself, ran to the raft, got his tomahawk, and attempted to dispatch Poe, the large Indian holding him fast in his arms with all his might, the better to enable his fellow to effect his purpose. Poe, however, so well watched the motions of his assailant, that, when in the act of aiming his blow at his head, by a vigorous and well directed kick with one of his feet, he staggered the savage, and knocked the tomahawk out of his hand. This failure, on the part of the small Indian, was reproved by an exclamation of contempt from the large one.

"In a moment the Indian caught up his tomahawk again, approached more cautiously, brandishing his tomahawk, and making a number of feigned blows in derision and defiance. Poe, however, still on his guard, averted the real blow from his head, by throwing up his arm, and receiving it on his wrist, in which he was severely wounded; but not so as to entirely lose the power of his arm. In this perilous moment, Poe, by a violent effort, broke loose from the Indian, snatched up one of the Indian's guns, and shot the small Indian through the breast, as he ran up the third time to tomahawk him. The large Indian was now on his feet, and grasping Poe by a shoulder and leg, threw him down on the bank. Poe instantly disengaged himself, and got on his feet. The Indian then seized him again, and a new struggle ensued, which, owing to the slippery state of the bank, ended in the fall of both combatants into the water. In this situation, it was the object of each to drown the other. Their efforts to effect their purpose, were continued for some time with alternate success, sometimes one being under the water, and sometimes the other. Poe at length seized the tuft of hair on the scalp of the Indian, with which he held his head under water until he supposed him drowned. Relaxing his hold too soon, Poe instantly found his gigantic antagonist on his feet again, and ready for another combat. In this they were carried into the water beyond their depth. In this situation they were compelled to loose their hold on each other, and swim for mutual safety. Both sought the shore, to seize a gun, and end the contest with bullets. The Indian being the best swimmer, reached the land first. Poe seeing this, immediately turned back into the water, to escape, if possible, being shot, by diving. Fortunately the Indian caught up the rifle with which Poe had killed the other warrior. At this juncture, Andrew Poe arrived upon the spot. Missing his brother from the party, and supposing from the report of the gun which he shot, that he was either killed, or engaged in a conflict with the Indians, hastened in the direction whence the firing came. On seeing him, Adam called out to him to 'kill the big Indian on shore.' But Andrew's gun, like that of the Indian's, was empty. The contest was now between the white and the Indian, who should load and fire first. Very fortunately for Poe, the Indian in loading drew the ramrod from the thimbles of the stock of the gun with so much violence, that it slipped out of his hand, and fell a little distance from him. He quickly caught it up, and rammed down his bullet. This little delay gave Poe the advantage. He shot the Indian as he was raising his gun to take aim at him."

During the contest between Poe and the Indians the rest of the party had overtaken the remaining five of them. A desperate conflict ensued, in which all of the Indians were killed, save one who alone escaped to tell the melancholy tale of the fate of his fellows. There was great grief in the Wyandot nation. The big Indian, and four of his brothers, who were all killed in this conflict, were distinguished chiefs, and their fall caused universal mourning.

MISCELLANEOUS ANECDOTES.

In one of the numerous partisan encounters in the South, Capt. Falls, a gallant and heroic officer, while leading a body of militia against a detachment of tories, was shot through the heart, and fell dead. He had been accompanied to the battle by his son, a youth of fourteen. "When the captain fell, this high-minded stripling, moved by an instinctive impulse of affection, sprang from his horse, to embrace the body, and protect it from insult. One of the enemy, believed to be the same that had shot the captain, advancing with a view to plunder the corpse, the son, suddenly snatching the sword of the deceased, plunged it into the bosom of the marauder, and thus, at once, punished audacity, and nobly revenged his father's death."

At the battle of Eutaw Springs, the following ludicrous incident occurred. The Americans had pursued the English so closely that they had taken refuge in a brick dwelling, while in their haste to close the door upon the rapidly advancing Americans they shut out some of their own officers, who were immediately surrounded by their captors. The Americans were now exposed to a galling fire, from those within the building, and they only found safety by interposing the persons of their captives between themselves and the marksmen at the windows. Among the British officers taken, was one Major Barry, who without the slightest resistance, began only with a profound solemnity to enumerate his many titles. "Sir, I am Henry Barry, Deputy Adjutant General of the British army, Secretary to the commandant of Charleston, captain of the 52d regiment, &c." "Enough, enough," replied Col. Manning, in whose hands he had fallen. "You are just the man I was looking of. Fear nothing: you shall *screen me* from danger, and I shall take especial care of you," and with the pompous major held before his person, the American officer secured a safe retreat.

WHEN the British obtained possession of Charleston, General Gadsden was lieutenant-governor of South Carolina, and he was among those paroled by the English commanders. But irritated by the popular outbreaks under Marion and Sumter, the English so far lost their sense of justice, as to arrest a large number of the citizens, among whom was Gadsden. He was arrested in his house, and conveyed on board a prison-ship, and thence to St. Augustine. Here he was offered his parole on condition, that he should do nothing "prejudicial to the British interests." Gadsden received the proposition with scorn. "With men," said he, "who have once deceived me, I can enter into no new contract. I gave one parole, and although I strictly observed its conditions, I have been seized, hurried from my family and home, and in the most unlawful manner. And now I am asked for more pledges by those who will be bound by none. No, sir; I will give no new parole" "Think better of it," was the reply of the British officer. "Your rejection of this officer, consigns you to a dungeon." "I am ready for it—prepare it," was the answer; "I will give no parole, *so help me God!*" He was thrown into the dungeon of the castle of St. Augustine, where he lay for ten months, kept from all intelligence, without society, and even prevented from seeing his fellow captives.

The *sobriquet* of "Game Cock," was applied to Sumter, the renowned partisan chief of South Carolina, which he received, it is said, under the following circumstance. While he was seeking recruits, he applied one day to several brothers, by name Gillespie, who were remarkably fond of cock-fighting. They had in their possession a blue hen, of the fighting species, whose progeny were celebrated for their courage. Among them was one named Puck, which had never been defeated in a conflict. Sumter suddenly appeared among the brothers, while they were engaged in their sport, and with ill-disguised contempt, he pronounced their employment child-like and cruel, and abruptly told them, that if they would go with him, he would give them worthier game, "and teach them how to fight with men." Struck with his courageous and fiery bearing, they took him at his word, and cried out, " Puck for ever! He is one of the 'Blue Hen's chickens!'" The *sobriquet* stuck to him always and afterwards, and he was known among his enemies, as well as among his men, by the *nom de guerre* of the "Game Cock."

One morning, during the seige of Charleston, Gen. Moultri was awakened by a more than ordinary furious cannonading from the enemy, and just as he leapt from his bed, a cannon ball came crashing through the house, traversing the entire length of the bed, tearing it to pieces, and scattering the fragments in every direction, after which mischief it continued on its career.

In the celebrated battle of Fort Moultrie a most remarkable coolness was manifested by the Americans. Moultrie, as well as several of his officers, smoked their pipes during the action, and only removed them when they had occasion to issue orders. Moultrie, in his Memoirs, gives us the following little incident, which speaks well for the coolness of his men. "When the action begun (it being a warm day,) some of the men took off their coats and threw them upon the top of the merlons. I saw a shot take one of them and throw it into a small tree behind the platform. It was noticed by our men, and they cried out, 'Look at the coat !'"

When General Greene was retreating from the Catawba, an incident occurred which admirably illustrates the sacrificing spirit of the American women. On the line of his retreat he stopped at a house for repose and refreshment. He had ridden all the day in a severe rain storm, and he was wet, fatigued, and his heart was sad and burdened with gloomy forebodings. His landlady observed his despondency, and upon asking him about his condition, he replied that he was "tired, hungry, and penniless." Refreshments were provided for him, and after he had partaken of them, the good woman drew him into a private apartment, and placing in his hands two bags of specie—all her wealth, made up of the little savings of years, she said, "Take these; I can do without them, and they are necessary to you."

In one district of the South during the war the young women at harvest time, formed themselves into a company of reapers. and went to all the farms of the neighborhood, and if the reply to the question—" Is the owner out with the fighting men ?" was in the affirmative, they would set to, cut and garner all the grain It was generally no small undertaking, and five or six weeks of unceasing toil were necessary to complete their rounds. Similar companies were formed in New York and Long Island. A whig paper of July 25th, 1776; says: "The most respectable ladies set the example, and say they will take the farming business on themselves so long as the rights and liberties of their country require the presence of their sons, husbands, and lovers in the field."

On one occasion a person by the name of Mills, belonging to Sumter's troops, was despatched to Charleston to draw money for the troops. He soon observed that he was dogged by an individual of a suspicious appearance, and just as he was preparing to leave the city, he managed to enter into a friendly conversation with the man, and invited him to his room. The stranger complied, but no sooner had he entered than Mills closed and locked the door, then produced a decanter of brandy, and told the man e must drink up the brandy on penalty of being shot. There was no alternative, and the fellow was obliged to comply. When e became hopelessly drunk, Mills left him, mounted his horse nd left the city.

"Mary Knight was one of those devoted women who contributed to the relief of Washington's army at Valley Forge—cooking and carrying provisions to them alone, through the depth of winter, even passing through the outposts of the British army in the disguise of a market-woman. And when Washington was compelled to retreat before a superior force, she concealed he brother, Gen. Worrell (when the British set a price on his head. in a cider hogshead in the cellar for three days, and fed him through the bung-hole; the house being ransacked four differen times by the troops in search of him, without success."

In the battle of Monmouth a gunner was killed, and a call was made for another to supply his place, when the wife of the fallen soldier, who had followed him through the wars, advanced and took his station, expressing a wish to do her duty, and impelled by a desire to revenge his death. The gun was well managed, and Washington was so much pleased at the report of her conduct, that after the battle he summoned her before him, and gave her a lieutenant's commission. She was afterwards called in the army, *Captain Molly.*

The British troops in their expedition into Connecticut passed through the village of Danbury, when the following incident occurred. As the enemy were advancing along the old Reading road, one of the inhabitants of the town rode his horse up to the summit of an eminence, directly in their front. Waving his hat with his sword, and turning his face as though he was addressing u. army behind him, he thundered out, "*Halt the whole Universe! break off by kingdoms!*" The Britishers, astounded by such an incident, came to a halt. Their cannon were brough forward, and flanking parties sent out to make discoveries. Mr. Halcourt, which was the name of this eccentric individual, finding himself on the point of being surrounded, made a rapid retreat and escaped from his pursuers.

At the battle of Bennington an old farmer had five sons in the field. When it was over a friend came to him, and said, "I have sad news for you." "What is it," replied the father; "have my sons run away from the fight?" "No," replied the friend, "but one is dead." "Bring him to me," replied the old man with an unchanged countenance. The lifeless form of his dead boy was laid before him. There was not a tear in the old man's eye, and not a groan escaped from his lips. He stooped to wipe the blood from the wounds, and to gaze into the pallid face before him. "It is the happiest day of my life," said he, "to know that my five sons have fought nobly for freedom, even though one has fallen on the altar of his country." A similar incident has immortalized the Roman Cato, but how few are acquainted with this instance of sublime patriotism, manifested by an obscure country farmer!

"Some time in the year '76, the British sloop-of-war, Unicorn, put into Holme's Hole, on the island of Martha's Vineyard, and having landed a detachment of marines, pressed into service a number of pilots. Upon this island, a liberty-tree had been erected, around which the citizens were wont to assemble, and pledge their fortunes and their sacred honors in the cause of liberty. Now his Majesty's ship was in want of a spar, and as the only stick of timber on the island that would answer for the purpose, was the liberty-tree, down it must come. The panic stricken citizens consented to sell it to them, and on the morrow it was to be delivered on board. But there was a numerous party who did not agree to this contract, and resolved to prevent its execution. Three young girls, named Parnel Manter, Horial Allen, and Mary Milman, whose young eyes had not yet beheld the frosts of sixteen winters, met together on that evening around the sacred tree, and by means of augurs, pierced it with numerous holes, which they filled with gunpowder; they then cautiously applied the match, and their emblem of liberty was shattered in many pieces." A few years since, the only living member of the heroic trio, who ought to be immortalized in song, Mary Milman was in age and distress, and was obliged to apply to congress for relief.

At the battle of Monmouth, among the Americans wounded, was Lieut. Tallman. He was shot through the throat, and crawled behind the barn to die. Two soldiers came to his relief, and raising him from the ground, were retreating with him across an orchard, when a musket ball passing through the hat of one of them, he hastily abandoned his charge and ran away. The other supported him to the dwelling of a Mr. Cook, in the vicinity, where also was carried another wounded officer, Mr. Nealey. Here they both received the kindest treatment and both officers recovered. But Captain Neally in receiving balm for the injury in his flesh, became wounded in a more tender point. There arose between him and a daughter of Mr. Cook, who had hovered over his couch in the shape of a " 'ministering angel," a romantic attachment, which finally resulted in marriage.

On one occasion, when Baron Steuben was reviewing a regiment, he heard the name of Benedict Arnold called in the muster roll. He commanded the person bearing the offensive name, to immediately advance from the line. The baron after surveying him for a few moments, said, " change your name, brother soldier; you are too respectable to bear the name of a traitor." " What name shall I take, general ?" inquired the young man. " Take any other; mine is at your service." He accepted it, and immediately had his name entered as Frederick William Steuben.

THE ladies of the revolution in Middlesex county, Massachusetts, obtained considerable celebrity, by an adventure of a daring and interesting nature. Rumors having come, that a party of the British were advancing, burning and destroying as they progressed, several of the leading ladies in the county, met together and resolved to organize an opposition to their approach. The male members of the community had most of them departed to join the continental army; these ladies therefore clothed themselves in their husband's apparel, and armed with muskets, pitchforks, and such other weapons as they could find, including no doubt, the household instruments, which legend has always associated with the prowess of women, and proceeded to Jewett's bridge, over the Nashua, between Peperell and Groton. Here they took their stand, and declared that no foe, foreign or domestic, should pass that bridge. They selected Mrs. Wright of Peperell, as their commander.

They were not long stationed here, before one Captain Whiting, a notorious tory, who was supposed to be engaged in conveying treasonable intelligence to the enemy, was observed advancing on horseback towards the interdicted passage. His surprise in finding himself confronted by such specimens of soldiery must no doubt, have been great, but the imperative commands of

Sergeant Wright, left no question as to their determination of purpose. He was unhorsed without ceremony, searched, and the treasonable correspondence discovered concealed in his boots. He was then sent to the proper authorities, and the ladies returned to their voluntary duties.

The Hon. James Schureman, who after the war, served four years in congress, was then sent to the United States Senate, and still later became Mayor of New Brunswick, was a prominent and influential man in New Jersey, during the revolution. On one occasion, the militia of New Brunswick were called out, to go against the enemy. Their captain made a speech, urged them to volunteer; but not one complied. Schureman, then in the ranks stepped out, and after volunteering himself, addressed them so eloquently, that a company was immediately formed, which went to Long Island, and was engaged in the battle there. In the course of the war, Schureman and George Thomson, were taken prisoners by a party of British horse. They were confined for a short time in the guard-house in New Brunswick. From this place, they were conveyed to New York, and confined in the sugar-house While here, they succeeded in enlisting the sympathy of Philip Kissick, a tory, who furnished them with money, with which they procured food. They bribed the guard, to give them the privilege of the yard; and one night having supplied them with some liquor, into which they had put a quantity of laudanum, they dug through the wall and escaped to the upper part of the city, near where the old prison stood. There they got on board a small fishing-boat, and with a single oar, paddled across the Hudson to Powles' Hook, and thence proceeded to Morristown, where they joined the American army.

"At the battle of Monmouth, the Marquis de Lafayette, having approached, with a small escort, within reach of the enemy's guns, for the purpose of reconnoitering their position, his aid-de-camp and friend was struck by a ball, and fell at his side. The officers and soldiers fled precipitately from the spot; but the general would not abandon his friend, while a chance remained of saving his life. He hastened to his side, and, leaning over him, addressed him in tones of kindness and affection, But it was too late; the work of death was already done. Turning away with deep emotion, he left the place with slow and mournful steps, and presently rejoined his escort, who awaited his coming at a safe distance from the fatal battery. It is said that Sir Henry Clinton was present in person at this scene; and recognising the young marquis, by the snow-white charger which he always rode, was so touched by his heroic magnanimity and manly grief, that he commanded the gunners to cease firing, and suffered him to retire unmolested."

About the time of the invasion of General Burgoyne, when the people were flying in terror before his army, an attempt was made to assasinate General Schuyler, by introducing a savage into his house for that purpose. "It was at the hour of bed time, in the evening, and while the general was preparing to retire for the night, that a female servant, in coming in from the hall, saw a gleam of light reflected from the blade of a knife, in the hand of some person, whose dark outline she discovered behind the door. The servant was a black slave, who had sufficient presence of mind, not to appear to have made the discovery. Passing directly through the door into the apartment, where the general was yet standing near the fire-place, with an air of unconcern, she pretended to arrange such articles as were disposed upon the mantel piece, while in an undertone she informed her master of her discovery, and said aloud, 'I will call the guard.' The general instantly seized his arms, while the faithful servant hurried out by another door into a long hall, upon the floor of which lay a loose board which creaked beneath the tread. By the noise she made in trampling rapidly upon the board, the Indian, for such he proved—was led to suppose that the Philistines were upon him in numbers, sprang from his concealment, and fled. He was pursued, however, by the guard, and a few friendly Indians attached to the person of the general, overtaken, and made prisoner."

On one occasion during the war of the Revolution, a stranger applied to the residence of Governor Clinton, for hospitality, and was received, and while refreshments were preparing for him, the Governor entered into conversation with him, in the course of which, in reply to some questions proposed by the host, he manifested so much uneasiness, that the suspicions of the family were aroused. These suspicions became confirmed in their minds by observing him take something very cautiously from his pocket and swallow it. Mrs. Clinton immediately conceived of a plan to make him disgorge his secret. She proceeded to the kitchen, and put a dose of tartar emetic in the cup of coffee preparing for him. The man partook of the beverage, and ere long he began to show signs of indisposition; he soon grew violently sick, and the result was, a small silver ball was discharged from his stomach. The ball was unscrewed, and found to contain an important communication from Sir Henry Clinton to Gen. Burgoyne. The man was arrested as a spy, and "out of his own mouth", as it was wittily said, he was convicted. He suffered death.

CAPTAIN RICHARDSON, of South Carolina, was so vindictively pursued and hunted by the British, that he was obliged to keep himself concealed in Santee Swamp. Large rewards were offered for his apprehension, and straggling parties were out continually in search of him. Notwithstanding all these dangers, he, on one occasion, ventured out of his retreat, in order to pay a visit to his family. Scarcely had he been admitted into his residence, when a party of the enemy were discovered approaching the spot. The moment was one of peril. But the presence of mind of Mrs. Richardson saved him. She hastened to the door, and so managed to detain them, and engage their attention, that he was enabled to rush out of the back door, and reach his place of retreat, before they were admitted.

"IN the battle of Long Island, part of the British army marched down a road, leading from Brooklyn to Gowanus, pursuing the Americans. Several of the American riflemen, in order to be more secure, and at the same time more effectually to succeed in their designs, had posted themselves in the high trees near the road. One of them, whose name is not now known, shot the English Major, Grant; in this he passed undiscovered. Again he loaded his deadly rifle, and fired; another English officer fell. He was then discovered, and a platoon ordered to advance and fire into the tree; which order was immediately carried into execution, and the rifleman fell to the ground, dead. After the battle was over, the two British officers were buried in a field near the place, and their graves fenced in with some posts and rails, where their remains still rest. But, for 'an example to the rebels,' they refused to the American rifleman the rites of sepulture, and the body lay exposed on the ground, until the flesh was rotten, and torn off the bones by the fowls of the air. After a considerable length of time, in a heavy gale of wind, a large tree was uprooted; in the cavity formed by which, some friends to the Americans, notwithstanding the prohibition of the English, deposited the soldier's skeleton, to mingle in peace with its kindred earth."

At one time during the war, Colonel Washington compelled the surrender of Colonel Rugely, who was posted in a very strong redoubt, by a very ingenious method. He ordered a pine log to be cut and mounted on wheels, so as to resemble a cannon. With this he approached the British commander, and summoned him to surrender. Rugely perceiving, as he thought, artillery in the ranks of the enemy, and knowing it impossible to maintain his post against cannon, yielded to the summons. This circumstance afforded the Americans in South Carolina, a great deal of merriment, and the Englishmen suffered a corresponding degree of mortification. Cornwallis, speaking of it in a letter to Tarleton, very significantly remarks, "*Rugely will not be made a Brigadier.*"

"While Enoch Crosby, the Westchester spy, was on duty in the vicinity of Teller's Point, a British sloop-of-war came up the river, and anchored in the stream opposite the Point. With an unconquerable predilection for stratagem, our hero immediately concocted a plot for the sole purpose, as he says, of affording 'a little sport for the soldiers.' He accordingly proceeded down the Point, accompanied by six men, all of whom, save one, concealed themselves in the woods which grew a short distance from the shore, while the other paraded the beach so as to display his uniform in so conspicuous a manner, as to attract the notice of the officers on board the vessel. The enemy swallowed the bait; and a boat was soon put off from the sloop-of-war, manned with eleven men, under the command of a lieutenant, to make a prisoner of this one Yankee, who precipitately fled into the woods as the barge approached the shore. The Englishmen followed, threatening to shoot the fugitive unless he stopped and surrendered. As soon as the pursuers had passed his little party, which were scattered in various directions, Crosby exclaimed,

"'Come on my boys! now we have them!'

"At this signal every man sprang up in his place, with a shout that made the welkin ring; making at the same time such a rustling in the bushes, that the British, thinking themselves surrounded by a superior force, surrendered without resistance."

"At one period in the revolution, Captain Roger Lyon, of North Castle, New York, had the honor of entertaining Gen. Washington and suite, on their route to White Plains. It is related by his grand-son, that during the entertainment, Captain Lyon being blind, handed the General a draught of good cheer, with these words, 'General! the ladies say you are a very handsome man but I cannot see.' 'Tell the ladies,' rejoined Washington, 'I am afraid they are as blind as yourself.'"

"Near Peekskill, on the road to Albany, is situated the 'Sodiers Spring,' which derived its name from the following tragical incident. The British had landed on Verplanck's Point, and commenced so vigorously to cannonade the village of Peekskill, that the Americans had to retire hastily. Their enemies kept up a constant firing upon them as they sought various avenues of retreat. A soldier stopped in his flight to refresh himself at the spring. While on his hands and knees, in the act of drinking, a ball which struck on the eminence above him, glanced obliquely, and descending the road with rapid bounds, finished its course by shattering the thigh of the soldier. Unable to move, he remained bleeding, and in agony, in the same position, until a wagon passing by rescued him. The wound proved fatal.

In one of the incursions of Indians upon our frontier settlements during the revolution, a very romantic incident occurred. The celebrated chief Cornplanter made an attack upon the neighborhood of Fort Plain, burning and destroying, and among the prisoners he captured was one John Abeil, an old inhabitant. The party had not travelled but a few miles on their return when was discovered that this Abeil was almost as well acquainted with their language as the Indians themselves. This fact interested the chief, and on inquiring of his captive his name, Cornplanter knew at once that he stood before *his own father*. Abeil, twenty-five years before, had been a trader among the Indians of Western New York, and in one of his visits became enamored of a pretty squaw, and the result of this affection was the graceful and celebrated warrior, whom the father now for the first time saw standing before him. The chief had learned from his mother the history of his parentage, and his father's name. The meeting was certainly extraordinary to a degrée. The young chief held out strong inducements to his white father to accompany him to his tribe, but paternal affection did not seem so strong in the heart of Abeil as his love for the comforts and luxuries of a white man's home, and so he chose rather to be restored to liberty and be returned to his friends. This was yielded, and he wa conducted in honor back to the settlements. Thus singularly me and parted the father and son.

GEN. SULLIVAN in his expedition into the Genessee Valley, fired daily, while in the Indian country, a morning and evening gun, to notify the scouting parties which were constantly kept out of his position. In one instance a pleasing incident was the result of these signal guns. The firing of a gun alarmed a party of Indians who were near, and they scampered off in great haste, leaving a female, who was in their company, who finding herself thus abandoned, went towards the American camp. On being brought before Col. Butler she stated that she was a native of Danbury, Connecticut; had been married several years before, and was living at Wyoming on the occasion of the massacre, when her husband was killed, an infant at her breast snatched from her arms and brained, and two other children carried away by one party of Indians as prisoners, while she herself was retained as captive by another party. When she arrived with her captors at their place of destination, she was compelled to live with an Indian as his wife, in which position she had remained until the signal gun in frightening away her companions gave her liberty. When she came into the American camp she had an infant child which was the fruit of her late unhappy connection. The child died not long after, and it was suspected that an American soldier, from sympathy to the woman, had given it poison. On the return of the army, she went back to her friends in Connecticut.

On one occasion when a party of Indians attacked the house of Lieut. Vrooman, on the New York frontier, he caught up his infant child and fled to a corn-field, followed by his wife leading her little daughter. He seated himself against the trunk of a tree, and his wife was concealed a few rods from him in the corn. All would probably have been well had not Mrs. Vrooman, not knowing where her husband was, called to him, which informed the enemy of their place of concealment. Her call was scarcely uttered ere a bullet pierced her side, and she fell writhing in death. An Indian now approached and scalped her little daughter, while another savage approached the husband and thrust a spear at him, which he parried, and the infant in his arms smiled. Another pass was parried and the infant again smiled. At the third blow of the spear, which Vrooman succeeded in warding off, the child, but five months old, laughed outright at the supposed sport, and this so awakened the sympathy of the savage that he forebore in his attack, and made Vrooman a prisoner.

"At the commencement of the revolutionary struggle, General Heath's division of the American army was stationed at Morrisania, on Harlem River, N. Y. From his Memoirs we gather the following particulars. A picket from our general's division, of four hundred and fifty men, constantly mounted, by relief, at Morrisania, from which a chain of sentinels, within half gun shot of each other, were planted, from one side of the store to the other, and near the water passage, between Morrisania and Montressor's island, which in some places is very narrow. The sentinels on the American side were ordered not to presume to fire at that of the British, unless the latter began; but the British were so fond of beginning, that there was frequently a firing between them. This having been the case one day, and a British officer walking along the bank, on the Montressor's side, an American sentinel, who had been exchanging some shots with a British sentinel, seeing the officer, and concluding him to be better game, gave him a shot, and wounded him. He was carried up to the house on the island. An officer with a flag soon came down to the creek and called for the American officer of the picket, and informed him that if the American sentinels fired any more, the commanding officer of the island would cannonade Col. Morris's house, in which the officers of the picket were quartered. The American officer was directed to inform the British officer that the American sentinels had always been instructed not to fire upon sentinels unless they were first fired upon, and then to return the fire; that such would be their conduct; as to the cannonading of Col. Morris's house, they might act their pleasure. The firing ceased for some time; but a raw Scotch sentinel having been planted one day, he very soon after discharged his piece at an American sentinel nearest to him, which was immediately returned; upon which a British officer came down, and called to the American officers, observing that he thought there was to be no firing between the sentinels. He was answered, that their own began; upon which he replied, 'he shall answer for it then.' There was no firing between the sentinels at that place, any more, and they were so civil to each other on the posts, that one day, at a part of the creek where it was practicable, the British sentinel asked the

American if he could give him a chew of tobacco; the latter having a thick, twisted roll, sent it across the creek to the British sentinel, who after taking off his bite, sent the remainder back."

IN December, 1777, while Washington was at Valley Forge and the enemy was in Philadelphia, Major Talmadge was stationed between the two places with a detachment of cavalry, to make observations and to limit the range of British foragers. On one occasion, while performing this duty, he was informed that a country girl had gone into Philadelphia—perhaps by Washington's instigations, ostensibly to sell eggs, but really and especially to obtain information respecting the enemy; and curiosity led him to move his detachment to Germantown. There the main body halted while he advanced with a small party towards the British lines. Dismounting at a tavern in plain sight of their outposts, he soon saw a young girl coming out of the city. He watched her till she came up to the tavern; made himself known to her, and was about to receive some valuable intelligence, when he was informed the British light horse were advancing. Stepping to the door he saw them in full pursuit of his patroles. He hastily mounted, but before he had started his charger, the girl was at his side begging for protection. Quick as thought, he ordered her to mount behind him. She obeyed, and in that way rode to Germantown, a distance of three miles. During the whole ride, writes the Major in his Journal, where we find these details "although there was considerable firing of pistols, and not a little wheeling and charging, she remained unmoved, and never once complained of fear."

OF all the heroines whose names are imperishably connected

with our history, that of Elizabeth Zane stands foremost. In 1777, Fort Henry in Ohio county, Virginia, was attacked by the Indians. The defence was made with vigor, but suddenly the ammunition became exhausted, and surrender seemed the only alternative. There was a keg of powder in a house about twelve rods distant, which to obtain would prolong the defence, and perhaps preserve the lives of the whole garrison. It was resolved that one person should venture out, and, if possible, secure and bear into the fort the valued prize. The Indians having retired a little distance, a favorable opportunity was afforded, but it became difficult to decide who should undertake the service, as every soldier was emulous for the honor of performing the perilous, but honorable enterprise. Their contention, however, was cut short by Miss Zane, who claimed to be chosen for performing the duty, giving as reasons, that the life of a soldier was more valuable in the defence of the fort, than was her own, and that her sex might preserve her errand from suspicion, and secure the success of the plan. Her resolute manner and urgent arguments overcame the scruples of the officer, and she was permitted to make the attempt. The Indians observed her depart from the fort, but from some unknown cause, offered her no molestation. She reached the house, eized the powder, and hastened to return. But by this time the avages comprehended the object of her visit without the fort. They fired a volley after her, as she with speed ran rapidly along to the gate of the fort. Fortunately not a bullet injured her They only gave activity to her movements, and reaching the fort, she was admitted, to the unbounded joy of the garrison. Animated by so noble an instance of heroism, the besieged fought with a bravery and vigor which the enemy could not overcome. and they raised the seige.

During the revolutionary war, while Fort Motte, situated on Congaree river, in South Carolina, was in the hands of the British, in order to effect its surrender, it became necessary to burn a large mansion standing near the centre of the trench. The house was the property of Mrs. Motte. Lieut. Colonel Lee communicated to her the contemplated work of destruction with painful reluctance, but her smiles, half anticipating his proposal, showed, at once, that she was willing to sacrifice her property if she could thereby aid in the least degree towards the expulsion of the enemy and the salvation of the land. The reply she made to the proposal was that she was " gratified with the opportunity of of contributing to the good of her country, and should view the approaching scene with delight !"

" Governor Griswold was once indebted to a happy thought of his wife for his escape from the British, to whom he was extremely obnoxious. He was at home, but expected to set out immediately for Hartford, to meet the legislature, which had commenced its session a day or two previous. The family residence was at Blackhill, opposite Saybrook Point, and situated on the point of land formed by Connecticut river on the east, and Long Island Sound on the south. British ships were lying in the sound; and as the governor was known to be at this time in his own mansion, a boat was secretly sent ashore for the purpose of securing his person. Without previous warning, the family were alarmed by seeing a file of marines coming up from the beach to the house. There was no time for flight. Mrs. Griswold bethought herself of a large meat barrel, or tierce, which had been brought in a day or two before, and was not yet filled. Quick as thought, she decided that the governor's proportions—which were by no means slight—must be compressed into this, the only available hiding-place. He was obliged to submit to be stowed in the cask and covered. The process occupied but a few moments, and the soldiers presently entered. Mrs. Griswold was of course innocent of all knowledge of her husband's whereabouts, though she told them she well knew the legislature was in session, and that business required his presence at the capital. The house and cellar having been searched without success, the soldiers departed. By the time their boat reached the ship, the governor was galloping up the road on his way to Hartford.'

"A BRITISH officer, distinguished by his inhumanity and constant oppression of the unfortunate, meeting Mrs. Charles Elliot in a garden, adorned with a great variety of flowers, asked the name of the Camomile, which appeared to flourish with peculiar luxuriance. 'The Rebel Flower,' she replied. 'Why was that name given to it?' inquired the officer. 'Because,' rejoined the lady, 'it thrives most when most trampled upon.'"

"MRS. DANIEL HALL having obtained permission to pay a visit to her mother on John's Island, was on the point of embarking, when an officer stepping forward in the most authoritative manner, demanded the key of her trunk. 'What do you expect to find there?' asked the lady. 'I seek for treason,' was the reply. You may then save yourself the trouble of search,' said Mrs Hall. 'You may find plenty of it at my tongue's end.'"

"MRS. THOMAS HEYWARD, in two instances, with the utmost firmness, refused to illuminate for British victories. An officer forced his way into her presence, and sternly demanded of Mrs Heyward, 'How dare you disobey the order which has been issued; why, madam, is not your house illuminated?'—'Is it possible for me, sir,' replied the lady, with perfect calmness, 'to feel a spark of joy? Can I celebrate the victory of your army, whil my husband remains a prisoner at St. Augustine?'—'That,' rejoined the officer, 'is of but little consequence; the last hopes of rebellion are crushed by the defeat of Green at Guildford. You shall illuminate.'—'Not a single light,' replied the lady, 'shall be placed with my consent, on such an occasion, in any window of my house.'—'Then, madam, I will return with a party, and, before midnight, level it with the ground.'—'You have power to destroy, sir, and seem well disposed to use it; but over my opinions you possess no control: I disregard your menaces, and resolutely declare—I will not illuminate!'"

"A REMARKABLE scene is related by Dr. Ramsay, to have occurred on the occasion of Fort Augusta, commanded by Colonel Browne, being taken, which well deserves to be recorded. Passing through the settlement where the most wanton waste had recently been made by the British, both of lives and property, a Mrs. M'Koy having obtained permission to speak to Colonel Browne, addressed him in words to the following effect: 'Colonel Browne—in the late day of your prosperity, I visited your camp, and on my knees supplicated for the life of my son; but you were deaf to my entreaties. You hanged him, though a beardless youth, before my face! These eyes have seen him scalped by the savages under your immediate command, and for no better reason than that his name was M'Koy. As you are a prisoner to the leaders of my country, for the present I lay aside all thoughts of revenge; but when you resume your sword, I will go five hundred miles to demand satisfaction at the point of it, for the murder of my son.'"

SHORTLY after the commencement of the war, the family of Dr Channing, then residing in England, removed to France, and sailed in a stout and well-armed vessel for America. They had proceeded but a little way when they were attacked by a privateer A fierce engagement ensued, during which Mrs. Channing kept the deck, handing cartridges, aiding the wounded, and exhorting the crew to resist until death. Their fortitude, however, did not correspond with the ardor of her wishes, and the colors were struck. Seizing the pistols and side-arms of her husband, she threw them into the sea, declaring that she would rather die than see him surrender them to an enemy."

"THE haughty Tarleton, vaunting his feats of gallantry, to the great disparagement of the officers of the continental cavalry, said to a lady at Wilmington—'I have a very earnest desire to see your far-famed hero, Colonel Washington.'—'Your wish, colonel, might have been fully gratified,' she promptly replied, 'had you ventured to look behind you, after the battle of the Cowpens.'

"It was in that battle that Washington had wounded Tarleton, which gave rise to a still more pointed retort. Conversing with Mrs. Wiley Jones, Colonel Tarleton observed: 'You appear to think very highly of Colonel Washington; and yet I have been told that he is so ignorant a fellow, that he can hardly write his own name.'—'It may be the case,' she readily replied, 'but no man better than yourself, colonel, can testify, that he knows how to make his mark.'"

"PRE-EMINENT in malignity stood the Engineer Moncrief. The instances of oppression issuing from his implacable resentment, would fill a volume. I shall confine myself to one anecdote.

"Mrs. Pinkney, mother of C. C. Pinkney, solicited as a favor that he would not suffer certain oak trees of remarkable beauty on a farm which he occupied, to be destroyed, as they were highly valued by her son, having been planted by his father's hand. 'And where is your son, madam?'—'At Haddrels, sir, a prisoner.' —'And he wishes me, madam, to have these trees preserved?'— 'Yes, sir, if possible.'—'Then tell him, madam, that they will make excellent firewood, and he may depend upon it they shall be burnt.' Colonel Moncrief was no jester. The promptitude of his actions left no room for suspense. An opportunity was offered to injure and to insult, and he embraced it. The trees were burnt."

"MARGARET WHETTEN, the wife of Capt. William Whetten, of New York, was one of the true mothers of the Revolution. During a part of the war, she resided on Cliff street, near the rear of St. George's chapel. There, if we mistake not, she became a widow; and though not left in affluent circumstances, she made her house an asylum, especially for the wounded and suffering whigs. For a long time she prepared food daily for the imprisoned soldiers, and often visited them and cheered their drooping hearts by her lively and hope-giving conversation. She was also accustomed to visit the hospitals; and even the Provost was not aroused, though the marshal was surly and abusive. Nor did she forget the prison-ships; their hapless inmates were often the recipients of favors which she caused to be sent.

"At one time a party of soldiers was sent to her house in pursuit of a suspected enemy of the crown. Being notified of their approach, she hastily slipped a dressing gown and night-cap on him; and placing him in a large easy chair, and handing him a bowl of gruel, she pointed the soldiers to the seeming invalid, whose fears doubtless contributed to his paleness. Thinking he must be too feeble, just then, to travel, they went away. The leader of this duped band was reprimanded for leaving him to his gruel, and ordered back: meanwhile the invalid had become rapidly convalescent, changed his suit, and gone out to try the air."

"When Col. Washington of the dragoons was engaged with Tarleton's cavalry, at the battle of ———— in South Carolina, his impetuosity separated him from his troops, and he was furiously beset by an officer and a dozen of British dragoons. In defending himself, he broke his sword, and was in a most perilous situation. While defending himself with his broken sword, the enemy pressing upon him with the fullest confidence of destroying him, Sergeant Everhart, of Frederick Co., Maryland, gallantly rushed up to him and handed him his well-tried sword, with which Washington soon extricated himself, cutting down his antagonists, until he was joined by his troops. Col. Washington ever afterwards, attributed the preservation of his life to the timely relief afforded by Everhart, gratefully acknowledging it, and enrolled him on the list of his dearest friends; and he never passed through Frederickstown without spending a day or two with his faithful sergeant."

"At the commencement of the Revolution, Mrs. Wright, a native of Pennsylvania, a distinguished modeler of likenesses and figures of wax, was exhibiting specimens of her skill in London. The king of Great Britain, pleased with her talents, gave her liberal encouragement, and, finding her a great politician, and an enthusiastic republican, would often enter into discussion relative to passing occurrences, and endeavored to refute her opinion with regard to the probable issue of the war. The frankness with which she delivered her sentiments, seemed rather to please than to offend him; which was a fortunate circumstance, for, when he asked an opinion, she gave it without constraint, or the least regard to consequences. I remember to have heard her say, that on one occasion, the monarch, irritated by some disaster to his troops, where he had prognosticated a triumph, exclaimed with warmth: 'I wish, Mrs. Wright, you would tell me how it will be possible to check the silly infatuation of your countrymen, restore them to reason, and render them good and obedient subjects.' 'I consider their submission to your majesty's government is now altogether out of the question,' replied Mrs. Wright: 'friends you may make them, but never subjects; for America, before a king can reign there, must become a wilderness, without any other inhabitants than the beasts of the forest. The opponents of the decrees of your parliament, rather than submit, would perish to a man; but if the restoration of peace be seriously the object of your wishes, I am confident that it needs but the striking off of *three heads* to produce it.'—'O, Lord North's and Lord George Germaine's, beyond all question; and where is the third head ?' O, sir, politeness forbids me to name *him*. Your majesty could never wish me to forget myself, and be guilty of an incivility.'

"In her exhibition room, one group of figures particularly attracted attention; and by all who knew her sentiments, was believed to be a pointed hint at the results which might follow the wild ambition of the monarch. The busts of the king and queen of Great Britain, were placed on a table, apparently, intently gazing on a head, which a figure, an excellent representation of herself, was modeling in its lap. It was the head of the unfortunate Charles the First."

"On one occasion, two young subalterns, who had been wounded, were taken prisoners, and on parole, took up their residence at a place called Dobb's Farm. One day, as they were sitting down to dinner, a swarthy man, of bold and full countenance, entered the room where they sat, and without announcing himself, asked how they liked their situation, and how they were treated? They answered in such a manner, as gave pleasure to their good host and hostess. The stranger expressed his satisfaction also; and begging leave to dine with them, placed himself at table, without waiting for an answer. When dinner was over, a couple of yagers made their appearance, and desired to know the stranger's commands. "You will bring the wine hither," said he; "get some refreshment yourselves, and saddle at five o'clock." The yagers withdrew, and their commander seeing the surprise of the officers, said, "Gentlemen, my name is Morgan, a major-general in the service of America." They interrupted him by apologies for the unceremonious reception he had met with which he begged not to hear, saying, that he had come on pur pose to see them, and to render them any assistance they might require; adding, that he was very glad to see them so well accommodated. Then filling a glass of wine, to which the officers had been sometime strangers, he gave, "A speedy peace," in which he was pledged most cordially. The bottle was quickly circulated, and the healths of the principal commanders in both armies drank in succession. A song was proposed; and after one of the officers had complied, the general won the hearts of his auditors, by singing, in allusion to his former profession, "When I was driving my wagon one day."

It was now five o'clock; the yagers presented themselves for orders, and General Morgan took his leave in a most friendly manner, assuring them he would use the best efforts for their speedy exchange, but adding, very gallantly, "though I have no desire to meet such men in arms against me." He left two hampers of wine which had been brought for the prisoners by the yagers, and which proved of infinite service to them, in aiding the recovery of their health."

The following anecdote, says a correspondent in the American "Village Record," comes from a source entitled to perfect credit. During the revolutionary war, two British soldiers, of the army of Lord Cornwallis, went into a house, and abused the inmates in a most cruel and shameful manner. A third soldier, in going into the house, met them coming out, and knew them. The people acquitted him of all blame, but he was imprisoned because he refused to disclose the names of the offenders. Every art was tried, but in vain; at length he was condemned by a court-martial to die. When on the gallows, Lord Cornwallis, surprised at his pertinacity, rode near him.

"Campbell," said he, "what a fool are you to die thus. Disclose the names of the guilty men, and you shall be immediately released; otherwise you have not fifteen minutes to live."

"You are in an enemy's country, my lord," replied Campbell "you can better spare one man than two."

Firmly adhering to his purpose, he died.

Does history furnish a similar instance of such strange devotion for a mistaken point of honor?

One day in the middle of winter, General Greene, when passing a sentinel who was barefooted, said, "I fear my good fellow, you suffer much from the severe cold." "Very much," was the reply, "but I do not complain. I know I should fare better, had our general the means of getting supplies. They say, however, that in a few days, we shall have a fight, and then I shall take care to secure a pair of shoes."

"During the traitor Arnold's predatory operations in Virginia, in 1781, he took an American captain prisoner. After some general conversation, he asked the captain "what he thought the Americans would do with him if they caught him." The captain declined at first giving him an answer; but upon being repeatedly urged, he said, "Why, sir, if I must answer the question, you will excuse my telling you the truth; if my countrymen should catch you, I believe they would first cut off your lame leg, which was wounded in the cause of freedom and virtue at Quebec, and bury it with the honors of war, and afterwards hang the remainder of your body on a gibbet."

"At the disastrous battle of Camden, while acting as Aid-de-Camp to General Gates, General Thomas Pinckney, was desperately wounded and made a prisoner. His patience and fortitude remained unshaken. Conveyed into the town, it was night when he reached *Mrs. Clay's* house (then by the fiat of power, converted into a Hospital). The family had retired, and Major Pinckney was placed on a table in the piazza, where he lay till morning, suffering under a compound fracture of both bones of his leg, as he would not permit the rest of an oppressed and patriotic female to be disturbed. This calm and happy temper of mind, contributed in no small degree to the preservation of his life, for an exfoliation of the broken bones following soon after his removal to quarters, and no surgical aid at hand, he was obliged to direct the dressing of his wound, and to point out to his anxious and intrepid wife, the splinters that occasioned the greatest agony, while, with tenderness she removed them. The trial was, indeed, a severe one, to a lady of uncommon sensibility; but there is no exertion to which the female heart, under the influence of its affections, is not equal. The duty performed, the fortitude of Mrs. Pinckney was no more; her emotion, on seeing her husband's sufferings, so totally overpowered her, that she fainted and fell. The recollection of such tender and heroic conduct cannot be lost: 't must ever command the admiration of the world, and to her sex, afford a fascinating example for imitation."

"An American officer, during the war of independence, was ordered to a station of extreme peril, when several around him suggested various expedients, by which he might evade the dangerous post assigned him. He made them the following heroic reply: "I thank you, my friends, for your solicitude—I know I can easily save my life, but, who will save my honor, should I adopt your advice ?"

"COLONEL HENDRICK FREY, (a colonel of colonial troops under Sir William Johnson, in the French war), a wealthy royalist, who resided in Schoharie County, N. Y., and who feigned neutrality the day after the battle of Oriskany, was visited by a party of hostile Indians. As they assembled around the table to eat, a sister of Frey who was awaiting upon them, discovered upon the person of one, the shirt of Major John Frey, a brother on the patriotic side—one sleeve of which had been perforated by a bullet and left very bloody. Her worst fears were aroused, and nearly letting fall something she held, she ran to her brother Hendrick, placed her hands on his shoulders, and exclaimed in a tone of real sorrow: "Brother John is dead!" assigning as her reason for such belief, the sight of the bloody trophy before them. The colonel who could speak the Indian dialect well, desired his sister not to show any emotion before the Indians; and endeavored to quiet her fears, by remarking, that probably the shirt had belonged to some one else. The agitated maiden could not be persuaded into this belief, as the garment had been the workmanship of her own hands; and her mental agony seemed almost insufferable.

"In a short time the Indians left the house, followed by Col. Frey, who overtaking them, inquired of the possessor where he got the shirt, which covered his brawny frame. He replied, that he had wounded an officer the day before, in the Oriskany contest, in an arm which he had exposed from behind a tree, had made him his prisoner, and after taking from him such portion of his clothing as he desired, had sold him to a British officer, who would possibly take him to Canada. This statement tended somewhat to calm the apprehensions of the brother and sister. It was found to be true. Major Frey was taken to Canada, and after two years confinement, was restored to liberty."

"The following anecdote, which is too well authenticated to be disputed, furnishes one instance, among thousands, of that heroic spirit and love of liberty, which characterized the American females during the struggle for independence.

"A good lady,—we knew her when she had grown old,—in 1775, lived on the sea-board, about a day's march from Boston, where the British army then was. By some unaccountable accident, a rumor was spread, in town and country, in and about there, that the *regulars* were on a full march for that place, and would probably arrive in three hours.

"This was after the battle of Lexington, and all, as might be well supposed, was in sad confusion: some were boiling with rage, and full of fight; some, in fear and confusion, were hiding their treasures; and others flying for life. In this wild moment, when most people, in some way or other, were frightened from their property, our heroine, who had two sons, one about nineteen years of age, the other about sixteen, was seen by our informant preparing them to discharge their duty. The eldest she was able to equip in fine style: she took her husband's fowling-piece, 'made for duck or plover,' (the good man being absent on a coasting voyage to Virginia,) and with it the powder-horn and shot-bag. But the lad thinking the duck and goose shot, not quite the size to kill regulars, his mother took a chisel, cut up her pewter spoons, hammered them into slugs, and put them into his bag, and he set off in great earnest, but thought he would call one moment and see the parson, who said, 'Well done, my brave boy! God preserve you!' and on he went in the way of his duty. The youngest was importunate for *his* equipments, but his mother could find nothing to arm him with, but an old rusty sword. The boy seemed rather unwilling to risk himself with this alone, but lingered in the street, in a state of hesitation, when his mother thus upbraided him: 'You John H*****, what will your father say, if he hears that a child of his is afraid to meet the British? —go along: beg or borrow a gun, or you will find one, child: some coward, I dare say, will be running away: then take his gun, and march forward; and if you come back, and I hear you have not behaved like a man, I shall carry the blush of shame on my face to the grave.' She then shut the door, wiped the tear from her eye, and waited the issue. The boy joined the march. Such a woman could not have cowards for her sons. Instances of refined and delicate pride and affection occurred, at that period, every day, in different places; and, in fact, this disposition and feeling was then so common, that it now operates as one great cause of our not having more facts of this kind recorded. What few there are remembered, should not be lost. Nothing great or glorious was ever achieved, which women did not act in, advise, or consent to."

"At the massacre of Wyoming, a tory found a brother secreted, and on recognizing him, said, "so it is you, is it?" The unarmed man approached his brother, fell upon his knees and besought him to spare his life; promising, if he would, to live with him and become his servant. "All this is mighty fine," rep"ed the human fiend, "but you are a d——d rebel!" at the same moment he raised his gun, heedless of the frantic prayers of his brother, and discharged its contents into his victim's body."

"During the siege of Yorktown, Baron Steuben, giving a breakfast to several of the field officers of the army, in the course of the entertainment, while festivity was at its height, and in anticipation of the honors which awaited them, mirth and good humor abounded, a shell from the enemy fell into the centre of the circle formed by his guests. There was no time for retreat; to fall prostrate on the earth afforded the only chance of escape; every individual stretched himself at his length; the shell burst with tremendous explosion, covering the whole party with mud and dirt, which rather proved a source of merriment, than serious concern, since none of the party sustained any further inconvenience."

"About the period of the final departure of the British from New York, an excellent repartee, made by Major Upham, aid-de-camp to Lord Dorchester, to Miss Susan Livingston, has been much celebrated. "In mercy, Major," said Miss Livingston, "use your influence with the commander-in-chief, to accelerate the evacuation of the city; for among your incarcerated belles, your Mischianza Princesses, the *scarlet* fever must continue to rage till your departure." "I should studiously second your wishes," replied the Major, "were I not apprehensive, that freed from the prevailing malady, a worse would follow, and that they would be immediately tormented with the *Blue Devils*."

"The wife of Colonel William Fitzhugh, of Maryland, while he was absent at one time, during the Revolution, was surprised by the news that a party of British soldiers was approaching her house. She instantly collected her slaves; furnished them with such weapons of defence as were at hand; took a quantity of cartridges in her apron, and, herself forming the van, urged her sable subalterns on to meet the foe. Not looking for resistance, the advancing party, on beholding the amazon with her sooty invincibles, hastily turned on their heels and fled."

"On a subsequent occasion, a detachment of soldiers marched at midnight to Colonel Fitzhugh's house, which was half a mile from the shore, and near the mouth of the Patuxent river, and knocked at the door. The Colonel demanding who was there, and receiving for reply that the visitants were "friends to King George," told the unwelcome intruders that he was blind and unable to wait upon them, but that his wife would admit them forthwith. Lighting a candle and merely putting on her slippers, she descended, awoke her sons, put pistols in their hands, and pointing to the back door, told them to flee. She then let the soldiers in at the front door. They inquired for Colonel Fitzhugh, and said he must come down stairs at once, and go as a prisoner to New York. She accordingly dressed her husband—forgetting meanwhile, to do as much for herself—and when he had descended, he assured the soldiers that his blindness, and the infirmities of age unfitted him to take care of himself, and that it could hardly be desirable for them to take in charge so decrepit and inoffensive a person. They thought otherwise; and his wife, seeing he must go, took his arm and said she would go too. The officer told her she would be exposed and must suffer, but she persisted in accompanying him, saying that he could not take care of himself, nor, if he could, would she permit a separation."

"It was a cold and rainy night, and with the mere protection of a cloak, which the officer took down and threw over her shoulders before leaving the house, she sallied forth with the party. While on the way to their boat, the report of a gun was heard, which the soldiers supposed was the signal of a rebel gathering. They hastened to the boat, where a parole was written out with trembling hand, and placed in the old gentleman's possession. Without even a benediction, he was left on shore with his faithful and fearless companion, who thought but little of her wet feet, as she stood and saw the cowardly detachment of British soldiers push off, and row away with all their might for safety."

"On the occasion of an anticipated attack on the Middle Fort, Schoharie Co., orders were given that the women and children should retire into a long cellar, within the fort. Upon hearing of this order, Mary Haggidorn, a lass of goodly proportions, stepped up to the commandant, and thus addressed him: "Captain, I shall not go into that cellar! should the enemy come, I will take a spear, which I can use as well as any *man*, and help defend the fort." Captain Hager, gratified in finding a soldier where he least expected one, and in admiration of her dauntless spirit, replied, "Then take a spear, Mary, and be ready at the pickets to repel an attack." She armed herself with this weapon, took her post, and did not abandon it until the danger was past."

"In the battle of Guilford, in the South, occurred one of those sanguinary personal conflicts, that frequently arose from the bitter hatred existing between the whigs and tories. The combatants were Colonel Stuart, of the enemy, and Captain John Smith, of the continental army. Both were men distinguished by nerve and muscle. They had met before, and a personal provocation had resulted in the mutual declaration, that their next meeting should end in blood. The present contest was seized upon as a fitting occasion, and they singled out each other, with a fierce passion for revenge, which made them totally regardless of the horrors of the contest. Their weapons were at once crossed, with a desperate fury, which promised but one result. A moment decided the conflict. The adroit pass of Stuart's small-sword, was admirably parried by the left hand of the American, while with his right, he drove the edge of the heavy sabre through the head of his enemy, cleaving him to the very spine. The next moment, he himself was brought to the ground, stunned, not slain, by the graze of a pistol-shot, sent by a devoted follower of the fallen Briton, who was stricken to the heart, almost in the same moment, by the bayonet of an American, who was equally watchful of the safety of his superior."

" An unfortunate whig, flying before a party of the enemy, intent upon his destruction, rushed into the dwelling house of Mr. Trapier, and entering the apartment of Miss Newman, an inmate of the family, exclaimed—'Protect me, Madam, or I am lost.' 'Quickly conceal yourself,' replied the lady, 'be silent, and rest assured, that I will do all that I can to save you.' She had scarcely time to compose herself, before admission was demanded from without, and an officer presenting himself, insisted that the place of concealment to which the fugitive had retired, should be immediately pointed out. 'It is little probable,' said Miss Newman, 'that a soldier, to whom I am probably altogether unknown, would, even under the terrors of death, seek security by intruding himself into my chamber; but, as I am confident that no credit will be given to my assertions, and that the power of search rests with you, its indulgence must necessarily follow; yet, I trust, from your character as a soldier, and appearance as a gentleman, with the delicacy due to a lady's feelings.' The composure so happily assumed, calmed the violence of the party, and the officer, believing that it could alone be exhibited from an entire ignorance of the hiding place of the object of his pursuit, bowed and retired."

"In one of the revolutionary battles, Colonel Jessup, suspecting that his troops had expended nearly all their cartridges, passed along the rear of the line, to make inquiry as to the fact. Several soldiers who lay mortally wounded, some of them actually in the agonies of death, hearing the inquiry, forgot for a moment, in their devotion to their country, both the pain they endured and the approach of death, and called out, each one for himself, 'Here are cartridges in my box, take and distribute them among my companions.'"

"A soldier in the line exclaimed to his commander, 'My musket is shot to pieces.' His comrade, who lay expiring with his wounds at the distance of a few feet, replied, in a voice scarcely audible, 'My musket is in excellent order—take and use her.'"

"It is no extravagance to assert, that an army of such men, commanded by officers of corresponding merit, is literally invincible."

An officer calling out to General Huger, "General, I plainly see one of the enemy's riflemen taking deliberate aim to destroy you." "That is no concern of mine," said the General. "If you think proper, order one of your men to take the fellow off."

"Dodge, or change your position," rejoined the officer, "or you are a dead man." "I will neither dodge nor quit my post," replied the General, "be the consequence what it may."

"THE Baron Steuben after the defeat of Gates in Carolina was engaged in raising a regiment in Virginia; men sufficient to form a regiment had with difficulty been collected; the corps was paraded, and on the point of marching to Carolina. A good looking man on horseback, with his servant as it appeared, also well mounted, rode up, and introducing himself to the baron, informed him he had brought a recruit. 'I thank you, sir,' said the baron, 'with all my heart, he has arrived in a happy moment. Where is he, colonel?' for the man was a colonel in the militia. 'Here, sir,' ordering his boy to dismount. The baron's countenance altered; a sergeant was ordered to measure the lad, whose shoes when off, discovered something by which his height had been increased. The baron patted the child's head, with a hand trembling with rage, and asked him how old he was? He was very young, quite a child; 'Sir,' said the baron, turning to him who brought him, 'you think me a rascal!' 'Oh, no baron, I don't.' 'Then, sir, I think you are one, an infamous scoundrel, thus to attempt to cheat your country! Take off this fellow's spurs, place him in the ranks, and tell General Greene from me, Colonel Gaskins, that I have sent him a man able to serve, instead of an infant, whom he would have basely made his substitute. Go, my boy, carry the colonel's horses and spurs to his wife; make my respects to her, and tell her that her husband has gone to fight, as an honest citizen should, for the liberty of his country. By platoons! to the right wheel! forward march!'"

"In the battle of Princeton, Capt. M'Pherson, of the 17th British regiment, a very worthy Scotchman, was desperately wounded in the lungs and left with the dead. Upon General Putnam's arrival there, he found him languishing in extreme distress, without a surgeon, without a single accommodation, and without a friend to solace the sinking spirit in the gloomy hour of death. He visited and immediately caused every possible comfort to be administered to him. Capt. M'Pherson, who contrary to all appearances recovered, after having demonstrated to Gen. Putnam the dignified sense of obligations which a generous mind wishes not to conceal, one day in familiar conversation, demanded—' Pray, sir, what countryman are you?' 'An American,' answered the latter. 'Not a Yankee!' said the other. 'A full-blooded one,' replied the general. 'Indeed, I am sorry for that,' rejoined M'Pherson, 'I did not think there could be so much goodness and generosity in an American, or, indeed, in anybody but a Scotchman.'"

In the terrible massacre of Wyoming the most unheard of barbarities were practiced, and, what history scarcely affords a parallel of, the acts that exceeded all others in fiendishness were those committed by men upon their own kindred. One man named Partial Terry had sent repeated messages to his father, saying that "he hoped one day to wash his hands in the old man's heart's blood," and his wishes were but too well answered, for on this occasion, *after having murdered and scalped his own mother, brothers, and sisters, he cut off his father's head!* Another man, named Thomas Hill, killed his mother, his father in-law, and his sisters. It is difficult for us to realise that these atrocities could have been performed, and were they not accredited by unimpeachable testimony, would be considered as monstrous fictions.

"General Nash, in the battle of Germantown, October 4th, 1777, was severely wounded in the thigh, the bone of which was shattered by a grape-shot. While they were carrying him off the field, a friend coming up, began to condole with him on his situation, and asked him how he felt;—'It is unmanly,' said the dying hero, 'to complain; but it is more than human nature can bear.'"

"In the commencement of the American revolution, when one of the British king's thundering proclamations made its appearance, the subject was mentioned in a company in Philadelphia; a member of Congress who was present, turning to Miss Livingston, said, 'Well, Miss, are you greatly terrified at the *roaring of the British lion?*' 'Not at all, sir, for I have learned from natural history, that that *beast roars loudest when he is most frightened.*'"

In August, 1775, Gen. Gage sent two armed schooners from Boston to Machias, with cash, to buy live stock, and gave orders to take the stock by force, if the inhabitants would not sell it. They did refuse,—the crews of the schooners then attempted to take off the stock by force, upon which the inhabitants rose, made all the men prisoners, seized on the schooners and cash and shared about 5*l.* sterling a man.

When Marion's brigade was once engaged in battle, captain Gee was supposed to be mortally wounded. A ball passed through the cock of his hat, very much tearing, not only the crown, but also his head. He lay, for many hours, insensible; ut, suddenly reviving, his first inquiry was after his hat: which being brought to him, a friend at the same time lamenting the mangled state of his head, he exclaimed: 'Oh, I care nothing about my head: time and the doctors will mend that; but it grieves me to think that the rascals have ruined my new hat forever.'"

An affair in which Major Postell was concerned, may serve to show the spirit of the times, and, especially, the indifference for property which then prevailed. A captain of the royal army, with twenty-five grenadiers, having taken post in the house of Postell's father, the major placed his small army of twenty-one militia, so as to command its doors, and then called on them to surrender. This being refused, he set fire to an out-house; was proceeding to burn the dwelling in which they were posted; and nothing but their immediate submission restrained him from sacrificing his father's valuable establishment for the interest of his country.

"It happened in 1776, that the garden of a widow, which lay between the American and British camps in the neighborhood of New York, was frequently robbed at night. Her son, a mere boy, and small for his age, having obtained his mother's permission to find out and secure the thief, in case he should return, concealed himself with a gun among the weeds. A strapping highlander, belonging to the British grenadiers came, and having filled a large bag, threw it over his shoulder; the boy then left his covert, went softly behind him, cocked his gun, and called out to the fellow, 'You are my prisoner: if you attempt to put your bag down, I will shoot you dead; go forward in that road.' The boy kept close behind him, threatened, and was constantly prepared to execute his threats. Thus the boy drove him into the American camp, when he was secured. When the grenadier was at liberty to throw down his bag, and saw who had made him prisoner, he was extremely mortified, and exclaimed, 'a British grenadier made prisoner by such a brat!' The American officers were highly entertained with the adventure, made a collection for the boy, and gave him several pounds. He returned, fully satisfied for the losses his mother sustained. The soldier had side arms, but they were of no use, as he could not get rid of his bag."

"LADY HARRIET ACKLAND accompanied her husband to Canada in the beginning of the year 1776. In the course of that campaign, she traversed a vast space of country, in different extremities of the seasons, and with difficulties that an European traveller will not easily conceive, in order to attend her husband in a poor hut at the Chamblée, upon his sick-bed. In the opening of the campaign of 1777, she was restrained from offering herself to a share of the hazard expected before Ticonderoga, by the positive injunction of her husband. The day after the conquest of that place he was badly wounded, and she crossed Lake Champlain to join him."

"As soon as he recovered, Lady Harriet proceeded to follow his fortunes through the campaign. Major Ackland, her husband, commanded the British grenadiers, who formed the most advanced post of the army, which required them to be so much on the alert, that frequently, no person slept out of their clothes

In one of these situations a tent, in which the Major and Lady Harriet slept, suddenly took fire. An orderly sergeant of grenadiers, with great hazard of suffocation, dragged out the first person he caught hold of; it proved to be the major. Fortunately his lady at the same moment escaped under the canvass of the back part of the tent."

"This accident neither altered the resolution nor the cheerfulness of Lady Harriet, who was in a hut during the whole of the action which followed, and close to the field of battle. In a subsequent engagement, Major Ackland was desperately wounded and taken prisoner. Lady Harriet sustained the shock with great fortitude, and determined to pass to the enemy's camp, and request General Gates' permission to attend her husband."

"Having obtained permission of General Burgoyne, Lady Harriet, accompanied by the chaplain of the regiment, one female servant, and the major's valet-de-chambre, rowed down the river to meet the enemy. The night was far advanced before the boat reached the enemy's outpots, and the sentinel would not let it pass, nor even come on shore. In vain was the flag of truce offered, and the state of this extraordinary passenger strongly represented. The guard, apprehensive of treachery, and punctilious in obedience to his orders, threatened to fire into the boat if they offered to stir before daylight. Her anxiety and sufferings were thus protracted through seven or eight dark and cold hours; and her reflections on that first reception, could not give her very encouraging ideas of the treatment she was afterwards to expect. But in the morning, as soon as her case was made known to General Gates, he received her with all the humanity and respect due to her rank and exemplary conjugal virtue, and immediately restored her to her husband."

"When a British fleet menaced a part of the American coast during the revolution, a man promulgated that he had discovered a combustible matter which could be easily conveyed uninjured to the ships, and then taking fire, produce a dreadful conflagration. With a knowledge of the inventions of Franklin and others, it was no wonder that this intimation, which was soon purposely conveyed to the English naval commander, should induce him to act with caution.

At an appointed day, a number of barrels were set on float, which made their way towards the ships, while the artist was embarked with a complicated apparatus, in a little boat. Shortly after, one of the barrels exploding with considerable blaze and report, the fleet, whose cables were already slipped, departed with precipitate haste, leaving the inventor, whose dangerous scheme was now entirely exhausted, in full possession of the coast for many miles."

"Gen. Putnam is known to have been decidedly opposed to duelling, on principle. It once happened that he grossly affronted a brother officer. The dispute arose at a wine table, and the officer demanded instant reparation. Putnam, being a little elevated, expressed his willingness to accommodate the gentleman with a fight; and it was stipulated that the duel should take place on the following morning, and that they should fight without seconds. At the appointed time, the general went on to the ground armed with sword and pistols. On entering the field, Putnam who had taken a stand at the opposite extremity, and at a distance of about thirty rods, levelled his musket, and fired at him. The gentleman now ran towards his antagonist, who deliberately proceeded to reload his gun."

"'What are you about to do?' exclaimed he;—'is this the conduct of an American officer, and a man of honor?'

"'What are you about to do?' exclaimed the general, attending only to the first question; 'a pretty question to put to a man whom you intended to murder. I'm about to kill you; and if you don't beat a retreat in less time than 'twould take old Heath to hang a tory, you are a gone dog;' at the same time returning his ramrod to its place, and throwing the breech of his gun into the hollow of his shoulder.

"This intimation was too unequivocal to be misunderstood; and our valorous duellist turned and fled for dear life."

When our gallant countryman, Major Pinckney, received the wound at Gates' defeat, which placed him in the hands of the enemy, the generous feelings of an old school-fellow, Captain Charles Barrington M'Kenzie, of the 71st British regiment, under the blessing of Heaven, preserved his valuable life. Applying to Tarleton for his interposition in behalf of his suffering friend, he immediately received an order to call from the field his surgeon, whose early attention, in all probability, prevented the catastrophe which befel General Porterfield and other officers, whose wounds not being dressed for thirty-six hours, from exhaustion and loss of blood, expired. The character of the wounded prisoner had excited a deep interest in his bosom. The ferocity of his temper was laid aside. He ordered, that every attention should be paid him that could mitigate the severity of his wound—supplied him amply with port wine, considered essential to prevent the spasms that threatened his life—tendered the restoration of the horses recently impressed from his family at Fort Motte—and urged with the generous spirit of a soldier, the free and unlimited use of his purse. I could pardon him a thousand errors for this emanation of generous sympathy. Such attentions were received with the gratitude they were well calculated to excite. The sincerest acknowledgments were expressed for all—though neither the horses nor purse were accepted. This gave an opportunity to M'Kenzie to display a trait of chivalric gallantry that cannot be too much admired. "Give me his charger, then;" he feelingly exclaimed, "it shall never be said, that the horse that carried Tom Pinckney, was ever employed against the friends and the cause that were dear to him."

"GENERAL WASHINGTON had two favorite horses; one, a large elegant parade horse of a chestnut-color, high-spirited, and of a gallant carriage; this horse had belonged to the British army: the other was smaller, and his color sorrel. This he used always to ride in time of action; so that whenever the general mounted him, the word ran through the ranks, 'We have business on hand.'

"AT the battle of Germantown, General Wayne rode his gallant roan, and in charging the enemy, his horse received a wound in his head, and fell, as was supposed, dead. Two days after, the roan returned to the American camp, not materially injured, and was again fit for service."

"AT a review at Morristown, a Lieutenant Gibbons, a brave and good officer, was arrested by Baron Steuben, and ordered in the rear, for a fault which it appeared another had committed. At a proper moment, the commander of the regiment came forward.

and informed the baron of Mr. Gibbons' innocence and worth, and of his acute feelings under this unmerited disgrace. 'Desire Lieutenant Gibbons, said the baron, 'to come in front of the troops.' 'Sir,' said he to him, 'the fault which was committed by throwing the line into confusion, might in the presence of an enemy, have been fatal; and I arrested you. Your colonel has informed me, that you are in this instance blameless. I ask your pardon; return to your command, I would not do injustice to any one, much less to one whose character is so respectable.' All this was said with his hat off, and the rain pouring on his reverend head! Was there an officer who saw this, unmoved with feelings of respect and affection? Not one, who had the feelings of a soldier."

"WHEN the news of a skirmish at Lexington reached Barnstable, a company of militia immediately assembled and marched off to Cambridge. In the front rank, there was a young man, the son of a respectable farmer, and his only child. In marching from the village as they passed his house, he came out to meet them. There was a momentary halt. The drum and fife paused for an instant. The father suppressing a strong and evident emotion, said, 'God be with you all, my friends! and John, if you, my son, are called into battle, take care that you behave manfully, or else let me never see your face again.' A tear started into every eye, and the march was resumed."

IT is certainly a very singular circumstance, that Andre should, in a very satirical poem, have foretold his own fate. It was called the "*Cow Chace*," and was published by Rivington, at New York, in consequence of the failure of an expedition undertaken by Wayne for the purpose of collecting cattle. Great liberties are taken with the American officers employed on the occasion With

"Harry Lee and his Dragoons, and Proctor with his Cannon."

But the point of his irony seemed particularly aimed at *Wayne* whose entire baggage, he asserts, was taken, containing

"His Congress dollars, and his prog,
H's military speeches:
His cornstalk whiskey for his grog,
Black stockings and blue breeches."

And concludes by observing, that it is necessary to check the current of satire,

"Lest the same warrio-drover Wayne,
Should catch--and hang the Poet."

He was actually taken by a party from the division of the army immediately under the command of Wayne.

The house of Captain Charles Sims, who resided on Tyger river, South Carolina, was often plundered by tories; and on one of these occasions, when his wife was alone and all the robbers had departed but one, she ordered *him* away, and he disobeying she broke his arm with a stick, and drove him from the house.

While the husband of Mrs. Dissosway, of Staten Island, was in the hands of the British, her brother Nathaniel Randolph, a captain in the American army, repeatedly and greatly annoyed the tories; and they were anxious to be freed from his incursions. Accordingly, one of their colonels promised Mrs. Dissosway to procure her husband's release, if she would prevail upon her brother to leave the army. She scornfully replied : "And if I could act so dastardly a part, think you that General Washington has but one Captain Randolph in his army?"

REV. THOMAS ALLEN was the first minister of Pittsfield. When the American Revolution commenced, he, like the great body of the clergy, ardently espoused the cause of the oppressed colonies, and bore his testimony against the oppression of the mother country. When, in anticipation of the conflict which finally took place at Bennington, the neighboring country was roused to arms, he used his influence to increase the band of patriots, by exciting his townsmen to proceed to the battle ground. A company was raised in his parish and proceeded. Some causes, however, were found to retard their progress on the way. Hearing of the delay, he proceeded immediately to join them, and by his influence quickened their march, and soon presented them to Gen. Stark. Learning from him that he meditated an attack on the enemy, he said he would fight, but could not willingly bear arms against them until he had invited them to submit. He was insensible to fear, and accordingly proceeded so near as to make himself distinctly heard in their camp, where, after taking a stand on a convenient eminence, he commenced his pious exhortations, urging them to lay down their arms. He was answered by a volley of musketry which lodged their contents in the log on which he stood. Turning calmly to a friend, who had followed him under cover of the breast-work which formed his footstool, he said—" Now give me a gun ;" and that is said to be the first gun which spoke on that memorable occasion. He continued to bear his part till the battle was decided in favor of the American armies, and contributed honorably to that result.

THE circumstances of the murder of Miss Jane M'Crea have been variously given, but the following version is supposed to be correct: "Miss M'Crea belonged to a family of royalists, and had engaged her hand in marriage to a young refugee, named David Jones, a subordinate officer in the British service, who was advancing with Burgoyne. Anxious to possess himself of his bride, h despatched a small party of Indians to bring her to the British camp. Her family and friends were strongly opposed to her going with such an escort; but her affection overcame her prudence and she determined upon the hazardous adventure. She set forward with her dusky attendants on horseback. The family resided at the village of Fort Edward, whence they had not proceeded half a mile before her conductors stopped to drink at a spring. Meantime, the impatient lover, who deserved not her embrace for confiding her protection to such hands, instead of going himself, had despatched a second party of Indians upon the same errand. The Indians met at the spring; and before the march was resumed, they were attacked by a party of the Provincials. At the close of the skirmish, the body of Miss M'Crea was found among the slain, tomahawked, scalped, and tied to a pine-tree, yet standing by the side of the spring, as a monument of the bloody transaction. The ascertained cause of the murder was this: The promised reward for bringing her in safety to her betrothed was a barrel of rum. The chiefs of the two parties sent for her by Mr. Jones quarreled respecting the anticipated compensation. Each claimed it; and, in a moment of passion, to end the controversy, one of them struck her down with his hatchet."

An act similar to that recorded of the gunner's wife at the battle of Monmouth, was performed by Mrs. Corbcu, at the attack on Fort Washington. Her husband belonged to the artillery and in the early part of the conflict was shot down. Standing by his side and seeing him fall, without pausing to heed her private grief, or give way to the agony of her heart, she hastened to fill his place and perform his duties. Although severely wounded, she heroically maintained her post to the last. Her services were rewarded by the honorable notice of Congress.

At the darkest period of the Revolution, New Jersey was, for a short time, full of British soldiers, and Lord Cornwallis was stationed at Bordentown. He visited Mrs. Borden one day, at her elegant mansion, and made an effort to intimidate her. He told her that if she would persuade her husband and son, who were then in the American army, to join his forces, none of her property should be destroyed; but if she refused to make such exertions, he would burn her house, and lay waste her whole estate. Unintimidated and patriotic, she made the following bold reply, which caused the execution of the threat: "The sight of my house in flames would be a treat to me, for I have seen enough to know that you never injure what you have power to keep and enjoy. The application of a torch to my dwelling I should regard as the signal for your departure." And such it was.

"An intrepid action of Sergeant Mitchell, merits particular notice. There were no ensigns attached to the command, and when it was ascertained that a contest must ensue with Tarleton, the adjutant selected Mitchell to bear the colors, as he had always been distinguished for correctness of conduct, and was connected with a family of high respectability. In the progress of the battle, Tarleton led an attack on the centre of the line where Mitchell was posted with his standard. The intrepid sergeant was cut down, and the staff of his colors broken. Grasping the part to which the colors were attached, he retained it firmly in his hands, while dragged to a distance of fifteen yards. The British dragoons now gathered round him, and would immediately have mangled him to death, but Captain Kinloch dismounted and protected him from their rage, declaring that so gallant a soldier, though an enemy, should not perish. Mitchell survived his wounds, though severe, removed, at the close of the war to Georgia, became, from his acknowledged merits, a brigadier-general, and was, but a few years back, a hale and hearty man."

INCIDENTS ON THE BORDER.

"At one time during the war, a detachment of seventy men, while ascending the Ohio river, were surprised by a party of Indians, and nearly exterminated. Among those who escaped both death and captivity, were Captain Robert Benham and another man, whose cases, together, form a novel and romantic adventure. Benham was shot through both hips, and the bones being shattered, he instantly fell. Still, aided by the darkness, he succeeded in crawling among the thick branches of a fallen tree, where he lay without molestation through the night and during the following day, while the Indians, who had returned for that purpose, were stripping the slain. He continued to lie close in the place of his retreat until the second day, when, becoming hungry and observing a raccoon descending a tree, he managed to shoot t, hoping to be able to strike a fire and cook the animal. The crack of the rifle was followed by a human cry, which at first tartled the captain; but the cry being repeated several times, the voice of a Kentuckian was at length recognised; the call was returned, and the parties were soon united. The man proved to be one of his comrades, who had lost the use of both his arms in the battle. Never did mercy find more welcome company. One of the party could use his feet, and the other his hands. Benham, by tearing up his own and his companion's shirts, dressed the wounds of both. He could load his rifle and fire with readiness, and was thus enabled to kill such game as approached while his companion could roll the game along the ground with his feet, and in the same manner collect wood enough to cook their meals. When thirsty, Benham could place his hat in the teeth of his companion, who went to the Licking, and wading in until he could stoop down and fill it, returned with a hatful of water. When the stock of squirrels and other game in their immediate neighborhood was exhausted, the man of legs would roam away, and drive up a flock of wild turkeys, then abundant in those parts, until they came within range of Benham's rifle. Here they lived for six weeks, when they discovered a boat upon the Ohio, which took them off. Both recovered thoroughly from their wounds."

GENERAL BENJAMIN LOGAN, a Virginian by birth, resided during the war in a small settlement called Logan's Fort, in Kentucky. Here, on one occasion, he distinguished himself by an act of courage and generosity unexcelled in the history of romantic and chivalrous daring.

"In the month of May, 1777, as the women of his family were engaged in milking the cows at the gate of the little fort, and some of the garrison attending them, a party of Indians appeared and fired upon them. One man was shot dead, and two more wounded, one of them mortally. The whole party, including one of the wounded men, instantly ran into the fort, and closed the gate. The enemy quickly showed themselves upon the edge of a canebreak, within close rifle-shot of the gate, and seemed numerous and determined. Having a moment's leisure to look around, Logan beheld a spectacle, which awakened his most ively interest and compassion.

"A man named Harrison had been severely wounded, and still lay near the spot where he had fallen, within view both of the garrison and the Indians. The poor fellow was, at intervals, endeavoring to crawl in the direction of the fort, and had succeeded in reaching a cluster of bushes, which, however, were too thin to shelter his person from the enemy. His wife and family were in the fort, and in deep distress at his situation. The Indians undoubtedly forbore to fire upon him, from the supposition that some of the garrison would attempt to save him, in which case, they held themselves in readiness to fire upon them from the canebrake. The case was a trying one. It seemed impossible to save him without sacrificing the lives of several of the garrison; and their numbers were already far too few for an effectual defence, having originally amounted only to fifteen men, of whom three had already been put *hors de combat*.

"Yet the spectacle was so moving, and the lamentations of the wounded man's family so distressing, that it was difficult to resist making an effort to rescue him. Logan tried to persuade some of his men to accompany him in a sally, but so evident and appalling was the danger, that all at first refused; one herculean fellow observing that he was a 'weakly man,' and another declaring that he was sorry for Harrison, but that 'the skin was closer than the shirt.' At length, John Martin collected his courage, and declared his willingness to accompany Logan, saying, that 'he could only die once, and that he was as ready now as he ever could be.' The two men opened the gate, and started upon their expedition, Logan leading the way.

"They had not advanced five steps, when Harrison perceiving them, made a vigorous effort to rise, upon which Martin, supposing him able to help himself, immediately sprang back within the gate.

"Harrison's strength almost instantly failed, and he fell at full length upon the grass. Logan paused a moment after the desertion of Martin, then suddenly sprang forward to the spot where Harrison lay, rushing through a tremendous shower of rifle-balls which was poured upon him from every quarter around the fort, capable of covering an Indian. Seizing the wounded man in his arms, he ran with him to the fort, through another heavy fire, and entered it unhurt, although the gate and picketing near him were riddled with balls, and his hat and clothes pierced in several places."

"In the year 1782, the war-chief of the Wyandot tribe of Indians of lower Sandusky sent a young white man, whom he had taken prisoner, as a present to another chief, who was called the Half-king of Upper Sandusky, for the purpose of being adopted into his family, in the place of one of his sons, who had been killed the preceding year. The prisoner arrived, and was presented to the Half-king's wife, but she refused to receive him; which, according to the Indian rule, was in fact a sentence of death. The young man was therefore taken away, for the purpose of being tortured and burnt on the pile. While the dreadful preparations were making, and the unhappy victim was already tied to the stake, two English traders, Messrs. Arundel and Robbins, moved by feelings of pity and humanity, resolved to unite their exertions to endeavor to save the prisoner's life, by offering a ransom to the war-chief; which, however, he refused, saying it was an established rule among them to sacrifice a prisoner when refused adoption, and besides, the numerous war captains were on the spot to see the sentence carried into execution The two generous Englishmen were however not discouraged and determined to try another effort. They appealed to the well known high-minded pride of an Indian.—'But,' said they 'among all these chiefs whom you have mentioned, there is none who equals you in greatness; you are considered not only as the greatest and bravest, but as the best man in the nation.' 'Do you really believe what you say?' said the Indian, looking them full in the face. 'Indeed we do.' Then, without speaking another word, he blackened himself, and taking his knife, and tomahawk in his hand, made his way through the crowd to the unhappy victim, crying out with a loud voice, 'What have you to do with my prisoner?' and at once cutting the cords with which he was tied, took him to his house, which was near that of Mr. Arundel, whence he was conveyed in safety."

"A soldier in Western N. Y., one day was out on a scouting party. Being a man of courage, enterprize, and sagacity, he was determined, if possible, to obtain an accurate knowledge of the position of the enemy. For this purpose he ventured to separate from his companions. In the course of his reconnoitering alone, in the open field, he approached a wood, the under brush of which was very thick. His watchful eye discovered what he supposed to be some animal among the bushes. He immediately saw his mistake—it was an Indian crawling on his hands and feet, with his rifle in his hand, and watching the soldier, evidently with the intention of advancing sufficiently near to make him a sure mark. For the soldier to retreat was now impossible; he thought he could not escape, and he remembered too, that his father had told him never to return with a *backside wound*. He pretended not to see the Indian, and walked slowly towards him with his gun cocked by his side, carefully observing all his movements. They approached nearer and nearer; at length he saw the Indian bringing the gun to his shoulder—at that instant the soldier fell to the ground—the ball whistled its deadly music over his head. The soldier lay motionless. The Indian uttered the dreadful yell which signifies the death of an enemy, and drawing the bloody scalping-knife, (but forgetting to reload his piece), advanced with hasty strides, thirsting for murder, and anticipating the reward for the scalp. The soldier, motionless, permitted him to approach within ten paces, he then with the utmost composure sprung upon his feet. The savage stood aghast! The soldier with deliberate aim, put two balls directly through his heart. A hoarse groan was the only sound that issued from the fallen savage. This son of the forest was at least six feet five inches in height."

"WHEN the war of extermination between the Indians and Kentuckians was at its height, those who inhabited the back parts of the state of Kentucky, were obliged to have their houses built very strong, with loop-holes all around; and doors always fastened, so as to repel any attack from the Indians. While the owner of one of these domestic fortresses was with his slaves, at work on the plantation, a negro who was posted near the house, saw approaching a party of Indians. He immediately ran to the house, and the foremost Indian after him. The Indian was the fleetest, and as the door opened to admit the negro, they both jumped in together. The other Indians being some distance behind, the door was instantly closed by the planter's wife within, when the Indian and negro grappled. Long and hard was the struggle, for as in the case of Fitz James and Roderick Dhu, the one was the strongest and the other more expert, but strength this time was the victor, for they fell, the Indian below; when the negro, placing his knees on his breast, and holding his hands, kept him in that position, until the woman, seizing a broad axe, and taking the Indian by his long hair, at one blow severed his head from his body. The negro, then seizing the guns, fired them at the other Indians, which as fast as discharged, were loaded again by the planter's wife, until the party from the field, hearing the firing, arrived, and the Indians took to flight."

"CAPTAIN HENRY ECKLER, was out with a friend in the vicinity of Fort Herkimer, and unexpectedly fell in with Brant and a party of his warriors. The chief, who was well acquainted with Captain Eckler, addressed him by name, and asked him if he would surrender himself his prisoner. "Not by a d———d sight, as long as I have legs to run!" and suiting the action to the word, he turned and fled at the top of his speed, and his companion with him. The surprise took place near a piece of woods, into which the fugitives ran, pursued by a band of yelling savages. Eckler had proceeded but a little distance in the woods when he found it would be impossible for him to run far with th speed requisite for his escape by flight; and passing over a knoll which hid him from the observation of his pursuers, he entered head first, a cavity at the root of a wind-fallen tree. He found its depth insufficient, however, to conceal his whole person, and like a young ostrich or partridge, that, with its head concealed, feels secure, if it remains still, he resolved to keep silence and trust to Providence for the issue. The party pursuing him, soon arrived upon the knoll, and halted almost over him, to catch another glimpse of his retiring form. But they looked in vain and while they stood there, and he heard their conversation, h expected every moment would be his last, as he was sure if his foes looked down, they could not fail to see at least, one half his person. He felt that if they did but listen, they could hear the heart in his breast beat like the thumping of a hammer. Supposing Eckler had fled in an opposite direction, his pursuers overlooked his place of concealment, and expressing to each other their surprise at his sudden exit, and declaring that a spirit had helped him escape, they withdrew, when he backed out of his hiding place, and regained his home in safety."

"In the massacre of Cherry Valley, a Miss Jane Wells, a young lady of superior character and exalted piety, having escaped by the door, sought safety in the wood-pile; but an Indian discovered her, and, after deliberately wiping his scalping-knife on his legging, sheathed it, and seized her by the arm, at the same time, brandishing his tomahawk. The captive remonstrated with him in the Indian language, with which she had some acquaintance; and one of the tories among the invading party, named Peter Smith, who had once lived with the family of Mr. Wells as a servant, interposed and begged the savage to spare her life, pretending that she was his sister. But this availed only to procure short delay. The next moment the interesting young lady fell dead from the blow of a tomahawk.

The house of the venerable pastor was entered by the enemy, and his aged wife immediately put to death; but one of the Mohawk chiefs, named Little Aaron, led him out of the house, and kept him under his protection. An Indian, running by, pulled off the old gentleman's hat; and the chief pursued him and brought it back. The old man was thus rescued from massacre but the shock he received was so great, that, although he was set at liberty soon after, he died a few months subsequently. The fort was not taken by the enemy: but, on the first alarm, a gun was fired from it, which gave intimation of the attack."

HISTORY OF NANCY HART.*

ONE among the most remarkable women that any country has ever produced, resided in Elbert. We give our readers various particulars concerning her, derived from conversations which we have had with persons who were acquainted with her, and from notes kindly furnished by the Rev. Mr. Snead, of Baldwin County, Georgia, a connection of the Hart family. We are also under obligations to the Hon. Thomas Hart Benton, to whom we addressed a letter asking for information in regard to the relationship existing between the family of the Harts and himself, who promptly favored us with all that we desired.

NANCY HART's maiden name was Morgan. She was married to Benjamin Hart, and soon afterwards came to Georgia. Her husband was brother of the celebrated Colonel Thomas Hart, of Kentucky, who married a Miss Grey, of Orange County, North Carolina. This gentleman was the father of the wife of the Hon. Henry Clay, and maternal uncle of the Hon. Thomas Hart Benton. The family of Mr. Snead removing to Georgia, in consequence of the relationship between them and the Harts, *Aunt Nancy*, as she was usually called, came to see them. Mr. Snead says he well remembers her appearance, and many anecdotes related of her. He describes her pretty much as she is made to appear in the Yorkville sketch below, but says she was positively not cross-eyed. He represents her as being about six

* From Historical Collections of Georgia, by the Rev George White.

feet high, very muscular, and erect in her gait; her hair light brown, slightly sprinkled with gray when he last saw her, being at that time about sixty years of age. From long indulgence in violent passion, her countenance was liable, from trivial causes, to sudden changes. In dwelling upon the hardships of the Revolution, the perfidy of the Tories, and her frequent adventures with them, she never failed to become much excited.

Among the anecdotes remembered by Mr. Snead is the following:

On one evening she was at home with her children, sitting round the log-fire, with a large pot of soap boiling over the fire. Nancy was busy stirring the soap, and entertaining her family with the latest news of the war.

The houses in those days were all built of logs, as well as the chimneys. While they were thus employed, one of the family discovered some one from the outside peeping through the crevices of the chimney, and gave a silent intimation of it to Nancy. She rattled away with more and more spirit, now giving exaggerated accounts of the discomfiture of the Tories, and again stirring the boiling soap, and watching the place indicated for a re-appearance of the spy. Suddenly, with the quickness of lightning, she dashed the ladle of boiling soap through the crevice full in the face of the eavesdropper, who, taken by surprise, and blinded by the hot soap, screamed and roared at a tremendous rate, whilst the indomitable Nancy went out, amused herself at his expense, and, with gibes and taunts, bound him fast as her prisoner.

Soon after the close of the Revolution, she removed with her family to Georgia, and settled at Brunswick, then a frontier place. She was the mother of six sons (Morgan, John, Ben,

Thomas, Mark, Lemuel) and two daughters (Sally and Reziah). Her eldest daughter, Sally, married a man by the name of Thompson, who partook largely of the qualities of Mrs. Hart. Sally and her husband followed Mrs. Hart to Georgia several years afterwards. Upon their journey, a most unfortunate affair occurred. In passing through Burke County, they camped for the night on the roadside. Next morning a white man, who was employed as a wagoner, on being ordered by Thompson, in a peremptory manner, to do some particular thing, returned rather an insolent answer, and refused. Thompson, enraged, seized a sword, and with a single blow severed his head from his body. He then, with apparent unconcern, mounted the team, and drove on himself, until he came to the first house, where he stopped and told the inmates he had "just cut a fellow's head off at the camp, and they had best go down and bury him!" He then drove on, but was pursued and taken back to Waynesborough, and confined in jail. This brought the heroic Nancy to the up-country again. She went to Waynesborough several times, and in a few days after her appearance thereabouts, Thompson's prison was one morning found open, and he gone!

Mrs. Hart, speaking of the occurrence, said rather exultingly, "That's the way with them all. Drat'em, when they get into trouble, they always send for me!"

Not long after their removal, Nancy lost her husband. But, after paying suitable respect to his memory, she consoled herself, like most other good wives who have the luck, by marrying a *young man*, with whom she lifted up her stakes, and, in the language of the annexed sketch, set out among the earliest pioneeers for the "wilds of the West."

The following sketch of this extraordinary woman, which

originally appeared in the *Yorkville (S.C.) Pioneer*, is believed to be the first account of her that ever found its way to the public:—

Nancy Hart and her husband settled before the Revolutionary War a few miles above the ford on Broad River, in Elbert County, Georgia. An apple orchard still remains to point out the spot.

In altitude, Mrs. Hart was a Patagonian, and remarkably well-limbed and muscular. In a word, she was "lofty and sour." Marked by nature with prominent features, circumstances and accident added, perhaps, not a little, to her peculiarities. She was horribly cross-eyed, as well as *cross-grained*; but, nevertheless, she was a sharp-shooter. Nothing was more common than to see her in full pursuit of the bounding stag. The huge antlers that hung round her cabin, or upheld her trusty gun, gave proof of her skill in gunnery; and the white comb, drained of its honey and hung up for ornament, testified to her powers in bee-finding.

Many can testify to her magical art in the mazes of cookery —being able to get up a pumpkin in as many forms as there are days in the week. She was extensively known and employed for her profound knowlege in the management of all ailments.

But she was most remarkable for her military feats. She professed high-toned ideas of liberty. Not even the marriage knot could restrain her on that subject. Like the ' Wife of Bath," she held over her tongue-scourged husband

"The reins of absolute command,
With all the government of house and land,
And empire o'er his tongue and o'er his hand."

The clouds of war gathered, and burst with a dreadful explosion in this State. Nancy's spirit rose with the tempest. She declared and proved herself a friend to her country, ready " to do or die."

All accused of Whiggism had to hide or swing. The lily-livered Mr. Hart was not the last to seek safety in the canebrake with his neighbors. They kept up a prowling, skulking kind of life, occasionally sallying forth in a sort of predatory style. The Tories at length, however, gave Mrs. Hart a call, and in true soldier manner ordered a repast. Nancy soon had the necessary materials for a good feast spread before them. The smoking venison, the hasty hoe-cake, and the fresh honey-comb were sufficient to have provoked the appetite of a gorged epicure! They simultaneously stacked their arms and seated themselves, when, quick as thought, the dauntless Nancy seized one of the guns, cocked it, and with a blazing oath declared she would blow out the brains of the first mortal that offered to rise, or taste a mouthful! They all knew her character too well to imagine she would say one thing and do another.

" Go," said she to one of her sons, " and tell the Whigs that I have taken six base Tories." They sat still, each expecting to be offered up, with doggedly mean countenances, bearing the marks of disappointed revenge, shame, and unappeased hunger.

Whether the incongruity between Nancy's eyes caused each to imagine himself her immediate object, or whether her commanding attitude, stern and ferocious fixture of countenance, overawed them; or the powerful idea of their unsoldierlike conduct unnerved them; or the certainty of death, it is not easy to determine. They were soon relieved, and dealt with according to the rules of the times.

This heroine lived to see her country free. She, however, found game and bees decreasing, and the country becoming old so fast, that she sold out her possessions, in spite of the remonstrances of her husband, and was "among the first of the pioneers who paved the way to the wilds of the West."

The following, from Mrs. Ellet's "Women of the Revolution," will be read with interest, although it does not coincide exactly with the Yorkville account:

In this county is a stream, formerly known as "War-woman's Creek." Its name was derived from the character of an individual who lived near the entrance of the stream into the river. This person was NANCY HART, a woman ignorant of letters and the civilities of life, but a zealous lover of liberty and the "liberty boys," as she called the Whigs. She had a husband, whom she denominated "a poor stick," because he did not take a decided and active part with the defenders of his country, although she could not conscientiously charge him with the least partiality towards the Tories. This vulgar and illiterate, but hospitable and valorous female patriot, could boast no share of beauty—a fact she herself would have readily acknowledged, had she ever enjoyed an opportunity of looking in a mirror. She was *cross-eyed*, with a broad, angular mouth, ungainly in figure, rude in speech, and awkward in manners, but having a woman's heart for her friends, though that of a Catrine Montour for the enemies of her country. She was well known to the Tories, who stood in fear of her revenge for any grievance or aggressive act, though they let pass no opportunity of worrying and annoying her, when they could do so with impunity.

On the occasion of an excursion from the British camp at Augusta, a party of Tories penetrated into the interior, and having savagely murdered Colonel Dooly in bed, in his own house, they proceeded up the country for the purpose of perpetrating further atrocities. On their way, a detachment of five of the party diverged to the east, and crossed Broad River, to make discoveries about the neigbborhood, and pay a visit to their old acquaintance, Nancy Hart. On reaching her cabin, they entered it unceremoniously, receiving from her no welcome but a scowl, and informed her they had come to know the truth of a story current respecting her, that she had secreted a noted rebel from a company of King's men who were pursuing him, and who, but for her aid, would have caught and hung him. Nancy undauntedly avowed her agency in the fugitive's escape. She told them she had at first heard the tramp of a horse rapidly approaching, and had then seen a horseman coming towards her cabin. As he came nearer, she knew him to be a Whig, and flying from pursuit. She let down the bars a few steps from her cabin, and motioned him to enter, to pass through both doors, front and rear, of her single-roomed house, to take the swamp, and secure himself as well as he could. She then put up the bars, entered her cabin, closed the doors, and went about her business. Presently some Tories rode up to the bars, and called out boisterously to her. She muffled her head and face, and opening the door, inquired why they disturbed a sick, lone woman. They said they had traced a man they wanted to catch, near her house, and asked if any one on horseback had passed that way. She answered no, but said she saw somebody on a sorrel horse turn out of the path into the woods, some two or three hundred yards back. "That must be the fellow," said the Tories; and asking her direction as to the way he took, they turned about and went off, "well fooled!" said Nancy, "in an opposite course to that of my Whig boy; when, if they had not been so lofty-minded, but had looked on the ground inside the bars, they would have seen his horse's tracks up to that door, as plain as you can see the tracks on this here floor, and out of t'other door down the path to the swamp."

This bold story did not much please the Tory party, but they could not wreak their revenge upon the woman who thus unscrupulously avowed her daring aid to a rebel, and the cheat she had put upon his pursuers, otherwise than by ordering her to aid and comfort them by giving them something to eat. She replied, "I never feed King's men, if I can help it. The villains have put it out of my power to feed even my own family and friends, by stealing and killing all my poultry and pigs, except that one old gobbler you see in the yard."

"Well, and that you shall cook for us," said one, who appeared the head of the party; and raising his musket, he shot down the turkey, which another of the men brought into the house, and handed to Mrs. Hart, to clean and cook without delay. She stormed and swore awhile—for Nancy occasionally swore—but seeming, at last, resolved to make a merit of necessity, began with alacrity the arrangements for cooking, assisted by her daughter, a little girl some ten or twelve years old, and sometimes by one of the soldiers, with whom she seemed in a tolerably good humor, exchanging rude jests with him. The Tories, pleased with her freedom, invited her to partake of the liquor they had brought with them, an invitation which was accepted with witty thanks.

The spring, of which every settlement has one near at hand, was just at the edge of the swamp, and a short distance within it was a high snag-topped stump, on which was placed a conch-shell. This rude trumpet was used by the family to give information, by means of a variation of notes, to Mr. Hart, or his neighbors, who might be at work in the field or clearing just beyond the swamp, that the "Britishers" or Tories were about, that the master was wanted at the cabin, or that he was to "keep close," or "make tracks" for another swamp. Pending the operations of cooking, Mrs. Hart had sent her daughter, Sukey, to the spring for water, with directions to blow the conch in such a way as would inform him that there were Tories in the cabin, and that he should "keep close," with his three neighbors who were with him, till he heard the conch again.

The party had become merry over their jug, and sat down to feast upon the slaughtered gobbler. They had cautiously stacked their arms where they were in view, and within reach; and Mrs. Hart, assiduous in her attentions upon the table and to her guests, occasionally passed between them and their muskets. Water was called for, and as there was none in the cabin—Mrs. Hart having so contrived that—Sukey was again sent to the spring, instructed by her mother to blow the conch so as to call up Mr. Hart and his neighbors immediately. Meanwhile, Mrs. Hart had slipped out one of the pieces of pine which constitutes a "chinking" between the logs of a cabin, and had dexterously put out of the house, through that space, two of the five guns. She was detected in the act of putting out the third. The party sprang to their feet. Quick as thought, Mrs. Hart brought the piece she held to her shoulder, and declared she would kill the first man who approached her. All were terror-struck, for Nancy's obliquity of sight caused each one to imagine her aim was at him. At length one of them made a motion to advance upon her. True to her threat, she fired. He fell dead upon the floor! Instantly seizing another musket, she brought it to the position in readiness to fire again. By this time Sukey had returned from the spring, and taking up the remaining gun, carried it out of the house, saying to her mother, "Daddy and them will soon be here." This information increased the alarm of the Tories, who understood the necessity of recovering their arms immediately. But each hesitated, in the confident belief that Mrs. Hart had one eye, at least, upon him for a mark. They proposed a general rush. No time was to be lost by the bold woman; she fired again, and brought down another Tory. Sukey had another musket in readiness, which her mother took, and, posting herself in the doorway, called upon the party to "surrender their d——d Tory carcasses to a Whig woman." They agreed to surrender, and proposed to "shake hands upon the strength of it;" but the conqueror kept them in their places for a few moments, till her husband and his neighbors came up to the door. They were about to shoot down the Tories, but Mrs. Hart stopped them, saying they had surrendered to *her*, and, her spirit being up to boiling heat, she swore that "shooting was too good for them." This hint was enough. The dead man was dragged out of the house, the wounded Tory and the others were bound, taken out beyond the bars, and hung. The tree upon which they were hung was pointed out, in 1838, by one who lived in those bloody times, and who also showed the spot once occupied by Mrs. Hart's cabin, accompanying the designation with the emphatic remark, "Poor Nancy—she was a honey of a patriot, but the devil of a wife."

APPENDIX.

HISTORY OF THE SONS OF LIBERTY.

In the year 1765, ISAAC SEARS, afterward, better known by the name of KING SEARS, a man of great personal intrepidity, forward in dangerous enterprises, and ready at all times to carry out the boldest measures, became the originator and leader of a patriotic band, who associated themselves together under the name of the "SONS OF LIBERTY." Their organization soon pervaded every part of the colonies, and was the *germ* of the Revolution. By their intrepidity the spirit of the masses was aroused, and by their persevering industry and zeal, the people were excited to oppose all efforts to enslave them. These bold spirits formed the nucleus of the future armies of the Revolution; and it is to the moral courage which they displayed, and the indomitable resolution with which they braved all danger, that the world is indebted for the illustrious example set by the infant colonies to Europe, and the foundation of a great and glorious republic.

The intent of the first association of the "Sons of Liberty" was to put down the stamp-act; and when this was effected, the objects of the society appeared to be accomplished. But the acts of parliament, simultaneous with, and subsequent to the repeal, gave to the more sagacious a cause for alarm greater than the obnoxious bill which had been rescinded. The billeting act, or mutiny bill, by establishing a standing army in the colonies at their own charge, was intended to strengthen the arm of the royal authority, to overawe the assembly, and to coerce the people to acquiesce in the impositions of the parliament.

History is full of the resistance to the enormous assumptions of the mother-country by New England, and at the south; but little is said of the attitude of New York in that dangerous crisis. And yet in that colony, where the power of the sovereign was almost omnipotent, notwithstanding the exertions of the most wealthy inhabitants whose large estates were held by grants from the crown, and whose subservience to the royal mandates influenced the assembly, and all those who subsisted by the royal bounty, there was found a chosen few who remained constant to the last; and who, when all seemed lost, kept alive the spirit of resistance, until from a feeble and hopeless minority, they were enabled to triumph over the power of the colonial government and prostrate the royal authority for ever.

The association of the "Sons of Liberty" was organized in 1765, soon after the passage of the stamp-act, and extended throughout the colonies, from Massachusetts to South Carolina. It appears that New York was the central post from which communications were despatched to and from the east, and to the south, as far as Maryland; which province was the channel of communication to and from its neighbors of Virginia and the Carolinas.

As the post-offices were under the control of the government, and the riders not at all times reliable, the committee of New York (and probably the other provinces adopted the same course), upon extraordinary occasions, despatched intelligence by special messengers; and if need were, a part of their members visited in person the neighboring associations to insure the perfect organization of the patriotic league.

The New York association had a correspondent in London, to whom an account was given of their proceedings, and from whom intelligence was from time to time transmitted of their proceedings and the supposed designs of the ministry, which in its turn was disseminated among the people by the association at home. A record of the names of the most active of their leaders would be a desirable document, but as this would be difficult to be obtained without great labor, and, perhaps, by a single individual impossible, a list of the committees in the different provinces, so far as they can be ascertained, from the remaining papers of the committee of New York, might be the means of initiating inquiry in other quarters toward producing the desired result.

Those from Maryland will appear from the following extract from the proceedings of the "Sons of Liberty," March 1, 1766.

APPENDIX. 43

"The Sons of Liberty of Baltimore county, and Anne Arundel county, met at the court house of the city of Annapolis, the first day of March, 1766.

"On motion of a Son of Liberty to appoint a moderator and secretary, the Rev. Andrew Londrum was chosen moderator, and William Paca, secretary.

"Joseph Nicholson, of Kent county, presented an address from that county, signed, William Ringgold, William Stephenson, Thomas Ringgold, jr., Joseph M'Hard, Gideon M'Cauley, Daniel Fox, Benjamin Binning, William Bordley, Jarvis James, William Stukely, Joseph Nicholson, jr., James Porter, Thomas Ringgold, James Anderson, Thomas Smyth, William Murray, Joseph Nicholson, George Garnet, S. Boardley, jr., Peroy, Frisby, Henry Vandike, and John Bolton."

William Paca, Samuel Chase, and Thomas B. Hands, were the Anne Arundel county committee.

John Hall, Robert Alexander, Corbin Lee, James Heath, John Moale, and William Lux, were the Baltimore county committee.

Thomas Chase, D. Chamier, Robert Adair, Patrick Allison, and W. Smith, were the Baltimore town committee.

Pennsylvania.—William Bradford and Isaac Howell, were the correspondents at Philadelphia.

New Jersey.—Daniel Hendrickson, minister, Peter Imlay, jr., Jos. Holmes, jr., Peter Covenhoven, jr., and Elisha Lawrence, jr., were the committee of Upper Freehold—Richard Smith of Burlington, and Henry Bickers of New Brunswick.

Connecticut.—Jo. Burrows; Jonathan Sturgis, Fairfield; John Durker, Norwich; Hugh Leollie, Windham.

New York.—Isaac Sears, John Lamb, William Wiley, Edward Laight, Thos. Robinson, Flores Bancker, Chas. Nicoll, Joseph Allicoke, and Gersham Mott.

Jeremiah Van Rensselaer, Mynhard Roseboom, Robert Henry, and Thomas Young, Albany.

John S. Hobart, Gilbert Potter. Thos. Brush, Cornelius Conklin, and Nathaniel Williams, Huntington, Long Island.

George Townsend, Barack Sneething, Benjamin Townsend, George Weeks, Michael Weeks, and Rowland Chambers, Oyster Bay, Long Island.

The first organization of the Sons of Liberty, was dissolved at the repeal of the stamp-act; and while the hope was strong that similar associations would no longer be necessary, the committee received a letter from their faithful correspondent in London, of the following import:—

LONDON, 28*th July*, 1766.

Gentlemen: I flattered myself to have heard from you by the last ships, but am informed your society is dissolved, which I am glad to hear, as the cause of your complaint is removed. But I think it necessary to assure you that the continual account we had of the Sons of Liberty, through all North America, had its proper weight and effect.

As our gracious sovereign rules over none but free men, and in which he glories, it therefore cannot offend him that his numerous and faithful subjects in America claim the appellation of Sons of Liberty. Permit me, therefore, to recommend ten or twenty of the principal of you, to form yourselves into a club, to meet once a week, under the name of Liberty Club; and forever, on the 18th of March, or first day of May, give notice to the whole body to commemorate your deliverance, spending such day in festivity and joy. I beg pardon for taking the liberty to advise you; but I am firmly of opinion it will have such effect as you wish.

I have the honor to be, gentlemen, your most humble servant.

NICHOLAS RAY.

P. S.—The commercial acts and free ports which we lately sent to all the colonies, I believe will give you pleasure.

To the Sons of Liberty, New York.

To this letter the committee returned the following reply:—

NEW YORK, *October* 10*th*, 1766.

SIR: Your esteemed favor of the 28th July last, we have duly received; and observe with the greatest regret your disappointment at not hearing from us, agreeably to your expectations, which, permit us to assure you, was not owing to any remissness on our part, or want of respect; but to the dissolution of our society, which happened immediately upon the repeal of the stamp-act.

Your proposal with regard to a number of us forming ourselves into a club, we have already had under consideration. But as it is imagined that some inconvenience would arise, should such a club be established just at this time, we must postpone the same till it may appear more eligible; at the same time we take the liberty to assure you, and all our good friends on your side of the water, who so nobly exerted themselves in behalf of us, and the expiring liberties of their country, that we still do, and ever shall retain the most grateful sense of the favors we have received; and that we shall use our utmost endeavors, consistent with loyalty, to keep up that glorious spirit of liberty which was so rapidly and so generally kindled throughout this extensive continent. In order to which, we shall not fail hereafter to celebrate the anniversary of the repeal, with every demonstration of gratitude and joy, on the memorable eighteenth day of March.

We have the honor to be, in behalf of the Sons of Liberty, sir your most obedient and obliged humble servants,

    ISAAC SEARS,   EDWARD LAIGHT,
    FLORES BANCKER, JOHN LAMB,
    CHAS. NICOLL,   JOSEPH ALLICOKE.

To Mr Nicholas Ray, merchant, London.

It was not long before the necessity for reorganization became apparent, and most of the committee, who had acted with so much vigor and zeal, were found equally vigilant on every emergency. Of the persons before named of the New York association, Mr. Allicoke alone is known to the writer to have espoused the cause of the king. But with the exception of Messrs. Nicoll and Bancker, whose names do not appear on any of the subsequent committees; the others were the most determined opposers of the crown and steadfast adherents to the revolutionary party.

THE APPOINTMENT OF GEORGE WASHINGTON

TO THE SUPREME COMMAND, JUNE 18TH, 1775.

"The army was assembled at Cambridge, Massachusetts, under General Ward, and Congress was sitting at Philadelphia. Every day new applications in behalf of the army arrived. The country were urgent that Congress should legalize the raising of the army as they had what must be considered, and was in law considered, only a mob—a band of armed rebels. The country was placed in circumstances of peculiar difficulty and danger. The struggle had begun, and yet everything was without order. The great trial now seemed to be in this question, Who shall be the commander-in-chief? It was exceedingly important, and was felt to be the hinge on which the contest might turn for or against us. The southern and the middle states, warm and rapid in their zeal, were for the most part jealous of New England, because they felt that the real physical force was there. What then was to be done? All New England adored General Ward: he had been in the French war, and went out laden with laurels. He was a scholar and a statesman. Every qualification seemed to cluster in him; and it was confidently believed that the army could not receive any appointment over him. What then was to be done? Difficulties thickened at every step. The struggle was to be long and bloody. Without union, all was lost. The country, and the whole country, must come in. One pulsation must beat through all hearts. The cause was one, and the army must be one. The members had talked, debated, considered, and guessed, and yet the decisive step had not been taken. At length Mr. Adams came to his conclusion. The means of resolving it were somewhat singular, and nearly as follows: he was walking one morning before Congress hall, apparently in deep thought, when his cousin, Samuel Adams, came up to him and said:—

"'What is the topic with you this morning?'

"'Oh, the army, the army,' he replied. 'I'm determined to go into the hall this morning, and enter on a full detail of the state of the colonies, in order to show an absolute need of taking some decisive steps. My whole aim will be, to induce Congress to appoint a day for adopting the army as the legal army of these united colonies of North America, and then to hint at my election of a commander-in-chief.'

APPENDIX. 439

"'Well,' said Samuel Adams, 'I like that, cousin John; but on whom have you fixed as that commander?'

"'I will tell you—George Washington, of Virginia, a member of this house.'

"'Oh,' replied Samuel Adams, quickly, 'that will never do—never.'

"'It must do—it *shall* do,' said John, 'and for these reasons the southern and middle states are both to enter heartily in th cause, and their arguments are potent: they say that New England holds the physical power in her hands, and they fear the result. A New England army, a New England commander, with New England perseverance, all united, appal them. For this cause they hang back. Now, the only course is to allay their fears, and give them nothing to complain of; and this can be done in no other way but by appointing a southern chief over this force, and then all rush to the standard. The policy will blend us in one mass, and that mass will be resistless.'

"At this, Samuel Adams seemed to be greatly moved. They talked over the preliminary circumstances, and John asked his cousin to second the motion. Mr. Adams went in, took the floor, and put forth all his strength in the delineations he had prepared, all aiming at the adoption of the army. He was ready to own the army, appoint a commander, vote supplies, and proceed to business. After his speech had been finished, some objected, and some feared. His warmth increased with the occasion, and to all these doubts and hesitations he replied thus:—

"'Gentlemen, if this Congress will not adopt this army before ten moons have set, New England will adopt it, and she will undertake the struggle alone—yes, with a strong arm and a clean conscience, she will front the foe single-handed.'

"This had the desired effect. They saw New England was neither playing nor to be played with, and they agreed to appoint a day. A day was fixed: it came: Mr. Adams went in, took the floor, urged the measure, and after some debate it passed.

"The next thing was to get a commander for this army, with supplies, etc. All looked to Mr. Adams on the occasion, and he was ready. He then took the floor, and went into a minute delineation of the character of General Ward, bestowing on him the encomiums which then belonged to no one else. At the end of the eulogy, he said: 'But this is not the man I have chosen.' He then went into the delineation of the character of a commander-in-chief, such as was required by the peculiar situation of the colonies at that juncture. And after he had presented the qualifications in his strongest language, and given the reasons for the nomination he was about to make, he said :—

"'Gentlemen, I know these qualifications are high, but we all know they are needful, at this crisis, in this chief. Does any one say they are not to be obtained in this country? In reply, I have to say, they are; they reside in one of our own body, and he is the person whom I now nominate—GEORGE WASHINGTON, OF VIRGINIA.'

"Washington, who sat on Mr. Adams' right hand, was looking him intently in the face, to watch the name he was about to announce, and, not expecting it would be his, sprang from his seat the minute he heard it, and rushed into an adjoining room. Mr. Adams had asked his cousin Samuel to ask for an adjournment as soon as the nomination was made, in order to give the members time to deliberate—and the result is before the world.

"I asked Mr. Adams, among other questions, the following:

"'Did you ever doubt of the success of the conflict?'

"'No, no,' said he, 'not for a moment. I expected to be hung and quartered, if I was caught; but no matter for that—my country would be free; I knew George the Third could not forge chains long enough and strong enough to reach around these United States.'"

A REVOLUTIONARY RELIC.

THE following interesting document was found among the papers of Major John Jacob Schæfinyer, a deceased patriot of the Revolution. It is a discourse delivered on the eve of the battle of Brandywine, by Rev. Joab Trout, to a large portion of the American soldiers, in presence of General Washington, General Wayne, and other officers of the army.

REVOLUTIONARY SERMON.

"They that take the sword shall perish by the sword."

Soldiers and Countrymen:

We have met this evening perhaps for the last time. We have shared the toil of the march, the peril of the fight, and the dismay of the retreat alike; we have endured the cold and hunger, the contumely of the internal foe, and the courage of the foreign oppressor. We have sat, night after night, beside the camp fire; we have together heard the roll of the revellie, which called us to duty, or the beat of the tattoo, which gave the signal for the hardy sleep of the soldier, with the earth for his bed and the knapsack for his pillow.

And now, soldiers and brethren, we have met in the peaceful valley on the eve of battle, while the sunlight is dying away beyond yonder heights, the sunlight that to-morrow morn will glimmer on scenes of blood. We have met, amid the whitening tents of our encampment; in the time of terror and gloom have we gathered together—God grant that it may not be for the last time.

It is a solemn moment. Brethren, does not the solemn voice of nature seem to echo the sympathies of the hour? The flag of our country droops heavily from yonder staff—the breeze has died away along the green plain of Chadd's Ford—the plain that spreads before us glittering in sunlight—the heights of the Brandywine arise gloomily and grand beyond the waters of yonder stream—all nature holds a pause of solemn silence on the eve of uproar and bloodshed and strife of to-morrow.

"They that take the sword, shall perish by the sword."

And have they not taken the sword?

Let the desolated plain, the blood-sodden valley, the burned farm-house blackening in the sun, the sacked village, and the ravaged town, answer—let the whitening bones of the butchered farmer strewn along the fields of his homestead, answer—let the starving mother, with her babe clinging to the withered breast that can afford no sustenance; let her answer with the death rattle mingling with the murmuring tones that marked the last struggle of her life; let the dying mother and her babe answer.

It was but a day past, and our land slept in the quiet of peace. War was not here; wrong was not here. Fraud and woe, and misery and want dwelt not among us. From the eternal solitude of the greenwoods, arose the blue smoke of the settler's cabin, and golden fields of corn looked forth from amid the waste of the wilderness, and the glad music of human voices awoke the silence of the forest.

Now, God of mercy, behold the change. Under the shadow of a pretext, under the sanctity of the name of God, invoking the Redeemer to their aid, do these foreign hirelings slay our people! They throng our towns—they darken our plains, and now they encompass our posts on the lonely plain of Chadd's Ford.

"They that take the sword, shall perish by the sword?"

Brethren, think me not unworthy of belief when I tell you the doom of the British is near. Think me not vain when I tell you that beyond the cloud that now enshrouds us, I see gathering thick and fast the darker cloud and blacker storm of Divine retribution!

They may conquer us to-morrow. Might and wrong prevail, and we may be driven from this field: but the hour of God's own vengeance will come!

Aye, if in the vast solitude of eternal space, if in the heart of the boundless universe, there throbs the being of an awful God, quick to avenge, and sure to punish guilt, then will the man George Brunswick, called King, feel in his brain and his heart, the vengeance of the eternal Jehovah! A blight will be upon his life—a withered brain, and an accursed intellect; a blight will be upon his children and on his people. Great God, how dread the punishment.

A crowded populace, peopling the dense towns where the man of money thrives, while the laborer starves: want striding among the people in all its forms of terror: and ignorant and God-defying priesthood chuckling over the miseries of millions; a proud and merciless nobility adding wrong, and heaping insult upon the robbery and fraud: royalty corrupt to the very heart, and aristocracy rotten to the core; crime and want linked hand in hand, and tempting men to deeds of woe and death—these are a part of the doom and retribution that come upon the English throne and the English people.

Soldiers—I look around upon your familiar faces with a strange interest. To-morrow morning we will go forth to the battle—for need I tell you that your unworthy minister will march with you invoking God's aid in the fight—we will march forth to battle! Need I exhort you to fight the good fight, to fight for your homesteads, for your wives and children?

My friends, I might urge you to fight by the galling memories of British wrongs. Walton—I might tell you of your father butchered in the silence of the night on the plains of Trenton; I might picture his grey hairs dabbled in blood; I might ring his death shriek in your ears. Shelmire—I might tell you of a butchered mother, and a sister outraged; the lonely farm-house, the night assault, the roof in flames, the shouts of the troopers as they dispatched their victims, the cries for mercy and the pleadings of innocence for pity. I might paint this all again in the vivid colors of the terrible reality, if I thought your courage needed such wild excitement.

But I know you are strong in the might of the Lord. You will march forth to battle on the morrow, with light hearts and determined spirit, though the solemn duty—the duty of avenging the dead—may rest heavy on your souls.

And in the hour of battle, when all around is darkness, lit by the lurid cannon glare, and the piercing musket flash, when the wounded strew the ground, and the dead litter your path—then remember, soldiers, that God is with you. The eternal God fights for you—he rides on the battle cloud, he sweeps onward with the march of the hurricane charge—God the awful and infinite, fights for you, and you will triumph.

"They that take the sword, shall perish by the sword."

You have taken the sword, but not in the spirit of wrong or ravage. You have taken the sword for your homes, for your wives, for your little ones. You have taken the sword for truth, and justice, and right, and to you, the promise is—be of good cheer, for your foes have taken the sword in defiance of all that men hold dear, in blasphemy of God—they shall perish by the sword.

And now, brethren and soldiers, I bid you all farewell. Many of us may fall in the battle of to-morrow. God rest the souls of the fallen! Many of us may live to tell the story of the fight to-morrow, and in the memory of all will ever rest and linger the quiet scenes of this Autumnal night.

Solemn twilight advances over the valley; the woods on the opposite heights fling their long shadows over the green of the meadow; around us are the tents of the continental host, the suppressed bustle of the camp, the hurried tramp of the soldiers to and fro among the tents, the stillness and awe that marks the eve of battle.

When we meet again, may the shadows of twilight be flung over a peaceful land. God in heaven grant it. Let us pray.

PRAYER OF THE REVOLUTION.

Great Father, we bow before thee; we invoke thy blessings, we deprecate thy wrath; we return thee thanks for the past, we ask thy aid for the future. For we are in times of trouble, oh, Lord, and sore beset by foes, merciless and unpitying. The sword gleams over our land, and the dust of the soil is dampened with the blood of our neighbors and friends.

Oh! God of mercy, we pray thee to bless the American arms

Make the man of our hearts strong in thy wisdom; bless, we beseech thee, with renewed life and strength, our hope, and thy instrument, even George Washington; shower thy counsels on the honorable the Continental Congress; visit our host, comfort the soldier in his wounds and afflictions, nerve him for the fight, prepare him for the hour of death.

And in the hour of need, oh, God of Hosts, do thou be ou stay; and in the hour of triumph, be thou our guide.

Teach us to be merciful. Though the memory of gallin wrongs be at our hearts, knocking for admittance, that they may fill us with the desire of revenge; yet let us, oh, Lord, spare the vanquished, though they never spared us, in the hour of butchery and bloodshed.

And in the hour of death, do thou guide us to the abode prepared for the blest; so shall we return thanks unto thee, through Christ our Redeemer. God prosper the cause. Amen.

Standard and Popular Books

PUBLISHED BY

Porter & Coates, Philadelphia, Pa.

WAVERLEY NOVELS. By Sir Walter Scott.

- *Waverley.
- *Guy Mannering.
- The Antiquary.
- Rob Roy.
- Black Dwarf; and Old Mortality.
- The Heart of Mid-Lothian.
- The Bride of Lammermoor; and A Legend of Montrose.
- *Ivanhoe.
- The Monastery.
- The Abbott.
- Kenilworth.
- The Pirate.
- The Fortunes of Nigel.
- Peveril of the Peak.
- Quentin Durward.
- St. Ronan's Well.
- Redgauntlet.
- The Betrothed; and The Talisman.
- Woodstock.
- The Fair Maid of Perth.
- Anne of Geierstein.
- Count Robert of Paris; and Castle Dangerous.
- Chronicles of the Canongate.

Household Edition. 23 vols. Illustrated. 12mo. Cloth, extra, black and gold, per vol., $1.00; sheep, marbled edges, per vol., $1.50; half calf, gilt, marbled edges, per vol., $3.00. Sold separately in cloth binding only.

Universe Edition. 25 vols. Printed on thin paper, and containing one illustration to the volume. 12mo. Cloth, extra, black and gold, per vol., 75 cts.

World Edition. 12 vols. Thick 12mo. (Sold in sets only.) Cloth, extra, black and gold, $18.00; half imt. Russia, marbled edges, $24.00.

This is the best edition for the library or for general use published. Its convenient size, the extreme legibility of the type, which is larger than is used in any other 12mo edition, either English or American.

TALES OF A GRANDFATHER. By Sir Walter Scott, Bart. 4 vols. Uniform with the Waverley Novels.

Household Edition. Illustrated. 12mo. Cloth, extra, black and gold, per vol., $1.00; sheep, marbled edges, per vol., $1.50; half calf, gilt, marbled edges, per vol., $3.00.

This edition contains the Fourth Series—Tales from French history, and is the only complete edition published in this country.

CHARLES DICKENS' COMPLETE WORKS. Author's Edition. 14 vols., with a portrait of the author on steel, and eight illustrations by F. O. C. Darley, Cruikshank, Fildes, Eytinge, and others, in each volume. 12mo. Cloth, extra, black and gold, per vol., $1.00; sheep, marbled edges, per vol., $1.50; half imt. Russia, marbled edges, per vol., $1.50: half calf, gilt marbled edges, per vol., $2.75.

*Pickwick Papers.
*Oliver Twist, Pictures of Italy, and American Notes.
*Nicholas Nickleby.
Old Curiosity Shop, and Reprinted Pieces.
Barnaby Rudge, and Hard Times.
*Martin Chuzzlewit.
Dombey and Son.
*David Copperfield.
Christmas Books, Uncommercial Traveller, and Additional Christmas Stories.
Bleak House.
Little Dorrit.
Tale of Two Cities, and Great Expectations.
Our Mutual Friend.
Edwin Drood, Sketches, Master Humphrey's Clock, etc., etc.

Sold separately in cloth binding only.
*Also in Alta Edition, one illustration, 75 cents.
The same. Universe Edition. Printed on thin paper and containing one illustration to the volume. 14 vols., 12mo. Cloth, extra, black and gold, per vol., 75 cents.
The same. World Edition. 7 vols., thick 12mo., $12.25. (Sold in sets only.)

CHILD'S HISTORY OF ENGLAND. By CHARLES DICKENS. Popular 12mo. edition; from new electrotype plates. Large clear type. Beautifully illustrated with 8 engravings on wood. 12mo. Cloth, extra, black and gold, $1.00.
Alta Edition. One illustration, 75 cents.

"Dickens as a novelist and prose poet is to be classed in the front rank of the noble company to which he belongs. He has revived the novel of genuine practical life, as it existed in the works of Fielding, Smollett, and Goldsmith; but at the same time has given to his material an individual coloring and expression peculiarly his own. His characters, like those of his great exemplars, constitute a world of their own, whose truth to nature every reader instinctively recognizes in connection with their truth to darkness."
—*E. P. Whipple.*

MACAULAY'S HISTORY OF ENGLAND. From the accession of James II. By THOMAS BABINGTON MACAULAY. With a steel portrait of the author. Printed from new electrotype plates from the last English Edition. Being by far the most correct edition in the American market. 5 volumes, 12mo Cloth, extra, black and gold, per set, $5.00; sheep, marbled edges, per set, $7.50; half imitation Russia, $7.50; half calf gilt, marbled edges, per set, $15.00.
Popular Edition. 5 vols., cloth, plain, $5.00.
8vo. Edition. 5 volumes in one, with portrait. Cloth, extra, black and gold, $3.00; sheep, marbled edges, $3.50.

MARTINEAU'S HISTORY OF ENGLAND. From the beginning of the 19th Century to the Crimean War. By HARRIET MARTINEAU. Complete in 4 vols., with full Index. Cloth, extra, black and gold, per set, $4.00; sheep, marbled edges, $6.00, half calf, gilt, marbled edges, $12.00.

HUME'S HISTORY OF ENGLAND. From the invasion of Julius Cæsar to the abdication of James II, 1688. By DAVID HUME. Standard Edition. With the author's last corrections and improvements; to which is prefixed a short account of his life, written by himself. With a portrait on steel. A new edition from entirely new stereotype plates. 5 vols., 12mo. Cloth, extra, black and gold, per set, $5.00; sheep, marbled edges, per set, $7.50; half imitation Russia, $7.50; half calf, gilt, marbled edges, per set, $15.00.
Popular Edition. 5 vols. Cloth, plain, $5.00.

GIBBON'S DECLINE AND FALL OF THE ROMAN EMPIRE. By EDWARD GIBBON. With Notes, by Rev. H. H. MILMAN. Standard Edition. To which is added a complete Index of the work. A new edition from entirely new stereotype plates. With portrait on steel. 5 vols., 12mo. Cloth, extra, black and gold, per set, $5.00; sheep, marbled edges, per set, $7.50; half imitation Russia, $7.50; half calf, gilt, marbled edges, per set, $15.00.
Popular Edition. 5 vols. Cloth, plain, $5.00.

ENGLAND, PICTURESQUE AND DESCRIPTIVE. By JOEL COOK, author of "A Holiday Tour in Europe," etc. With 487 finely engraved illustrations, descriptive of the most famous and attractive places, as well as of the historic scenes and rural life of England and Wales. With Mr. Cook's admirable descriptions of the places and the country, and the splendid illustrations, this is the most valuable and attractive book of the season, and the sale will doubtless be very large. 4to. Cloth, extra, gilt side and edges, $7.50; half calf, gilt, marbled edges, $10.00; half morocco, full gilt edges, $10.00; full Turkey morocco, gilt edges, $15.00; tree calf, gilt edges, $18.00.

This work, which is prepared in elegant style, and profusely illustrated, is a comprehensive description of England and Wales, arranged in convenient form for the tourist, and at the same time providing an illustrated guide-book to a country which Americans always view with interest. There are few satisfactory works about this land which is so generously gifted by Nature and so full of memorials of the past. Such books as there are, either cover a few counties or are devoted to special localities, or are merely guidebooks. The present work is believed to be the first attempt to give in attractive form a description of the stately homes, renowned castles, ivy-clad ruins of abbeys, churches, and ancient fortresses, delicious scenery, rock-bound coasts, and celebrated places of England and Wales. It is written by an author fully competent from travel and reading, and in position to properly describe his very interesting subject; and the artist's pencil has been called into requisition to graphically illustrate its well-written pages. There are 487 illustrations, prepared in the highest style of the engraver's art, while the book itself is one of the most attractive ever presented to the American public.

Its method of construction is systematic, following the most convenient routes taken by tourists, and the letter-press includes enough of the history and legend of each of the places described to make the story highly interesting. Its pages fairly overflow with picture and description, telling of everything attractive that is presented by England and Wales. Executed in the highest style of the printer's and engraver's art, "England, Picturesque and Descriptive," is one of the best American books of the year.

HISTORY OF THE CIVIL WAR IN AMERICA. By the COMTE DE PARIS. With Maps faithfully Engraved from the Originals, and Printed in Three Colors. 8vo. Cloth, per volume, $3.50; red cloth, extra, Roxburgh style, uncut edges, $3.50; sheep, library style, $4.50; half Turkey morocco, $6.00. Vols. I, II, and III now ready.

The third volume embraces, without abridgment, the fifth and sixth volumes of the French edition, and covers one of the most interesting as well as the most anxious periods of the war, describing the operations of the Army of the Potomac in the East, and the Army of the Cumberland and Tennessee in the West.

It contains full accounts of the battle of Chancellorsville, the attack on the monitors on Fort Sumter, the sieges and fall of Vicksburg and Port Hudson; the battles of Port Gibson and Champion's Hill, and the fullest and most authentic account of the battle of Gettysburg ever written.

"The head of the Orleans family has put pen to paper with excellent result. .... Our present impression is that it will form by far the best history of the American war."—*Athenæum, London.*

"We advise all Americans to read it carefully, and judge for themselves if 'the future historian of our war,' of whom we have heard so much, be not already arrived in the Comte de Paris."—*Nation, New York.*

"This is incomparably the best account of our great second revolution that has yet been even attempted. It is so calm, so dispassionate, so accurate in detail, and at the same time so philosophical in general, that its reader counts confidently on finding the complete work thoroughly satisfactory."—*Evening Bulletin, Philadelphia.*

"The work expresses the calm, deliberate judgment of an experienced military observer and a highly intelligent man. Many of its statements will excite discussion, but we much mistake if it does not take high and permanent rank among the standard histories of the civil war. Indeed that place has been assigned it by the most competent critics both of this country and abroad."—*Times, Cincinnati.*

"Messrs. Porter & Coates, of Philadelphia, will publish in a few days the authorized translation of the new volume of the Comte de Paris' History of Our Civil War. The two volumes in French—the fifth and sixth—are bound together in the translation in one volume. Our readers already know, through a table of contents of these volumes, published in the cable columns of the *Herald*, the period covered by this new installment of a work remarkable in several ways. It includes the most important and decisive period of the war, and the two great campaigns of Gettysburg and Vicksburg.

"The great civil war has had no better, no abler historian than the French prince who, emulating the example of Lafayette, took part in this new struggle for freedom, and who now writes of events, in many of which he participated, as an accomplished officer, and one who, by his independent position, his high character and eminent talents, was placed in circumstances and relations which gave him almost unequalled opportunities to gain correct information and form impartial judgments.

"The new installment of a work which has already become a classic will be read with increased interest by Americans because of the importance of the period it covers and the stirring events it describes. In advance of a careful review we present to-day some extracts from the advance sheets sent us by Messrs. Porter & Coates, which will give our readers a foretaste of chapters which bring back to memory so many half-forgotten and not a few hitherto unvalued details of a time which Americans of this generation at least cannot read of without a fresh thrill of excitement."

HALF-HOURS WITH THE BEST AUTHORS. With short Biographical and Critical Notes. By CHARLES KNIGHT.
New Household Edition. With six portraits on steel. 3 vols., thick 12mo. Cloth, extra, black and gold, per set, $4.50; half imt. Russia, marbled edges, $6.00; half calf, gilt, marbled edges, $12.00.
Library Edition. Printed on fine laid and tinted paper. With twenty-four portraits on steel. 6 vols., 12mo. Cloth, extra, per set, $7.50; half calf, gilt, marbled edges, per set, $18.00; half Russia, gilt top, $21.00; full French morocco, limp, per set, $12.00; full smooth Russia, limp, round corners, in Russia case, per set, $25.00; full seal grained Russia, limp, round corners, in Russia case to match, $25.00.

The excellent idea of the editor of these choice volumes has been most admirably carried out, as will be seen by the list of authors upon all subjects: Selecting some choice passages of the best standard authors, each of sufficient length to occupy half an hour in its perusal, there is here food for thought for every day in the year: so that if the purchaser will devote but one-half hour each day to its appropriate selection he will read through these six volumes in one year, and in such a leisurely manner that the noblest thoughts of many of the greatest minds will be firmly in his mind forever. For every Sunday there is a suitable selection from some of the most eminent writers in sacred literature. We venture to say if the editor's idea is carried out the reader will possess more and better knowledge of the English classics at the end of the year than he would by five years of desultory reading.

They can be commenced at any day in the year. The variety of reading is so great that no one will ever tire of these volumes. It is a library in itself.

THE POETRY OF OTHER LANDS. A Collection of Translations into English Verse of the Poetry of Other Languages, Ancient and Modern. Compiled by N. CLEMMONS HUNT. Containing translations from the Greek, Latin, Persian, Arabian, Japanese, Turkish, Servian, Russian, Bohemian, Polish, Dutch, German, Italian, French, Spanish, and Portuguese languages. 12mo. Cloth, extra, gilt edges, $2.50; half calf, gilt, marbled edges, $4.00; Turkey morocco, gilt edges, $6.00.

"Another of the publications of Porter & Coates, called 'The Poetry of Other Lands,' compiled by N. Clemmons Hunt, we most warmly commend. It is one of the best collections we have seen, containing many exquisite poems and fragments of verse which have not before been put into book form in English words. We find many of the old favorites, which appear in every well-selected collection of sonnets and songs, and we miss others, which seem a necessity to complete the bouquet of grasses and flowers, some of which, from time to time, we hope to republish in the 'Courier.'"— *Cincinnati Courier.*

"A book of rare excellence, because it gives a collection of choice gems in many languages not available to the general lover of poetry. It contains translations from the Greek, Latin, Persian, Arabian, Japanese, Turkish, Servian, Russian, Bohemian, Polish, Dutch, German, Italian, French, Spanish, and Portuguese languages. The book will be an admirable companion volume to any one of the collections of English poetry that are now published. With the full index of authors immediately preceding the collection, and the arrangement of the poems under headings, the reader will find it convenient for reference. It is a gift that will be more valued by very many than some of the transitory ones at these holiday times."— *Philadelphia Methodist.*

THE FIRESIDE ENCYCLOPÆDIA OF POETRY. Edited by HENRY T. COATES. This is the latest, and beyond doubt the best collection of poetry published. Printed on fine paper and illustrated with thirteen steel engravings and fifteen title pages, containing portraits of prominent American poets and fac-similes of their handwriting, made expressly for this book. 8vo. Cloth, extra, black and gold, gilt edges, $5.00; half calf, gilt, marbled edges, $7.50; half morocco, full gilt edges, $7.50; full Turkey morocco, gilt edges, $10.00; tree calf, gilt edges, $12.00; plush, padded side, nickel lettering, $14.00.

"The editor shows a wide acquaintance with the most precious treasures of English verse, and has gathered the most admirable specimens of their ample wealth. Many pieces which have been passed by in previous collections hold a place of honor in the present volume, and will be heartily welcomed by the lovers of poetry as a delightful addition to their sources of enjoyment. It is a volume rich in solace, in entertainment, in inspiration, of which the possession may well be coveted by every lover of poetry. The pictorial illustrations of the work are in keeping with its poetical contents, and the beauty of the typographical execution entitles it to a place among the choicest ornaments of the library."—*New York Tribune.*

"Lovers of good poetry will find this one of the richest collections ever made. All the best singers in our language are represented, and the selections are generally those which reveal their highest qualities. . . . . The lights and shades, the finer play of thought and imagination belonging to individual authors, are brought out in this way (by the arrangement of poems under subject-headings) as they would not be under any other system. . . . . We are deeply impressed with the keen appreciation of poetical worth, and also with the good taste manifested by the compiler."—*Churchman.*

"Cyclopædias of poetry are numerous, but for sterling value of its contents for the library, or as a book of reference, no work of the kind will compare with this admirable volume of Mr. Coates. It takes the gems from many volumes, culling with rare skill and judgment."—*Chicago Inter-Ocean.*

THE CHILDREN'S BOOK OF POETRY. Compiled by HENRY T. COATES. Containing over 500 poems carefully selected from the works of the best and most popular writers for children; with nearly 200 illustrations. The most complete collection of poetry for children ever published. 4to. Cloth, extra, black and gold, gilt side and edges, $3.00; full Turkey morocco, gilt edges, $7.50.

"This seems to us the best book of poetry for children in existence. We have examined many other collections, but we cannot name another that deserves to be compared with this admirable compilation."—*Worcester Spy.*

"The special value of the book lies in the fact that it nearly or quite covers the entire field. There is not a great deal of good poetry which has been written for children that cannot be found in this book. The collection is particularly strong in ballads and tales, which are apt to interest children more than poems of other kinds; and Mr. Coates has shown good judgment in supplementing this department with some of the best poems of that class that have been written for grown people. A surer method of forming the taste of children for good and pure literature than by reading to them from any portion of this book can hardly be imagined. The volume is richly illustrated and beautifully bound."—*Philadelphia Evening Bulletin.*

"A more excellent volume cannot be found. We have found within the covers of this handsome volume, and upon its fair pages, many of the most exquisite poems which our language contains. It must become a standard volume, and can never grow old or obsolete."—*Episcopal Recorder.*

THE COMPLETE WORKS OF THOS. HOOD. With engravings on steel. 4 vols., 12mo., tinted paper. Poetical Works; Up the Rhine; Miscellanies and Hood's Own; Whimsicalities, Whims, and Oddities. Cloth, extra, black and gold, $6.00; red cloth, paper label, gilt top, uncut edges, $6.00; half calf, gilt, marbled edges, $14.00; half Russia, gilt top, $18.00.

Hood's verse, whether serious or comic—whether serene like a cloudless autumn evening or sparkling with puns like a frosty January midnight with stars—was ever pregnant with materials for the thought. Like every author distinguished for true comic humor, there was a deep vein of melancholy pathos running through his mirth, and even when his sun shone brightly its light seemed often reflected as if only over the rim of a cloud.

Well may we say, in the words of Tennyson, "Would he could have stayed with us," for never could it be more truly recorded of any one—in the words of Hamlet characterizing Yorick—that "he was a fellow of infinite jest, of most excellent fancy." —D. M. MOIR.

THE ILIAD OF HOMER RENDERED INTO ENGLISH BLANK VERSE. By EDWARD, EARL OF DERBY. From the latest London edition, with all the author's last revisions and corrections, and with a Biographical Sketch of Lord Derby, by R. SHELTON MACKENZIE, D.C.L. With twelve steel engravings from Flaxman's celebrated designs. 2 vols., 12mo. Cloth, extra, bev. boards, gilt top, $3.50; half calf, gilt, marbled edges, $7.00; half Turkey morocco, gilt top, $7.00.

The same. Popular edition. Two vols. in one. 12mo. Cloth, extra, $1.50.

"It must equally be considered a splendid performance; and for the present we have no hesitation in saying that it is by far the best representation of Homer's Iliad in the English language."—*London Times.*

"The merits of Lord Derby's translation may be summed up in one word, it is eminently attractive; it is instinct with life; it may be read with fervent interest; it is immeasurably nearer than Pope to the text of the original. . . . . Lord Derby has given a version far more closely allied to the original, and superior to any that has yet been attempted in the blank verse of our language."—*Edinburg Review.*

THE WORKS OF FLAVIUS JOSEPHUS. Comprising the Antiquities of the Jews; a History of the Jewish Wars, and a Life of Flavius Josephus, written by himself. Translated from the original Greek, by WILLIAM WHISTON, A.M. Together with numerous explanatory Notes and seven Dissertations concerning Jesus Christ, John the Baptist, James the Just, God's command to Abraham, etc., with an Introductory Essay by Rev. H. STEBBING, D.D. 8vo. Cloth, extra, black and gold, plain edges, $3.00; cloth, red, black and gold, gilt edges, $4.50; sheep, marbled edges, $3.50; Turkey morocco, gilt edges, $8.00.

This is the largest type one volume edition published.

THE ANCIENT HISTORY OF THE EGYPTIANS, CARTHAGINIANS, ASSYRIANS, BABYLONIANS, MEDES AND PERSIANS, GRECIANS AND MACEDONIANS. Including a History of the Arts and Sciences of the Ancients. By CHARLES ROLLIN. With a Life of the Author, by JAMES BELL. 2 vols., royal 8vo. Sheep, marbled edges, per set, $6.00.

COOKERY FROM EXPERIENCE. A Practical Guide for House-keepers in the Preparation of Every-day Meals, containing more than One Thousand Domestic Recipes, mostly tested by Personal Experience, with Suggestions for Meals, Lists of Meats and Vegetables in Season, etc. By Mrs. SARA T. PAUL. 12mo. Cloth, extra, black and gold, $1.50.
Interleaved Edition. Cloth, extra, black and gold, $1.75.

THE COMPARATIVE EDITION OF THE NEW TESTAMENT. Both Versions in One Book.

The proof readings of our Comparative Edition have been gone over by so many competent proof readers, that we believe the text is absolutely correct.

Large 12mo., 700 pp. Cloth, extra, plain edges, $1.50; cloth, extra, bevelled boards and carmine edges, $1.75; imitation panelled calf, yellow edges, $2.00; arabesque, gilt edges, $2.50; French morocco, limp, gilt edges, $4.00; Turkey morocco, limp, gilt edges, $6.00.

The Comparative New Testament has been published by Porter & Coates. In parallel columns on each page are given the old and new versions of the Testament, divided also as far as practicable into comparative verses, so that it is almost impossible for the slightest new word to escape the notice of either the ordinary reader or the analytical student. It is decidedly the best edition yet published of the most interest-exciting literary production of the day. No more convenient form for comparison could be devised either for economizing time or labor. Another feature is the foot-notes, and there is also given in an appendix the various words and expressions preferred by the American members of the Revising Commission. The work is handsomely printed on excellent paper with clear, legible type. It contains nearly 700 pages.

THE COUNT OF MONTE CRISTO. By ALEXANDRE DUMAS. Complete in one volume, with two illustrations by George G. White. 12mo. Cloth, extra, black and gold, $1.25.

THE THREE GUARDSMEN. By ALEXANDRE DUMAS. Complete in one volume, with two illustrations by George G. White. 12mo. Cloth, extra, black and gold, $1.25.

There is a magic influence in his pen, a magnetic attraction in his descriptions, a fertility, in his literary resources which are characteristic of Dumas alone, and the seal of the master of light literature is set upon all his works. Even when not strictly historical, his romances give an insight into the habits and modes of thought and action of the people of the time described, which are not offered in any other author's productions.

THE LAST DAYS OF POMPEII. By Sir EDWARD BULWER LYTTON, Bart. Illustrated. 12mo. Cloth, extra, black and gold, $1.00. Alta edition, one illustration, 75 cts.

JANE EYRE. By CHARLOTTE BRONTÉ (Currer Bell). New Library Edition. With five illustrations by E. M. WIMPERIS. 12mo. Cloth, extra, black and gold, $1.00.

SHIRLEY. By CHARLOTTE BRONTÉ (Currer Bell). New Library Edition. With five illustrations by E. M. WIMPERIS. 12mo. Cloth, extra, black and gold, $1.00.

www.ingramcontent.com/pod-product-compliance
Lightning Source LLC
Chambersburg PA
CBHW022145300426
44115CB00006B/351